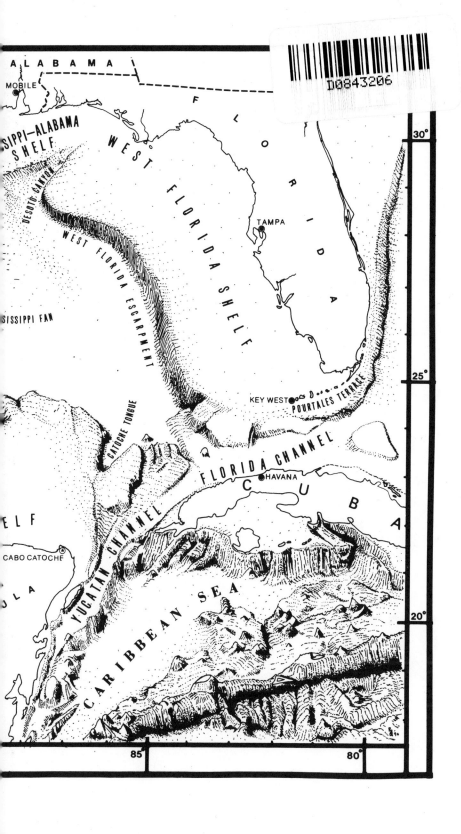

THE GULF OF MEXICO

Endsheet. Physiography and physical geography of the Gulf of Mexico.
The physiographic complexity of the Gulf is revealed in this schematic view (with exaggerated vertical scale) of the major submarine features. Factors that have shaped, and continue to shape, the geology and biology of the Gulf are easily seen. Among these are the deep channels that direct the flow of major surface currents; extensive sedimentary fans deposited by the Mississippi River; the broad continental shelves ringing the central depression of the Mexico Basin; the large, offshore canyons furrowing the West Florida, Texas, and Louisiana shelves and slopes; and the petroleum-rich slope and plateau off Louisiana and Texas. All surround the wide, deep, relatively flat Sigsbee Plain which lies in the central western portion of the Mexico Basin. [Modified and redrawn from U.S. Dept. of the Interior, Minerals Management Service. OCS Regional Office, Gulf of Mexico, visual no. 9, 1981.]

The McGowan-Davis
Map (1781) of the Gulf of
Mexico. By the end of the
18th century the geography
of the Gulf of Mexico had
been reasonably well
charted, with important regions of commerce and population more clearly
delineated than financially
less critical areas. Interesting features include the
"New Kingdom of Leon"
(Mexico and Texas) and the
territories of West and East
Florida (the former extending to the vicinity of the
present-day Louisiana-Ala-
bama border). Note also the
numerous "islands" that
purportedly made up the
southern tip of the Florida
peninsula which at that time
was still very much tierra
incognita.

Pineapple Press, Inc.
Sarasota, Florida

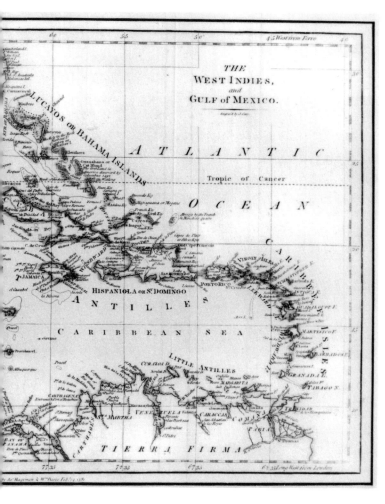

THE GULF OF MEXICO

A Treasury of Resources in the American Mediterranean

Robert H. Gore

Pineapple Press, Inc.
P.O. Drawer 16008
Southside Station
Sarasota, Florida 34239

LIBRARY OF CONGRESS CATALOGING IN PUBLICATION DATA

Gore, Robert H.
    The Gulf of Mexico: a treasury of resources in the American Mediterranean /by Robert H. Gore. -- 1st ed.
       p. cm.
    Includes bibliographical references.
    ISBN 1-56164-010-7: $24.95
    1. Mexico, Gulf of. 2. Natural resources
    -- Mexico, Gulf of.
3. Pollution -- Mexico, Gulf of. I. Title.
F296.G67 1992
333.95'2'0916364 -- dc20   91-44386
                                                CIP

All photographs and illustrations not otherwise credited are by the author.

Design by Frank Cochrane Associates
Composition by Millicent Hampton-Shepherd

Printed and bound by Arcata Graphics in Fairfield, Pennsylvania

To the vanished coastal Indians
of the Gulf of Mexico,
who knew what they were losing,
and to the present coastal populace,
who may not.

Contents

Acknowledgments

The immense amount of data available on the Gulf of Mexico is matched only by the difficulty in obtaining or assembling it all into one place. Several organizations aided in this process, providing publications of importance, and I am indebted to The Conservancy, Inc., and the Rookery Bay National Estuarine Research Reserve (RBNERR), in Naples, Florida; the U.S. Fish and Wildlife Service, Patuxent Wildlife Research Center, Laurel, Maryland; the Department of the Interior, Minerals Management Service (MMS), New Orleans, Louisiana, and Washington, DC; the Environmental Protection Agency (EPA), Region IV (Atlanta) and Region VI (Dallas); and Shell Offshore, Inc., New Orleans, Louisiana.

The following persons at EPA were particularly helpful in providing information on superfund activities in the Gulf region: Mr. Arthur Collins, Superfund Supervisor for Alabama, Georgia and Mississippi; Mr. Eric Hughes, Regional Wetlands Planning Expert; Mr. H. Kirk Lucius, Chief, Waste Programs Branch, Superfund Program, Region IV; and Mr. Thomas L. Neesmith, Chief, Policy, Planning, and Evaluations Branch, Region IV; and the public relations staff from Region VI.

Several persons at the Minerals Management Service (MMS) offices supplied valuable information and/or literature dealing with OCS activities, leasing terminology, and procedures for petroleum and sulfur exploration in the Gulf of Mexico, including Ms Carol Hollingsworth, Headquarters, Public Affairs Office, Washington, DC; Mr. Chuck Hopson, Chief, Leasing Activities Section, Dr. Robert M. Avent, Oceanographer, and Ms Pat Bryars, Statistical Assistant, OCS Gulf Region, New Orleans, Louisiana.

The final manuscript benefited greatly from the suggestions and criticisms of numerous reviewers, including Dr. John Compton, University of South Florida at St. Petersburg; and Dr. C. E. Proffitt, St. Petersburg Junior College, St. Petersburg, Florida; Dr. Richard C. Dodge and Dr. Charles Messing, Nova University Oceanographic Center, Dania, Florida; Dr. Darryl L. Felder, University of Southwestern Louisiana, (USL) Lafayette, Louisiana; Dr. R. Grant Gilmore, Harbor Branch Oceanographic Institute (HBOI), Ft. Pierce, Florida; Dr. Kenneth L. Heck, Jr., Marine Environmental Sciences Consortium (MESC), Dauphin Island Sea lab, Dauphin Island, Alabama; and Dr. James A. Henry, University of Florida (UF), Gainesville, Florida.

The following people provided much information, or clarified certain points in their respective areas of expertise: Dr. Robert M. Avent, MMS, on marine mammals, hydrothermal vent organisms, and oil drilling platforms; Ms Julie Firman, and Dr. Peter Glynn, Rosenstiel School of Marine and Atmospheric Sciences, University of Miami, Florida, on pesticide contamination of the Florida reef tract; Ms Julie Garrett, Florida Marine Research Institute, Florida

8

Department of Natural Resources (FDNR), St. Petersburg, Florida, on taxonomy of red tide dinoflagellates; Mr. Daniel G. Gore, Lockheed Aerospace Inc., Cape Canaveral, Florida, for data and illustrations on hurricane and tropical storm tracks; Ms Wendy Jacobs, Public Affairs Department, Shell Offshore, Inc., New Orleans, Louisiana, for photographs and information on OCS platforms; Mr. Dean Letzring, Manager for Marine Operations, and Dr. Denis Wiesenburg, Geochemical and Environmental Research Group, Texas A&M University, Galveston, Texas, for maps and data on the Orca basin in the Gulf; Mr. Greg Linscombe, Louisiana Department of Wildlife and Fisheries, New Iberia, Louisiana, on prescribed burns in salt marshes; Mr. David Maehr, Florida Game and Freshwater Fish Commission (FGFWFC), Naples, Florida, on endangered Florida wildlife species; Mr. Hank McAvoy, Bureau of Seafood Marketing (FDNR), and Mr. Les McLeod, Senior Attorney, Florida Department of Agriculture, Tallahassee, Florida, on Florida fisheries; Ms Elizabeth Mehl, Legislative Director, Office of Congressman Andy Ireland, Washington, DC for discussion of pertinent legislation; Professor Fazil Najafi, Department of Civil Engineering, (UF), on the potential effects of petroleum spills in south Florida; Ms Nancy Olsen, Collier County Museum, Naples, Florida, for bibliography and references on Calusa and other Florida Indians; Mr. Steve Rabalais, Louisiana Universities Marine Consortium Laboratory (LUMCON), Cocodrie, Louisiana, on biological effects of the IXTOC-1 oil spill; and Mr. Lawrence Rozas (LUMCON), on salt marsh fires. My thanks to them all. As always, any errors of interpretation or fact are mine alone.

Photographs, illustrations, charts, or other materials were provided by Dr. Robert M. Avent (MMS); Mr. Ted Below, Audubon Corkscrew Swamp Sanctuary, Naples, Florida; Dr. Darryl L. Felder (USL); Dr. Gene Feldmann, Goddard Space Flight Center, Greenbelt, Maryland; Mr. Will Gould and Ms Laura K. Metcalf, National Climatic Data Center, Satellite Data Information Services, Washington, DC; Mrs. Maura Kraus, Collier County Natural Resources Management Department, Naples, Florida; Mr. Darrel Land, (FGFWFC); Mr. Miles Laurence, NOAA, National Hurricane Center, Miami, Florida; Dr. Betty E. Lemmon (LUMCON); Mr. Gary Lytton and Mr. Stephen Bertone (RBNERR); Ms Dixie Lee Nims, Florida Department of Commerce, Division of Tourism, Tallahassee, Florida; Ms. Joanna Norman, Florida State Archives, Tallahassee, Florida; Ms Gwen Pitman, National Aeronautics and Space Administration (NASA), Washington, DC; Dr. Scott Ritchie, Collier Mosquito Control District; Mr. Ed Stein, Rocky Mountain News, Denver, Colorado; Dr. and Mrs. Kris Thoemke, Naples, Florida; and last but certainly not least, Dr. Marsh M. Youngbluth (HBOI). They all have my gratitude for responding so generously or under such short notice. Their contributions, as can be easily seen, improved the book immensely.

Editors are an author's worst nemesis and greatest salvation. Ms Lisa Compton not only edited the copy on two earlier drafts but gently showed me (in spite of my disputation) how to write in the English language once again. Ms June Cussen, Executive Editor of Pineapple Press, patiently, and with much understanding, helped assemble all the discordant and scattered pieces into the final work. Millicent Hampton-Shepherd translated my computerized ramblings into a final composition and Pat Hammond helped with the proofreading and indexing. These four ladies, above all, were instrumental in compiling and sorting through the text. To them my heartfelt appreciation and thanks. In advance, many thanks to Mary Pasieka, who will be using her promotion skills to let readers know about this book. And my gratitude to David Cussen must be mentioned. Without his foresight and publishing acumen, this book would never have come to this full fruition.

Finally, and let it here be said without further comment—it might not ever have been finished without Seána-Rhu.

Preface

THIS IS AN AGE in which citizens in Gulf coastal states find a host of environmental issues included in the agenda of the city council, the county/parish government, and the state legislature. Many such issues ultimately end up on the ballot, where the citizen is forced to choose the candidate, amendment, millage, or make the environmental decision that in substantial part will determine the fate and future of many of our coastal areas. Alteration and preservation of coastal and wetland habitats are debated at length in the public forum, with reporters and feature writers or television commentators serving to chronicle and sometimes interpret the course of events. Courtrooms are swamped with litigation that bears on coastal and marine environments, with the issues ranging from injunctions against ocean dumping or offshore incineration of toxic materials to suits seeking recovery of damages for a plaintiff's loss of livelihood from destruction of oyster leases or other fisheries. Politically active environmental groups have come to full blossom, and compete for the citizens' financial support, just as does some pending new tax millage for amelioration of coastal erosion or the purchasing of a new coastal wetland reserve. The motives and ethics of the land developer or industrialist, as well as the preservationist or environmentalist, are cross-challenged, often with communication becoming reduced to little more than heated name-calling and acrimonious debate.

What can the citizen do? Where does one find facts, balance, and good judgment in all of this? The answers are certainly not simple and the background to many issues is often extremely complex. Thus, the citizen seeking knowledge and wishing to be informed is easily tempted to forego involvement as voter, jury member, activist or politician, and leave the decision-making process to others who may appear to know more, or have more of a "vested interest" in the question at hand. The resources involved—biological, environmental, economical, or sociological—are not identified as a personal birthright or a gift over which the average citizen does indeed have stewardship.

Yet, any observant resident of the Gulf of Mexico can testify to the incredible changes that have occurred in times as short as decades in coastal landscapes, populations of coastal sportfishes, the health of coral reefs, and even in the appearance of local beaches. Who has not experienced the loss of a favorite coastal fishing spot or campsite? Who has not viewed with disgust the oil slick or raft of garbage ten or twenty miles at sea? Who has not witnessed the littering or oiling of a once pristine strip of sandy beach? Or reacted with dismay at the construction of multi-story condominiums within a once-favorite coastal panorama? Or decried the diminishing populations of coastal wading birds and migrant waterfowl? And in so doing, who has not asked what decisions, what outcry, what leverage could have been made by the everyday citizen that might have modified or prevented these events? In short, how, when, where, and to what degree should the non-specialist, the everyday citizen of America, Mexico or Cuba become involved and make the "right" decision?

The obvious answer to these questions lies in information and education. However, the present body of literature on these many subjects is often highly technical, and aimed more at the college or postgraduate-level scientist, engineer and lawyer than it is to the everyday citizen. A weighty terminology can bog down the most determined reader, and promote the impression that the layman is neither conversant, nor welcome to be, with the issues.

The present work attempts to rectify this disparity. Prepared intentionally as an introduction and synopsis of salient factors operating in the Gulf today, it is "user-friendly" and meant to avoid the intimidating terminology and theoretics in more technical works. As such, it is offered both as a tool and a resource for those who desire this information. But the format, albeit understandable and readable at the intelligent laymen's level, does not soft-peddle the issues or, more importantly, ignore the critical background that fostered or promulgated these same issues in the first place. For the non-biologist, non-engineer, and non-attorney, this book provides a much needed guide that can substantially improve the understanding of the environments as well as the environmental issues that are having such an impact on the Gulf of Mexico today. And having such knowledge is the first step toward making the correct decisions.

Dr. Darryl L. Felder
Director, Center for Crustacean Research
University of Southwestern Louisiana

Author's Introduction

WHAT YOU ARE ABOUT TO READ is a synopsis. As such, it must consist of generalizations, admittedly not the best way to treat any subject, let alone one as vast and as complex as the Gulf of Mexico. Some will think my treatments too simplistic; others will consider the material treated in too much detail. And therein lies the dilemma faced by any author.

There is an absolute wealth of material available about the Gulf of Mexico. Fortunately, most of it is recent, comprehensive, relatively uncomplicated, and most importantly, readily accessible to the diligent seeker. The dilemma thus lies not in having insufficient data, but rather in how to best present those aspects in order to introduce the general reader to this immense amount of material.

For those whose favorite topics or pet theories seem perfunctorily treated herein, let me state that it was not from lack of interest, but rather owing to the constraints of time and space. The astute reader will quickly see that every chapter in this book could easily be expanded into its own particular volume.

For those who seek and find egregious errors I ask your forbearance, and request that you send me the corrections. I have endeavored to address the most pertinent topics fairly, presenting both sides of any pertaining arguments. If you disagree, or if there are topics that should have been more thoroughly addressed please let me know and I will add them to an alreading expanding list of subject matter that may be covered in a subsequent edition. I do not claim to have the final word on any topic in this book. My purpose is to introduce, not adjudicate.

Throughout the following chapters I have continually emphasized that the Gulf of Mexico, our own American Mediterranean Sea, is a treasury of resources—natural, demographic, historical, economic. But the greater wealth is that lying in the storehouses of knowledge about this great body of water. That wealth is available to anyone who would have it. The word "introduction" comes from the Latin, *introducere*—to lead within. The door to the treasury is open. And so let us enter.

Prologue

ON JUNE 16, 1497, AFTER A VOYAGE of 37 days westward across the trackless blue waters of the Atlantic Ocean, a small Spanish fleet made its maiden entry into the Gulf of Mexico. The captains and crew members of these ships, all hardened men and seasoned seafarers, had embarked from Cádiz, Spain, on a voyage of discovery. Their purpose: to find new lands and fill the coffers of Don Ferdinand de Castilla, the king of Spain, with gold. Although they were the first Europeans to enter and navigate along the primeval coastlines of the Gulf, the glory of having their names associated with the discovery of this great body of water would be lost in the dusty pages of history. But one of the officers on board was a middle-aged Italian merchant, erstwhile astronomer, and sometime mapmaker. On his return to the Old World he would write letters describing his discoveries, letters that others—men of courage, of God, and of avarice—would read. His name, now familiar to every schoolchild, was Amerigo Vespucci. [1]

Turning northward, the ships sailed along the wild and verdantly forested coast of what is now Honduras and entered a pristine harbor that would eventually be named Campeche Bay, on the Yucatán Peninsula of Mexico. Here they were met by Indians. The first encounter between Old World adventurers and the New World coastal inhabitants on this yet unnamed sea resulted in a brief but fierce battle. The Spaniards withdrew, leaving 15 to 20 Indians dead, and sailed for home.

Did these swarthy seafarers from Cádiz and the Alboran Sea, the first Europeans to sail into the Gulf of Mexico, realize what lay within their grasp? Did they know that the vast blue waters on which they sailed were circumscribed almost completely by the lands of a great continent? Were they aware that there were but two narrow entrances into this sea? If so, in a flash of insight they certainly would have remembered their native Mediterranean. And recalling that ancient and fabled sea, wine road of the Greeks, pathway to commerce and war for the Romans, bridge to discovery and conquest for the great Moorish kingdoms, and now point of embarkation for His Catholic Majesty's *navegadores*, the strategic and commercial possibilities could not have been missed. Truly España would soon become most favored among all of God's kingdoms. But it was a favoring that, because of ineptitude, mischance, and lack of foresight, would last less than 300 years.

The Spanish exploitation and eventual loss of the area would be a precursor for events yet to come. The rush to spend the material and human resources would be matched by other nations in the following centuries. And half a millennium later the dark swirls of pollution from both local and world-wide sources would taint the once pristine waters and wash ashore on the beaches of this great enclosed sea. In the Gulf of Mexico, from the time of the Old World empires of Spain, France, England, and Holland to that of the present countries of the New World, some things never change.

THE GULF OF MEXICO

The Pelican God from the Court of the Pile Dwellers.
A reconstruction of a Calusa Indian wooden effigy referred to as the "Pelican God" shows the skill and aesthetic creativity of these now vanished peoples. The original, discovered buried in the mud of a mangrove forest on Key Marco (now Marco Island) in southwestern Florida, was excavated by Frank Hamilton Cushing in 1896 but has deteriorated since. The age of the mask, based on associated potsherd stratigraphy and radio carbon dating, is estimated to be between 800-1600 A.D. [Author, from example in Collier County Museum]

Part One

"The Richest Country in the World"

Gold is most excellent. Gold is treasure, and with it, whoever has it may do what he wants in the world, and may succeed in taking souls to Paradise.

Cristobal Colón, 1503
Lettera Rarissima

Spanish Discovery and Exploration

JUST EIGHT SHORT YEARS after Christopher Columbus first arrived in the New World, the general boundaries of the large enclosed sea between the Antilles and the Central American land mass then known as Nova España had already been drawn.[1] Juan de la Cosa, owner and pilot of the *Santa María*, flagship of the Columbus expedition, produced the first map in 1500. The large island called Isabela (Cuba), previously known from Columbus's expeditions, was clearly delineated. By 1513 that ill-fated seeker of eternal health, Juan Ponce de León, had crudely defined the peninsula of *Pascua Florida*, the chain of barely emergent coral keys called *Los Mártires* (the Martyrs) at its tip, and the small reef-ringed turtling grounds to the westward named *Las Tortugas*. He also discovered the vagaries of the great current that would one day be called the Gulf Stream.

Because the Spanish, at least in European eyes, all but controlled this great land-encircled sea, it had been given a variety of names by the cartographers of Seville: *Golfo de Florida*, *Golfo de Cortés*, *Sinus Magnus Antillarum* (in reference to the Antilles), and even *Mare Cathaynum* (Chinese Sea). Old beliefs—including the misconception that Columbus had, in fact, reached the East Indies—died hard in the Old World. Not until 1550 was a map clearly labeled *Golfo de Mexico*. It was not a popular name. Another map in 1593 called the sea *Golfo Mexicano*. As late as 1728 the Spanish Admiralty charts still referred to it as *Golfo de Nueva España* (another name for Mexico), *Ensenada Mexicana,* or *Seno Mexicano*. Only in the mid-1600s did the appellation Gulf of Mexico become firmly and finally established, and then usually by nations other than Spain (see Frontispiece).

No matter its name. Once the region became mapped, reports from other adventurers and explorers over the next 50 years began flooding back to Seville. We can imagine the astonishment of the admirals as the cartographers spoke. Here was a great ocean ringed with mountains on its west; there, coastal plains and forested hills on the north; to the east lay savannahs and wetlands; and there, on the great island of Cuba to the south, more mountains and plains. So many harbors! And the rivers! Majestic, mighty freshwater torrents that beckoned conquistadore, priest, and merchant to the interior of what could only be a large and previously unknown continent. *Madre de Dios*! Certainly much fortune awaited therein!

21

The admirals and merchants alike were intrigued. The fact that both sea-lanes into this *Mare Nostrum*, this new Spanish Sea, were guarded by peninsulas, and thus were easily controlled, could not have been lost on the schemers and planners at court. Even more important, a swift ocean current passed into this sea at the western entrance and looped to exit with even more rapidity to the east. It seemed that even the sea gods were in favor of hurrying the colonizing galleons inward and then sending them, fully laden, groaning and top-heavy with booty, rapidly on their way back to Spain. To the Castilians it was as if the keys to a bottomless treasure chest had been dropped in their laps. But the maps to this treasure were to be drawn in blood and violence.

To bring some kind of order to the forthcoming expeditions, the Casa de Contratacíon was established in Seville in 1503 to let contracts for expeditions, assess the returning information, ensure the proper disposition of royal tithes and goods, arbitrate or adjudicate disputes, and regulate commerce and navigation with the New World. Amerigo Vespucci was appointed to the post of Pilot Major in this organization in 1508 and served until his death in 1512.[2]

In 1517 a slaving expedition sailed west from Havana, Cuba, to Yucatán and roamed along the rugged wild coastline, charting many bays and inlets and finally reaching and naming Campeche Bay. Here the coastal Indians quickly repaid the earlier debt incurred by the Vespucci expedition, killing many soldiers in the landing party and mortally wounding Francisco Hernández de Córdoba, the expedition leader. His pilot, Antón de Alaminos, also wounded, sailed quickly for home but arrived too late in Cuba to save his compatriot Córdoba, who died of his wounds shortly thereafter.

But Alaminos was destiny's child, participating in several later expeditions, including that led by the slave-taker Juan de Grijalva in 1518, which finally found the metal the Spaniards so coveted. The coastal Indians, wearing hand-beaten gold amulets, could not have misconstrued the probing questions and the bright gleam of avarice in the eyes of their Spanish visitors. They told of a land of abundances to the west, called Mexico. By this ploy the rustic coastal Indians betrayed the pagan city-kingdoms of the feather-headdressed Aztecs and Mayas to the steel-helmeted Christians from Castile. Grijalva returned to Cuba richer by 20,000 pesos worth of Indian gold, and priceless information on a new land. Grijalva's expedition had knoocked once, but subsequent expeditions kicked open the door of the Mexican treasury. The stone-templed empires fell quickly under sword, crossbow, harquebus, and armor. Again, we can imagine the astonishment of the conquerors. So much wealth! So many slaves! So quickly taken! And so easily shipped back to Cuba and Spain via the newly charted sea-lanes listed on the Spanish Admiralty maps as *La Mar del Norte*.

Even the worldly-wise conquistadores were surprised at the vast amounts of wealth yielded by the land of this New World Mediterranean: gold, silver, copper, and the new liquid metal called quicksilver (mercury) so useful in amalgamation; the translucent stone as green as a breaking wave, called jade; the speckled sky-blue mineral turquoise; chocolate, vanilla, peppers, beans, corn, squash, potatoes, yams, tomatoes, and a wealth of other fruits and vegetables; sisal for rope; indigo and cochineal for dyes; the miraculous "Jesuit's Powder" that seemed to cure malaria; and the new leaf for smoking called *tabac*; in short, all the items of trade and commerce passing from the inland through the ports of Havana, Pensacola, Galveston, and Vera Cruz. The list was seemingly endless and all of it was free or relatively inexpensive for the taking.

Expedition followed expedition, beginning in 1519 with Hernando Cortés, and another under Don Alonzo Alvarez de Pineda. Cortés headed west and then north up the Mexican coast and discovered the Rio Grande; Alvarez de Pineda sailed north to Florida and then up the west coast of this Land of Flowers until he arrived at the mouth of a majestically large freshwater river he named Rio del Espiritu Santo. Today we know it as the Mississippi.[3]

In 1528 Pánfilo de Narváez, accompanied by a young grandee named Álvar Núñez Cabeza de Vaca, put ashore at Bahia de Santa Cruz (Tampa Bay) to seek a fabled land of gold, called by the Indians Abalachi, or Apalachee. They found instead a country filled with swamps, ravening hordes of insects, and murderously hostile Indians. Forging northwestward, Narváez crossed a river he named Rio de Magdalena (either the Apalachicola or St. Mark's), and continued past Santa Rosa Sound and Chandeleur Sound. After several months of fruitless wanderings, the expedition crumbled. Many had died in combat, others from sickness and hunger. Narváez himself was racked with malaria. Trying to cross the mouth of the Mississippi River during a violent storm, Narváez added his name to an ever-lengthening list of those who died for gold, gospel, and the glory of Spain.

His companion Cabeza de Vaca and several others survived, living for six years among Indian tribes, some friendly, most hostile. Suffering extreme hardship, the Spaniards made their way westward across the Mississippi, and through Texas to Mexico, the Gulf of California, and civilization. Cabeza de Vaca's observations and experiences proved so valuable they were summarized and sent back to the cartographers in Seville. Thus grew the power of Spain in the 1500s.

In 1539 Hernando de Soto, newly wealthy from his plundering of the Inca empire in Peru, left Havana with seven ships and 700 soldiers, bent on exploring the land Cabeza de Vaca called "the richest country in the world."[4] Like that of his predecessor Narváez, de Soto's diplomacy toward the Indians was violently simple: intimidation, terror, and enslavement. Landing at Tampa Bay, he too marched overland, while his captain Diego Maldenado sailed along the coast to Pensacola Bay. Following his own golden will-o'-the-wisp, de Soto wandered as far north as the Savannah River before returning to Mobile Bay. But his hourglass, filled with the sands of the Mississippi, was soon to run out. In 1542, marching north up this great river, he caught a fever and joined his bones with those of his predecessor Narváez.

In spite of these setbacks, in just 50 short years Spain had expanded its foothold into a controlling interest. By the turn of the century the first trade routes had been established and the booty from pillaged Indian empires and slave labor flowed back to Cádiz, Barcelona, Madrid, and Seville in amounts that left even Spanish grandees gaping in astonishment. It is estimated that in a single year, between 1533 and 1534, the conquistadores sent back to Spain from just the Inca Empire citites some 10 metric tons (22,000 pounds) of 22 carat gold, and another 70 metric tons (154,000 pounds) of fine silver. This booty was plundered at an average rate of 60 pounds of gold and 421 pounds of silver a day. In 1992 values that is approximately $347,000 and $33,700 per day, respectively, for a total of $126.7 million in gold and $12.3 million in silver. During the sixteenth century Spain received a return of nearly $187,000 on every nickel invested by Ferdinand and Isabella in the Columbus expeditions.[5] By then the names Pizarro, Cortés, de Soto, de León, Grijalva, and others were household words. All of Spain rallied around the seemingly tautological motto on de Soto's ensign: *Possunt quia posse videntur!* We are able because we seem able!

Throughout the sixteenth and seventeenth centuries the litany of bloodshed begun by the Spanish a hundred years earlier continued as other nations turned covetous eyes toward the region. The Gulf of Mexico became both passageway to plunder and waterway for commerce and settlement as the Spanish, Portuguese, French, Dutch,[6] and British raced each other westward to claim the riches of the New World and nurture their growing colonies. The colonizers battled each other as well. Religious murder, rapine, and destruction became a way of life, committed on each other by French Huguenot, Spanish Catholic, and English Protestant colonists. Survivors were left to the local Indians, who were only too happy to take their own slaves or sacrificially cleanse their lands of the hated white invaders.

By the late seventeenth and early eighteenth centuries, the great mercantile routes of the Spanish Main were in full operation. Caravels and galleons, heavy with the wealth of the West Indies, plowed along the Gulf coast on well-worn sea paths. Vera Cruz–Havana–Spain read the manifests. Return voyages brought supplies, horses, and men. Offshore, French, English, and Dutch buccaneers, using maps pirated from Spain and revised in northern Europe, lay in wait, ready to sack the great floating treasure chests[7] as they wallowed slowly eastward. Those that escaped the freebooters often fell victim to hurricanes, spilling their bounty across the seafloor and along the desolate beaches of the mainland, to be collected again by the Indians or lost forever in the shifting barrier island sands.

But if Spain controlled the seas, others desired the land, particularly the silver treasure chests of Mexico. Away from the main sea routes the wilderness around the Gulf of Mexico remained tantalizingly unexplored, a highly desirable tierra incognita. To pluck this plum the British set up a pincer, descending from Virginia and Georgia to the north and ascending from the island of Jamaica in the Caribbean.[8] The French chose the back and side doors, coming down the Mississippi from Canada and upward from the Caribbean island of Santo Domingo. It was, in retrospect, a fascinating game of military and mercantile chess, with continuing checks but no checkmates (see Figure 1).

In 1682, Robert Cavelier, Sieur de La Salle, descended the Mississippi River and entered the Gulf. Stepping ashore somewhere on the delta, he raised a cross

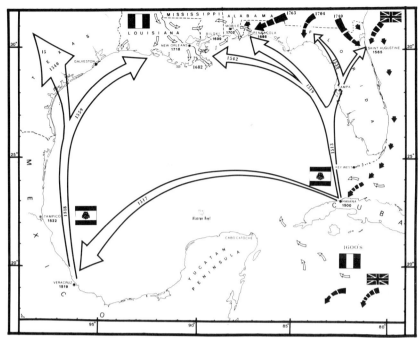

Figure 1. The geopolitical situation in the Gulf of Mexico during the late 1700s.
The beginning of the end of European imperialism occurred in the military and mercantile rivalry between Spain and France, with England circling the combatants like a hungry wolf, eager to steal the spoils. In a series of moves and countermoves, Spain (large open arrows), still a formidable sea power, attempted to maintain its control of all the Gulf-ring lands while sending colonizing expeditions westward into Texas and California. France (small open arrows) attempted interdiction through Louisiana, Mississippi, and Alabama. England (closed arrows) made repeated forays into Spanish Florida. English and French pirates also continued to harass Spanish colonies from bases in the Caribbean. But by the turn of the century war and revolution had effectively eliminated French and English competition, and Spain was left to contend with the land designs of the newly formed United States. In short order the admission to statehood of Louisiana (1812), Mississippi (1817), Alabama (1819), Florida and Texas (1845) ended forever Spain's dominion in the northern Gulf above 25° N latitude. First or major expeditions (large numbers) and founding dates of cities (small numbers) are indicated.

and claimed all the land drained by this majestic river and its tributaries for France. Ever aware of his political responsibilities, although certainly unaware of the vast amount of land now claimed for France, La Salle named the area *La Louisiane*, after the French monarch, Louis XIV. Two years later, France sent La Salle back to the Mississippi River to implement some original ideas. By colonizing Louisiana, France could, in effect, connect Canada to the Caribbean via the Mississippi River, provide a buffer against east coast British imperialism, and split Spanish Florida from Spanish Mexico. And if France could beat England to the Mexican silver mines of Nueva Viscaya, so much the better—even if it was outright invasion!

Unfortunately, ambition exceeded ability. Sailing westward along the northern Gulf coast, La Salle overshot his destination and came ashore somewhere in the vicinity of Matagorda Bay in Texas. With two ships wrecked and a third deserting his command, La Salle and his company were placed in dire straits. Eventually, owing to vicissitudes of weather and his own harsh treatment, La Salle's colony, just as many others, failed. La Salle then chose a small party of men, abandoned the area and attempted to return upriver toward Illinois. Soon after he departed, his fort and the remaining score or so of colonists was destroyed by Indians in retaliation for La Salle's theft of their canoes. Shortly thereafter, La Salle himself was assassinated by the disgruntled and starving survivors in his party as he made his way back to Canada.

Alarmed by continuing thrusts of the "French thorn into the heart of [Spanish] America," the Spanish government, beginning in 1686, outfitted four large expeditions with orders to find and eradicate the failed French colony, and at the same time survey the Gulf of Mexico more completely. As a result the entire coastline from Vera Cruz eastward to Apalachicola was mapped. More importantly for Spanish aims, both Pensacola Bay and Mobile Bay were more clearly charted. The former soon developed into an important colony, port, and military garrison in Spanish West Florida; the latter, along with Biloxi, was occupied by the French in 1702. Once again, check, but no checkmate.

England's aims in the Gulf were never realized. After a series of skirmishes, failed sorties, and impotent military maneuvers against Spanish Florida, the British finally gained the territory in exchange for relinquishing the city of Havana, captured during the Seven Years' War in 1763. Just 13 years later, on a hot July day in 1776, British plans in the Gulf would be thwarted forever by a band of rebellious colonists in a meeting hall in Philadelphia. A new political power came on the scene, secured by "their lives, their fortunes and their sacred honor."

It was apparent, however, that by the eighteenth century cartography had become a primary means for enhancing commerce, settlement, and the inevitable military operations that accompanied them. In 1719 the French geographer Guillaume de L'Isle recharted much of the maritime lands along the northern Gulf, recognized the area of Texas (*Los Teijas*), and provided a sound basis for all future mapping of the great western portion of the continent. At the same time, the observations of his countryman Bernard de la Harpe resulted in charts clarifying the coastline from the Louisiana bayous south to the Yucatán Peninsula. By 1754 the French navy was using a somewhat stylized but heavily annotated chart of the entire Gulf of Mexico and the Antilles.

Not to be outdone, the British, with their ill-fated designs on colonial America, also gathered cartographical intelligence. John Mitchell's map of 1775 was used after the surrender of Cornwallis to settle the many boundary disputes arising between the fledgling United States and the Old World imperial powers. One year earlier Bernard Romans had completed a chart of the Florida coastline, published in his book on the natural history of the Floridas (East and West as they were known at that time).

But the clock of rebellion was ticking. By the late 1700s, the glory of exploration and the exploitation of riches from the New World was fading. Spanish power, taxed by continued military excursions against the impudent French and tenacious English, was waning. And if that were not enough, monarchies themselves were in danger. An upstart ragtag group of English colonists were speaking and then engaging in rebellion against England's George III. The French Revolution turned western Europe upside down, and Spain's own New World colonies were fomenting revolt. With the French, English, and Dutch snapping at its heels, and the Americans and their sometime Indian allies blocking further continental advances, the Spanish lion was beset from all quarters. It could roar but no longer bite.

In a series of military and diplomatic blunders, beginning with a colonial uprising originating in New Orleans in 1768, Spain quickly let the Louisiana Territory, gained at the Treaty of Fontainebleau, slip through her fingers. In 1803, the land-hungry French, short of monies to consolidate their expanding Old World empire, sold the territory to the new United States, thereby giving the fledgling nation its first major outlet from New England into the Gulf. By 1821, eaten from within by revolution of its own colonies, and harried from without by the hordes of American frontiersmen, Spain also agreed to sign over its possessions in East and West Florida. Licking its wounds, the Spanish lion retreated to its remnant domains in California, Mexico and Cuba. There, the remaining power of the New Kingdom of Leon would last less than 100 years. The continent-ringed portion of the great body of water once considered by the Spanish as their own New World mediterranean sea became, finally, the northern portion of the American Mediterranean.

> Una va pasada
> y en dos muele;
> mas molera
> si mi Dios querra.
> *Mariner's nightwatch song*
> *ca. 15th century*[9]

New World Indians and Early Spanish Contacts

I T IS A CURIOUS FACT, and a commentary on the outlook and philosophy of the time, that when the Spanish first arrived in the New World and saw their first Indians, they accepted the presence of these peoples as if they had expected to find them there all along. They apparently never considered the possibility that this great new land might be uninhabited. To the Spanish merchant, explorer, priest, or friar, and many of the later Europeans, the New World Indians were an accepted fact of life, placed there, no doubt, by the same Christian God who had peopled the Old World—and therefore must be dealt with accordingly. This philosophy—which included a rationalized dichotomy of both deliberate and inadvertent genocide—was a mirror image of religious persecution that had already occurred in Europe, and so dictated events for the indigenous peoples of the Gulf region for the next 250 years. During this time the Spanish (and later the French and British) initiated four types of contact with the numerous tribes of New World Indians: for slavery, for conversion, for trade, and (when these failed) for war.

JUSTIFIED INHUMANITY—CONQUEST, CHRISTIANITY, SLAVERY AND THE LAW

To properly understand the events that transpired after the first Spanish contacts, it is necessary to consider briefly the following points. First, in medieval law, a monarch was considered to legally own *all* resources—animal, vegetable, mineral, and human—on any lands claimed through discovery or conquest. This was clearly acknowledged by Columbus, who wrote in his log of 20 December: ". . . I already consider them [the Indians] to be Christians and subjects of the Sovereigns of Castile. *They belong to the Sovereigns even more than do the people of Castile"* [Author's emphasis].[1] Thus, for the later conquistadores, taking slaves was first rationalized as merely the acquisition of royal property for the greater good and glory of the pertinent throne.

Second, concurring with the tenor of the times, heathens or infidels needed to be Christianized. Queen Isabella had forbade the taking of Indians as slaves unless it was necessary to save their heathen souls. This gave the Spanish slavers the loophole they were looking for, and they employed their own inimitable style of salvation to convert tens of thousands of New World Indians and send them on to heaven.

Third, ecclesiastical law needed to address the thorny problems of the origin and status of these new peoples. New World Indians, at first, were not even considered humans by some Europeans because there was no mention of "red men" in the Bible. Cohabitation by the early sailors and conquistadores soon disproved this fallacy. But good Catholics were specifically forbidden to cohabit with heathens. So, in order to allow such socializing, the Indians had to be baptized as Christians, thus saving body and soul together.

In a later rationalization, European ecclesiastical law defined the Indians as "infants in the faith", that is, having the same agnostic state as newborn children, and thus not responsible for the lamentable state of their souls. So seriously was this belief held that Pope Paul III, in the papal Bull issued in 1537, specifically forbade "apostates" (read Lutheran or Jew), under pain of excommunication or death, from going to the New World, so as not to infect and pervert the innocence of the Indians by giving bad example. But the means directed toward their salvation were often overly zealous—questionable at best and extremely cruel at worst. In 1539, for example, the Mexican bishops decreed that whipping and flogging of Indians were not appropriate ways to induce catechismical learning or enforce adherence to religious tenets.[2]

Thus, conquest, christianizing, and slavery went hand in hand, in spite of another legal point (conveniently overlooked by many, beginning with Columbus) that any peoples found in a land claimed as a possession of the Spanish king became, *ipso facto*, Spanish citizens. Spanish citizens could not make slaves of other Spanish citizens. But Christians could, and did, hold slaves.

THE CHRISTIAN CROSS AND PAGAN DOUBLECROSS

Among the first Indians met during the Spanish conquest were the Taino, distant relatives of the South American Arawaks. These primitive Indians, originally migrating up from South America, inhabited Cuba and many of the Bahamian islands but existed as disorganized small villages and so had little intercourse with, and provided even less threat to, the newly-arrived Spanish. Other small tribal-village units that interacted with the Spanish included the Guaniguanicos and Guanahacabibes, belonging to the Ciboney nation, who lived in the western portion of the island. These coastal and inland Indians lived without clothing in the numerous caves of the foothills and mountains and were primarily hunter-gatherers of fish, turtles, and local vegetables and fruits. According to Bartolome de las Casas, some three million Indians lived in Cuba at the time of the Spanish contact, although how he arrived at this figure is conjectural. More believable is his statement that the numbers were reduced to a mere 300 by the middle of the sixteenth century, most having been killed or captured and either impressed into the expeditionary forces or put into slavery under royal land grants called *encomiendas*, which gave the grantee rights to all the people thereon. These last were the most unfortunate, being made to work the great cassava (manioc) fields of Cuba in a manner that would be reflected 300 years later with African negroes on cotton plantations of the American South.

The main population center for the Taino Indians was on the island of Hispaniola and the eastern part of Cuba. A quiet, reserved, and seemingly gentle people, the Taino formed groups or tribes that lived in large villages and practiced extensive agriculture. While not properly Gulf coast Indians, they are important because they showed that perfidy and chicanery would not be merely a Spanish bailiwick. Christopher Columbus was the first European to learn this when he made contact with these industrious and accomodating Indians.

After the *Santa Maria* had accidently run aground and broken up, Columbus ordered part of the crew to stay behind on shore and establish a small settlement among the Tainos. Upon his return a year later, in a precursor of events to come in the sixteenth century, Columbus found the village burned to the ground and the sailor-colonists killed. The Taino chief, Guacanagari, was properly and ostentatiously sorrowful, but the suspicion remained that his political machinations, which involved kowtowing to other, stronger Taino chiefs, were at least in part responsible for the colony's destruction. In Guacanagari's defense it must be remembered that the Spaniards of the colony of La Navidad had been almost continuously at sea for more than 140 days. The enforced celibacy of the ships (excluding any homosexual relief while on board) was exacerbated by Columbus's high-minded instructions to the crew. He explicitly forbade social interactions with any island Indians who, in addition to walking about totally naked, were all too willing to give to the sailors (whom the natives believed had come from heaven) any favor they wished in exchange for glass beads and hawks' bells. With Coumbus away, his colonists did play—and apparently made themselves something substantially more than *personae non gratae*. The gentle Tainos soon learned just how demanding, earthbound (and mortal) their erstwhile gods were. And they responded accordingly.

In the end, the Europeans had the last word. Slowly, over the next several years as the Spanish populated Hispaniola and began to work the people and the land for gold, the Taino Indian society collapsed. Eventually, Spanish authority and power, technology, ruthless slave-taking, Old World diseases, and outright genocide inexorably triumphed and destroyed the population completely.[3]

DARK NEMESIS AND THE LAND OF FLOWERS

But other lands and other Indians lay waiting. Approximately 700 miles to the northwest of Hispaniola lay the peninsula of land that would be named *Pascua de Florida* by Juan Ponce de León. Along the southwestern coast, from the vicinity of Charlotte Harbor southward, lived a large, fiercely warlike tribe of tall, well-armed Indians who worshiped the sun. They called themselves Ka-la-loo-sa, "the dark strong people." The name would be slurred by the Spaniards as "Calusa." For many Spaniards in the coming decades, the howling warwhoops of the nearly naked, tattooed, and feather-plumed Calusas would be the last thing they heard on earth.

The Calusa were a powerful tribe, ruled by a chief (cacique) and several subchiefs and priests in a sort of council. The Calusa villages were large and carefully laid out, composed of the cacique's house, individual residences, and other ceremonial houses surrounding a central plaza, and all protected by tall, closely set fortifications made of sharpened cabbage palm tree trunks. The largest villages usually had a temple mound[4] constructed of mollusc shells. One branch of the tribe even built houses on stilts out over the shallow waters of the coastal lagoons, presumably to escape the ravenous hordes of mosquitos that infested much of the peninsula.

Primarily hunter-gatherers, the Calusas apparently had not even a rudimentary agriculture. The abundant provender of seafood plus deer, wolves, turkey, alligators, lizards, snakes, and other forest animals was supplemented by maize, tubers, several types of squash, beans, and various naturally occurring fruits. Tobacco may have been grown as well.

The Calusa were also accomplished seafarers. Large dugout canoes with outriggers allowed these Indians to sail for miles offshore in pursuit of shark and other marine fish and mammals. Onshore, some settlements even excavated large canals connected to the Gulf. Incoming tides brought the bounty of the sea which was easily trapped for food. The bones of animals and fish, and the empty shells of oysters, conchs, and whelks were discarded into piles called middens. Over the decades they accumulated into huge shell mounds, many of which still exist along the Florida coastline today.

The Calusas, as with many coastal Indians, found trade an important means for supplementing certain geographical and geological deficiencies. Florida is a limestone land, born of the sea, shaped by its rising and falling, and one that will eventually return to the sea. No metal ores or dense, rocky minerals exist.

Lacking hard stone to work for grain grinders (called *metates*), hammers, and weapon points, the Calusa are known to have traded with more northerly tribes. Copper from the Appalachian mountains, heavy granitic stones from the rivers and streams of the southeastern coastal plains, and gold ornaments from the Georgian foothills have all been found in their moundlike middens.

When the clumsy galleons and caravels laden with gold, silver, and emeralds began to stumble ashore—pushed by hurricanes, errant currents, and poor hydrographical knowledge, their hulls riddled by shipworms—the Calusas were first on the beaches to loot the cargoes and strip the iron nails, bandings, and plating. As a consequence, they were (albeit inadvertently) one of the richest tribes in Florida, with a net worth on the Spanish market of well over a million dollars. Only the Ais Indians, the accomplished looters of the great Silver Plate fleets along the Indian River region in central eastern Florida, were in any way equal.

A fierce nature, capable trading abilities, and shrewd alliances made the Calusa a powerful tribe—so much so that several other tribes in Florida, notably the Tequesta, Jeaga, and Ais on the east coast, the Mayaimi of Lake Okeechobee, and occasionally the Tocobaga on the west coast, were held in a sort of fiefdom. Yearly feoffments (required gifts) of food, livestock, and material goods—including Spanish cargo—were paid to the cacique (called "Calos" or perhaps "Carlos"). In return, the Calusa would grant these tribes membership in a loose federation and provide limited protection under vaguely stipulated conditions. For the weaker and less organized tribes it was an offer they couldn't refuse.[5]

The Calusa first met the Spaniards on hostile terms, setting a trend that would continue in the Gulf region for more than two centuries. Spanish slavers had roamed the western coast of Florida beginning about 1502, seeking Indians to work the mines and the fields of Cuba and Hispaniola or to be sent back to Spain as prizes. It didn't take long for the Calusa to learn that the sight of a Spanish sail meant death, destruction, or certain slavery. The Indians fought back with all the means at their disposal—primitive bows and fire-hardened reed arrows, stone knives and axes against state of the art chainmail, sword, halberd and harquebus. Over the next 70 years, hostile encounters were the norm,[6] and the Calusas managed to hold their own. But fortune was not on their side and the military power of Spain would eventually take its toll.

Sporadic attempts by the Spanish to subdue or enjoin the Calusa from their hostilities failed. In one instance, an uneasy truce was formed in 1566 when the sister-wife of the cacique Carlos was "married" to Pedro Menéndez de Avilés, the Spanish governor-administrator of the still mostly unsettled peninsula. Baptized as Doña Antonia, she was sent to Cuba for further religious instruction and to become "civilized." Menéndez, good Catholic that he was, and already married, refused to consummate the marriage. When the cacique's sister returned to Florida she gave her brother an earful of this insult. Hostilities broke out again and any Spanish soldiers, sailors, or priest who were unlucky enough or foolish enough to come ashore were fair game—with slavery and sacrificial death by burning their ultimate fate. The Calusas learned their lessons well from their Spanish instructors.

Over the next century the Spanish explorers continued to make inroads all along both Florida coasts, and the Calusas suffered accordingly. Eventually, the last of the Calusas, those not killed in warfare or by disease,[7] were captured and shipped to Cuba or Hispaniola. Some few allegedly escaped this fate and retreated deep into the wilds of the lower peninsula where, nearly two hundred years later, they would join their lineage with another group of outcast Indians of Creek and Cherokee extraction that had migrated downward from the north—and who called themselves "Seminole."

Several other tribes were of periodic importance during the early Spanish contact period. Along the Florida Keys the Cuchiyaga and Guaragunve (sometimes lumped together with the Bahamian "Lucayos," a sub-Taino group) fished and gathered the seemingly unending bounty of the warm, blue tropical waters. For other tribes in this area, most consisting of one or two small villages, we have no names except that given them by the Spanish: the Martires (named after *Los Martires*, the Spanish name for the chain of Florida Keys),[8] the Organos, and the Tortugas. All fell prey to the rapacious Spanish slavers or other Indians. Except for some scattered middens and artifacts, no trace of them remains today.

Above Tampa Bay, the Apalache (or Abalachi) and the previously mentioned Tocobaga inhabited the central and northwestern Florida coast with several smaller tribes. The Mayaca and Mayatuaca ranged along the northeastern coast. They became associated with a larger tribe called the Timucua in the north central part of Florida and thus formed their own loose federation. These groups traded in shells, hides, some produce, and freshwater pearls taken from small clams living in the cold rivers running down from the Appalachian foothills. Both the Timucua and the Apalache proved daunting foes to the Spaniards of the Narváez and de Soto expeditions.

THE INDIANS OF LA TIERRA INCOGNITA

Father north and west into the Florida panhandle lived the Tallahassee and Yamassee, primarily farmers and livestock growers, but slavers themselves when the occasion and rewards warranted. The Yamassee, under the direction of a white slave trader in the early 1700s, were responsible for capturing the last of the Ais, Jeaga, Tequestas, and nearly all the remaining Calusas and selling them into slavery. Farther west, the Alabamas, Chickasaws, Chiscas, Choctaws, Coosas, Mobilas, Panzacolas, and several smaller tribes inhabited the area extending from western Florida to around Mobile Bay. The Alabamas, Coosas, Choctaws, and Mobilas were fierce tribes of savage warriors that often skirmished both with their native American neighbors as well as with the Spaniards. The Choctaws allegedly practiced ritualistic cannibalism to boot. Most of the others were hunter-gatherers, doing a little farming on the side and living more or less peaceably in forest villages and along the coast. Trade items consisted mostly of what was hunted and gathered, as well as items from exchange from other tribes. But they could be fierce warriors when provoked, and their flint-tipped and bone-tipped arrows also pierced many a Spanish cuirass during the 15th and 16th centuries.

These Indians occupied La Tierra Incognita, the unknown land that surrounded the northern part of the Gulf. It was thus their destiny to be exposed to several continuing contacts with Spanish explorers, beginning with Hernando de Soto. They soon learned the character of the average conquistadore and the eccentricities of their brown-robed religious men. Although some villages provided food for the often-starving Spaniards, whom fate, usually with a little help from the elements, cast into their midst, others remained hostile, constantly harassing any Spanish settlements, particularly the Franciscan missions, throughout the 1600s. Eventually, these Indians also were subdued, enslaved, or exterminated. Meanwhile, some factions of the Creek Indians began to move slowly into Florida from northern Alabama, Georgia, and the Carolinas, assuming or usurping the gradually vacated lands of the traditional inhabitants. Along the Texas coast, barrier islands, and into northern Mexico were numerous tribes, small villages and roving bands of Indians. These included the periodically hostile, agriculturally inclined Tejas or Teijas, and the generally warlike Eyeish(Ais), Asinai, Karankawas, Atakapas, Chichimecas, Coahuiltecas, and fully two dozen other groups.[9] Most resisted Spanish (and later, French) pacification efforts but eventually fell before the onslaught of the European explorers and slavers, their diseases, and starvation.

THE EMPIRE OF THE SUN AND RAIN

The greatest of the mainland coastal Indians along the Gulf of Mexico, without a doubt, were the Mayans and the Mejicas, or Aztecs. The Mayan cultural area extended broadly on the north from the vicinity of Villahermosa in the Mexican state of Tabasco to the present Guatemalan border with Mexico on the Pacific coast, and in the south from about Puerto Cortes, Honduras, on the Caribbean side to El Salvador on the Pacific. The Mayans, however, were already in decline as a great empire when the first Spaniards walked ashore in Central America about 1511. But their origins were long in history. Beginning with small, scattered tribal units, the Mayans quickly united into a more complex civilization as early as 3,000 years ago. The first of the great flat-topped pyramids for worshiping sun, rain, moon, and a veritable pantheon of other natural forces were constructed in the southern lowlands of Guatemala some 2,100 years before Columbus anchored near the Bay Islands of Honduras on his fourth voyage to the New World. The conquistadores would see the horrifying evolutionary end point, in the forbidding, stone-serpent temples of Chac-mool, the rain god, receiver of beating human hearts. It would not be the last time. Later, and farther north, they would view other temples adorned with facades of twisted, intricately carved, blood-soaked stone, and dedicated to a similar deity, one the Aztecs called Tlaloc.

Although usually recognized today more for their great temple-cities, wars of conquest, and their seemingly barbarous customs and religious ceremonies,[10] these same Indians were nevertheless hardy seafarers and astute and shrewd tradesmen. The Mayans constructed large dugout canoes from the then widely growing mahogany tree and plied the Gulf coasts from Yucatán northward to Texas and southward to Panama. These dugout merchantmen could carry 25 to 50 people at a time, including the wives and children of the merchants, Indian slave rowers and bearers, plus trade goods consisting of cotton cloth and clothing, obsidian (volcanic glass) knives, wooden swords, pottery, perfumed woods and incense,[11] cacao and other produce, livestock, and even corn beer. There is evidence, from carved jade amulets and a hammered Mayan Sun God effigy found in middens (refuse heaps) of central Florida, that they may have periodically traded with eastern and northeastern Gulf coastal tribes as well, sailing with the currents and the winds from Yucatán northward, in a route that would later be exploited by Antón de Alaminos, the great Spanish pilot and navigator.

As trade progressed, trading centers naturally developed. Large bustling ports lined the Yucatán and upper Central American coasts, lying safely within natural harbors or reef-fringed lagoons. Island harbors included Isla de Cozumel, Isla de Mujeres, and Isla Contoy along the upper northeastern Yucatán coast. Cerritos, an island on the northern tip of Yucatán, was a major harbor and port facility, with numerous wharves and an artificial breakwater more than 1,000 feet long that provided safe harbor to large numbers of trading dugouts. Archaeologists have located over two dozen harbors and trading ports along the Yucatán peninsula and nearby islands. Here, coastal trade intermeshed with that of the interior. Sea salt, marine shells, and a diversity of seafood ranging from fish

Figure 2. Remnants of a vanished civilization.
Europeans first making contact with the inhabitants of the New World did not appreciate the depth or complexity of the civilizations they were about to destroy. Today, we are left with tantalizing glimpses of the Indians' artistic capabilities in the multihued ceramics called polychrome ware (A, a sitting woman, perhaps an icon for childbirth) and in the monochrome animal effigy bowls (B, a tripod bowl supported by stylized jaguars; and (C, a toucan and a tortoise) created by the coastal and inland tribes from Mexico, Central America, and Peru. [Collections of the author, and Dr. and Mrs. Kris Thoemke]

and shellfish to manatees, seals, crocodiles, and sea turtles were traded for obsidian weaponry and utensils, animal pelts, cotton cloth, cacao (chocolate), and spices. Mexican turquoise and copper, Costa Rican and Panamanian gold, Guatemalan jade, and finely worked ceramics were also important items of commerce (see Figure 2).

So extensive was this trade that by the time the first Spaniards arrived there already was a thriving commercial network, controlled by the wealthy nobility, fostering interchange of artisans and tradespeople, and conveying all the couriers, ambassadors, and statesmen so necessary for government functioning. Cities consisting of a central temple, surrounded in circles outward by the thatched and brightly decorated houses of the priests, chiefs, wealthy individuals and leading men, and finally the common folk, sprang up throughout Yucatan and Central America. Outside the cities lay the farm fields full of cotton, corn, and other vegetables known and grown for well over 3,000 years, and village after village rising away into the distant uplands and the slopes of the mountains themselves. While it might not be considered a peaceable kingdom owing to continuing incursions by various subtribes on one another, the Empire of the Sun was, for the most part, satisfied and prosperous.

With the arrival of the Spanish the ancient civilization quickly shattered. The natural inclination of the Maya for internecine warfare was not lost on the Spanish, who often manipulated one village or tribe against another as a means of population control and reduction. Throughout, the Spanish engaged in a continuing series of skirmishes for conquest and slave-taking, with unbelievable atrocities committed as a matter of course, or disguised under the pretense of conversion to Christianity. The continuing encroachment and settlement by the Spanish, and their "privatization" of the gold mines, salt pans, cotton manufacturing centers, and cacao plantations, brought a rapid end to the Golden Age. The introduction of iron tools and weapons, European ceramics, horses,[12] firearms, and Christianity sounded the death knell. The priests and ruling class were killed, imprisoned, or stripped of their rank. Books and libraries were burned.[13] Stone gods, their temples, and their ancient ceremonies were abolished as being both idolatrous and satanic. With the loss of centralized government and all its accompanying rituals for harvest and warfare, the common people left the burning cities and retreated into the surrounding forests. With this flight, one of the oldest mercantile and scientific civilizations in the western hemisphere collapsed, and 3,000 years of history, development, and progress sank beneath the tangled green sea of the jungle.

From the Mayan *Books of Chilam Balam,* a transliterated series of texts from Mayan into Spanish (ca. 1550) by a cult known as the Jaguar Priests, an apocalyptic chant reads in part:

> On that day, a strong man seizes the land,
> On that day, things fall to ruin,
> On that day, the tender leaf is destroyed,
> On that day, the dying eyes are closed,
> On that day, three signs are on the tree,
> On that day, three generations hang there,
> On that day, the battle flag is raised,
> And they are scattered afar in the forests.[14]

PEOPLE OF THE NAVEL OF THE MOON—THE AZTECS

The Aztecs were both an end point and a beginning of the indigenous Mexican Indians. The Aztecs stood on the shoulders of earlier giants—the Olmecs and the Toltecs. The Olmecs, whose great sneering monolithic heads lie scattered in seeming abandon throughout the jungles of upper Central America, were the innovators of two concepts—organized state religion and the priest rulers to both interpret and enforce its precepts. The large pyramid at La Venta, in the state of Tabasco on the Gulf, and another cultural center at Tres Zapotes, near Vera Cruz, contain buildings both architecturally rich and diverse. From the Olmecs came the idea of measuring time, a phonetic alphabet, and the calendar, all ideas that would be expanded by the later Mayans and Aztecs. Their great cathedral cities dotted the countryside from Mexico to Guatemala, culminating in Teotihuacan, the "Place where the Lords were buried."[15] The largest settlement in Middle America, it was located some 25 miles north of present-day Mexico City.

The Toltecs arrived later, and are thought to have originated near Tula, approximately 50 miles north of present-day Mexico City. A warlike group, they founded many fortified cities throughout the Valley of Mexico. From them arose a legend of a priest of the plumed serpent god Quetzalcoatl who opposed human sacrifice. Running afoul of the prevailing beliefs (and the military-royalty complex) of the time, the priest left Mexico, vowing to return one day from the east and reestablish his kingdom. As will be seen, the effect of this ancient belief would have far-reaching consequences for the Toltec descendants in 1521. Several other warlike tribes existed in the vicinity, but the one of most importance to our story was a small, disorganized, and poorly led group called the Mejicas. These marauding Indians, distant relatives of tribes from Nevada and the Pueblos of New Mexico, were once the serfs of other, more powerful tribes in the basin called the Valley of Mexico. Eventually, through war and intermarriage, they gained their ascendancy over the once powerful Toltecs. Uniting the remaining warring factions, including the Texcocans, Cholulans, and Chalcans, and adopting much of the Toltec culture, they stepped onto the stage of history in the fifteenth century as the militaristic Aztecs. They called themselves the People of the Navel of the Moon.[16]

These great tribes of the Valley of Mexico all spoke a common language, called *nahuatl*. The common religion involved human and animal sacrifice on a monthly basis to the Sun God, Huitzilopochtli, in order to keep him moving through the sky.[17] The toll could reach thousands per year. The temple at Tenochtitlan was consecrated with 20,000 souls.

The great cities that soon followed were constructed similarly to those of the Mayans, with a central large pyramidal temple and an open plaza for marketing or religious ceremonies, surrounding offices, and residences of the ruling elite and officials of lesser importance. The peasant farmers remained scattered in villages throughout the rest of the country. By 900 AD the cathedral cities of Monte Alban, Tajin, near Vera Cruz, and Cholula had risen along the Gulf coast, held sway, and then decayed. Some 400 years later the capital city of Tenochtitlan, was founded, replacing Teotihuacan which had burned about 800 AD. Another architectural masterpiece was Texcoco, established at about the same time on the lake of the same name.

Here architecture, the arts, writing, scientific calendars, astronomy, herbal medicine, law, a well-regulated commerce, an educational system, and a complex religion flourished—the summarization of some 3,000 years of previous thought, philosophy, and accomplishments—in a melding of arts, science, statehood, politics, and high barbarism.

Not all the Aztecs were philosophers, of course. Most were rural farmers, but there was a thriving and powerful merchant class; still others were international traders. Corn (maize) was the staple throughout the Valley of Mexico where they lived. Slash-and-burn agriculture predominated in which the fields were cleared by cutting and burning, planted, harvested, and then reburned for the succeeding harvest until the soil was exhausted (see Figure 3). The Aztecs also built irrigation canals and developed hydrological engineering into a well-versed science—an important accomplishment in a country that might

Figure 3. Slash and burn agriculture.
Some agricultural practices by the early Indians of the Gulf of Mexico remain little changed even today. Small plots of tropical forest are cleared, usually with machetes and axes (the "slash"), and are then cleaned of underlying debris and planted. After the crop is harvested the fields are set afire (the "burn"), to clear invading weeds and undergrowth, and then replanted. The cycle continues until the soils are exhausted. The Indians then move to another part of the land and begin again. The grueling intensity of the slashing method is evident in this small field located in a forest along the lower Yucatán coastline.

periodically undergo drought. The agricultural base allowed development of trade and commerce. Marine shells, uncut or intricately carved jade and turqouise, copper artifacts and utensils, fine clay pottery, and cotton cloth were traded both within the country or exported up and down the coast and undoubtedly across the Gulf.

But it was gold that delineated much of Aztec society, culture, and religion—gold ranging from secular jewelry and artifacts to offerings for tribute, religious amulets, and sacred temple ornaments. The amounts and complexity of the artifacts were simply astounding—ritualistic granaries filled with golden corn plants; idols, statues, effigies gilded or cast in solid gold; golden images of the sun as large as cartwheels, intricately hammered; golden weapons, golden armor, golden utensils. Gold used in every conceivable way to make every conceivable object, from the most mundane to the most spiritual. Gold whose luster flamed into the eyes of the conquistadores and dimmed them forever toward any perception or appreciation of humanity in the goldsmiths. Gold that superseded even the most basic tenets of Christianity—that fomented war, rapine, pillaging, atrocities, and death, and paid the invoices of an emerging European empire while toppling a 3,000-year-old people in one year's time.

If religion elevated the Aztec civilization to the heights that it achieved, it was also responsible in part for bringing it down. Moctezuma, the Aztec Emperor at the time of the Spanish contact, made a major messianic misinterpretation when he thought that Hernando Cortés, newly arrived on the Mexican coast, was the plumed serpent-god Quetzalcoatl returning from the east with his retinue to reestablish his earthly kingdom. Moctezuma, a philosopher and something of a mystic, was a wily, shrewd protagonist against the Spanish. But, uncertain as to the origins and omnipotence of the Spaniards, he finally paid with his life for his dilatory action.

The end came quickly. Hernando Cortés, desirous of acquiring Mexico "for God, for his king, for himself, and for his friends,"[18] landed near present day Vera Cruz in 1519 and began his march up the coast. Surviving a series of political machinations and skirmishes with competing conquistadores, he consolidated his forces. Cortes was not only a brilliant military commander but an astute politician, able to hold his own against the intrigues of both Castillian nobleman and Indian cacique alike. After securing his power base at Vera Cruz he marched northward at the head of a group of some 700 Spaniards and Indian allies and 15 horses, entering Tenochtitlan in November, 1519, and arresting the ruler Moctezuma. Six months later he and his troops were expelled by the Aztecs, in a night rued forever after as *la noche triste,* the "night of sorrows." Undaunted, Cortés regrouped with a mighty army of 40 horses, more than 500 Spaniards, and thousands of Indian allies or conscripts. Returning to Tenochtitlan in 1521, Cortés sacked the capital. Twenty centuries of Mexican Indian heritage, crowned by Aztecan civilization and power, swirled upward into the sky in the plumes of black smoke from the burning buildings. Tenochtitlan, the Aztecan wonder, the gleaming white metropolis on the lake, called by Bernal

Díaz del Castillo "The Enchanted City," had endured for less than 200 years.

The Aztecs of today are isolated in small villages throughout the mountains of Mexico. Others have intermarried with the Spanish, lost their lineage and are called *mestizos*. Many of the surviving Indians live in poverty, often on the edge of existence. These scattered remnants of a once-great empire poignantly illustrate a stanza of poetry written by the renowned poet-king, Nezahualcoyotl of Texcoco, shortly before the Spanish arrived in the New World:

> Not forever on earth; only a little while here.
> Although it be jade, it will be broken.
> Although it be gold, it is crushed.
> Although it be quetzal feather, it is torn asunder.
> Not forever on earth; only a little while here.[19]

Let Bernal Díaz del Castillo, chronicler of Cortés, provide the final epitaph:

> Of all these wonders that I then beheld
> to-day all is overthrown and lost,
> nothing left standing.[20]

Other Nations, Other Sorrows

FRENCH, BRITISH, AND AMERICAN CONTACTS

A LTHOUGH THE SPANISH, first into the Gulf of Mexico, were responsible in large part for much of the demise of Indian civilization in the Gulf region, they were not alone in their actions—just more efficient. The French and the British also made substantial inroads into the indigenous people's populations, but both of these European nations preferred to make the Indians allies to aid in achieving their territorial objectives. Moreover, few of the other Gulf-ring tribes had anywhere near the complexity of civilization seen in their southern neighbors. Most villages were small, composed of hunter-gatherers, and thus offered neither major resistance nor long-term threat to English or French colonists or the marauding privateers and pirates. Never well organized, most Indian skirmishes were little more than guerilla raids rather than pitched battles, unless alliances were formed. Both the French and British then reciprocated by forming alliances with their respective tribal pawns when the political issues so warranted. By pitting tribe against tribe and exacerbating old enmities, the two European nations divided from within and eventually conquered.

THE MISSISSIPPI SUN—THEOCRACY ON THE RIVER

A large and powerful tribe of heavily tattooed Indians, called (by the French) the Natchez, lived along the banks of the Mississippi River. Of uncertain origin but known to belong to a culture called "Mound Builders," these Muskhogean-speaking Indians had some early interchange with the Spanish, particulary de Soto's intrepid explorers who dared to ascend the Mississippi River. But most of our knowledge of these vanished Indians comes from the French who lived and traded with them during the turn of the seventeenth century.

The Natchez were interesting for two reasons: they were mound builders—every village had both a temple mound for sun worship and a special residential mound for the chief; and they were one of the few Indian tribes that was organized around an absolute monarchy. The chief, called the Great Sun, was considered a brother of the sun and therefore divine. He had total despotic control over the life and death of any of his people. The Great Sun ruled over three other castes: the Nobles, the Honored Men, and the common people, called Stinkards. The latter, consisting of Natchez tribespeople and captives, had approximately the same rights and privileges as the untouchable caste of India and were considered the lowest of the low.

The Natchez tribe was clearly ruled as a theocracy, with a conclave of priests subject only to the Great Sun. But in a most unusual turnabout, every Great Sun chief was mandated to marry a Stinkard woman. Any of his offspring were immediately reduced one step to the Noble class. Matrilineal descent ruled, with higher-class women determining the rank of their offspring. For example, the children of a Noblewoman and a Stinkard husband remained Noble, those of a Nobleman and a Stinkard woman fell one step further downward to Honored Man, and so on. Only the Great Sun's sister, herself a female Sun, could produce a successor to the Great Sun. Thus, the next Great Sun was the present chief's nephew.

The Natchez were an agrarian and hunting tribe, subsisting on maize (corn), wild vegetables, fruits, nuts, and a variety of game including bison, bear, turkeys, deer, and an occasional village dog. The common people's lot in life was to provide not only for themselves but sufficient excess to support the ruling castes and particularly the Great Sun and his retinue.

Regardless of the alleged solar magnificence, the onslaught of the French beginning in 1699 soon brought an early sundown. By 1704 fully one third of the estimated 4,500 Natchez had died off, victims of disease, skirmishes, and starvation, giving place "on God's wishes" (so the French believed), to the newly arrived Europeans. In 1729 the Natchez had had enough and rose up in open rebellion, attacking a French trading post and massacring 200 white people. The French, no doubt taking their cue from the Spanish, formed an alliance with the Choctaw Indians and put down the uprising so completely that the Natchez, for all intents and purposes, ceased to exist. The approximately 400 captives, along with the Great Sun, were sold into slavery on Santo Domingo in the Caribbean. Only a few escaped and were absorbed into neighboring tribes. For the Natchez, as with other northern Gulf tribes, the long night was just beginning.

THE FIRST FINAL SOLUTION

The next half century brought more incursions by the whites. The American frontier was opening westward along two riverine pathways—the Ohio and the Mississippi—both conduits to the Gulf. The British and the French, fighting for furs as well as territory, fanned the embers of intertribal hatred. In 1763 the northeast erupted into the flames of the French and Indian War. And the new Americans were beginning to realize how vast and rich a country the old Americans still occupied.

The successful conclusion of the American Revolutionary War, and the subsequent War of 1812, brought a new force onto the Indians' horizon. Land-hungry settlers began the long intrusions into the remaining territories and hunting grounds allowed to the Indians. By 1848, the fledgling eagle of the United States was now nearly half-feathered, with 13 new states added to the Union. Statehood meant settlement, particularly on Indian-owned lands. Tentative contacts became push, push turned to shove, and shove became retaliation. The administration of Andrew Jackson was the standard bearer for genocide. Earlier, in 1830, the Gulf coastal Indians east of the Mississippi had been given two choices by the Hero of New Orleans—relocate, or die. The final battlegrounds would be located on the peninsula first circumnavigated by Juan Ponce de León just 300 years earlier.

FLORIDA UNTAMED—THE SEMINOLE UPRISINGS

With the extermination of the Calusas and most of the other indigenous tribes of Indians, the peninsula of Florida became an empty niche that beckoned to both Indian and white settler alike. For a number of years some groups of Creek Indians, one speaking a language called Hitchiti, the other speaking a Muskhogean dialect, had been migrating into north Florida. These people were a polyglot mixture of purebred Creek, escaped negro slaves, remnant indigenous tribes, and Spanish settlers. The Spaniards called them "cimmarones" which, according to the commonly accepted interpretation, meant "wild, untamed" (in reference to their outcast status with the original Creek Confederation). The name was slurred by other whites and became "Seminoles."

The Seminoles were an industrious group, for all of their questionable status. They established villages and began to farm the land and raise cattle, horses, and pigs. At first, the newly immigrating white settlers lived more or less peacefully with these Indians, setting up trading posts and exchanging gunpowder, ammunition, cooking utensils, the usual beads and trinkets, and rum and whiskey for pelts. But as Spain's influence in the New World, and particularly in Florida, continued to wane, more and more settlers continued to enter Florida. The new arrivals noticed that many of the Indian settlements were located on prime agricultural lands. In yet another replay of the sad history between white man and red man, the Seminoles began to be pushed from their lands. Villages were raided for cattle and negroes, whom the Seminoles kept as slaves. Political machinations from the lowest local level all the way up to Washington, D.C., resulted in a series of treaties which little by little robbed the Seminoles of their land and their livestock. The Indians responded with counter-raids, killing a few settlers and inflaming a far larger number, who immediately petitioned the federal government for redress and removal of the upstarts. The culmination of these events, which began as far back as 1763, took place in 1823 at Moultrie Creek below St. Augustine, where a treaty of the same name was signed by some 150 Seminole chiefs. This brought to a close the First Seminole War. In return, the Indians were promised large sums of money for their land and their livestock. Little of this remuneration was ever paid, and still fewer Indians ever saw it.

In 1832, in an arrogant move fully equal to anything the Spanish had ever done in Mexico, the U.S. government appointed a new Indian commissioner and told him to prepare the Seminoles for their ultimate removal. In a series of deceitful parleys and promises, the Indians once again were made to sign a treaty, this time agreeing to their transfer to reservations in Oklahoma Territory, west of the Mississippi. The powder keg that had had its lid loosened in 1823 at Moultrie Creek now was kicked over. The spark that touched it off came three years later when the U.S. Army was sent to Florida to forcibly remove any Seminoles who did not leave for the west on their own volition.

The Second Seminole War exploded in Florida, between 1835 and 1842, when several groups of the Miccosukee and Seminole tribes, provoked by the broken treaties, U.S. government chicanery, and land-stealing settlers (and scornful of their leaders who acquiesced), began a series of guerrilla raids on isolated cabins, settlements, and military outposts. Led by several charismatic war chiefs, including Asi-sin-yahola (Osceola), Coacoochee (Wildcat), and Chekika, the Seminoles changed guerilla warfare from an art to a fine military science. In skirmishes up and down the peninsula, atrocities were committed on both sides. The U.S. military soon learned all over again the hard lessons taught the Spanish—fighting a foe on his own ground, in the swamps, forests, and waterfilled prairies of Florida, was not the way to win a war. Yet in the end, with the deaths of more than 1,500 white soldiers and the expenditure of some $40 million, the United States prevailed. All but a small group of fiercely independent Seminoles were sent to Oklahoma. Deep in the steaming swamps of the Big Cypress and Everglades regions, the remaining Seminoles escaped and took up their new lifestyle.

The Third Seminole War began as a series of retributional murders by Indians responding to provocations by the continually encroaching white settlers. Again the U.S. military was sent in, this time offering a $250 bounty for every Seminole captured. The hostilities ended with the kidnapping and holding hostage of Chief Billy Bowlegs' granddaughter. Giving up the fight, he and another old war chief named Tiger Tail conceded defeat. On the steamer carrying them to New Orleans and transfer points west, Tiger Tail, wracked with grief and despair committed suicide. Behind was an unknown number of unrepentant and unrepatriated Miccosukees and Seminoles now hiding deep in the swamps of south Florida.

By 1855, the few other surviving Gulf coast Indian tribes were settled on reservations, made Christians, and considered "pacified." Now, the contenders for Gulf wealth could get on with the business of colonization. What the Spanish conquistadores had begun 350 years earlier was now concluded by American frontiersmen.

In 1835, on the eve of the Second Seminole War, Alexis de Tocqueville prophetically wrote in his *Democracy in America*:

> The Spaniards, by unparalleled atrocities. . . did not succeed in exterminating the Indian race and could not even prevent them from sharing their rights; the United States Americans have attained both these results with wonderful ease, quietly, legally, and philanthropically, without spilling blood and without violating a single one of the great principles of morality in the eyes of the world. It is impossible to destroy men with more respect to the laws of humanity. [1]

In the final analysis, as Peter Farb so succinctly noted, just two mistakes were made—one by each side. The red man suspected the white man might be a god; the white man considered the Indian to be an animal.[2]

Development of U.S. Interests in the Gulf

LTHOUGH THE MAJOR commercial and exploratory efforts in the Gulf of Mexico during the nineteenth century were being made by the British, the new and rapidly expanding United States still shared the lands around the Gulf almost exclusively with Spain. The ex-colonial merchants were quick to appreciate the Gulf of Mexico as a sea-lane. Inland rivers from the Rio Grande eastward provided the water routes. By the early 1800s the Mississippi River had assumed the dominant role in U.S. commerce it has held ever since, connecting the interior via the Ohio and Missouri rivers to New Orleans, the Gulf, and the world.

The admission of the five Gulf-ring states to the Union (Louisiana in 1812, Mississippi in 1817, Alabama in 1819, and Florida and Texas in 1845) solidified the southern territorial integrity of the United States and provided a necessary bufferzone on the Gulf toward preventing further expansionist aims by any European nation. Primarily agricultural in economy, these five states began to establish the empire of King Cotton, with the resulting large plantations that could only be economically operated through slave labor. New Orleans remained the largest, most centralized, and best organized port for shipping cotton and other agricultural and manufactured goods of the deep south to the world.

With the demand increasing for more accurate navigational charts to guide the often heavy, unwieldy sailing vessels through the nearshore shoals and reefs, the United States Coast Survey (now the U.S. Coast and Geodetic Survey) began to work in earnest in the region in 1845. They investigated tides, seawater chemistry, the physical contours and make-up of the sea floor, and traced the origins of the ever- shifting, perpetually flowing currents spilling out of the Gulf. First discovered by Antón de Alaminos, pilot for Juan Ponce de León in 1513, they constitute one of the greatest of oceanic highways, the Gulf Stream.

The nineteenth century saw blossoming trade and westward expansion of the American frontier. The ports of Mobile, New Orleans, Galveston, Vera Cruz, and Havana formed a mercantile polygon whose points focused the sea routes now beginning to thread through the Gulf. Goods arriving from Europe and the Antilles were exchanged for cotton, lumber, tobacco, indigo, sugar, and many other products produced by the United States. And when the clouds of civil war gathered, the ports of Brownsville, Mobile, and New Orleans assumed even greater importance to the Confederacy, becoming the escape channels from the stranglehold of the Union blockade at Charleston, Norfolk, and other Atlantic ports.

With the conclusion of the Civil War, the predominant interests of the newly re-United States in the Gulf of Mexico were directed toward rebuilding an almost completely shattered economy. The southern half of the Confederacy struggled back to its feet, fought carpetbag rule, and attempted to establish a viable economic structure in which slavery could no longer play a part. Agriculture remained a prime and easily reestablished source of income, but coal and iron industries began to appear in Mobile and Birmingham, forestry assumed a new role in Mississippi, Texas expanded the cattle industry for which it still remains famous, and Florida— well, Florida remained essentially a vast savannah and swampland, farmed mostly by some farsighted (some said benighted) souls who planted citrus. And then somebody else (we shall never really know who) proposed the idea that Florida had the perfect climate for invalids and those wishing to escape the northern winters. And suddenly, the Land of Sunshine had an entirely new industry, and one which has supported it ever since—the Yankee tourist.

Scientific interests around the Gulf were more mundane, directed primarily toward biological and fishery investigations. In the 1880s the explorations of the recently formed U.S. Fish Commission were making the hidden regions and inhabitants of the deep Gulf of Mexico as well known as the flora and fauna of the land.

At the turn of the century, the U.S. Navy Hydrographic Office implemented an innovative plan requesting all vessels sailing the Gulf to log daily certain parameters (ship's speed, direction, wind speed, water temperature, and other factors). The data summarized in 1914 produced the most complete picture of water currents in the Gulf to that time. It is intriguing to wonder, had this information, so vital for shipping, been available 300 years earlier to the Spanish, whether the Gulf of Mexico today might still be a Spanish sea.[1]

By the turn of the century, the "old South" was rapidly becoming the "New South." Railroads pushed their way into the wildernesses and sewed the great cities together with iron, ties, and ballast. Railways and roadways supplemented or replaced riverways. Mississippi flatboats gave way to paddlewheel steamers, and these, in turn, to boxcars, cattlecars, coal gondolas and pulpwood flatcars. The poleboatsmen's halloo was exchanged for the piercing bellow of the riverboat and the lonely wail of the railroad steam whistle. The wealth of this newest country of the new world was being shipped both within and abroad. And suddenly, along the coasts, in the ever expanding harbors, above the levees, villages became towns and towns turned into cities. For the maturing United States, the Gulf of Mexico was now more important than ever.

Florida, the first southern land of the continent to be discovered, was among the last to be settled and developed. But where galleons failed, iron rails succeeded. In Tallahassee, the state legislature and the Trustees of the Internal Improvement Fund fell over themselves attempting to sell "useless swampland" to the burgeoning timber interests and would-be railroad magnates. Hamilton Diston, a Philadelphia tool maker bought 4 million acres for 25 cents an acre, and immediately began dredging a canal to connect the lower west coast with the center of the state. By 1885, Henry Plant's railroads had connected Georgia and central Florida to the coastal village of Tampa. In a few short years that city became a bustling deepwater port where coastal steamers, freighters, lumber boats and cattle ships crowded the newly built wharves. Just inland, in 1888, pebble and hard-rock phosphates were discovered, triggering a speculative land rush for Florida's own white gold. Henry Flagler's Florida East Coast Railway, the "Railroad That Went to Sea," was completed in 1912, allowing rail travelers and freight handlers to make connections from every major city in the north served by railways to the continental tip at Key West. Population explosion, land boom and bust, recovery and stabilization followed. The new grandees wore silk shirts and buttondown vests, and blue-shirted conquistadores conquered the land with steam dredge and dragline. Pensacola, Tampa, Sarasota, Charlotte Harbor, Key West—the Calusa and Timucuan Indian city names would remain—but the land would never be the same.

LOOKING TOWARD THE FUTURE

Today, exploration and exploitation continue throughout the Gulf of Mexico. Ships from U.S. and foreign oil companies roam the continental shelf. Research vessels from the U.S. military, federal and state agencies, and academic institutions join those from Mexico and Cuba, crisscrossing the open offshore waters. Cruise ships ply the tropical sea-lanes off Yucatán. Shrimping fleets sail from Louisiana, Texas, Mississippi, Alabama, Florida, and from numerous ports along the Mexican coast to harvest grounds as near as their own coastlines and as far as the Tortugas and Yucatán. Long-liners and drift netters from Cuba, the Far East, and the once Soviet Union reap a continuing harvest from the open sea. And merchant vessels from tramp steamers to supertankers ply the offshore trade routes carrying the consumer goods of the world, and to the world.

But the picture is not completely rosy. Population impacts on the coastal regions are increasing, pressure for coastal and offshore oil and gas exploration continues, many commercial fisheries are overexploited, recreational open space is deteriorating because of pollution, coastal habitats are undergoing constant degradation, and demands for cleaner waters and waterways are becoming more strident. Solutions to these problems are no longer simple, and many are environmentally damaging. Less affluent nations like Mexico and Cuba, backed into a financial corner and burdened with hungry populations, cannot afford the methodical, long-term solutions to many of these problems such as have been espoused by the United States.

But with time and experience has come, finally, an increasing awareness of the fragility of these marine ecosystems, and the study and exploration of the Gulf of Mexico has entered a new era. Policymakers in the Gulf-ring nations have agreed that the emphasis should now be directed toward wise conservation of natural resources and preservation of environmentally critical areas. Acknowledging not only national interests but an implicit requirement for sharing this great marine treasure chest has brought a new maturity to political thinking. Just how successful this new policy direction will be remains to be seen.

Weather along La Mar del Norte.
Thousands of cumulus clouds, propelled by the trade winds, sail row upon row like a vast armada of puffy white galleons along the southeastern margin of the Loop Current (lower left corner). To the north, above the clear area, a second line of coalescing large cumulus clouds marks the boundary of a disturbed weather system that will eventually produce thunderstorms and rain-squalls. [U.S. Geological Survey, EROS Data Center, Sioux Falls, South Dakota.]

Part Two

The Sea Where the Gulf Stream Begins

Sailing south . . . all the three ships . . . saw a current which, although they had a good wind they could not stem. It seemed that they advanced well, but they soon recognized that they on the contrary were driven back, and that the current was more powerful than the wind.

Ponce de León, 1513

Sea, Stone, and Sand

THE MANY PARTS THAT MAKE THE WHOLE

THE NOTED GEOLOGIST H. K. Brooks wrote in 1973: "The Gulf of Mexico and the adjoining land has received more attention from geologists than any other region in the world." Much of this information was the product of oil and gas explorations along the coast and offshore continental shelf in the northwestern and northeastern Gulf. Data from this and other research indicate that the basin which delimits the Gulf has both geological and hydrological connections to the Caribbean Sea. The formation and structural complexities of the Gulf, therefore, require it to be considered not as an isolated area but rather in conjunction with both the North American continent, to which it belongs, and the basins and islands of the Greater Antilles archipelago, to which it also shows some geological relationships (see endsheets).

DEFINING THE AMERICAN MEDITERRANEAN

While it may be safe to say that most laymen know where the Gulf of Mexico is, few know just what it is. Oceanographers define the Gulf of Mexico as a mediterranean-type sea, that is, a semi-enclosed, partially land-locked, intercontinental, marginal sea (lying on the margin of a major ocean). Such mediterranean-type water bodies are separated from the adjacent ocean by a sill or ledge rising high up from the adjacent oceanic floor. These marginal seas have water masses and water movements that often differ substantially from those in the ocean.

Looking at the endsheets it can be seen that the basin of the Gulf is circumscribed by the North American continent, including the states of Texas, Louisiana, Mississippi, Alabama, and Florida on the north, by Mexico on the west, and by Florida on the east. The southern boundary is more complex and is formed by the Straits of Florida north of the island of Cuba and a line arbitrarily drawn from Cabo Catoche on the Yucatán Peninsula to Key West, Florida.[1]

In the Gulf three physiographic features stand out: a shoreline bordered by coastal plains and mountains; a surrounding, generally wide, continental shelf; and a large, deep, off-central basin. Together, these features and their boundaries not only constitute the Gulf but define the northern portion of what oceanographers call the American Mediterranean Sea, which includes the Gulf of Mexico and the Caribbean Sea.

The general shape of the Gulf of Mexico is roughly oval and resembles a gigantic pit with a wide, shallow rim (continental shelf) grading into relatively steep sides (continental slope) that drop from 100 to 1,700 fathoms (180 to 3,100

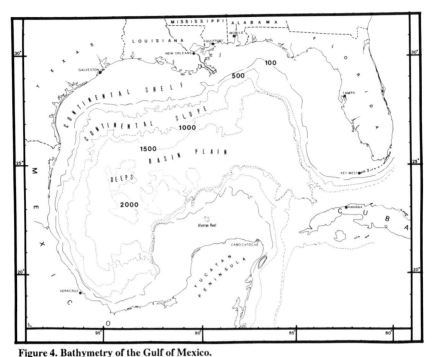

Figure 4. Bathymetry of the Gulf of Mexico.
Isobaths (contour lines showing depth measurements in fathoms) show the Gulf to be a deep, irregularly shaped pit surrounded by a Continental shelf of varying width. The Continental slope declines more gradually off Texas and Louisiana than off Florida and Yucatán, where enormous, clifflike escarpments occur. On the floor of the Mexico Basin Plain several irregularly shaped depressions, termed deeps, delineate the deepest oceanic portions of the Gulf. Within this region of the Gulf occurs the maximum recorded depth to date, 2393 fathoms (14,358 ft). [Modified and redrawn from J. I. Jones et al. (eds.), 1973, and U. S. Hydrographic Office bathymetric charts]

meters) where they meet the Mexico Basin Plains, composed of the Sigsbee and adjacent Florida Plains that form the deep ocean floor of the Gulf (see Figure 4). Although these plains may appear generally flat, areas of noticeable relief do occur. There is a great deal of water in this pit, some 3.35 million cubic kilometers, which equates to nearly 265 trillion gallons/cubic kilometer.

The maximum width of the Gulf is approximately 1,000 miles in an east-west direction; north to south its narrowest width is about 500 miles on a line from the Mississippi Delta to the tip of the Yucatán Peninsula.

The total area of the Gulf of Mexico is about 1.5 million square kilometers, equivalent to nearly 600,000 square miles. Submerged shallow and intertidal areas (less than 10 fathoms or 20 meters deep) comprise about 38% of the total area; continental shelf (10-100 fathoms or 20-180 meters deep) about 22%; continental slopes (100-1,500 fathoms or 180-3,000 meters) 20%; and the abyssal or deep-sea basins (greater than 1,700 fathoms or 3,000 meters) another

20%. The deepest part of the Gulf of Mexico is the Sigsbee Deep at 2,393 fathoms (4,384 meters), one of a series of depressions located in the southwestern portion of the Mexico Basin Plain.

THE SHORELINE

The marine continental shoreline extends from Cape Sable, Florida, to the tip of the Yucatán Peninsula, about 3,600 miles. The northwest coast of Cuba would add another 240 or so miles.[2] However, the total tidal shoreline, including all the bays, inlets, and other features is over 17,000 miles long in the United States alone. Of this shoreline, 1,553 miles are sandy beach (much of it on barrier islands), some 1,370 miles are barrier islands, and the remainder is a profusion of topographical features including beach ridges, keys, barrier reefs, pocket harbors, and coastal embayments, lagoons, marshes, bayous, and mangrove forests. Putting this into perspective, to sail along an equivalent length of other U.S. coastlines would require a run from southern California to north of Washington state, or from Providence, Rhode Island, all the way to Miami.

The shorelines of the Gulf of Mexico exhibit a complex array of features (see Figure 5). Because the climate throughout the area ranges from warm-temperate to tropical, a wide variety of maritime regions also occurs. Geologically interesting areas include (progressing clockwise) the drowned limestone shelves (or karst region) on the northwestern Florida coast; the great mangrove ridge of the Ten Thousand Islands; the Colorados Barrier Reef on Cuba's northwestern shore; the rain-forest deltas of Yucatán; the volcanic regions around Vera Cruz; the offshore submerged mountain chains, and salt domes east of Tampico; the hypersaline Laguna Madre in southwest Texas and Mexico; the extensive bayou and brackish-to-saline marsh regions on the Louisiana coast; and the great sedimentary deposits of the Mississippi Delta depositional fan. Also included are the ring of barrier islands found on nearly every Gulf coast shore.[3]

In geological terms the Gulf of Mexico coastline is young; relatively newly formed mountains border the southern coasts, particularly on the island of Cuba, and in the southwestern quadrant in Mexico, where they have been traced northeastward into the Gulf off the mouth of the Rio Grande River. A higher range is found extending 50 miles offshore east of Tampico, Mexico, where the mountains rise 5,800 feet (1,770 meters) off the seafloor and approach to within 33 feet (10 meters) of the sea surface.

The southwestern shore of the Gulf is an ancient rim of fire that remains geologically active. Volcanic mountains of the Gulf region occur in the vicinity of Vera Cruz and southward. They form an extension of the Sierra Neo-Volcanica, a series of eruption-formed peaks extending across Mexico from the Pacific coast, through Mexico City, to the Gulf. The San Martín Tuxtla range south of Vera Cruz is also associated with the Sierra and boasts some of the highest peaks in Mexico, including Orizaba (5,700 meters or 18,696 feet) and Cofre de Perote (4,280 meters or 14,048 feet). El Chichón, a recent volcano in Chiapas State, is currently over 3,000 feet high (see Figure 6). Beachside and nearshore cliffs to 1,000 feet occur at Roca Partida and Punta Delgada, while

Figure 5. Some interesting shoreline features around the Gulf.
Gulf coastlines are a variegated mixture of calcareous sands, karst limestones, castellated mudlumps, and volcanic rocks, with numerous other intergradations. (A) A derelict bastion in an empty sea, Fort Jefferson National Monument sits in red-bricked splendor on the calcareous sandy keys of the Dry Tortugas. The islets in turn rest on the backbone of an ancient coral reef that once extended from near Miami south and westward nearly 220 miles around the peninsular tip of Florida and into the Gulf of Mexico. (B) Like mossy hummocks, the karst limestones of northwestern Florida reach into the Gulf washed by waves and tides. These limestones of relatively recent age (100,000 years or less) overlay at least part of the Suwannee Limestone, a marine formation of Oligocene age (greater than 15 million years old). (C) The stratified battlements of Mississippi mudlumps rise along their namesake river delta in Louisiana. Built out of silty sediments contributed by much of the eastern United States, mudlumps form extensive deposits on the delta shore of the Gulf. (D) Storm-borne breakers crash ashore on the dark and rocky volcanic coastline near El Moro, Mexico. The mountains that helped form this coast can be seen dimly through the mist sweeping down toward the beach. Here, the ceaseless war between charging breakers and the tumbled breastworks of volcanic shorelines continues unabated. What the land laid down eons ago by volcanism the sea will soon claim by erosion. [Courtesy Darryl L. Felder]

offshore a cluster of hillocks and knolls disappearing into deep water provides additional evidence of volcanic activities.

THE CONTINENTAL SHELF

The submerged continental shelf is nearly continuous around the entire basin, being broken only at the Yucatán Channel and Straits of Florida. The shelf varies in width from 8 to 135 miles. The widest portions are found off western Florida (117 miles), off the mouth of the Sabine River on the border of Texas and Louisiana (110 miles), and north of the Yucatán Peninsula (135 miles). Total shelf area is over 4,300 square miles.

At least three large submarine canyons (the De Soto Canyon off Panama

City, Florida, the Mississippi Trough south of that river, and the Alaminos Canyon off Matagorda Bay, Texas) interrupt the shelf and mark the site of ancient river valleys from times of lower sea levels. These canyons rise in relief from 200 to 600 meters (600 to 1,970 feet) above the seafloor. The longest and deepest can be traced in water from 20 fathoms deep nearshore to over 900 fathoms deep offshore (120 feet or 37 meters to 5,400 feet or 1,645 meters).

For an ancient sea basin the Gulf of Mexico seems remarkably free of major surface features. Geologists have mapped drowned dunes, submerged rocky outcrops and ledges, salt domes, shelf-edge pinnacles, sinkholes, troughs, and ancient (relict) reef structures on the continental shelves and slopes.[4] Yet other than the coastal barrier islands, some limestone keys off Florida, and a few coral-sand and lava-rock islets off Mexico, no large offshore islands occur (see endsheets).

THE CONTINENTAL SLOPE AND DEEP SEA

The continental slope, the physiographic feature that forms the deepening seaward extension of the continental shelf, is variable in both steepness and width and runs like a great cliff or escarpment around the entire Gulf basin. Great valleylike notches occur irregularly along its length, the most prominent being the Catoche Tongue on northeast Yucatán (see endsheets).

The Mexico Basin, a large, triangular area with depths greater than 2,000 fathoms (12,000 feet), is the only basin of the five found in the American Mediterranean that occurs in the Gulf. The Sigsbee Deep, the deepest part of the Gulf of Mexico, is also found here. Along the abyssal Sigsbee Plain occur several prominent features, including hummocks, knolls, and ridges. The hummocks or salt domes off Louisiana, often capped by assemblages of deep-sea corals and related organisms, are well-known topographical features that may rise up to 2,500 feet above the seafloor, whereas associated troughs and depressions may be up to 2,000 feet deep.

Guyots, distinctive flat-topped prominences submerged in hundreds of fathoms of water, are scattered throughout the Mexico Basin. Isolated, irregularly peaked seamounts, such as the Jordan Knoll, the Sigsbee Knolls, and others, also form distinct features rising from the Basin floor.

A curious feature found only near the mouth of the Mississippi River are mudlumps and mudlump islands. These are mounds of mud, often sculpted into small cliffs up to 10 feet high, having a core of fine-grained clay surrounded and/or capped by clay and silt. Their origin remains speculative, but they appear to have been formed when excessively heavy sediment deposits from the Mississippi River forced the surrounding mud to bulge upward into mounds (see Figure 5c).

Oil seeps, freshwater and saltwater springs, and cold saline seeps also occur along the continental slope in some parts of the Gulf of Mexico. Oil seeps, naturally occurring flows of oil from the earth, have been found all along the continental margins from DeSoto Canyon westward to salt domes off Texas. Several springs producing either fresh or saline waters occur on the nearshore

Figure 6. The mark of El Chichón.

El Chichón volcano, whose name in Spanish means "the swelling," erupted in early 1982. Located in Mexico's Sierra Neo-Volcanica (approximately at the point of the left-hand arrow) the volcano quickly spewed an ash cloud over several thousand square miles of the Yucatán Peninsula, Belize, Honduras, El Salvador, and parts of Nicaragua. While not a particularly catastrophic volcano by world standards, the magnitude of the ash cloud provides a glimpse of how the fires and smoke of the earth, in conjunction with the weather, can affect large areas of the land and sea. [National Climatic Data Center, Satellite Data Information Service]

continental shelf, such as those found on a large deep-sea limestone platform off northwestern Florida.

Of greater interest is recent evidence which reveals that some biologically strange clam and tube worm communities occur from about 900-3,000 feet in certain oil seep areas. These regions are termed "seismic wipe-out" zones[5] because they are presumed to have been produced through geological alterations of the seafloor. They occur along the Texas-Louisiana shelf, and at cold saline seeps at the fractured base of the Florida Escarpment. The saline seeps, and the "wipe-out" seeps, while not thermally analogous to the well-known deep-sea hydrothermal (superheated gas and steam) vents found on the eastern Pacific rise and on the Mid-Atlantic ridge, nevertheless exhibit some biological similarities to the latter. Both appear to support an indigenous clam and tubeworm fauna similar to that found at the vents. These organisms are of great interest to marine scientists because they are chemosynthetic; that is, they seem to be nutritionally dependent on hydrogen sulfide and/or methane gas that either bubbles up naturally from the substrate, or is produced by bacterial decomposition of the seeping oil (see Plates 1, 2A).

Yet another interesting deep-Gulf community is associated with deep-sea pockmarks, cavities that form with the expansion, eruption and subsequent collapse of a gaseous dome. These contain beds of mussels that can somehow exist in pools of hypersaline brines (up to three times normal seawater concentrations) that seep into the "popped" pockmark. Even more amazing is that the mussels survive in an almost total lack of oxygen. These molluscs also apparently rely on symbiotic bacteria inside the mussel tissue to provide food.

Origins of the Gulf of Mexico

A S WITH MANY THEORIES on beginnings, the genesis of the Gulf of Mexico is still not clearly understood. Most geologists are now convinced that the basin itself formed through subsidence, that is, some mechanism which forced the seafloor downward. They disagree on how that mechanism occurred. At present three explanations appear most likely. The first two hold that the Gulf is simply a continental plate that collapsed downward (foundered) either through down-faulting or sedimentary overload; the third hypothesis is that it was formed by continental enclosure or accretion, as a consequence of seafloor rifting and associated crustal movements (called plate tectonics). This chapter looks at each of these hypotheses in some detail.

FORMED FROM A SUNKEN CONTINENT?

The foundered-plate hypothesis, originally proposed at the turn of the century, suggests that the Gulf was once an elevated landmass of an ancient continental region that formed part of the entire American Mediterranean (that is, the Caribbean Sea, the Antillean chain, and the Gulf of Mexico). During the Cretaceous period (135 million years before present, abbreviated as mybp) this plate underwent tectonic alteration (earthquakes, volcanism, and mountain building) and collapsed downward, forming the present oceanic basin lying today in more than 12,000 feet of seawater, bounded by Yucatán on the west and the island of Cuba to the south.

This hypothesis, however, does not account for the substantial accumulations of land- and sea-borne sediments on the deepest part of the present-day seafloor, sediments which normally are laid down by river flows. Geologists think that insufficient time has elapsed to allow for so much sediment accretion (that is, accumulating by filtering down) through deep-sea water columns. They suggest instead that these deposits were present before any hypothesized collapse. Geologists also point to recent evidence from plate tectonics (the movement of the earth's large crustal plates, sometimes called continental drift) which shows that Cuba, now a continental-like oceanic island, was at one time attached to Yucatán but became separated when Caribbean oceanic plates slid beneath Central American continental plates. Thus, neither Yucatán nor Cuba could have had any direct relationship in the formation of the Gulf.

An alternative hypothesis suggests that the Gulf originally began as a shallow sea that gradually filled with river-borne sediments washed down from the surrounding coastal plains. Beginning about 400 mybp the seafloor began

58

to slowly subside under the combined action of the weight of these sediments and seafloor instability until it reached its present depth of more than 12,000 feet below sea level.

The compelling evidence for this view lies in the large accretions of sediments that occur in terraces from areas as far inland as Oklahoma, Missouri, Kentucky, and Tennessee. These sediments also seem to overlie even the deepest seafloors, and are found in the large sediment fans that still form today at the mouths of the great rivers. Such sediment loading can be enormous. For example, the accumulation of several thousand feet of sediments on top of basaltic basement rock in the Sigsbee Deep, the deepest part of the Gulf of Mexico, indicates that before it began to be filled in the Cenozoic era (about 60 mybp) it was even deeper, perhaps by as much as 25,000 feet.

Some geologists support a third hypothesis (linked to the second) which holds that the Gulf of Mexico could have been formed from a geosyncline, a fancy word that describes a trough caused when a geologically unstable land area collapses and becomes filled with sediments. For evidence they are able to trace just such a geosyncline all around the Gulf with deviations from land into sea at Mississippi, Texas, and the Rio Grande area in Mexico. This geosyncline is still active today and sedimentary evidence suggests millions of years of loading, which produced a subsidence of over 30,000 feet!

While the sedimentary hypotheses seem to carry the most weight, a serious problem exists in explaining how and why extensive areas of salt (presumably formed in shallow evaporative seas in the Jurassic period, about 180 mybp) came to lie under these same seafloor sediments.

AN ANCIENT BASEMENT FORMED BY FIRE

The combination of seafloor spreading and plate tectonics are responsible for the origins and current positions of the continents and the oceans on earth. To see how this activity affects the Gulf of Mexico we must go back in time some 180 million years to a period before the Atlantic Ocean existed. Liquified rock (magma) from deep in the earth and under intense heat and pressure began to rise vertically to the earth's surface beneath a gigantic proto-continent geologists called Pangaea. As the magma reached the earth's solid outer crust it had three effects: first, it caused the continent to crack apart; second it raised a continuous series of large mountainous ridges between the separating continental plates; and third, it both created and began to push primeval seafloor laterally away from the ridges. The crack, and its defining ridges, formed a submerged moutain range called the Mid-Atlantic Ridge. This ridge today snakes more or less longitudinally from the tip of Iceland soutward to east of the tip of South America.[1]

As the magma continued to rise, new mountains formed on either side of the crack, and the seafloor continued to spread outward, carrying the older mountains and the split continental plates (now called Laurasia and Gondwanaland) either westward or eastward away from the central ridge at about 1 - 2 inches per year. Gradually, the large continental masses stabilized. Then, as the westward-moving sea floor of the new Atlantic Ocean met the Caribbean and

Continental American plates it began to slip under them in a tectonic process called *subduction*. This process also caused these plates to rotate and grind slowly past each other, much like gigantic paving stones. The resulting mountain-building and crustal faulting, beginning about 150 mybp, was responsible not only for the north-south extension of the Caribbean Sea, but also for the configuration of the entire American Mediterranean, including the formation of all the deep basins both in the Gulf of Mexico and the Caribbean Sea.[2]

Nor can the volcanic prehistory of the Gulf be ignored. Stratigraphic data (derived from the way rocks of different ages form layers) have shown that the deep Gulf basin is formed of basaltic rock, erupted from volcanoes and deposited in pre-Cambrian seas over 600 mybp. These remnant areas of deep Gulf seafloor, along with their more southerly sister plates in the Yucatán and Caribbean basins, thus have great antiquity. Further evidence that these deep plates are both ancient and quite extensive was provided in 1935 when it was shown that the basement plate of the Gulf of Mexico extended from Tabasco in Mexico to as far north as southern Illinois and included portions of Texas, Arkansas, the Florida peninsula, and the northern Bahama banks. This evidence suggests that the Gulf of Mexico may be, in its basement, a very ancient ocean indeed.

PUTTING IT ALL TOGETHER

So what's the final assessment as to how the Gulf of Mexico formed? Probably a combination of all three hypotheses. The evidence of large-scale geological processes operating in the Gulf is incontrovertible and easily seen in the deep-sea fractured blocks along the Florida Escarpment and off the Yucatán Peninsula (see endsheets). The data suggest that the Gulf basin, first created in the Paleozoic era, filled in with riverine sediments and collapsed about 300 million years ago, either because of the weight of these sediments or owing to tectonic processes, or both. Continued sediment loading throughout the Mesozoic and Cenozoic eras filled the basin margins (the geosynclines) and (perhaps) deepened the basin floor. Episodes of mountain building from as near as southern Mexico and as far away as the Rocky Mountains, seafloor spreading in the Atlantic and Caribbean, and resulting crustal deformation—all of these both altered the basin configuration and contributed to additional sedimentation. This sedimentation, in turn, extended the continental margins and (like pouring sand in a floating Dixie cup) tilted and forced them downward. So, although the overall basin may look simple, its origins are fairly complex and reflect processes that continue even today.

Yet for all of its previously shaky beginnings, the Gulf of Mexico remains reasonably stable today. No major earthquakes have ever occurred in the northeastern shelf area of Mississippi, Alabama, and Florida. And all volcanic activity is today restricted to Mexico. Indeed, the Gulf of Mexico is considered one of the most geologically stable areas in the world.

Water, Ice, and Life

THE CREATION OF SEA AND LAND

G EOLOGISTS LOOK AT the Gulf of Mexico and see four major factors operating. First, the Gulf basin is bounded by continental landmasses threaded with numerous rivers, all of which empty their waters into the sea. Second, it is a basin both formed by, and being filled by, terrigenous (land-borne) sediments primarily from four large river systems. Third, the eastern and western basin margins support extensive carbonate limestone banks. Fourth, only in southern Mexico are volcanism and earthquakes important to Gulf coastal physiography. To coastal and marine geologists this says quite simply that, so far as geological processes creating and shaping the Gulf of Mexico are concerned, sedimentation is the name of the game.

The Gulf of Mexico is without a doubt a very large and extremely efficient sediment trap. The sediments come from three major sources: erosion of the land by glaciation (glaciers and their movements), transport of clastics (broken rock and fossil fragments) by rivers, and organic mineral deposits—the deposition of the remains of marine organisms. The end result is a complex and highly mixed sedimentary potpourri that will keep geologists happily sampling for decades to come. Where the sedimentation process began and where it is going is our story now.

SEA FROM THE LAND, LAND FROM THE SEA

The first of these depositions began long ago in the shadowed yesteryears of the early earth. These sediments need not concern us today because most of them are now compressed into rock. Our interest is in the more recent past, that geological era known to geologists as the Cenozoic, when earth, air, fire, and water were finishing their shaping of our present land and sea. It was a time of changing sea levels, when the earth's oceans rose and fell with almost periodic regularity, clocked by the great ice ages, and events transpired in thousands rather than millions of years. Then massive glaciers rumbled southward across the Eurasian and North American continents, gouging hills and valleys, while howling blizzards and rainstorms ground mountains into foothills. The water required for such glaciers ultimately comes from one place: the sea. With so much seawater tied up as ice,[1] sea levels were greatly lowered; in the Gulf the sea may have receded by as much as 300 to 450 feet. But glaciers are never forever. As they melted, the runoff coalesced, beginning as trickles and merging into streams and eventually into mighty rivers. The flowing waters eroded the rocks and soils, and the particles were swept toward the sea. As they bumped and clattered down the ancient river courses, these particles added their own abrasion, creating more and more sediments that eventually were deposited in large and ever-expanding deltaic fans at the numerous river mouths opening along the edge of the Gulf. Creeping outward across the shallow and deeper seafloor, they wrote their names and their history in the particulate inks that geologists read today.

With the melting and eventual retreat of the glaciers across the land, the seas of the earth once again began to refill. In the newly expanded Gulf of Mexico, the great offshore river valleys of Tampa, Charlotte Harbor, Mobile Bay, Mississippi, and Rio Grande were drowned by Gulf waters and new beaches and shores were created. Wave-action ground their old sediments still finer and the winds and rains redistributed them along the newly defined coasts.

Along the beaches primeval lines of dunes appeared, consolidated, and were washed away or inundated. Behind the beaches ancient estuaries were created, filled with muds, drowned, and were re-created farther and farther inland. Saline lagoons baked slowly into gray-white hardness in the long Pleistocene summers, their evaporated salts forming great beds of minerals. Coastal forests were drowned, and their peat layers, often tens of feet thick, were swallowed by the sea and changed into a mute and spongy shroud covering their graves. And still the rivers flowed,

Figure 7. The erosion of ancient seabeds.
Cascading through its geological history, a small stream in northern Alabama tumbles through cross-bedded limestones laid down by marine organisms tens of millions of years ago when the waters of the ancient Gulf and Atlantic Ocean washed shores farther inland than today. Fractured and twisted through geological processes, and now eroded through the continual rush of water, the rocks provide mute testimony of the immense amounts of sediment and the magnitude of the forces that were operating around much of the Gulf of Mexico at that time.

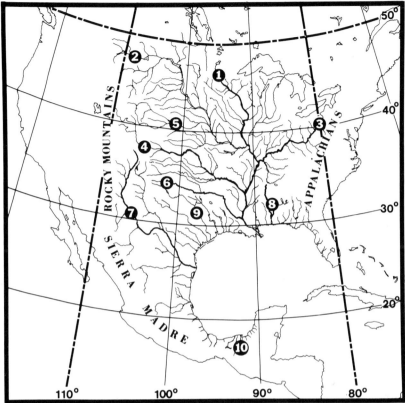

Figure 8. Surface water drainages into the Gulf of Mexico.
Surface waters from 30 states and three other countries (Mexico, Cuba, and Guatemala) spill into the Gulf daily via a series of great river systems and their associated tributaries. These include (1) Mississippi, (2) Missouri, (3) Ohio, (4) Arkansas, (5) Platte, (6) Red, (7) Rio Grande, (8) Tombigbee-Alabama, (9) Colorado-Brazos-Trinity, and (10) a series of smaller rivers along the Mexican coast that drain the plains and mountains in the interior. In general, the Gulf is fed by all the flowing continental surface waters between 15 and 50° North latitude and 80 to 110° West longitude (dashed lines), or from nearly 2.8 million square miles of North and Central America. [Modified and redrawn from H. Brooks, in Jones et al. (eds.) 1973, and from several other sources]

the sediments washed down, and the Gulf basin continued to fill (see Figure 7).

It seems paradoxical that the shelf and basin of the Gulf would not exist without the great river drainages of the eastern United States. Yet these same rivers are racing to fill the Gulf basin with sediments eroded from the ancient mountain chains of Appalachia and Ouachita. The amounts of these consolidated depositions are astonishing: more than 6 million cubic miles have been deposited since the Mesozoic era, about 200 mybp. Most were laid down in the major trough or depression called the Gulf Coast geosyncline. Others fell onto the Atlantic coastal plain when that area was submerged under the Gulf. Still others repose today in the shallow and deep offshore waters of the Gulf basin. In places along the northern and western Gulf coast these sediments are over 30,000 feet thick. While it may seem farfetched to propose that so much sediment could be eroded and deposited, a glance at the river systems that eventually empty into the Gulf of Mexico dispels that uncertainty (see Figure 8).

FROM THE SMALLEST TO THE GREATEST

Our story turns now to biology. In the warm nearshore waters millions of marine invertebrates lived, reproduced, and died; their skeletons composed of calcium carbonate (limestone) settled on the seafloor, coalesced, and formed layer upon layer of limestone strata and reefs along ancient shores. Offshore, billions upon billions of tiny microscopic organisms, with macroscopic names like Foraminifera and Radiolaria, lived, reproduced in saline profligacy, and died in the great surface currents. Their minuscule skeletons, looking like lilliputian grape-clusters of limestone or exquisitely formed baskets of glass (silica), spiraled slowly to the seafloor, creating a clearly traceable pavement showing the course of ancient surface currents. Ages and ages of death and deposition produced sediment layers thousands of feet thick, composed of nearly pure accretions of limestone or silica. So it began then, and so it continues today.

And yet, for all of this, approximately 70% of all the unconsolidated sediments occurring in the Gulf today were deposited as recently as the last (Wisconsin) glacial epoch, 8,000 to 20,000 years ago. On the western Florida shelf, for example, several distinct zones can be recognized, progressing from shallow-water quartz sands and crushed shells (10 to 12 fathoms), to sands composed of fragmented, limestone-depositing algae (calcareous algal sand) along the outer continental shelf (100 fathoms), and finally at the shelf edge (100+ fathoms) zone composed of microscopic egg-shaped granules of nearly pure calcium carbonate, termed oolites. From here downward into the eternal darkness of the continental slope and abyss the sediments become an ooze of foraminiferan shells.

THE LAND RECLAIMS ITS OWN

Much of the broken and deformed sediments from the continent (called clastics), and particularly that carried by the great rivers such as the Mississippi, were deposited at river mouths where they slowly expanded outward. In the case of the Mississippi, great deltaic fans were formed, probably as a result of high-speed, extremely fluid mudflows called *turbidity currents*.[2] As time passed these sediment loads not only began to fill the nearshore basin but began to weigh heavily on it. This additional weight caused the seafloor to warp downward, while the adjacent continent rose in equilibrium; geologists call this process isostasy. The result? Additional land created or lost to the sea.

It is another paradox that sea-borne sediments also have played a role in land formation around the Gulf. The great limestone banks off Yucatán resulted from a combination of three events: biological growth and deposition, sea-level change, and subsidence of the land. Here the race was between the shallow water biota (life forms) that formed or incorporated limestone into their exoskeletons (outer body coverings) on the one hand, and sea-level changes resulting from glaciation or land subsidence on the other. These shelly materials, in reality mass graveyards of molluscs, corals, and bryozoans (often called moss animals because some form encrusting colonies), accumulated in large banks that eventually spread outward over the adjacent deeper seafloor. Off the Yucatán coast these banks extend for miles in shallow water. Yet on the west coast of Florida these reefs, formed in shallow water in Cretaceous times over 200 million years ago, subsided; today they are found 8,000 feet under the sea floor.

SALT DOMES: REMNANTS OF ANCIENT SEAS

There is one more element that needs to be added to the picture of land and sea, one that not only provides another glimpse into the distant past of the Gulf region, but also has important ramifications for the future. Let's look briefly at salt domes, their formation and their utility.

To do so we must start at the beginning, over 250 million years ago when a shallow basin was created, probably by the separation of two continental plates. Imagine pulling a lump of bread dough apart; the thinner portion that forms in the middle approximates the formation of this basin. The basin was hypothesized to have only a limited connection to the newly formed Atlantic Ocean. Nevertheless it was to form part of the prototype of the later Gulf. In the interim, the basin filled with water from the nearby proto-Atlantic and with runoff from the nearby continental mass. Soon, a shallow salty sea filled the basin. About 150 million years ago, under the burning sun of the Jurassic summers, the rate of evaporation of seawater in the basin increased. Evaporation made the remaining seawater more dense, and this brine settled slowly to the seafloor. As the sea continued to evaporate, the water became more and more briny and more and more dense. Gradually, the salt was deposited all across in the floor of the shallow basin, and soon formed massive layers called today *Louann Salt* after the Arkansas town where it was first detected. The Sigsbee Escarpment, a massive cliff some 100 miles offshore along the edge of the Texas–Louisiana Shelf, is a great wall of Louann Salt that migrated southward into the present-day basin of the Gulf.

The glaciers and rivers come next on stage, bringing their tons of sediments to swirl and drift across the salt bed. Year after year, century after century, millenium after millenium, the sediments swept down the Mississippi, Rio Grande, and other nearby rivers and out to sea, covering the salt layer with deposits that eventually rose miles above the original bed. This massive sedimentary deposit, called the *overburden,* gradually pushed downward onto the salt bed, squeezing it by its great weight. As the pressure increased, the salt became liquified and flowed upward through the overlying sediments, much like a large, slow-moving liquid bubble moving through a more dense medium. Remember our bread dough example? Lay your hands across the flattened dough and press slowly but firmly; some of the dough will squeeze out and upward between your fingers in a manner analagous to what happens to salt deposits in the geological layers.

Over millions of years a large series of salt columns rose upward toward the existing surface of the earth, some rising more than 10 miles upward from the originally deposited salt bed. This geological process is called *diapirism* and the resulting columns of salt are called *diapirs*. As the salt bubbles reached the surface they distend the overlying layer forming domelike structures two or more miles across, hence the name *salt dome*. More than 500 of these domes are presently recorded, spread in one series across a large area extending from southeast of Dallas, Texas, across northwestern Louisiana, southeastern Mississippi, and just north of Mobile, Alabama; a second and larger series extends along the coastal Gulf from Corpus Christi, Texas, to the Mississippi Delta and the adjacent offshore continental shelf. A large but unknown number of other domes occur in the deep Gulf.

Interestingly, not all salt domes form "domes." Some occur under swamps and other low-lying depressions, suggesting that the salt has been leached away, thereby allowing the overlying land (or seafloor in some cases) to collapse downward.

PILLARS OF SALT AND PETROLEUM POOLS

Salt domes are aptly named. They are almost 100% pure salt; geologists call this *halite*. Very small amounts of impurities, notably calcium sulfate ($CaSO_4$, or anhydrite) and gypsum (another form of $CaSO_4$), also occur. Although minuscule, the presence of anhydrite has important geological ramifications. If underground water dissolves the salt away, the remaining anhydrite forms a somewhat insoluble barrier. This anhydrite layer is then acted upon by anaerobic bacteria that convert $CaSO_4$ to $CaCO_3$, called calcite by geologists, and otherwise known as a type of limestone. Gypsum is theorized to form later, perhaps through the actions of rainwater percolating through the rock. The composite sedimentary overlayer of calcitic limestone, gypsum, and anhydrite above a diapir is known geologically as *caprock* and can range from several feet to over 1,500 feet thick. What is extraordinary about this conversion process is that it requires approximately 2,000 feet of salt to be dissolved to produce one foot of caprock!

Where do the anaerobic bacteria get the carbon necessary to reduce anhydrite to limestone? From hydrocarbons in petroleum products that accumulate in crevices and pockets along the edge of the dome. Another important resource is the large amount of sulfur deposits also found along the margins of salt domes. It is an interesting historical sidelight that the associated petroleum was first used as a source of energy to provide steam for mining the sulfur deposits. Today, salt domes are mined not only for their petroleum deposits, but for sulfur, gypsum for plaster of Paris, and of course, for salt.

SALT CELLARS IN THE GULF'S BASEMENT

Salt mining takes place in two ways: ordinary blasting and excavation, and injection of water and pump-out of the resulting brine. The first method, called room-and-pillar mining, produces gigantic cellars under the earth some 100 feet high by 100 feet wide, and up to several thousand feet in length. The second method, called solution mining, produces variably sized cavities depending on the amount of salt removed.

These empty cavities are excellent storage areas, and have been used as such for over 40 years. Liquefied petroleum gas has been stored in salt domes since 1951. The Strategic Oil Reserve Program presently stores nearly 600 million barrels of petroleum in six salt domes under Louisiana and Texas, with room for another 150 million barrels still vacant. In one dome in Mont Belvieu, Texas, some 160 million barrels of light hydrocarbon materials have been stored in 137 caverns inside the dome, making it the world's largest salt cellar. Other materials suggested for storage include hazardous chemical wastes and spent nuclear materials, options fraught with hazards and not considered viable by many scientists.

Dome operations are not without their own hazards. Collapsing pillars and ceilings, flooding from underground and surface waters, release of deadly hydrogen sulfide gas, explosions of methane gas liberated from pockets called *blowouts*, and surface subsidence produced by removal of supporting salt and rock from the cavern below ground, are all dangerous risks involved in the mining of salt and storing of hazardous materials.[3] In one of the most bizarre accidents, an oil drilling rig near Lake Peigneur in southern Louisiana penetrated a large salt mine 1,300 feet below the surface. The entire lake and much of the shoreline quickly began to drain into the punctured cavern, and as workers watched dumbfounded, a 50-foot waterfall formed rapidly and spilled into the now-increasing hole, sucking down the $5 million drilling rig, several salt barges, a tugboat, and ten acres of land![4] It may just be common salt that we are talking about, but clearly there is still much to be learned about getting it safely from Nature's cellar into those on our dining room tables.

The Sea Where the Gulf Stream Begins

IN ENVISIONING THE GULF as a major, marginal sea it helps to remember that it is really nothing more than a large rocky basin filled with water. And just as water can be made to surge around and around inside a hand-held washbasin, so the great current systems of the Gulf move in their own basin. The difference, of course, is that Gulf currents are driven by a variety of factors, among the most important of which are wind and the incoming oceanic currents of the Atlantic Ocean and the Caribbean Sea.

THE LOOP CURRENT

Just as all water in the Gulf comes from elsewhere, so do the forces driving these waters, the great oceanic currents. The most important current system in the Gulf of Mexico is the Loop Current, a tremendous mass of water transporting nearly 80 million gallons per second, born in the trade-wind-driven regions of the Caribbean Sea and impelled by the conjunction of two mighty water flows, the Equatorial Current and the Guiana Current. These great trans-Atlantic currents combine and enter the Gulf through the Yucatán Channel, east of the Yucatán Peninsula. Here, constricted in part by the Yucatán Channel, and driven by nearly constant easterly winds, this great mass of water "piles up"[1] and then bursts through into the Gulf at speeds ranging from 12-35 nautical miles per day. Velocities in the core of the Loop Current can exceed 4 nautical miles per hour in the summer, but may diminish to about 1 nautical mile per hour in the winter (see Figure 9A and B).

Immediately after passing into the Gulf the combined flow splits into two components. The left-hand or Gulf Basin component swings toward the west, passing the Campeche Banks in a band of water 56–93 miles wide before circumscribing a broad, meandering clockwise loop and exiting through the Florida Straits. The right-hand component is greater and flows eastward along the northern coastline of Cuba, then exits directly into the Florida Straits. This component, and not the Gulf Basin component, carries most of the water passing through the Yucatán Channel.

In its slow but inexorable journey northward and then eastward, the Loop Current generates a series of eddies and spirals, termed gyres. One of these occurs in the Bay of Campeche, another in the northeastern Gulf east of the Mississippi Delta, and a third off the west coast of Florida in an area called the Middle Grounds. Although these gyres spin off the main Loop Current, they circulate in a counterclockwise direction. In the summer the Mississippi Delta

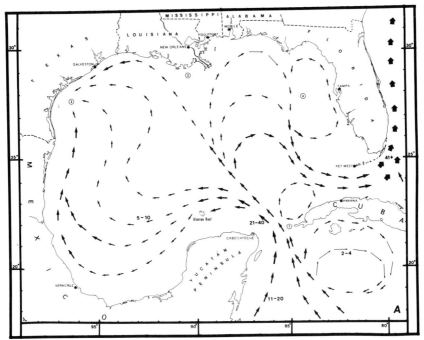

Figure 9A. Major surface currents in the Gulf of Mexico.
(A) Surface currents in June.
Two major physiographic features, the Yucatán Channel and the Straits of Florida, influence the surface currents in the Gulf. All seawater in the Gulf originates in the Caribbean Sea, enters through the Yucatán Channel and exits through the Straits of Florida. An imaginary line drawn from the western tip of Cuba (85° West) to Atchafalaya Bay, Louisiana (90° West) forms a general boundary between water flowing north and westward and that flowing east and southeastward. An anomalous area occurs southeast of Aransas Pass, Texas (96° West), where converging currents create a confused mass of waters known locally as "the graveyard of ships." Another is the large counterclockwise gyre off the west coast of Florida that conducts warm offshore surface waters onto the Florida shelf. [Modified and redrawn from D. F. Leipper, in Galtsoff, P. (ed.) 1954, and National Weather Service data.]

and Florida Middle Grounds gyres either coalesce or disappear, and a single large counterclockwise gyre takes their place. These gyres have important climatic ramifications because they bring a continual replacement of warm open-Gulf water onto the continental shelf, especially during the winter.

Oceanographers are quick to point out, however, that the Loop Current is not so much a clearly defined, unchanging hydrographical entity but rather the sum total of all the highly variable current patterns occurring offshore over a given season. The "loops" form ascending and descending arcs that may extend as far north as Mississippi-Alabama or as far south as west central Florida. The eddies and gyres along the Campeche, west Texas, Mississippi-Alabama, and

The Sea Where the Gulf Stream Begins **69**

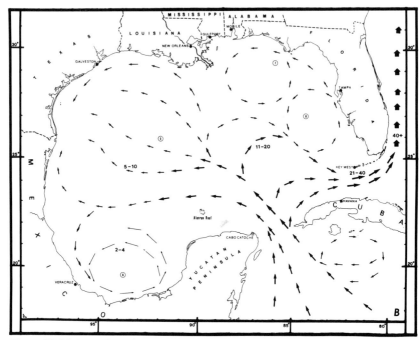

Figure 9B. Major surface currents in the Gulf of Mexico.
(B) Surface currents in December.
Winter currents show essentially the same distribution and direction as those in the summer, although the average velocities may differ. The imaginary east-west current boundary line shifts toward the southwest (92° West). A large counterclockwise gyre may develop in the Bay of Campeche (91-96° West), and the west Florida gyre may split into two discrete circulations, the northernmost to the west of Cape St. George, Florida (85° West), the southernmost forming off the Tampa area. Arrow widths and numbers approximate average miles per day travelled by each current portion.[Modified and redrawn from D. F. Leipper, in Galtsoff, P. (ed.) 1954, and National Weather Service data.]

west Florida shelves shift and change like smoke rings in the wind, and the paths of current-tracking buoys resemble nothing so much as the spiral scribblings of a child on the blue chalkboard of the sea surface. In fact, owing to its great variability, the actual "location" of the Loop Current at any given time is definable only in statistical terms (see Figure 10).

The Loop Current is not just an oceanic system. Its direction and flow are also affected in part by continental outpourings of water from the Mississippi and other large rivers. As it continues its journey around the Gulf and down toward the tip of peninsular Florida it is also subtly affected by the massive seasonal freshwater sheetflow leaking out from the Everglades–Big Cypress Swamp region in southwest Florida. Rounding Cape Sable, the Loop Current rejoins with its more powerful right-hand component off Cuba, and the combined masses of water surge into the Straits of Florida, often in gigantic pulses that attain speeds as high as 40 nautical miles per day.

Here, in this tremendous transport of water now called the Florida Current, lies the origin of the Gulf Stream system,[2] and "the current more powerful than the wind" so succintly noted by Juan Ponce de León. Metaphorically considered by early oceanographers as a gigantic river in the sea, the system transports more than 80 million tons of water per second (nearly 33 million cubic yards or 6.6 quadrillion gallons) along the edge of the western North Atlantic Ocean. So powerful is this stream that its warm waters may indirectly produce ameliorating effects on climate as far away as the British Isles and the continent of Europe.[3] By comparison, the *total* amount of water discharged into the Gulf of Mexico by that mighty Father of Waters, the Mississippi River, and all the other rivers and streams, is a relatively paltry 33,000 cubic yards/second, or about 6.7 million gallons by volume/second.

CREATING "THE CURRENT MORE POWERFUL THAN THE WIND"

To complete our synopsis of this great current system we must briefly turn to a concept of physical oceanography called *geostrophic flow* (*geos* = earth; *trophos* = motion). It is now known that wind blowing across the surface of the sea creates stress, called *wind drag*. This friction induces the water beneath the wind at the sea surface to move at a 45° angle to the right of the wind's direction. Thus, wind blowing from east to west causes a current that sets toward the northwest; wind blowing from the opposite direction (west to east) sets a surface current toward the southeast; and so on.

Now, the deeper one goes beneath the sea surface the more toward the right the underlying water "layers" move. But at the same time, these deeper water layers lose velocity owing to frictional interaction from the more shallow layers, so that they become slower as they turn more to the right. Thus, if current velocity at any given point in the sea is indicated by arrows, the longest arrow would appear at the surface, and the shortest arrow would be found at about 600 feet below and at nearly right angles to that of the surface. In between, the arrows would delineate a spiral of increasingly shorter (and more "right angle-ing") arrows from the surface to 600 feet. This current spiral is called the *Ekman spiral* after the Swedish oceanographer who first described it. The water parcel in which any Ekman spiral occurs is called the *Ekman layer*.

One other factor that must be considered is the Coriolis effect, named after the French mathematician who first described it. Briefly, the effect is caused by a combination of the earth's rotation and gravity. An observer above the earth would see moving particles or objects (air, water, artillery shells traveling over the earth) deflected to the right in the northern hemisphere. and to the left in the southern hemisphere. This effect is easily demonstrated using an orange and a black marker pen. Place the pen tip at the top ("north pole") of the orange. Now, holding the pen steady, slowly draw a vertical line downward toward the orange's "equator," while slowly rotating the orange at the same time west to east, or counterclockwise. Imagine the resulting spiral as wind or surface

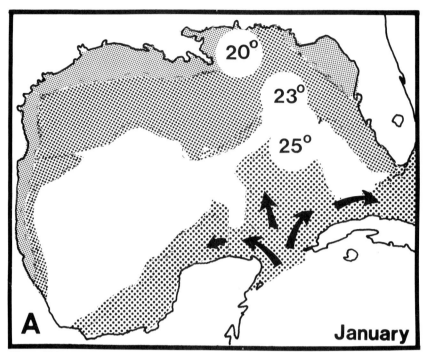

Figure 10A

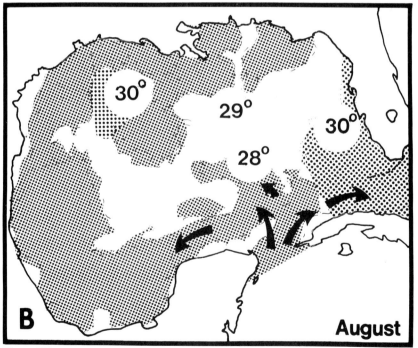

Figure 10B

currents and it is easily seen how they are deflected in a spiral to the right.

What has all this to do with the Loop Current or the Gulf Stream? Quite simply—everything. The flow of the trade winds from the east toward the west induces the surface water coming through the Yucatán Channel to move constantly to the right of the wind—in effect, causing it to move toward the center of its gyre. As the current meets and is deflected from the western land mass of Mexico it is channeled northward, eastward, and then southward around the Gulf, creating the great system called the Loop Current. Deep sea topography, gravity variations, sea level, water density, and the aforementioned Coriolis effect all add their own impulses. The end result of all of these complexities, best visualized in a daunting series of mathematical equations, is the Loop Current—and eventually the Gulf Stream itself. Antón Alaminos might have been perplexed by the mathematics, but he would certainly have appreciated the irony that "the current more powerful than the wind" was a partial product of the wind itself!

WATER MASSES IN THE GULF OF MEXICO

Seawater in the Gulf of Mexico comes from what might be considered unlikely places of origin. Oceanographers have shown that Gulf seawater consists of several components: Atlantic Surface Water (from both the North and South Atlantic), Subtropical Underwater (from the equatorial Atlantic and Caribbean Sea), and Subantarctic Intermediate Water (from between the lower southeastern coast of South America and Antarctica).

The South and North Atlantic Waters are warm surface waters (about 78°F) that extend to about 100 meters in depth. Below these, extending to a depth of about 500 meters, lies the Subtropical Underwater, a relatively cooler (60-68°F) water mass. At a depth between 800-1000 meters, the cold (about 40-45°F) Subantarctic Intermediate Water occurs. This water mass not only originates near the Antarctic continent, but continually moves northward throughout the entire Atlantic Ocean. Some of this water enters the Caribbean Sea and eventually spills over into the Gulf at the shallow sill of the Yucatán Channel, cascading downward like a frigid waterfall onto the bottom in the deep Gulf of Mexico. Below about 1,600 meters, the deep, icy-cold (<35°F) and perpetually dark

Figure 10. Finding the Loop.
Satellite photography and telemetry provide a day to day analysis of the average surface temperatures in the Gulf of Mexico and reveal the incredible complexity of water movements throughout the American Mediterranean. These data can also clearly show major current patterns. In these examples, average temperature values of the relatively warmer inflowing Caribbean Sea water are used to locate the Loop Current. The 25°C isotherm is used in winter (A), and the 28-29°C isotherms in the summer (B). Arrows show presumed directions of water flow. Fine, medium, and coarse shading show relatively colder, cooler, and warmer water, respectively.
[Synopsized and redrawn from OPC 14 KM MCSST charts provided by the National Oceanic and Atmospheric Administration, National Climatic Data Center, Asheville, NC]

waters of the Gulf of Mexico show such uniform characteristics that they cannot be easily differentiated into separate components.

Characterizing these water masses is important because the locations of prime commercial and sport fishing grounds are strongly influenced by the presence of the Loop Current. This is because plankton, the base of the oceanic food chain, become concentrated along the Loop Current margins. Predatory sport fishes, for example, are often caught in large numbers off the eastern edge of this current. Because the Loop Current shifts seasonally, changes size annually, and almost certainly meanders on a daily basis, any change in location will result in a shift of the prime fishing areas.

UPWELLING

A water movement of major importance to all marine life, *upwelling* is usually found along continental margins where cold water currents flow. In contrast to currents that usually carry water laterally, upwelling is a vertical movement of water. It is caused by two processes: wind displacing surface waters away from the coast, or by deep currents which drive into one another or are deflected upward against landmasses. In either case, nutrient-rich subsurface waters are raised to the sea surface. Areas of upwelling are almost always areas of extremely high biological productivity and represent rich commercial and sport fishing regions as well.

In the Gulf of Mexico at least two major regions of upwelling occur, one off the Yucatán Peninsula and the other along the west coast of Florida. Both are associated with the perimeter of the Loop Current, and both occur along the edges of the respective continental shelves. Such large-scale overturn of water can be seasonal or may be related to other climatic or oceanographic factors.

Upwelling has another effect. In cases where large amounts of deep cold water well upward to the surface and the air is warmer than the water, sea fogs may form. This is a common phenomenon along the Gulf coast in the winter months.

Time, Tides, and Sea-Level Rise

TIDES IN THE GULF OF MEXICO are of three types: diurnal (with one high and one low tide per 24.8-hour, or lunar, day), semidiurnal (two generally equal high and low waters per lunar day), or mixed diurnal (two unequal high and two unequal low tides per lunar day). In some areas, for example on the northwestern coast of Florida and in the Sanibel Island area of that state, there often may be just one tide per lunar day (see Figure 11).

Tidal ranges on peninsular Florida are about 2.0–4.5 feet and are the highest of any on the Gulf coast. Elsewhere the tidal range is not extensive, averaging about 1-2 feet, except during periods of strong onshore winds, tropical storms, or hurricanes. The presence of large outflowing rivers and streams or barrier islands alongshore with their associated inlets or passes can modify local tidal height substantially, producing extremely complex water movements.

Although Gulf of Mexico tides are essentially astronomical and controlled by the moon and sun, some meteorological phenomena often override the lunar component. One of these, called *wind-forcing,* may restrict or enhance normal tidal flows. Through the action of strong or just steady winds, water may be forced into, prevented from leaving, or blown out of enclosed bays and estuaries. Additional complications may be imposed owing to the irregular shape of the Gulf of Mexico basin and the existence of only two portals into the Gulf. Tides from adjacent areas (for example, the Atlantic Ocean, Straits of Florida, or the Caribbean Sea) can also interfere substantially with the tidal cycles in south-western Florida or along the Yucatán peninsula.

SEA-LEVEL RISE

The term *sea level* refers to the average height of the sea determined as if there were no rise and fall of the tide. Measurements of tidal heights consistently over a period of time (weekly, monthly or at longer intervals) reveal that the sea is, in fact, never "level" but actually fluctuates in height owing to vagaries in weather, barometric pressure, lunar periodicities, and other factors. Sea-level is thus a single value averaged from all the tidal heights on any particular coast over a 19-year period.

Another sea level can be obtained by comparing average tidal heights from different localities over a long period of time, say annually. These data reveal that sea level in the Gulf is lower in the first half of the year than in the second.

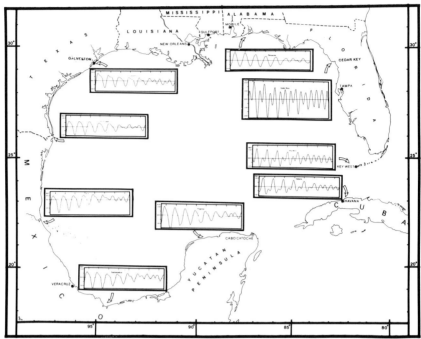

Figure 11. Tidal cycles in the Gulf of Mexico
Tidal records for the same 8-day period in June show dramatic differences in levels and periodicity around the Gulf. Tick marks within the boxes denote noon of each day. Compare the tidal height at Cedar Keys, Florida, where a 4-foot difference exists between the highest high and lowest low tide, with that at Galveston, Texas, where the difference between highest and lowest water never reaches 2 feet. Note that the tides in the eastern Gulf are almost all mixed semidiurnal (two highs, two lows for each 24-hour period), whereas those in the western and southwestern Gulf are mostly diurnal (one tide per day). [Modified and redrawn from H. A. Marmer, in Galtsoff, P. (ed.) 1954]

The reasons for this are not clear but may be related to seasonal winds forcing more water through the Yucatán Channel.

By using average tidal heights over even longer periods, such as decades or even in some cases a century, still another phenomenon can be observed, that of sea-level rise and fall. This observation is of extreme importance, particularly to coastal communities. For example, data from tidal stations in Florida progressing northward from Key West to Cedar Keys and Pensacola, and from Galveston, Texas, indicate that between 1909 and 1950 sea level rose approximately 0.3–1.0 feet. Furthermore, the rise was relatively more rapid between 1930 and 1950 than in the earlier decades. From about 1950 to 1980, sea level continued to rise, though at a less rapid rate. What does this portend for coastal regions in the Gulf? To answer this question we must first look at some causes.

Sea level change can be attributed to three different causes: the volume of seawater in a basin is increasing; the coastal area may be subsiding; or a combination of both factors is occurring. Data from climatologists and oceanographers clearly indicate that the volume of water in the world's oceans is increasing. U.S. Coast and Geodetic Survey records show, for example, that the general level of the sea has risen along our coastlines from 8 to 10 inches since 1870.

Scientists attribute this rise primarily to melting of the polar ice caps, which release their stored water into the sea. But another factor that may prove to be important is the continuing deposition of sediments into oceanic basins, which causes both a rise in sea level and a decrease in the depths of the sea. Like adding too much sugar to a cup of coffee, the liquid spills over the rim.

Sea-level alterations can also cause a kind of domino effect. The melting of polar glaciers and ice caps imposes subtle changes on weather patterns that, in turn, are translated into changes in wind direction and velocity onto coastal areas. For example, the effects of increasing water levels resulting from glacial melting can be exacerbated by onshore winds in low-lying coastal areas. Other changes brought about include modifications in sedimentation rates, alterations in biological processes and species distributions, changes in river levels, variation in shore erosion, and a host of lesser but clearly related factors.

Simple sea-level rise by itself is serious enough. If all the water in the ice caps of Antarctica and Greenland were returned to the world's oceans, sea level around the world would rise 200 to 300 feet. Such an increase in the Gulf would move the shoreline 50 to 250 miles inland along the continental coastal plain, and totally inundate most of Florida and much of Yucatán and coastal Mexico. But it need not be even that dramatic. A rise in sea-level of just six inches would inundate on a daily basis many existing shorelines along the resort coasts of the Gulf. Low-lying coastal plains and barrier islands would be particularly susceptible. The consequences of such inundations, coupled with any extra volume of water brought ashore, such as might occur during hurricanes, would be devastating.

In a scenario reminiscent of a Hollywood catastrophe film, a 1-meter rise in sea level by the year 2100 could inundate from 25% to 80% of the present coastal wetlands in the United States, flood 4,000 to 9,000 square miles of protected dry land shores, and 5,000 to 10,000 square miles of dry land if the shores remain unprotected. The latter result, of course, would exchange previously existing wetlands with new wetlands created by the 1-meter inundation. Good news for coastal wildlife in 2100 AD—but small comfort for the human populations who used to live there.[1]

Although sea level rise scenarios emphasize the effects of surface inundation, subsurficial effects may be just as catastrophic in another way. Salty marine waters encroaching into shallow freshwater aquifers can seriously contaminate a drinking water supply for an entire coastal area, particularly in those regions where porous limestones form the basement rock. The situation has already occurred in several parts of Florida, and promises to continue as the sea inexorably rises and mankind continues to drain away or use up the freshwater lenses that cap and hold back the intruding salt water.[2]

This problem has received increased attention in the last decade as concerned scientists look for better methods for predicting rate of change and wrestle with the legal and economic difficulties of protecting coastal areas and their residents. The most daunting aspect of the problem is the acknowledged fact that most present-day coastal dwellers refuse to accept what is inevitably coming. Or dismiss it as not their problem but one for future generations to solve. Economics is another factor. Coastal zone properties are often the most desirable, and therefore among the most expensive, lands on earth. The average beachfront landowner does not want to be told that in 50 years or so his or her property will be, to all intents, worthless. Education and acceptance are the necessary first steps in solving this complex problem. But we must hurry. The data clearly suggest that there is not much time. The data also suggest that there will be no easy solutions.

Seawater

ITS CHARACTERISTICS, CONSTITUENTS, AND IMPORTANCE

E VERYONE KNOWS that the Gulf of Mexico, like all large intracontinental seas, is filled with salt water. But the ramifications that seawater has for physics, chemistry, and biology may not be generally appreciated. Imagine, for example, that the Great Lakes were totally saltwater and the Gulf of Mexico and Atlantic Ocean were totally freshwater, and the importance of salt water versus fresh water becomes clearer. Yet all the differences, though producing wide-ranging effects, are actually relatively uncomplicated.

Seawater can be characterized quite simply using three major parameters: its temperature, its salinity (or saltiness), and the quantities and types of dissolved gases and organic substances in it. These characteristics not only tell oceanographers much about the seawater itself, but also allow them to make predictions regarding the effects these parameters will have on the biology and ecology of many marine organisms.

TEMPERATURE

Temperature is considered the most important physical parameter operating in the world's oceans, and it is no less important in marginal seas such as the Gulf of Mexico. Temperature as a physical factor has ramifications for both the hydrology (the study of water and all its properties) and the biology of a region, affecting everything from atmosphere above marine waters to the life processes of the organisms found on, in, or adjacent to the sea.

Surface temperatures in the Gulf exhibit decidedly seasonal changes (see Figure 12). Whereas the average summer surface temperature is an almost uniform 84°F (about 29°C) throughout the entire Gulf, in the winter a distinct gradient appears, ranging from 75°F (about 24°C) in the southern portion to 65°F (19°C) in the north. During cold snaps, seawater temperatures may plunge more than 30 degrees from the day's high temperature. One effect of such periodic freezes is large fish kills. In the shallow coastal waters of Texas, a region for which some of the most complete records are available, such freezes occur every 14 years on the average. The last major fish kill occurred in 1989.

Sea surface temperatures, however, may be distinctly different from those at depth. For example, during the summer, warm water temperatures are found from the surface downward to a certain depth. As with air, the warmer these waters are, the less dense they are. Below this depth, the water quite suddenly

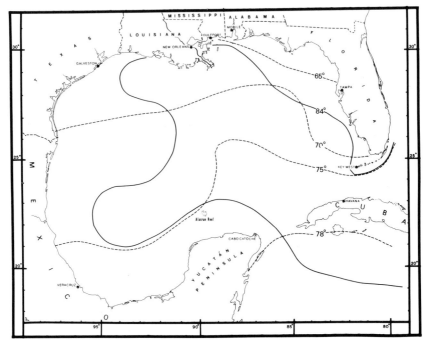

Figure 12. Average sea surface temperatures in the Gulf of Mexico.
Temperature contours, called isotherms, show the average seasonal differences between seawater temperatures in winter (dashed lines) and summer (solid line). Northern areas undergo a wider seasonal fluctuation in temperatures (15 to 20° F) compared to the more southerly regions (10°). With increasing depth, the temperature differences become less disparate, particularly below the thermocline at depths greater than 200 feet. [Modified and redrawn from D. F. Liepper, in Galtsoff (1954), and additional data from the National Hurricane Center, Miami, Florida]

becomes much cooler and therefore denser. The depth where this vertical temperature gradient changes so drastically is called a *thermocline*. Depending on the region in the Gulf, the thermocline may occur from just below the surface to as deep as 160 feet. During the winter part of the cycle, however, seawater becomes well mixed as a result of storms that cool the surface waters, increase their density, and promote mixing. Both the currents and the thermocline are then altered or destroyed.

As might be expected, cooler temperatures also occur near the deeper seafloor. For example, seawater temperatures above the seafloor on the inner continental shelf range between 63° and 68°F and are generally at least 5 degrees cooler than the surface waters above. At greater depths, seawater temperatures decline very rapidly, decreasing in approximately 10-degree increments at depths of 200 meters, 400 meters, and 800 meters. Below 1,000 meters (about 3,300 feet) temperatures are usually less than 40°F, the coldest in the Gulf.

SALINITY

Oceanographers refer to the total amounts (by weight) of dissolved solids in seawater as its salinity. This measurement can be made with relative ease because of a happy circumstance. Regardless of the absolute concentrations of the total dissolved salts, *the relative proportions (that is, the ratios) of the major dissolved salts remain nearly constant throughout the entire world's oceans.* Thus the "saltiness" of different seas can be compared with one another, providing a measure of standardization for seawaters around the world.

Yet for all its saltiness, seawater in a general sense isn't really very "salty." In fact, the concentrations (and their differences) are so small that they are measured in parts per thousand ($^0/oo$). But though these differences seem small and are, for the most part, not detectable to humans, they can be vitally important to marine organisms.

The two most abundant elements dissolved in seawater are, of course, sodium (whose chemical symbol is Na) and chlorine (Cl). These elements combine to form the chemical compound we know as common table salt. Chemists write the formula for table salt as NaCl, or sodium chloride. Both Na and Cl are dissolved in sea water as ions. Ions are atoms that have lost or gained more than their normal complement of electrons, and so exhibit a positive (+) or negative (-) charge, instead of being neutral. Thus, simple table salt in water solution consists of sodium ions (Na+) and chloride ions (Cl-). These, however, are not the only components found in seawater. A listing of other ions and their abundances is given in Table 1.

Water at the sea surface in the offshore central Gulf of Mexico is typically rather salty, its salinity measuring at least 36 $^0/oo$. Over the continental shelf and near the coastlines salinities may vary below this value, dropping to 35 $^0/oo$ nearshore, or to below 25 $^0/oo$ off passes and inlets owing to dilution from land runoff, rivers, rain, and other factors. Fresh water from the Mississippi River, for example, can dilute nearshore waters to less than 24 $^0/oo$ as deep as 50 feet, and for a distance of more than 150 miles offshore. Owing to mixing of deep seawater masses, salinities below 600 meters may decrease to 34 $^0/oo$.

Seasonal influx of other seawaters can change surface salinities dramatically. For example, at the mouth of the Yucatán Channel, incoming water from the Caribbean Sea in the springtime can raise salinity to 36.5 $^0/oo$. Elsewhere, surface waters over portions of the Florida Shelf and the Campeche Banks may be elevated above 36 $^0/oo$ as colder, more saline water wells upward onto the shelf during periods of summertime deep water overturns. Values approaching 37 $^0/oo$ have been recorded in the Straits of Florida.

Table 1

Major Constituents of Seawater and Their Approximate Relative Concentrations

Ion		o/oo
Chloride	Cl^-	18.98
Sodium	Na^+	10.56
Sulphate	$SO_4{-2}$	2.65
Magnesium	Mg^{2+}	1.27
Calcium	Ca^{2+}	0.40
Potassium	K^{2+}	0.38
Bicarbonate	HCO_3-	0.14
Bromide	Br^-	0.06
Boric acid	H_3BO_3	0.03
Strontium	$^{2+}$	0.01
Flouride	Fl^-	Trace

Source: Sverdrup, H. U., et al. 1942.

But the grand prize for the saltiest surface waters associated with the Gulf of Mexico goes to the Laguna Madre, a shallow, hypersaline coastal lagoon confined by coastal barrier islands in the Rio Grande drainage area south of Corpus Christi, Texas. Here, during the summer and in periods of drought and high evaporation, salinites may skyrocket to as high as 80^0/oo or greater. It is truly a briny lagoon.

In some offshore deep waters even more briny conditions occur. Two hypersaline basins have been discovered on the offshore continental shelf. One is located on the East Flower Garden Bank, a generally shallow, coral-capped promontory about 100 nautical miles southeast of Galveston, Texas, where a small deep "pool" has salinities reaching 160^0/oo. The other is found in over 2,000 meters of water in the Orca Basin, a small area 200 miles south of New Orleans, where salinities of 250^0/oo have been recorded. These pools, arising in part from dissolution of sodium chloride from salt domes, certainly give new meaning to the expression "briny deep."

Salinity, as a physical factor, is second in importance only to temperature in seawater. In conjunction with the latter, synergistic effects may predominate that outweigh either factor considered alone. Because the Gulf of Mexico and its immediately surrounding areas are a marine environment, salinity-temperature relationships often have an overriding role in the occurrence, distribution, and maintenance of marine and estuarine organisms and their communities. Thus, the attributes of salinity and temperature, either alone or in combination, are the prime determinants of which organisms will live where, and how well.

PRESSURE IN THE SEA: A DIFFERENT KIND OF STRESS

We need to consider two other factors that influence sea water. The first of these, pressure, is easily understood. Meteorologists, for example, measure atmospheric pressure (the weight of the atmosphere pressing down on the earth's surface) in millibars, or thousandths of a bar. At sea level, where atmospheric pressure is normally 14.7 pounds per square inch, the equivalent is 1013 millibars. This means that a person standing on the earth's surface has 14.7 pounds (1013 millibars) of atmosphere pressing down on every square inch of his or her body—or 1 atmosphere.

How does this fit into seawater? Well, consider this. The pressure equivalent of 1 atmosphere can also be produced by a column of water 30 feet high. Now, normally, no one goes around on the earth's surface carrying columns of water 30 feet high! But many people dive into the sea, and if they descend to 30 feet beneath the surface they have, in effect, a column of water 30 feet high above them. They are thus supporting the watery equivalent of 1 atmosphere of pressure, or about 15 pounds per square inch of body surface, at that depth. If they dive to 60 feet the water pressure increases to an equivalent 2 atmospheres, or about 30 pounds per square inch; 90 feet = 3 atmospheres or about 45 pounds per square inch; and so on. A quick and easy calculation is to take the depth in feet and divide by 2 to get the approximate number of pounds per square inch of water pressure. Looked at another way, every 30 feet of depth brings an increase of 1 atmosphere of pressure. Using the metric equivalents, every 10 meters of depth (approximately 30 feet) increases water pressure the equivalent of 1 atmosphere. Thus a person standing on the seafloor in 100 meters of water has the equivalent of 10 atmospheres or 150 pounds per square inch pressing down on him or her. One now begins to see how important a factor pressure is for living organisms.

Shallow living organisms (and shallow-diving humans) usually do not have to worry about pressure as a factor operating directly on their respective body surfaces. But the deeper an organism goes into the sea the more important a factor pressure becomes. Deep sea fishes living on or just above the Sigsbee Plain, for example, swim in nearly 15,000 feet of water. They are, in a sense, supporting a water column almost 3 miles high above them. Every square inch of their body surface is subject to immense pressures, approximately 7,500 pounds worth, 500 atmospheres, or the equivalent of almost 4 tons of weight per square inch!

COPING WITH LIFE UNDER PRESSURE

With such pressures the question naturally arises: Why aren't deep sea organisms squashed to jelly? The answer, much simplified, is that the hydrostatic pressure being exerted on the tissues of these organisms is almost exactly balanced by the pressure within these same tissues. Tissues are mostly water, and water is, to all intents and purposes, incompressible (that's why a belly flop in your swimming pool hurts so much!). So it's not the amount of tissue composing an organism that creates pressure problems, it's the amount of gas within those tissues. Were we humans able to extract oxygen from the surrounding sea water, and maintain a hydrostatic pressure equilibrium with the environment, we would be able to walk about three miles down on the Sigsbee Plain with almost as much ease as we do strolling along the sandy beaches of a barrier island.

Scuba divers are familiar with this effect. As long as they receive sufficient gas (air or any gas mixture being used) they find the surrounding sea pressures tolerable. The gas they breath from their scuba tanks is delivered to their lungs under a pressure equivalent to that of the surrounding sea. In effect, a scuba regulator is a ramjet that forces air, oxygen, helium-oxygen (heliox) or other gas mixtures into the lungs. To get a glimpse of how this works, try this: lie on your back in the shallow end of a swimming pool and attempt to breath through a hollow tube extending to the water's surface. The deeper you are lying the harder it will be to breathe—because of the pressure of the water on the outside of your body, which in turn affects the ability of your lungs to expand and thus inhale the needed oxygen. Recall, too, the discomfort that some people experience when an airliner is coming in to land. Here, the effect is reversed. The cabin air pressure is reduced, but the air pressure inside their sinus cavities is not, thus creating pain until the pressure is equalized by venting.

Marine organisms, particularly deep-living species, use a variation on this theme to compensate for, or overcome the tremendous pressures in the deep sea. Many fishes have well-developed swim bladders, internal sacs lined with gas-producing glands. By filling the bladder with gas obtained from the blood stream (oxygen, carbon dioxide, and nitrogen) these fish are able to float nearly weightless at a desired level in the water column. As the fish swims deeper, the hydrostatic pressure of the surrounding water increases, and squeezes the swim bladder and its contained gases. This not only reduces the size of the bladder, it also makes the fish heavier than the surrounding water. To maintain its equilibrium, so to speak, the fish must add gas to the bladder. When the fish swims higher in the water column, the gases expand, and the fish must then reabsorb the excess in its bloodstream and then vent it to the outside during respiration. If a fish rises too quickly upward (for example, if it is caught in a deep sea trawl) it may be unable to properly vent these gases (remember our airline passenger?). The result is the same as when a scuba diver rises "faster than the bubbles" to the surface—an embolism occurs. In the hapless fish the swim bladder is usually ruptured or forced completely out of the body via its mouth. The result in either case, fish or human, is fatal.

Not all fishes have swim bladders, and no invertebrates do. These deep sea species maintain their body shape and lifestyle by keeping their tissues in hydrostatic equilibrium with the surrounding water. Such animals are rather lightly built, with skimpy bones and fragile, thin tissues and muscles. Some jellyfish secrete or absorb gas in internal chambers or floats in a manner analagous to a fish's swim bladder. Deep benthic (bottom-dwelling) species (sea cucumbers, sea stars, anglerfish, blind lobsters, and many others) have little trouble existing in the abyssal regions, as long as they keep control of any internal gases. In fact, marine physiologists believe that it is not the rapid change in pressure that kills these organisms when they are brought up in the trawls, but rather the swift change in temperature, from the frigid and dark nether regions of the deep sea to the warm, bright waters of the sea surface.

DENSITY OF SEAWATER: THE COMPLEXITIES OF WEIGHT

The other factor to be considered is density. Density of seawater is a rather more complex concept than pressure. Yet the density of seawater depends not only on pressure, but on temperature and salinity as well. Density is equivalent to *specific gravity*, a term that represents the ratio at sea surface of the weight of a given volume of seawater to the weight of an equal volume of distilled water measured at its maximum density of 4°C. Thus, when more salts are dissolved in seawater, or reciprocally, when more water evaporates from a container, the seawater becomes more dense owing to the weight of the dissolved salts. However, a change in salinity (say, from 30 ^{0}/oo to 35 ^{0}/oo) at one temperature (say, 25°C) will produce a density different than the same changes of salinity taking place at 30°C. And, to further complicate matters, the depth at which these changes in salinity occur (because of the pressure factor) will also affect the density value.

Seawater density is important for two simple reasons, both tied to the physical properties of water itself. Any water, as it cools, becomes denser up to a certain point, and therefore sinks through warmer, less dense water. In fresh water, when 4°C (about 39°F) is reached the molecular structure of water changes and the water becomes less dense before it finally freezes. Less dense (albeit colder) water that turns to ice then rises and floats on the surface of the more dense, slightly warmer water. This is an important circumstance, because it means that any water body (including the sea) will always freeze primarily from the surface downward, rather than from the bottom upward. Were water to continuously increase in density with decreasing temperature then the ice that formed would become a permanent ice layer on the basin floor in boreal climates because the sun's heat would be unable to sufficiently warm the deeper layers.

But isn't seawater more dense than fresh water because of its dissolved salts? And won't this increasing density mean that seawater will continue to get heavier the colder it becomes? The answer is yes to both questions. But these same dissolved salts in the sea not only increase the density of sea water over that of fresh water, they also lower the freezing point. Increasing pressure also lowers the freezing point. Moreover, any seawater that does freeze forces the dissolved salts out in the process. The sea ice that forms is nearly fresh water, and so it, too, floats—this time on the surface of the sea. The remaining deep water, now being more salty, has its freezing point depressed even further. Thus, sea water has a series of freezing points determined by salinity, pressure, and density. Some of the coldest waters on earth are found in the deep sea off Antarctica where temperatures of -2.7°C (27°F) occur — well below freezing, but not frozen.[2]

A detailed discussion of seawater pressure and density is beyond the scope of this book.[3] Suffice it to say that, in general, an increase in seawater temperature decreases its density, whereas an increase in salinity, or an increase in pressure, increases the density. But since none of these factors occurs in isolation in seawater, each exerts its particular influence on the other. Cold, highly saline, deep sea water is denser than warm, less saline, surface sea water. But seawater undergoing high evaporation rates (for example, in enclosed shallow bays in the summer) is rendered more dense than its nearshore water counterpart. The end result is that the organisms living in these conditions must adapt to these changes or die.

DISSOLVED OXYGEN

Most marine organisms, whether plants or animals, require oxygen to exist. But it is often not realized that oxygen can only be added to the sea in the upper layers of water, either by being absorbed from the atmosphere immediately above or by being produced through photosynthesis by phytoplankton, marine algae, and sea grasses living at depths where there is sufficient light for this process to occur.[4] At the same time, oxygen can be lost by interaction with the atmosphere, through respiration by plants and animals, and by decompositional activities of bacteria. Although oxygen in seawater can unite with other materials in strictly chemical reactions, these are limited and occur, for the most part, either directly at the surface or on or under the seafloor.

Just as with dissolved salts, the amounts of dissolved oxygen in the sea are not large. Surface waters typically contain about 5 milliliters oxygen per liter of seawater (ml/l), or only about 5 parts oxygen per thousand parts of water. Even these low values decrease dramatically in deeper (>250 meters) waters and may continue showing a gradual decline to as little as 2.5 ml/l at 500–700 meters of water depth. At this depth a curious hydrochemical feature occurs, called the *oxygen minimum layer*, in which the amount of dissolved oxygen drops to a minimum value differing from that in waters above and below this layer. Several explanations have been offered for this feature, but oceanographers generally agree that high levels of organic decomposition (which tie up oxygen into other compounds) may be the cause. Yet other low-oxygen areas are found in very shallow coastal regions, including the northwestern Gulf (<2.5 ml/l) and over the Campeche Banks and West Florida Shelf (<2.7 ml/l). Large-scale biological activity that uses up oxygen as quickly as it is produced appears to be the most important contributing factor in these areas.

Oxygen concentrations in shallow water often depend largely on a combination of biological and physical activities. The presence or absence of seagrass beds, mangrove forests, carbonate sediments, large animal and plant communities, sewage and other pollutants, currents and waves, water temperature, and a number of other complex factors can all affect daily oxygen concentrations. In shallow areas the overall values thus fluctuate more widely than in the open sea. Surf-zone waters are typically high in oxygen owing to aeration by waves. In some cases, seawater over littoral (intertidal) seagrass beds may even become supersaturated with oxygen (>8 ml/l), especially during the summer when overlying waters are warmed by long, hot, sunny days and the rate of photosynthesis rises. On the debit side, daily concentrations may also be affected by oxygen requirements of infaunal organisms (those living in the sediments). Moreover, large-scale respiration, particularly that carried out during decompositional activities by bacteria and other microorganisms, can also "use up" an available supply. This usage is termed *biological oxygen demand,* or BOD.

pH AND CARBONATES: THE BUFFERING OF SEAWATER

Oceanographers use another relationship to characterize seawater. By measuring the concentration of hydrogen ions (H^+) to hydroxyl ions (OH^-) in a water sample they determine its relative acidity, or pH. This is plotted on a logarithmic scale ranging from 0 to 14. Pure fresh water, for example, has a pH of 7 because it is chemically neutral, that is, it is neither acidic nor "alkaline," or, as chemists would say, it is neither acidic nor basic. The pH of acidic water solutions is less than 7.0 whereas that of basic (alkaline) solutions is higher than 7.0. Common household vinegar (acetic acid) for example, has a pH of about 3.0; the pH of household ammonia solutions (being basic or alkaline) may be as high as 10.[5]

In general, surface seawater under normal conditions has a pH of 8.2, and is thus slightly basic. But it may range from 7.0 to 8.5. In the open waters of the Gulf of Mexico pH ranges from about 8.1 to 8.3 at the surface, decreasing to about 7.9 at 700 meters depth, before increasing again to about 8.0 in deeper water. Dramatically fluctuating values are seen in the shallow coastal systems. Here, where overland runoff, rivers, streams, swamps, lakes, lagoons, and other water bodies mix carbonate-impregnated fresh water with varying amounts of seawater, pH may range from a comparatively acidic 6.7 to a more basic 8.5. Natural inland waters, and those high in tannic acid from decaying leaves, may even drop in pH as low as 4.0 and consequently lower the pH of coastal waters when they meet and mix.

Industrial or agricultural activities can also affect natural waters, often creating highly acidic runoff with a pH even lower than 4.0. The effect of these waters on local coastal waters is wide-ranging and complex, and depends in large part on how well buffered the seawater is with other dissolved salts, particularly carbonates and bicarbonates. These salts act just like antacids in a person's stomach, "neutralizing" the excess acidity and bringing the seawater more toward neutrality.

Much of these carbonates and bicarbonates comes from carbon dioxide gas (CO_2) in the atmosphere. When the sea makes direct contact with the air, it can absorb up to 200 times more CO_2 than that normally and already found in solution. This CO_2 is dissolved as carbonic acid, the same acid (and gas) in seltzer water. Carbonic acid then dissociates into bicarbonate (HCO_3^-) and carbonate (CO_3^{2-}) ions. As a consequence, the world's oceans can be considered a large bicarbonate solution that is more or less in equilibrium with atmospheric carbon dioxide. The most important ramification of this fact is that it causes seawater to resist accepting additional amounts of acids or bases. Oceanographers say that seawater in this condition is "buffered" against such additions.

The presence and abundance of carbonate ion (CO_32-) is also of significance for marine organisms. It is a curious fact that seawater is supersaturated with calcium carbonate ($CaCO_3$) at the sea surface. Moreover, this supersaturation increases with increasing temperature (up to 300% saturation). Thus, the many marine organisms that require $CaCO_3$ find it in abundance in the warm surface waters of the tropical Gulf. And as they die and decompose, they leave their shells and exoskeletons behind, particularly in the great limestone banks off Yucatán and western Florida.

Supersaturation of $CaCO_3$ also has geological ramifications. The many layers of sedimentary limestone (termed strata), often hundreds to thousands of feet thick, give dramatic proof of the oceanic-atmospheric carbonate system in action over millions of years. Indeed, in the tropical and warm-temperate regions of the world, the presence of calcium and its carbonate salts can be considered directly responsible for the awesome amounts of marine life that existed long ago, died out, and became fossilized. It was certainly no accident that the overwhelming majority of marine organisms, including many algae, incorporated and depended upon $CaCO_3$ for their existence, their ecological development, and ultimately their evolution.

Nutrients in the Sea

THE BROTH OF LIFE

IT HAS BEEN SAID, with perhaps but slight exaggeration, that the sea is a rich organic soup from which all life on earth evolved, and which is still carried in the veins of mankind and many other animals. The origin of life, hypothesized to have occurred over 3.8 billion years ago, was quickly followed by the evolution of photosynthesizing bacteria some 3.4 billion years ago. The first organisms possessing a cellular nucleus appeared some 1.5 billion years later, followed by the metazoan animals approximately 700 million years ago. Yet none of this might have happened had these same orgnisms not been able to utilize as nutrients the many different kinds of elements dissolved in the Archaean seas that washed for eons against the barren, rockbound shores of the early earth.[1]

Yet it is a curious fact that of the 92 naturally occurring elements on earth only a few are of major importance in marine and estuarine ecosystems. These are carbon (as carbon dioxide and carbonates), nitrogen (nitrates and nitrites), phosphorus (phosphates), sulfur (sulfates and sulfides), as well as silicon (silicates), potassium (from potash), magnesium, oxygen, and calcium as previously discussed. In addition, copper, chromium, zinc, and manganese, all of which occur in only trace amounts (the trace elements) are important for growth and maintenance in many marine organisms. The effects of other trace metals have not been completely quantified, but several are believed to be of some importance for general viability. However, five other trace metals—lead, cadmium, arsenic,[2] mercury, and tin—are usually considered indicators of pollution and, depending on their ionic state and overall concentrations, can be highly toxic to marine life. How all of this applies to the Gulf flora and fauna is the next part of our investigation.

CARBON

Carbon is one of the fundamental elements of life on earth. It functions not only as a nutrient but also in photosynthesis and respiration by plants, and by incorporation as carbonates and carbohydrates in skeletal, exoskeletal, tissue, and muscle components. Organisms ranging from microscopic Foraminifera to massive reef corals, and from single-celled algae to the great whales, all depend on carbon as a structural component. More importantly, *primary production,* that is, the fixation of carbon by bacteria and phytoplankton, forms the basis for nearly every food chain on earth (see Figure 13A).

Yet the story of carbon on earth is one of overabundance and underutiliza-

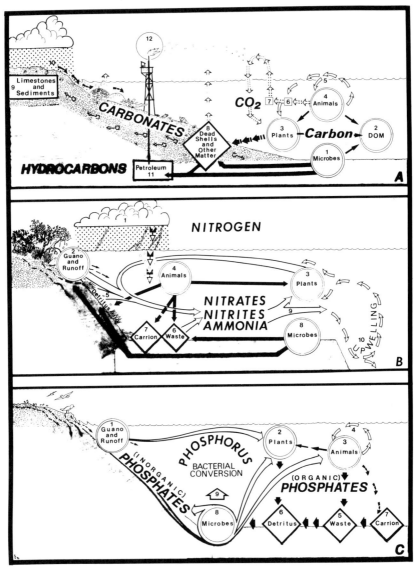

Figure 13. Nutrient cycles in the sea.

Figure 13. Nutrient cycles in the sea.

(A) Carbon.

Carbon in the marine environment comes primarily from carbon dioxide, produced through photosynthesis, respiration, and decay. MICROBES (1) produce DISSOLVED ORGANIC MATTER or DOM (2) in decay processes. DOM, rich in carbon compounds termed carbohydrates, is used by planktonic PLANTS (3) and ANIMALS (4). Higher ANIMALS, feeding on PLANTS or other ANIMALS (5) also recycle these compounds. All ANIMALS release Carbon Dioxide (CO_2) in respiration into the water, where it is eventually exchanged with the atmosphere at the WATER'S SURFACE (6). PLANTS (3) use both dissolved and atmospheric CO_2 in PHOTOSYNTHESIS (7) to produce their own organic carbon compounds. Dead plants and animals undergoing bacterial decomposition release additional CO_2. Their DEAD SHELLS AND OTHER CALCAREOUS MATTER (8) are gradually changed (lithified) into LIMESTONE AND CARBONATE SEDIMENTS (9). EROSION (10) by wind and rain redissolves these sediments releasing CO_2 and carbonate ions. The latter may again be recycled as carbonate exoskeletons. Organic remains covered by sediments are gradually converted by MICROBES (1) and other geological processes into PETROLEUM (11). COMBUSTION (12) of fossil fuels, and other carbonaceous materials, releases additional CO_2 into the atmosphere where it is recycled again in PHOTOSYNTHESIS (7).

B) Nitrogen.

The largest reservoir of nitrogen is the atmosphere but the gas is chemically inert and unavailable to living organisms, although small amounts of molecular nitrogen enter the sea through LIGHTNING AND RAIN (1). GUANO (bird droppings) AND LAND RUNOFF (2) carries far more dissolved nitrogen compounds (NITRATES, NITRITES, AND AMMONIA) into the water, particularly in estuaries. PLANTS (3) convert these compounds into amino acids, proteins, and other nitrogenous compounds. ANIMALS (4) incorporate them when they feed on PLANTS (3) and PLANT DETRITUS (5). DETRITUS (5), ANIMAL WASTE (6) and CARRION (7), all rich in nitrates, nitrites, and ammonia, are broken down by MICROBES (8) which remineralize the organic nitrogen or oxidize ammonia and shuttle it back into the marine system where it is once again utilized by PLANTS (3). Nitrogen compounds not used are LOST TO DEEPER WATERS (9) where they remain unavailable to PLANTS (3) until COASTAL UPWELLING (10) returns them to the surface to be reinserted into the cycle.

C) Phosphorus.

Phosphorus occurs most abundantly as *inorganic phosphate,* dissolved in LAND WATER RUNOFF (1) from land rocks. *Organic phosphate* in GUANO (1) may be locally prevalent. PLANTS (2) change dissolved *inorganic phosphate* to *particulate organic phosphate* and incorporate it into their cells, or excrete it as *soluble organic phosphate.* ANIMALS (3) eat plants and incorporate the *particulate organic phosphate* into animal cells. ANIMALS FEEDING ON OTHER ANIMALS (4) continue this exchange. Fecal WASTE (5) from animals, DETRITUS (6) from plants, CARRION (7), and *dissolved inorganic phosphate* are broken down by (8) MICROBES in a BACTERIAL CONVERSION PROCESS (9) that releases *soluble organic phosphate* back into the water column and sediments. The bacteria also change *soluble organic phosphate* back to *soluble inorganic phosphate* which is again taken up by PLANTS (2), thus completing the cycle all over again.

tion. Most of the carbon produced in the world's oceans is deposited as carbonates (73%) or organic carbon (26%) in the sediments. Small amounts are dissolved in the hydrosphere (the fresh and salt waters of the earth), and still less (about an order of magnitude smaller or 0.16%) is found in the biosphere (the living organisms) and atmosphere. Carbon dioxide, as a gas in seawater or in the atmosphere, makes up less than 2% of the total carbon on earth. On a yearly basis, photosynthesis by marine plants uses up about 1/280 of the total CO_2 available in the ocean. Thus organic carbon in living organisms actually comprises a very small amount of the total carbon available on earth.

PONDERABLES FOR OUR FUTURE

Fact: There are four main reservoirs for carbon in the earth's carbon cycle: the oceans, fossil fuels (geological), rocks on the earth's surface (terrestrial), and the atmosphere.

Fact: The oceanic reservoir (85%), estimated at about 38,000 billion tons (38,000 gigatons), is the major determinant of carbon dioxide (CO_2) in the atmosphere. The amount released depends on a multitude of mixing, chemical, and biological processes.

Fact: The amount of carbon presently held in the atmosphere, mainly as CO_2, is estimated at approximately 748 gigatons (1.6% of the total).

Fact: The amount of CO_2 transferred from sea to air, and from air to sea, is about equal, totalling approximately 100–115 gigatons in and out per year. The exchange is said to be in equilibrium.

Fact: Photosynthesis by plants removes another 100–120 gigatons of carbon (as CO_2) from the atmosphere each year. Respiration by plants, organic decay, and fires returns 90–120 gigatons each year. Thus this part of the cycle is also in equilibrium.

Fact: Remaining recoverable carbon held in all fossil fuel reservoirs on earth is estimated at about 4,000 gigatons (9%).

Fact: Burning of these fossil fuels (petroleum, natural gas, coal) adds more than 5 gigatons of carbon (as CO_2 and hydrocarbons) to the atmosphere each year and is therefore the dominant contribution to increasing levels of CO_2 in the atmosphere.

Fact: CO_2 in the atmosphere has increased about 16% since 1900.

Fact: If no other changes occur in the overall balance of the carbon cycle, all fossil fuel reservoirs will be exhausted in about 800 years—if a global warming catastrophe caused by increasing CO_2 levels in the atmosphere doesn't occur first.

Source: Post, W.M. et. al, ."The Global Carbon Cycle," *American Scientist*, 78, no. 4 (July-August, 1990).

NITROGEN

Equal in importance to carbon, nitrogen is widely distributed in the marine environment either as nitrate, nitrite, or ammonia compounds. Although atmospheric nitrogen gas itself is almost inert, its compounds are extremely reactive. Nitrogen-based compounds are absolutely essential for all living organisms because they combine with carbon chains to form proteins; enzymes; genetic material including DNA, RNA, purines, and amino acids; and other constituents of living cells.

Unlike carbon's simple pathways, nitrogen pathways can be incredibly complex. They begin with bacteria that, through a process called *nitrification*, change inert nitrogen into nitrate and nitrite compounds. These compounds are absorbed by plants and transferred to herbivores (plant-eating animals). They are further assimilated when herbivores are eaten by carnivores (meat-eating animals). Eventually, they are released back into the marine environment as nitrogenous waste, organic compounds such as urea and uric acid, or through release of ammonia (NH_3) via bacterial decomposition of dead animals and plants. In this latter respect the nitrifying bacteria play a significant role in making simple nitrates available again to plants, thus completing the cycle (see Figure 13B).

PHOSPHORUS

Phosphorus occurs as both inorganic and organic phosphate (tied to various organic molecules). Primarily a land-borne element in the Gulf of Mexico, phosphorus concentrations of surface waters gradually decrease as both the distance from shore and the depth increase. Inorganic phosphate, the most abundant form in the sea, is introduced primarily via dissolved sediments in rivers and streams. Large rivers can be an important phosphorus source. The Mississippi River, for example, is estimated to contribute approximately three pounds of phosphorus per second into the Gulf. Land-based runoff is also important. Waters entering Tampa Bay from the phosphate-rich areas of western Florida may contain exceedingly high amounts of soluble inorganic phosphate.

Organic phosphorus, on the other hand, is both abundant and rapidly cycled by living cells. Substantial quantities are available in fecal material produced by marine invertebrates and vertebrates. Bacterial decomposition of organic material may also release organic phosphate, which, in turn, is eventually converted to inorganic phosphate. Thus the cycle is relatively simple: inorganic phosphate—organism—organic phosphate—microbes—inorganic phosphate. (see Figure 13C).

Phosphates, either as inorganic or organic compounds, have great importance in coastal and estuarine areas. Here, their nutrient functions are well known, and they support large areas of sea grasses and phytoplankton, thus providing a firm basis for an extended food web. This is not to imply, however, that offshore phosphorus compounds are unimportant. Studies suggest that plankton blooms such as the toxic "red tides" that periodically occur are strongly influenced, and may be precipitated by, excess dissolved phosphates in the water column.

On the other hand, once phosphates sink from the water column and become incorporated into sediments, they usually are not found in appreciable amounts in the overlying waters. Even in areas of upwelling, for example along the western Florida continental shelf, no unusually large amounts of phosphate have been detected.

SULFUR

Sulfur occurs in the marine environment primarily in the form of sulfates, or as hydrogen sulfide (H_2S), although free or elemental sulfur can be deposited by some bacteria. Plants assimilate sulfate and incorporate it as amino acids and proteins. These, in turn, are passed on to animals when the plants are eaten. Sulfates are then released back into the environment via excretion or aerobic (oxygen-demanding) decomposition. However, in low- or depleted-oxygen situations, sulfides are produced instead of sulfates. These sulfides quickly unite with hydrogen to form hydrogen sulfide gas in a series of complex chemical reactions. Muds containing this compound are black and smell strongly of rotten eggs. Free or elemental sulfur itself has a relatively innocuous but characteristic odor.

Several kinds of bacteria use H_2S, as rotten as it smells, as an energy source in conjunction with light to engage in photosynthesis. This process differs from that seen in green plants in that no free oxygen is released; instead either elemental sulfur or sulfates will be produced, depending on available oxygen. Such organismic operations simply reinforce the fact that life has evolutionarily explored a multitude of pathways in its attempt to remain successful.

Sulfur-containing compounds have received additional attention of late when it was discovered that some bacteria associated with deep-sea hydrothermal vents are able, in the absence of light, to chemically synthesize carbon compounds from CO_2 by oxidizing sulfides. The process is called *chemoautotrophy*, or chemical self-feeding. The bacteria were found in large numbers in marine worms called pogonophorans, which lack mouths and digestive systems. This suggests that the bacteria may be acting as symbionts by producing dissolved nutrients that the worms are able to absorb directly. Originally discovered near rifts in the deep seafloor of the Eastern Pacific and mid-Atlantic Oceans, similar communities or their analogues are now known to exist in the Gulf of Mexico as well. Here, however, the communities are associated with cold saline seeps along the Florida Escarpment, and with hydrocarbon seeps adjacent to salt domes off Louisiana.

SILICON

Silicon, a primary component of glass, seems a bizarre element to be important to life. Indeed, in living organisms it is not required for nutrition in the strictest sense, but rather for formation of skeletal components, particularly in the one-celled planktonic organisms called diatoms and radiolarians (see Figure 34, Chapter 25). Yet, in spite of the element's apparent abundance in these organisms, the silicon cycle is not well understood.

For example, when diatoms or radiolarians die, the silica-based exoskeletons (called *frustules* or *tests*, respectively) sink into the deep sea where redissolution supposedly must take place. And, during the summer, excess amounts of silicates are detectable in deep-sea water columns. This implies that during the diatom/radiolarian bloom in the spring the cast exoskeletons have been rapidly redissolved, and that silicon may be regenerated and reused several times over a seasonal cycle.

But the organic fly in this glassine ointment is that the siliceous frustules and tests of both diatoms and radiolarians often show great resistance to dissolution and so accumulate over hundreds of thousands of years in massive fields of ooze that carpet the seafloor for thousands of square miles in depths hundreds to thousands of feet thick.[3] How can this be?

The answer lies partly in deep-sea water chemistry and partly in biology. As hydrostatic pressure increases in the deep sea, dissolved carbon dioxide dissociates, and the sea water becomes more acidic. This acidification decalcifies any calcium carbonate, but has relatively little effect on silicates, so that calcareous shells are more easily dissolved than siliceous ones. But at least some siliceous exoskeletons must be dissolved. Otherwise where do the high amounts of silicates periodically found in seawater come from? One hypothesis suggests that an organic layer of protein-like molecules may form a kind of a buffer on the tests, slowing or preventing dissolution of their silica compounds. On the other hand, those tests which have been eaten and therefore have passed through the stomachs of herbivores are often fractured and may have this layer removed, thus facilitating their ultimate dissolution when they are finally excreted into the sea. Whatever the explanation, one thing is certain: the chemistry of dissolved silica and silicates is still poorly known.

TRACE ELEMENTS

About 55 of the 92 elements that are found on earth (excluding the trans-uranium series) are always present and readily detectable in seawater. The remainder are either difficult to measure, or are nondetectable by present technology, and thus occur only in trace amounts. These trace elements comprise some 40% of all the elements on earth, both metallic and nonmetallic.

Trace elements seem to be a mixed blessing. Many of them are of prime importance in maintaining biological health (see Table 2). Their deficiency is often manifested in declining vigor of individuals or populations. Yet, other trace elements, particularly the "heavy metals" such as copper, cadmium, and lead, are extremely toxic—so much so that although their concentrations are able to be measured in parts per billion (ppb), the lethal doseage is often listed in tenths or hundredths ppb. Thus, low concentrations of such trace metals should not be equated to their significance in marine ecosystems.

The trace nonmetals also tend to remain dissolved in the water column, appearing as ions (such as hydrogen bromide) or undissociated acids (such as boric acid). In contrast, many trace metals form either simple chemical compounds (copper sulfide) or complex species containing organic molecules (methylmercury chloride) and become attached to detrital (particulate organic matter) and sediment particles where they are quickly removed from the water column. This makes these metals more available to benthic (bottom-dwelling) organisms, either through direct ingestion or assimilation, or to their predators via biological accumulation and magnification. Because many benthic organisms are detrital feeders, they are more rapidly and completely exposed to both necessary and harmful trace metals advected onto sediments.

Some of the most recently added trace metals have a deadly pedigree. Isotopes of radioactive cesium, strontium, and lead, called *radionuclides*, are turning up more and more in sediments. Although some of these forms occur through radioactive decay of naturally occurring isotopes, others have been shown to be the remnants of fallout from clouds produced by atmospheric testing of atomic weapons in the late 1950s and early 1960s and from accidental discharges at nuclear power plants. The wide-ranging and long-term effects of such radioactive trace metals released by the Chernobyl nuclear plant disaster, for example, remain either unclear or unassessable at present. It may be years before their effects, if any, appear.

Table 2
The More Important Inorganic Trace Elements in Seawater and
Their Significance for Marine Organisms

Iron	Blood constituent; photosynthesis regulator
Copper	Respiratory pigment; plant enzyme component
Boron	Plant cell growth regulator
Manganese	Chlorophyll component; plant growth regulator
Zinc	Plant enzyme component
Silicon	Growth and skeletal structure in marine diatoms
Cobalt	Enzyme component in nitrogen/vitamin metabolism
Iodine	Growth component in marine algae
Fluorine	Concentrated by some algae
Strontium	Skeletal component
Molybdenum	Enzyme component in nitrogen metabolism
Bromine	Concentrated by some algae
Vanadium	Respiratory pigment; nitrogen metabolism component
Titanium	Diatom skeletal component; red tide growth factor?
Aluminum	Mucous sheet component in bivalves
Gallium	Essential growth factor in some algae

Data synopsized from several sources.

BIOLOGICAL CONCENTRATION AND MAGNIFICATION

Toxic trace metals and sediments produce two problems of increasing environmental importance: biological concentration and biological magnification. Many trace metals when ingested are not excreted by an organism but are stored in body tissue, fat, liver cells, gonadal tissue, exoskeletal matter, or skeletal bone. Thus, over a period of time these compounds become highly concentrated in individuals. Although these concentrations may prove toxic to the organism, in many other cases they are tolerated with few outward effects.

When such organisms die or are eaten, the stored metals are released, either into the environment or incorporated into the feeding animal. Ingestion of many contaminated animals by a single predator thus magnifies the final concentration. As predation proceeds up the food chain, biological concentration increases, with the top predator or carnivore ultimately receiving the largest dose. From trace amount to lethal dose is thus often a matter of who has eaten how much of whom. While at first glance this may seem of no consequence to us, it cannot be dismissed so lightly. Humans, standing at the apex of the food web, are not immune, because the organisms we eat often carry the largest amounts of contamination. It is both ironic, and a sad commentary on our exploitative actions, that we may be poisoned by those lower organisms who are concentrating the very toxins we put into the environment in the first place.

Weather and Its Consequences

THE THREE MOST IMPORTANT FACTORS affecting the climate and weather patterns of the Gulf of Mexico are the Bermuda High, extratropical cyclones, and sea surface temperatures. The interaction of all three not only determines the weather of the day but also affects future weather patterns.

THE BERMUDA HIGH

The atmospheric high-pressure cell known as the Bermuda High is the overriding phenomenon controlling atmospheric circulation patterns in the Gulf, especially during the spring and summer (see Figure 14). One consequence is the prevalence of easterly and southeasterly winds throughout the basin. When such winds bring in moist, unstable air, thunderstorms appear. Westerly and northwesterly winds are less common and are associated with summer thunderstorms. In late summer the Bermuda High shifts more toward the north and another and more tropical atmospheric phenomenon called the Equatorial Low Pressure Belt is more influential on Gulf weather patterns. Thus, from March through September wind direction is generally clockwise, from the northeast and southeast; from October through February the wind direction is predominantly counterclockwise, coming from the northwest and southwest. As a general statement spring and summer winds are tropical in origin, whereas fall and winter winds are more polar in origin.

Surface winds range from 6 to 8 knots in the summer and 10 to 12 knots in the winter. The winter winds trend more from the east and a northerly component appears. When southeasterly winds occur they tend to carry moister, warmer air over the cooler northern regions, often leading to extended periods of fog. Such fogs appear primarily in midwinter in the Gulf region, being more prevalent in the north than in the south.

Wind and Waves

An important consequence of the mostly moderate winds that prevail over the Gulf is that moderate seas are the rule. Wave heights of less than 3 feet occur about 65% of the time over the year, while heights greater than 5 feet occur about 10–15% of the time, and heights greater than 12 feet happen only about 1% of the time. Offshore swell heights are equally moderate, with up to 80% being less than 6 feet from September through April and only 3% to 6% being higher than 12 feet. These percentages are of obvious importance to mariners, whether they are tanker or steamship captains, or just dad, mom, and the kids on a Sunday outing.

EXTRATROPICAL CYCLONES

When wind and waves unite to form large storm systems, these weather patterns then become of supreme importance to everyone in the coastal zone, seafarer and landlubber alike. Extratropical cyclones (originating outside the tropics) are large counterclockwise air circulations that result from warmer, moister air meeting the colder, drier air coming off the mountains and plains of the North American continent to the west and north. These cyclones occur on an average of ten times each year, usually when a cold air mass sweeps downward from the central plains. Beginning in October, they extend to April, with the greatest number of cyclones taking place during the winter months, particularly January. These systems generate the seasonal "northers," fierce storms that can produce large-scale erosion of beaches and subsequent destruction of coastal properties. These storms will be discussed later.

SEA SURFACE TEMPERATURES

Because the average sea surface temperature in the Gulf is about 84°F, air temperatures above the sea may also usually be uniformly warm, and differ by less than 1 degree. However, sea temperatures in general average about 5 degrees higher than air temperatures overall. This results from exchange of heat between the sea and the air. Moreover, during the winter a larger temperature gradient occurs, with sea surface temperature ranging from a warm 75°F and higher in the southern regions, to decidedly cooler temperatures of 65°F or less in the north. The warmer southern air thus produced is carried northward by the Equatorial Low Pressure Belt discussed above, and is responsible in large measure for the normally pleasant climate enjoyed in the maritime provinces around the entire Gulf.

STORMS AND OTHER ADVERSE WEATHER CONDITIONS

Storms are a result of several interacting factors, the most important of which are atmospheric circulation and atmospheric pressure. In the Gulf region the average sea-level atmospheric pressure varies from 30.00 to 30.15 inches of mercury; however, wide-scale variations can occur as a consequence of the three weather factors discussed above. Variations also result from the effects of tropical storms and hurricanes, as will be seen shortly.

Clouds and Cloud Cover

Weather produces clouds; clouds produce weather. Both cloudiness and adverse weather are a result of extratropical cyclones in the winter and convective thunderstorms in the summer. Throughout the Gulf, clouds cover from 40% to 60% of the sky, with the north and northwestern Gulf areas mostly obscured in the winter and spring, and the southeastern and southwestern portions having highest cloud cover in the summer and fall. The type of cloud formation and the height and direction of movement not only provide indications of coming

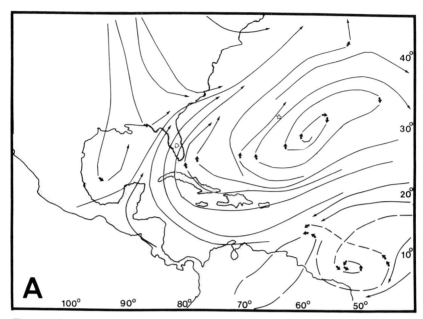

Figure 14A

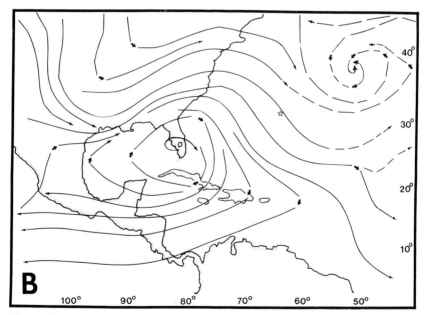

Figure 14B

changes in the weather but often indicate direction and patterns of the high-level, 200+ miles per hour, atmospheric windstream called the tropospheric jetstream over the Gulf as well. Weather forecasters use these higher-altitude cloud formations to predict long-term weather patterns.

One of the most common types of lower-level clouds are the typical puffy, flat-bottomed cumulus, which are responsible for rain. High-altitude photographs show that these clouds often extend in a distinct band from Yucatán toward the northwest. They occur as a consequence of evaporation of water from the sea surface, and along the sea-land interface (see Part Two Figure).

CLOUDS, WIND, RAIN, AND WEATHER

Cumulus clouds and, to a lesser extent, stratus clouds (those occurring in layers) produce most of the rain that falls. Rainfall (precipitation) amounts vary widely and depend on a multitude of factors. In the Gulf, rainfall averages range from 30 to 60 inches a year, with pockets of lower and higher averages resulting from locally prevalent conditions. For example, southern Gulf areas are less influenced by extratropical cyclones and passages of cold fronts, so rainfall in the winter is reduced. This produces the typical winter dry season in the southern areas of the Gulf. Increasing rainfall beginning in the summer (May or June) results in the typical subtropical wet season.

On the other hand, in the northern and western Gulf the climate is warm-temperate and influenced more by continental weather patterns. Rainfall and, more importantly, snowfall may vary substantially from the more southerly areas, with more precipitation (the sum of rain and snow) falling in winter than in summer.

Northers or Northeasters

Periodically, from November through March, cold, fast-moving winds accompanied by cold, driving rain sweep through the Gulf. These winter storms occur when a cold, high-pressure area (an anticyclone) drifts southward, pushing a warm, cloudy or rainy front ahead of it. Such weather systems can last from one to three days, and are termed "northers" by mariners. They bring frigid polar air southeastward, often accompanied by foul weather offshore. After a norther

Figure 14. The Bermuda High in summer and winter.
The Bermuda High, an atmospheric high pressure system (solid lines), is plotted by meteorologists using layers of equal atmospheric pressure termed isobars. The seasonal change of position of this important weather parameter from southeast of Bermuda (star) in late summer (A) to over Florida and the Gulf of Mexico in early winter (B) is apparent. The innocent-looking curlicue of counterclockwise low pressure circulation (dashed lines) in the lower right hand corner of (A) marks the ominous development of Hurricane Gilbert, one of the most destructive storms to ever occur in the Gulf of Mexico. The same pattern in the upper right hand corner of (B) delineates a North Atlantic winter gale system. [Data from Atlantic Tropical Ocean Lower Layer Analysis (A.T.O.L.L.) charts, courtesy NOAA, National Weather Service, National Hurricane Center, Miami, Florida]

front passes, the winds become calm and a two- to five-day period of clear, cold weather ensues. While sea temperatures in the Gulf rarely drop below 60°F, land temperatures may fall precipitously 25° to 50°F in three hours time or less. When such temperatures drop below freezing for an extended period of time they can produce "hard freezes" that may be catastrophic to agricultural areas in the normally warmer regions of the Gulf. Truly exceptional cold snaps have resulted in mass mortalities of marine and estuarine organisms as well. The January 1978 freeze in south Florida brought snow to Miami (and even the Bahamas) and produced a massive fish kill and nearly total decimation of estuarine mangrove forests along many parts of the coast.

Thunderstorms, Tornadoes, and Waterspouts

Perhaps the most important types of storms are those involving rapid air circulation. These bouts of violent weather can occur anytime but are more prevalent during summer and early fall. When high-humidity air masses at low levels become unstable they begin to rotate, forming what weathermen call convective circulation cells. These cells act like gigantic atmospheric whirlpools, carrying evaporated moisture rapidly into the upper atmospheric layer called the troposphere. Here the water vapor condenses into massive clouds, the tops of which may extend well beyond 40,000 feet. At this height tropospheric winds shear off the cloud tops, producing the typical anvil-shaped thunderhead cloud.

Now the stage is set for serious adverse weather. The contained cloud-water soon recondenses and falls either as rain or, if repeatedly recirculated and refrozen, as hail. Lightning displays are a prominent feature of such storm clouds, particularly during the summer. As the rising hot air collides with cold down-welling air, even more violent and rapid circulation patterns occur, resulting in tornadoes inland, and waterspouts offshore. Their whirling winds, circulating at 250 miles per hour or more, pick up dust, debris, or water and form the typical and terrifying funnel-shaped cloud that moves rapidly across land or sea surfaces.

Tropical Storms and Hurricanes

Tropical storms and hurricanes[1] are both products of the tropics, particularly warm equatorial sea surfaces. Born in the oceanic waters off western Africa and the Azores, and rocked in the circulating nursery of thunderstorms, they can mature rapidly, feeding on the warm, evaporating surface waters, and the lower atmospheric pressure that results when sea surface heat is transferred to the atmosphere. The process is similar to that occurring in a thunderhead: an area of vertical circulation formed at the sea surface climbs skyward, creating wind that rushes into the area from outside where atmospheric pressure is higher. A large-scale spiral rotation is produced which forms a "heat engine" that enhances additional heat transfer, producing more winds and thereby generating and driving the storm. Thus, tropical storms, hurricanes, cyclones, and tornadoes are just different manifestations of the same thing: a circulating weather pattern that

Figure 15. The monster that ate the Gulf.
In this remarkable satellite photograph, Hurricane Allen, one of the largest storms to ever enter the Gulf of Mexico, is shown at its position on August 8, 1989. The photograph emphasizes an often disregarded fact, that hurricanes are not simply small S-shaped characters plotted to latitude and longitude on colorful maps on the evening news, but are instead large, well-organized, circulating, violent weather systems containing destructive winds and tides, whose effects not only encompass, but adversely affect extremely large areas of the earth. [Courtesy of the National Climatic Data Center, SatelliteData Information Service]

can eventually spin out of control if conditions are right.

Hurricanes begin life as areas of disturbed weather and rainsqualls. When counterclockwise air circulation begins to occur, the atmospheric pressure drops at the center, wind speed increases, and a tropical depression forms. Continued circulation and forward movement results in still higher wind speed and the creation of a cloud wall containing rain bands. These bands begin to spiral around the depressed area. Once wind speeds in these bands attain 38 miles per hour (34 knots) the developing system is called a *tropical storm.*

As the rotating cell gains speed and definition, more rain bands form and spin off from the center carrying gales to the northeast and southwest quadrants of the storm. Wind speed rises and the rain bands spiral more rapidly around a defined calm central area, termed the "eye." Continued development increases the number and size of the rain bands and the speed of their contained winds. Soon these winds are roaring around the clearly circumscribed eye, the area of lowest pressure in the storm.

The size of the storm will now be defined by a complex of factors based on wind, rain, oceanic heat transfer, central atmospheric pressure, upper atmospheric winds, the system's forward movement, and speed. At wind speeds of 74 miles per hour (64 knots) the tropical storm becomes a hurricane. Central pressure may drop as low as 26 inches of mercury, winds in the wall cloud and the rain bands nearest the center may exceed 200 miles per hour, and the final storm diameter may exceed 500 miles (see Figure 15).

Now the hurricane is a monster offspring of sea, air, and earth. Movement and speed of the developing hurricane is controlled by sea surface currents, winds and pressure systems at the surface, and upper-level atmospheric winds, collectively called *steering currents*. But the direction the storm takes also becomes influenced by the *Coriolis effect*, an apparent force resulting from the earth's rotation that deflects moving objects in the Northern Hemisphere, including air and water currents, toward the right of their forward motion. These three factors unite to produce average forward speeds of 10 to 20 miles per hour, although faster and slower storms have been recorded. Generally, when first formed, the storm's movement is faster, but as the hurricane gains strength and diameter, movement slows. Many times the storm will be affected by other atmospheric phenomena such as cold or occluded (interacting cold and warm) fronts, which can stall its forward movement, change its direction, or sap its strength.

As long as a hurricane remains at sea it poses a threat only to shipping. But even this is a mixed blessing for land-dwellers, because the sea provides the heat necessary not only to maintain the storm configuration but also to increase its strength. In general, the longer a hurricane remains in warm seas, the stronger and more massive it becomes, building its four most destructive aspects: high-speed winds, massive waves, the storm surge, and prolonged rains.

Hurricane Winds

The force of hurricane winds is the result of several complex factors, including how much sea surface heat is transferred to the atmosphere and for how long, the extent and height of the vertically circulating component, and the intensity of the spiraling rain bands. Although furious gale-force winds are often found in the northeast (forward) and southeast (rear) quadrants of a hurricane, the highest winds occur in a region immediately surrounding the eye, where they blow with indescribable fury.

Hurricane Waves

Hurricanes always form at sea; consequently, they generate waves. Wave height, whether storm-associated or not, depends on three factors: the force of the wind acting on the water, the length of time it blows, and the distance, or "fetch," over which it travels. In a hurricane formed well offshore, the high winds thus create extremely rough seas and long, surging swells. As the storm approaches shallow water, these waves "feel" the bottom and change from great swells to mountainous breakers that thunder ashore with awesome force.

Storm Surge

Lowest atmospheric pressure is found within the eye.[2] Thus, the sea surface inside the eye responds to reduced pressure and bulges upward in a hurricane wave, or *storm surge*. In the open sea the difference is about three feet, but as the storm approaches shore the water bulge may increase to 20 feet higher than the sea surface outside of the eye. Moreover, wind-generated storm waves up to 60 feet high may be associated with this region or occur as long, rolling, massive swells that move outward from the center.

The highest and most dangerous area of storm surge is found on the onshore side of the storm: it may extend to 50 miles ahead of the center and precede the storm's actual arrival by three to five hours. Of little import while at sea, the storm surge can wreak terrible destruction as it comes ashore, particularly if it coincides with lunar high tides and strong onshore winds. The fearsome combination of massive wave action, joining with the bulging sea surface (storm surge) and high tides, can raise water levels 20 feet or more where the storm strikes land. The result of such large-scale differences in water height between storm and landfall areas is often catastrophic erosion and disastrous loss of life.

Hurricane Rains

Hurricanes are seawater storms—born, maintained, or dying depending on seawater conditions. Once hurricanes come ashore they lose the driving force of their heat engine, and wind speed and circulation begin to decrease. Heavy rains comprise any hurricane and both precede and follow the arrival of a hurricane onshore. Depending on the speed, intensity, and "wetness" of the hurricane, up to 15 inches or more of rain may fall in an area as the storm passes. Such rains, coupled with high winds and coastal flooding by onshore seas, may produce widespread inundation of low-lying areas, resulting in great property damage and loss of life.[3] In fact, most loss of life in hurricanes occurs from drownings and not from wind-carried debris.

Hurricanes in the Gulf of Mexico

Hurricanes have been described as gigantic but slower-revolving tornadoes. On the basis of higher wind speed, catastrophically low atmospheric pressures, general size, and short, violent duration, tornadoes are more locally destructive than hurricanes. But for sheer extended periods of destruction hurricanes exceed tornadoes. In fact, hurricanes are the most destructive of all natural disasters, exceeding even earthquakes and volcanic eruptions. The amount of energy in a typical hurricane is equal to dozens of atomic bombs going off at once, every minute. Truly massive storms such as Hurricane Betsy or Camille caused billions of dollars of damage in the coastal regions of the Gulf.

Hurricane damage is not limited to humans and their structures. Ecological effects of hurricanes can be equally widespread and long lasting. Heavy rains can produce high water, excessive river flows, and inundation and erosion. Sea surface waters may be abnormally cooled as much as 9°F, affecting the plant and animal communities of both the nearshore and offshore continental shelf.

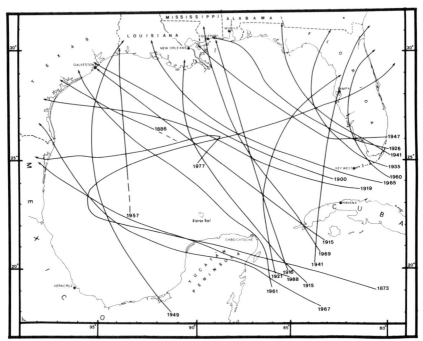

Figure 16. No place to run to, no place to hide.
Tracks of major storms from the late 1800s show that all parts of the Gulf are equally susceptible to hurricanes, whether the storms form within its boundaries or enter from the Caribbean Sea or Atlantic Ocean. From 1900 to 1989, at least 50 well-defined hurricanes have originated or passed through the Gulf, an average of about one every two years. Some of the largest and most economically devastating storms ever recorded in the Western Hemisphere spent a large portion of their life within the Gulf, a fact that seems to be ignored, dismissed, or lost on much of the present coastal populace. [Data from NOAA, National Weather Service, National Hurricane Center, Miami, Florida and other sources]

Hurricanes may have other destructive consequences. Natural and man-made pollutants may be injected in large pulses into estuaries, sediments may remain suspended for weeks, and entire bottom communities may be destroyed. High winds can devastate forested areas and mangrove swamps, killing or severely debilitating the flora and fauna therein. Salinity regimes can be massively altered, either by ingress of wind or wave-borne saline waters into freshwater systems, or by abnormally high freshwater input from rainfall and runoff into estuarine and marine systems.

About 80% of hurricanes form outside the Gulf, primarily near the Cape Verde Islands or in the lower Caribbean. The remaining 20% form within the Gulf, some 15% in the northern portion and the remaining 5% in the southern Gulf. But the point of origin of these massive storms has little bearing on whether a hurricane will eventually enter, or even remain in, the Gulf. As a general statement, hurricanes forming in June enter the Gulf from the south, whereas those forming in August and September enter from the southeast. On rare occasions some storms may form off the west coast of Florida. However, many storm track records show that several large hurricanes which apparently were bypassing the Gulf were suddenly diverted and entered it (Figure 16).

What's the probability of a hurricane or tropical storm forming in or entering the Gulf in any given year? About 1 in 2. The probability of two such storm events occurring in the area decreases to about 1 in 6. Or, in short, about the same probability of making your point in a crap game. Using a single die.

Mississippi ripline.
The massive outpouring of freshwater from the Mississippi River can easily be traced miles out into the Gulf where the differences in salinities and the velocity of the mighty river current unite to form a color break and a ripline between the smoother, lighter Mississippi water in the lower part of the photograph and the more choppy, darker water of the open Gulf in the upper part. [Courtesy Darryl L. Felder]

Part Three

Continental Shelf Physiography

When you approach the river's mouth, which you will by running about 4 miles on the above soft soundings, you will see the color of the water alter, and it will appear like a shoal; this is occasioned by the current of the river mixing with the sea; . . . when you are in (8 fathoms), you will see some mud islands about as large as a vessel of 150 or 200 tons; from among which you will perceive the rivers mouth . . . Unless in a case of utmost necessity . . . let not go an anchor, for its a thousand to one you will lose it if you do . . .

Bernard Romans, 1775
Directions for Going to the Mississippi

Offshore Reefs and Banks

OUT OF SIGHT, NOT OUT OF MIND

HUMANITY HAS ALWAYS had a fascination for reefs. This familiarity began in the earliest days of sailing when reefs were listed on hydrographic (navigational) charts as places to be avoided, and continues to the present, where some reefs are now recognized as complex ecological communities having a richness and diversity rivaled only by tropical rain forests. And although a picture may spring to mind when the word "reef" is mentioned, the image will be as different to each person as the individual's experience is with the habitat. One man's reef may be another man's rock pile.

Webster's Ninth New Collegiate dictionary defines a reef as "a chain of rocks or ridge of sand at or near the surface of water; a hazardous obstruction." While this definition is good as far as it goes, it is not complete. Marine scientists now recognize several different types of reef, not all of which are found at or near the water surface. Two major types occur: biologically formed and geologically formed. The former are constructed by living, or once-living organisms. The latter are the result of geological, hydrological, or sedimentological processes. Biologically formed reefs may be further subdivided into two categories, living and dead. Living reefs, called *bioherms* by oceanographers and geologists, are composed of hard substrates such as coral, mollusc shell, or sand, the materials produced or utilized by the animals actually forming the reef. Dead reefs are simply the remnant structures of once-living reefs.

Whether a reef is living or dead bears no relationship to its complexity or even its origin. A living coral reef is as different from a reef formed by vermetid molluscs as both are from the sandy-tubed structures built by sabellariid worms. Each type of reef supports its own particular flora and fauna, as will be described later in this chapter. On dead reefs, although the original animal-formed substrate may now be lifeless, the existing surfaces may be clothed with a living carpet of sessile (non-motile) animals and plants, including sponges, soft corals, sea whips, sea fans, algae, and a host of other associated organisms, none of which actually formed the reef. In the sea, as on land, Nature does not waste her potential living space.

REEFS AND CORAL IN THE GULF OF MEXICO

Just what are corals and how do some species of these tiny organisms form such massive living structures? Let's look at some background first. Suprisingly enough, corals are closely related to jellyfish, both in their shape and in their life processes. Corals, jellyfish, and their relatives are all classified by scientists as Cnidaria, a classical Greek word that means "nettle." And therein lies the tale of their relationship to each other, for every cnidarian animal, be it hard coral or soft, jellyfish or man-o'-war, sea whip, sea fan, or sea anemone, has movable, whiplike appendages called tentacles. These tentacles form a ring around the mouth of the organism. They may be quite long and trail behind the swimming animal, as they do in jellyfish, or they may be rather short and stubby, as they are in hard and soft corals, sea whips, and their relatives.

What does all this have to do with nettles? Well, every tentacle carries microscopic stinging cells along its length. These tiny cells, used both in feeding and defense, lie coiled like miniature harpoons until a hapless animal brushes against the tentacles. Then the stinging cells explode open, hurling their lilliputian harpoons, and a dose of deadly poison to boot, into the victim. Small organisms (larvae of fishes, crabs, molluscs, and numerous other marine creatures) die and are eaten; large organisms like humans are merely stung, but the result is very much as if they had brushed against a plant containing nettles. Sensations range from mild itching to violent pain, depending on how badly the person is stung.

Now let's turn to the reefs themselves. At first glance, a coral reef certainly doesn't show much resemblance to a soft jellyfish. But it does if we change our perspective. Take a jellyfish, shrink it drastically down in size to about ¼ inch, turn it on its back, surround its body with calcium carbonate (limestone), fix it firmly to the substrate, and presto! you have an individual coral animal called a polyp. A jellyfish is, in one sense then, simply a large, naked, swimming polyp. Or, looked at another way, a coral polyp is simply a miniaturized sessile jellyfish surrounded by limestone that it has secreted for protection and strength. The difference is that jellyfish are mostly solitary animals, whereas many corals are gregarious and settle onto certain substrates in large numbers. Here, they form colonies joined together by their mutual secretion of calcium carbonate.[1] Over time, the colonies enlarge, grow on or over each other, and become more and more massive. When different species of hard corals find the correct substrate and join together over a wide area of the seafloor, the resulting formation is a coral reef (see Plate 2B). Looking closely at any single coral species on a reef, one can easily see the millions of individual polyps punctuating its stony surface. They range from tiny, star-shaped cups to long, serpentine channels. Close up, even the small tentacles surrounding the polyp's mouth become visible.

Although most of the Gulf of Mexico is unsuitable for supporting large-scale coral reef growth, *hermatypic* (reef-building) corals do occur in scattered locations. Usually they are not sufficiently abundant or massive to form a true living reef platform. The three major exceptions are the Marquesas Keys–Dry Tortugas off Florida, the Alacran Reef and some associated smaller reefs near Vera Cruz off the Yucatán Peninsula, and the Colorados Barrier Reef along the northwestern coast of Cuba. The Flower Garden Banks off Texas, formed on a salt dome rather than a true reef platform, constitute a somewhat unique reef assemblage and will be discussed below (see Plate 3).

Extensive platform reefs occur on the coral islets of the Marquesas Keys and the Dry Tortugas, both located at the western termination of the Florida Reef Tract. These islets are not true atolls (formed around a sunken submarine volcano) but ring-shaped reefs built on the same Pleistocene fossil reef that forms the foundation for all the Florida Keys. Both the Marquesas and the Tortugas reefs, which stand in 3 to 6 fathoms of water, are composed of many of the 50 species of corals found on the Florida Reef Tract to the east.[2]

The Alacran Reef is the largest of a series of atoll-like formations located along the seaward margin of the Campeche Bank.[3] These reefs form a disconnected circular series of coral banks, in some 20 to 30 fathoms of water, about midway along the Campeche Shelf off the Yucatán Peninsula. Other coral reefs and reeflike structures are found off the mouths of rivers and streams in the same area, and northward off Vera Cruz and Tampico. Because of the remoteness of this coast, little is known of their ecology, although species censuses indicate similarities to coral assemblages off Florida and, to a lesser extent, in the Caribbean.[4]

The Colorados Barrier Reef off the northwestern coast of Cuba is a true barrier reef, that is, a reef of hermatypic corals built on a platform up to 20 miles offshore. A wide shallow lagoon separates the reef from the mainland. The Colorados Tract, ranging from 5 to 6 fathoms in depth, extends from Cape San Antonio on Cuba's westernmost tip to Bahia Honda in Pinar Del Rio Province. Farther to the east are a series of scattered reef tracts running from Nuevitas Bay to Havana, and the eastern shore of Cuba also supports scattered reefs. These, however, are Atlantic and not Gulf of Mexico reefs, although geologically they are part of the same platform system.

Elsewhere in the Gulf, small groupings of corals may occur anywhere on the shallow continental shelf where water of sufficient clarity and temperature (at least 68°F) and proper substrate conditions (rocky, permanent, with low amounts of silt) are found. These are often termed *patch reefs*. Although they may form substantial mounds of living coral, they usually are built on a basement of small sea mounts, rubble piles, or even shale mounds upthrust by emergent salt domes. The living and fossil corals found on these mounds are not as rich in species as those on the barrier and platform reefs, but the associated communities are often complex, consisting of numerous sponges, sea whips, sea anemones, polychaete worms, crabs, and shrimps, as well as a diverse fish fauna (see Plate 2B and Figure 17E).

Notably large associations are found off Texas at Padre Island (7½ Fathom Reef, Hospital Reef, Big Southern Reef), Freeport (Freeport Rocks), off Florida south of Pensacola, and widely scattered along the western Florida continental shelf (the Florida Middle Grounds). Among the best known and studied of these associations are the Flower Garden Banks. These banks are an extensive reef assemblage containing some 18 species of shallow hermatypic corals, plus a deeper grouping of sponges, algae, and black corals (antipatharians), growing on upthrusted salt domes in approximately 10 to 30 fathoms (20 to 60 meters) of water on the edge of the continental shelf 110 nautical miles southeast of Galveston. The Flower Garden Banks are unique in being the northernmost continental shelf reefs in the Western Atlantic as well as being the northernmost hermatypic reef in the Gulf of Mexico (see Plate 3B).

Ahermatypic (non-reef-forming) corals may also grow in large concentrations that appear as reeflike pinnacles on fathometers. Closer examination shows these assemblages to be more thicketlike and associated with protuberances such as mudlumps, small hillocks, and fossil or subfossil shell heaps on the seafloor along the edge of the continental shelf.

ROCK LEDGES AND BANKS

Much of the shallow continental shelf (less than 50 fathoms) appears to be relatively smooth and featureless, but such is not always the case. Close examination reveals a geological hodgepodge of ledges, solution holes, and fossilized sand ridges scattered all over its surface. Off the Louisiana and Texas coast, for example, large conglomerates of broken whelk and other molluscan shells, often partially fused, provide local relief and are called "piles" by shrimp fishermen. Mudlumps, 10-feet-high domes of fine, tough, structureless clay, are another feature recognized by shrimpers.

Another prominent localized feature is snapper banks, so called because of the large numbers of these fish (*Lutjanus* species) found in commercial quantities there. These banks are believed to be salt domes covered with a veneer of coralline (limestone-secreting) algae, shell hash, and fossil corals. Sponges and scattered living corals, including some normally deep-sea forms, are also present. Many of these same shallow-water banks (sometimes called "high relief fishing grounds") are well known for the extensive shrimp-harvesting grounds associated with them. Heald and Claypile Banks off Freeport, Texas, are two examples. Other major commercial and recreational fishery banks are listed in Table 3.

In the eastern Gulf are areas collectively called "live bottom." These contain characteristic assemblages of algae, sponges, sea whips and sea fans, corals, crinoids (sea lilies), and associated mobile organisms living on or above the seafloor, and termed "epifauna" (see Plate 2B). The Florida Middle Grounds, located northwest of Tampa in waters from 12 to 16 fathoms (75 to 100 feet deep), contain the northernmost reef coral assemblages in the eastern Gulf. They are biologically similar to the Flower Garden Banks noted above, but occur nearly 600 miles to the east.

OYSTER BARS AND OTHER REEFLIKE STRUCTURES

In addition to coral reefs, five other interesting biological communities often form extensive ledges and banks. These are the oyster bars, vermetid mollusc reefs, sabellariid worm reefs, serpulid worm reefs, and sponge banks (see Figure 17). The first four are usually (but not always) found in the intertidal zone; the last is always found subtidally.

Table 3
Some Important Banks and Fishing Grounds in the Gulf of Mexico

Region	Local Nomenclature	Type
Florida Keys	Tortugas Banks	Snapper grounds
	Tortugas Sanctuary*	Shrimp grounds*
Florida-Southwest	Florida Bay	Lobster/crab grounds
	Ten Thousand Islands	Crab grounds
Florida-Central	Sanibel Grounds	Shrimp grounds
Florida-Big Bend	Middle Grounds	Shrimp/fish/ scallop grounds
West Florida	No major banks present	
Florida-Alabama	Southeast Grounds	Fishing grounds
	Timberholes	Snapper grounds
Louisiana	Atchafalaya Shoals	Shrimp grounds
	Trinity Shoal	Shrimp/fish grounds
	Tiger Shoal	Shrimp/fish grounds
Louisiana-Texas	Sabine Bank	Shrimp grounds
Texas	Claypile Bank	Snapper banks
	Stetson Bank	Finfish banks
	Heald Bank	Shrimp grounds
	East Bank	Shrimp/fish grounds
	7 ½ Fathom Reef	Fish grounds
	South Texas Banks	Snapper banks
	Dream Bank	Snapper banks
	Small Adam Rock	Snapper banks
	Big Adam Rock	Snapper banks
	Blackfish Ridge	Snapper banks
	Steamer Bank	Snapper banks
	Seabree Bank	Snapper banks
Mexico	Yucatán Banks	Shrimp grounds

*Part of the Florida Keys National Marine Sanctuary; commercial fishing and scientific collecting (with permits) allowed.

Source: Beccasio, et al. (1982), and Florida Keys National Marine Sanctuary Office (personal communication).

Oyster Bars

Oyster bars are among the most important communities found in estuarine bays and lagoons. Usually occurring in shallow water of reduced salinity, and oriented transversely to incoming tidal currents, an oyster bar may have its upper portion exposed during lower than normal tides. General shape ranges from circular banks to elongated teardrop-shaped bars, often covering much of the bay bottom (see Figure 17A).

In some areas of the Gulf of Mexico, sufficient freshwater outflow occurs

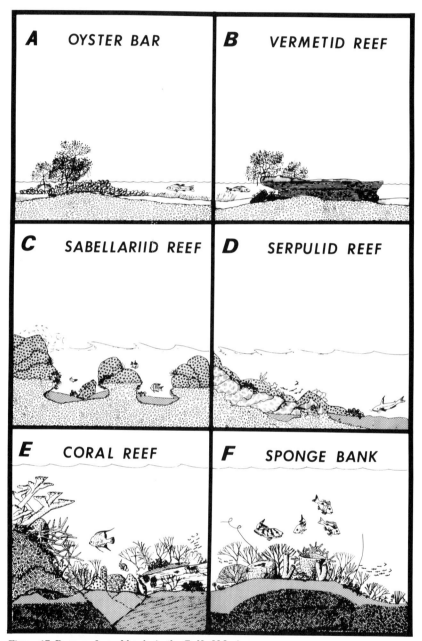

Figure 17. Bars, reefs, and banks in the Gulf of Mexico.

offshore to create brackish water conditions and thus allow establishment of oyster reefs outside the estuary. Such conditions occur off Louisiana's Atchafalaya Bay and Marsh Island, where some oyster bars are found up to five miles offshore. The submerged limestone banks (drowned karst subsector) north of Anclote Keys on the western Florida coast is especially notable for the large oyster bars occurring in apparently totally marine conditions one to two miles offshore. Elsewhere, one of the largest, nearly continuous oyster reefs in the world lies off Pass Christian, Mississippi.

Some oyster bars also occur offshore in the Ten Thousand Islands area of southwestern Florida, but still remain within the mangrove estuarine zone. Here they grow into distinct, reticulated ridges that snake and wind across the shallow, muddy bay floor (see Plate 3A, 10D). In this region the reticulated oyster ridges trap sediments and mangrove tree propagules and eventually become colonized by thriving stands of red and black mangroves.[5]

Vermetid Mollusc Reefs

Gastropod molluscs in the family Vermetidae are also reef-builders. These small snails with twisting, wormlike shells, settle and coalesce in large numbers on shallow rocky substrates just offshore, or within tidal passes of larger estuaries along the southwestern Florida coast. Called "worm rock" by local fishermen, the calcareous platforms often provide suitably stable substrate for mangroves and oysters that eventually, by their growth, enlarge the reefs into small islands in the estuary (see Plate 3C and Figure 17B).

Sabellariid Worm Reefs

Polychaete worms of the family Sabellariidae live in tubes formed of sand grains cemented together. They feed by filtering plankton from seawater and thus require their food to be in suspension. However, in order to build their tubes, they also need conditions where sufficient sand particles are continually suspended in the water column. Sabellariid worms are thus restricted to high-energy beaches with constant, if not heavy, surf. Individual worms settle in or just offshore of the surf zone, usually on exposed limestone ledges, although any semipermanent hard substrate will suffice. Here they collect sand and secrete their tubes. Eventually these coalesce into large, rounded colonies shaped by wave and current action (see Figure 17C).

Although small isolated colonies have been observed along Gulf beaches of

Figure 17. Bars, reefs, and banks in the Gulf of Mexico.
Schematic cross-sections of typical bioherms, or biologically formed reeflike structures. Members of four invertebrate groups predominate: molluscs in quiet estuaries (A, B), polychaete worms in surf zones and near shore (C, D), and corals and sponges on the continental shelf offshore (E, F). All are commonly constructed on preexisting carbonate ledges (A-C) and other rocks (D), or reef limestones and associated talus (E, F).

Florida, they never attain the height and extent of their counterparts on Florida's east coast. There, particularly along the Indian River region in central Florida, they form massive reeflike structures on the exposed coquina limestone shelves that parallel the shore. Sabellariid worm reefs at Punta Delgado near Vera Cruz are less well developed on volcanic rock outcroppings.

Serpulid Worm Reefs

Serpulid reefs are large, rocklike structures caused by the settlement, growth, and coalescence of polychaete worms belonging to the family Serpulidae. These worms, like sabellariids, are filter feeders. But they secrete calcium carbonate tubes, rather than collecting sand grains. The tubes form large, irregularly shaped colonies that eventually may coalesce into flat, platelike reefs or small, low islands. Confined to shallow intertidal waters, they have been recorded in the vicinity of Baffin Bay, Texas, and near Vera Cruz, Mexico (see Figure 17D).

Sponge and Antipatharian Coral Banks

These banks occur in subtidal and deeper waters from about 1 to 25 fathoms (sponge banks) and 25 to 50 fathoms (antipatharian coral banks) (see Figure 17F). Substrate ranges from muddy bottoms to slightly elevated rocky ridges or shell piles. Large numbers of individuals and species of sponges are found on the shallow bars; some are commercially valuable and are harvested by sponge fishermen. Also found growing with the sponges in deeper areas are several species of ahermatypic corals and alcyonarians. Major sponge banks are found along the continental shelf off western Florida, but lesser banks occur off northern Yucatán.

THE IMPORTANCE OF REEFS

All of the reef and reeflike structures discussed above can develop into large, shallow-water prominences forming potential hazards to fishermen and mariners. But their importance as biological communities should not be overlooked. Although each reef may be discretely oyster, polychaete worm, mollusc, or sponge, they all provide additional biological and topographical complexity in relatively homogeneous environments such as sandy surf zones or on shell-hash or muddy seafloors. Consequently, each reef provides potential habitat for invertebrate and vertebrate species that might not otherwise be able to exist in the vicinity. Species richness and diversity develops through colonization, establishment of feeding and breeding areas, and symbiotic associations involving other species. The reef ultimately becomes not only an ecological refuge (refugium), but also a self-supporting, functioning community in an otherwise inimical environment. Species richness, while not approaching that seen on Caribbean reefs, is nevertheless substantial. On the Flower Garden Banks, for example, more than 200 species of fish and nearly 400 species of invertebrates have been recorded so far.

FOOLING KING NEPTUNE: ARTIFICIAL REEFS AND OIL PLATFORMS

Naturally occurring rocky shores are scarce in the northern and eastern Gulf of Mexico. Yet, contrary to what might be expected, biological communities typically associated with hard bottoms and rocky shores are not necessarily rare. This results from the ability of various species to adapt to other types of hard substrates. It has long been known that any hard, more or less permanent, man-made object in the marine environment will quickly be colonized, primarily by sessile (permanently attached) species, particularly those called fouling organisms (hydroids, barnacles, sea squirts, and sponges, so called because they commonly "foul" the structure on which they grow). As they grow and reproduce, the sessile species soon attract both grazing and predatory fauna. Because these artificial structures mimic the habitat created by naturally occurring obstructions such as coral, serpulid worm, or oyster reefs, an active and flourishing community is soon established where such a community would normally not occur. Easily observed examples are seen on any shallow-water jetty, groin, or bulkhead.

Artificial Reefs

It did not take long for people to realize that artificial structures on the seafloor would attract a large, usually self-supporting and regenerating community. A serendipitous result was that game and sport fish populations also quickly became associated with such artificial reefs, so that their recreational and biological value was enhanced.

Today, more than 130 artificial reefs have been established throughout the shallow, nearshore waters of the Gulf. They run the gamut from sunken World War II liberty ships off Texas to cement-filled automobile tires and construction debris off Florida (see Plate 4). Regardless of the composition (concrete, steel, rubber) or the physical form (auto bodies, railroad cars, airplane fuselages, culverts), these reeflike structures are rapidly colonized by marine organisms. Coast Guard regulations require pinpointing their exact locations so that commercial shipping, charter fishermen, and private individuals can easily locate them (see Table 4).

Petroleum-Exploration Structures

Well over 3,000 petroleum exploration platforms and drilling rigs have been erected on the continental shelf of the northern and western Gulf (see Plate 4). These structures, often located above relatively homogeneous sandy plains, increase the ecological complexity of the area and provide artificial but no less usable habitats as well.[6] The growth of a typical invertebrate fouling community on platform pilings quickly attracts numerous species of fish normally associated with reefs. Thus, despite their drab utilitarian nature, many continental shelf oil rigs have become popular offshore recreational fishing areas for local sportsmen (see Figure 18). In this case, both science and industry have joined to fool King Neptune.[7]

Value versus Validity

The use of artificial reefs has generated some controversy as to whether they are actually beneficial or detrimental to fish populations. The arguments go as follows. Where no reefs exist, many good-sized "game" fish live and range over large areas of sea bottom. Thus they seldom, if ever, all occur in one spot. But because artificial reefs are usually well-marked piles of materials, they serve to

Figure 18. How to "pass a gar-anteed good time" off the rigs.
Forty pounds and 52 inches of fightin' silver fury was no match for Cajun determination, as this kingfish soon found out. Highly mobile predators, kingfish (sometimes called king mackerel) and other gamefish lurk near the invertebrate-encrusted legs and frameworks of OCS oil rigs and platforms seeking their own fishy prey while providing both fun and food for offshore anglers in the bargain. [Courtesy Darryl L. Felder]

attract not only a particular resident fish population but many of these same game fish as well, which come to feed on the residents. With both fish and anglers congregating around these sites and competing for the resident fish populations, these same populations may be depleted.

Although this argument seems intuitively correct, it is not always true, particularly in those cases where the artificial reef "pods" are placed far enough apart on the seafloor to be truly separate entities, yet are close enough to allow easy and frequent movement of resident fish species among them. Different species of resident fish may find the invertebrate "pickins" more to their liking on one pod than on the other. Provided recruitment and settlement of invertebrate larvae from the plankton continues, no artificial reef should ever become completely depleted of food supplies for fish.

Moreover, good management practices, including moving of buoy-markers from pod to pod (much like the agricultural practice of letting farm fields lie fallow for a year) should ensure continued build-up of resident fish stocks, while at the same time allowing community complexity to recover or advance. If these gamefish predators (much like people) find their prey declining or absent, they will simply "fish" somewhere else. This ecological fact by itself will aid in the reconstruction of artificial reef communities.

One other factor, not always considered, is of some importance in the artificial reef programs established by local municipalities. If artificial reefs are established and become productively self-sufficient, then restriction or prohibition of fishing over natural reef areas may then be reasonably considered. Such action would go far toward preserving or reestablishing the natural biological communities on these reefs, many of which are already under stress from overfishing, pollution, and disease. It would also reduce or eliminate the thoughtless damage caused by powerboat propellers, dragging anchors, and the disposal overboard of everyday litter. King Neptune himself couldn't ask for more.

TABLE 4
Some Examples and Locations of Artificial Reefs and Reeflike Structures

Area	Structure	Approximate locality
Florida-southwest (44)	Concrete culverts	Off Naples
	Concrete-filled tire	Off Cape Romano
	Vessels and vehicles	Off Charlotte Harbor
Florida-northwest (45)	Construction debris	Off Destin Inlet
Alabama (16)	Ships, concrete debris	Off Mobile Bay
Mississippi (5)	Ships, autos, tires	Off Pascagoula
Louisiana (Many)*	Oil platforms	Off Vermilion Bay
Texas (7)*	Oil platforms	Off Galveston Bay
	Liberty ship	Off Matagorda Bay
	Liberty ship	Off Redfish Bay

*Most oil platforms remain functioning.
Numbers in parentheses indicate number of reefs in the area.
Exact localities and type of reef structure can usually be obtained from local chambers of commerce or county governmental agencies.

Source: Gulf of Mexico O.C.S. Regional Office Map, visual no. 4.

Barrier Islands

LAND FROM THE SEA

B ARRIER ISLANDS, sometimes called coastal barriers or offshore bars, are among the most interesting physiographical features associated with the Gulf coastal areas. Although seemingly simple in form and structure, these landforms are a result of complex and continuing interactions among the sea, the air, and the land. And although the term itself implies that an island forms some type of "barrier" to the sea, there is more to it than just that. Both natural and man-made forces, working together or separately, often conspire to prevent the birth, interrupt the maintenance, and cause the ultimate demise of these geophysically fragile coastal features.

SCULPTURES BY NATURE: WIND, WAVES, AND SAND

At present there are two hypotheses regarding barrier island formation. The first holds that barrier islands form when waves and currents deposit sediments onto an offshore area that differs slightly in topography from the surrounding area— for example, on a ledge of limestone protruding above the seafloor. In parts of the Gulf these sediments often originate from modern or ancient river deltas. In other cases they may accumulate from wave-promoted breakdown of coastal shorelines. In either situation, as sediments are continually laid down a sand bar begins to form on and around the ledge or obstruction. The bar then acts to steal additional sediments from incoming waves or currents, thereby raising its height, which in turn causes more sediments to be deposited until eventually the bar breaks the surface of the sea.

Over time ranging from decades to thousands of years, the newly formed island grows, sculpted and refashioned by wind and wave until it attains stability. Colonization by dune-loving plants on the seaward side and mangroves or marshes on the landward side further stabilizes the island until, through botanical diversification, the island eventually becomes a thriving habitat for plants and animals alike (see Figure 19).

The second hypothesis states that barrier islands form when waves and wind carry sand deposits off a sandy mainland beach and drop them onto a more or less permanent geological formation (such as a limestone ridge). Thus the beach itself gradually moves offshore. This process, called *progradation,* may continue until sufficient sediments have been deposited offshore to form a barrier beach connected by a delta or peninsula. If further wave and current action destroys the connecting link, the barrier island is severed from the mainland. If

TABLE 5

TABLE 5
Types of Barrier Islands in the Gulf of Mexico

Type	Description	Example
Single Dune Ridge	A generally continuous dune ridge* "spine" close to the beach, backed by extensive vegetated wet or dry flats	North Padre Island, Texas
Multiple Dune Ridge	Multiple, parallel or curving rolling dune ridges and swales, supporting hardwood maritime forest on the ridge tops and freshwater marshes or savannahs toward the land	Cat Island, Mississippi
Washover Type	Dunes scattered in a zone of overwash-deposited sediments grading into halophilic vegetational assemblages on the back side	Dauphin Island, Alabama
Single Beach Ridge	Low height beach ridges made of a variety of depositional materials (cobbles to mud) forming a small linear wave-created berm and usually backed by extensive, low, and periodically inundated wetlands of salt marsh or mangroves	Grand Terre Island, Louisiana
Multiple Beach Ridge	A series of low, sandy parallel and coalescing wave-formed beach ridges* occurring linearly along the island. Vegetation along ridge tops well-developed; between ridges as savannahs and marshes	North Captiva Island, Florida
Chenier†	Low, curving or linear sand ridges, widely separated but lying more or less parallel to each other, the depressions being filled with extensive marshland, the ridges supporting upland hardwood (oak) forests.	Chenier au Tigre Louisiana

*Dune ridges are sand hills formed by wind or entrapment of sand by plants. Beach ridges are formed by waves or other action of the sea.
†"Chenier" in French means "oak"

Source: Synopsized from Schwartz, (1973).

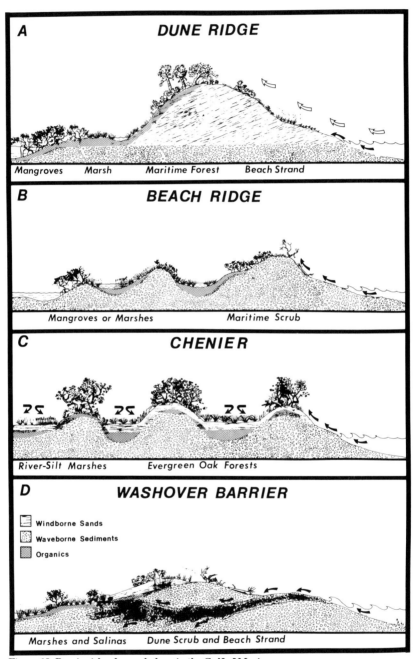

A DUNE RIDGE

Mangroves   Marsh   Maritime Forest   Beach Strand

B BEACH RIDGE

Mangroves or Marshes   Maritime Scrub

C CHENIER

River-Silt Marshes   Evergreen Oak Forests

D WASHOVER BARRIER

Windborne Sands
Waveborne Sediments
Organics

Marshes and Salinas   Dune Scrub and Beach Strand

Figure 19. Barrier island morphology in the Gulf of Mexico.

the barrier remains attached to the mainland it is called a barrier spit, bay barrier, or tombolo, depending on its physiographic characteristics.

Coastal geologists think that both processes occur at one time or another, each reinforcing the other. Researchers also agree that barrier islands can form only where there is a sufficient amount of sand and the necessary water currents and wave action (called a sand budget) to aid in their construction. If the sand budget is interrupted for any reason, for example by the insertion of jetties or groins, the latter structures can rob the downstream island of its sand source, resulting in serious erosion.

COASTAL NECKLACES OF SAND AND SHELL

Coastal geologists have classified barrier islands into a number of different categories based on their structure, geological attributes, and method of formation (Table 5). In general, however, all coastal barriers lie parallel to the shore they protect. In instances where they trend into or away from the shoreline they may eventually develop into headlands that may form capes or gradually coalesce with the shore. Cape San Blas in Florida and Cabo Rojo in Mexico are two examples.

As barrier islands grow and elongate they tend to enclose marine waters behind them, forming partial or complete lagoons. If river drainages occur along the mainland these lagoons may undergo salinity changes from nearly marine to nearly fresh, depending on tidal, current, weather, and freshwater flow conditions. Generally, a well-developed estuarine situation occurs that is enhanced by lengthening of the offshore barrier, thereby further enclosing the lagoon.

When a barrier island is breached by waves or currents, small inlets or tidal passes may form. Like the islands themselves, these passages are often ephemeral, opening and closing sporadically as hydrological conditions change. Under proper conditions the deposition of sand by waves and longshore currents may permanently close these inlets. In some cases extremely long, well-developed, and essentially permanent barrier islands can then develop. A prime example is Padre Island, Texas, which extends for more than 130 miles in an unbroken coast and is the longest intact barrier island in the world.

Barrier islands in the Gulf may range from less than a hundred yards to

Figure 19. Barrier island morphology in the Gulf of Mexico.
Schematic cross-sections of typical Gulf barrier islands show how sea, wind, and sand unite to produce these coastal landforms.
A) Dune ridge barrier, B) Beach ridge barrier, C) Chenier, D) Washover barrier. In each drawing the Gulf of Mexico lies to the right, back barrier lagoons and wetlands lie to the left. Open arrows (wind) and closed arrows (water) indicate major depositional method and general progression of sediments building each barrier. The figure is not drawn to scale, and vertical heights are exaggerated for clarity. Compare the drawing with Table 5.
[Modified and redrawn from P. J. Godfrey, 1976 (unpublished data) and F. P. Shepard, in F. P. Shepard et al. 1960)]

several miles in width, and from 10 to 60 feet in height. Typically, four physiographic features are present: beaches (sometimes divided into the foreshore and the backshore) and resulting beach ridges (formed by wave and current action); dune belts and ridges (formed by wind and plant colonization); back barrier flats (containing marshes, mangroves, and other wetlands), and the tidal passes or inlets that connect the sea to the interior lagoon or sound (see Figure 19).

Geological data indicate that most of the presently existing barrier islands in the Gulf began developing about 5,000 years ago, or about the time of the great Egyptian dynasties. But old age does not bring stability. Although seemingly immovable, barrier islands are in actuality quite dynamic. Series of aerial photographs taken over periods as short as a decade have shown that many barrier islands migrate along the direction of the prevailing current. In other cases, storm tides may breach an island, creating a series of washover deltas that develop into passes and, in turn, subdivide an island into several smaller islands. In still other instances, river sediments may fill in the depressions between the ridges, thus changing the topography.

If the vertical relief of barrier islands is primarily the result of wind, the overall shape is determined by the sea (see Plate 5). The general form may be a concave arc (for example, along the Texas coast), a series of shorter convex arcs (along the Louisiana coast), or a cape (Cape San Blas and Cape St. George, Florida). They may lie more or less parallel to the mainland (Captiva Island, Florida), actually coalesce as a headland (Marco Island, Florida) or form an incipient headland (Cape Romano, Florida).

The interior (lagoonal) shoreline is usually highly irregular and its form depends primarily on the backshore vegetational assemblages that occur there. Mangrove forests, salt marshes, clay hills, escalloped bays, and ephemeral passes and "cuts" are all locally common features.

THE SEA GIVETH; THE SEA TAKETH AWAY

As real estate, barrier islands have Jekyll and Hyde characteristics. On the one hand, their attractive sea views, the relatively isolated location, limited access, and the romance of island "ambience" have made them enticing targets for massive residential development. On the other, their constant exposure to the open sea, hydrological dynamics, relative impermanence, again their limited accessibility, and the fact that they are often first in line in the path of tropical storms and hurricanes make them areas of high or even deadly hazards.

Although attempts have been made to engineer safety into barrier islands, the unalterable fact is that these impermanent and shifting pieces of seashore were created by wind, wave, and current, and consequently can be as quickly altered or destroyed by these same forces. Whether the destruction is gradual, occurring over decades, or rapid and taking place over a three-day storm period, the results are the same: erosion of shorelines, destruction of structures, damages totaling millions of dollars, and almost invariably some loss of life. As any child who has ever gone to the beach knows, castles built on sand are always washed away by the tide.

Rivers, Bays, Lagoons, and Deltas

ESTUARINE LIFEWAYS INTO THE GULF

MORE THAN 150 RIVERS drain the continent of North America into the Gulf of Mexico. The exact number of smaller streams, creeks, and tributaries that also empty into the Gulf is unknown but certainly numbers in the thousands. Fresh water from the two largest river deltas in the United States, the Mississippi and the (five-river) Mobile Bay System, accounts for much of this input. These gigantic river systems, like a huge network of watery nerve cells, connect and ramify throughout continental North America. Water from as far north as eastern Canada and as far west as Montana eventually enters the Gulf (refer again to Figure 8).

The numerous bays lining the shoreline of the Gulf are another important physiographical and biological feature of the region. Known since the time of Spanish conquest, many of these embayments today are thriving ports (for example, Galveston) or connect to port cities farther upstream (such as New Orleans). Others lie behind offshore barrier islands (Apalachee Bay) or are sufficiently enclosed by the islands to be called lagoons (for example, Laguna Madre).

Although the quiet, sheltered waters are of obvious benefit for shipping, commerce, and industry, the river mouths, bays, and lagoons have an even greater biological importance. Here, around the entire continent-enclosed shoreline, where the rivers meet the sea, are found the Gulf's greatest ecological treasures, the numerous estuaries. Along the northern rim the system of bays is particularly well developed and opens to the Gulf via a series of narrow tidal inlets or passes at the ends of barrier islands or at the fronts of eroding marshes and river deltas.

To the southeast the bays become more diffuse, appearing as irregularly open water bodies choked with mangrove islands. At least 19 major estuaries are associated with embayments along the western Gulf of Mexico from Texas to Mexico. The inflowing rivers drain lands ranging from Texas grasslands to Mexican rain forests.

In general the river-bay-lagoonal systems around the Gulf range from areas of relatively low wave-energy off the Florida coast to high wave-energy areas off Texas, and from highly silted muddy bottoms to limestone shelf and shelly areas. This diversity of physical and sedimentological factors allows a concomitant diversity of ecosystems to become established and to flourish. Nearly every type of common warm-temperate or subtropical coastal ecosystem can be found somewhere along the shores of the Gulf of Mexico (see Table 6).

These great interlocking hydrological systems are pathways of life for the flora and fauna of the coastal Gulf of Mexico. Here, adults spawn, eggs and larvae are set adrift, postlarvae and juveniles settle and mature, food webs become established, and ecosystems flourish. It is a complex partnership of waters, fresh, brackish, and saline, that provides both the foundation and the continuing support for much of the biota of the Gulf. In this chapter we shall see just how complex these systems can be.

TABLE 6
General Classification of Common Gulf Coast Ecosystems

Area	Boundaries	Description
Florida Bay	Key West–Cape Sable Florida	Extensive mangrove swamps and islands, seagrass beds and mudflats, bordered by the Everglades National Park, southwestern Florida
Ten Thousand Islands	Cape Sable–Cape Romano, Florida	Complex mangrove swamp and island coastline, with tidal channels and reticulated oyster bars
Central Barrier Coast	Cape Romano–Tarpon Springs, Florida	Sandy beaches backed by coastal lagoons, marsh and mangrove swamps
Big Bend Limestone Coast	Tarpon Springs–Lighthouse Point Florida	Rugged shallow shoreline with rocky bottom, extensive oyster bars, seagrass beds
Appalachicola Delta Coast	Lighthouse Point–Cape San Blas, Florida	Barrier enclosed coast, smooth sandy beaches, shallow muddy bays, sparse sea grass
North Central Gulf Coast	Cape San Blas–Mobile Bay, Alabama	Extensive barrier island coast and dune system, white sand high-energy beaches
Mississippi Delta	Mobile Bay–Vermilion Bay, Louisiana	Barrier-enclosed coast, with extensive marsh and bayou systems, high silt and terrigenous sediment greatly influenced by Mississippi River drainage; numerous shallows

Area	Boundaries	Description
Chenier-Barrier Coast	Vermilion Bay– Galveston Bay, Texas	Chenier-based coastal topography, extensive fresh/salt marshes and associated freshwater river inflow
Texas Coastal Barriers	Galveston Bay–Rio Grande Delta, Mexico	Extensive lagoonal topography of drowned river mouths and sandy barrier islands; freshwater to hypersaline conditions
Mexican Coastal Barriers	Rio Grande Delta– Cabo Rojo, Mexico	Extensive barrier-enclosed lagoons, often hypersaline; sandy beach and scrub shorelines backed by desert or arid plains
Veracruzian Shelf	Cabo Rojo–Punta Roca Partida, Mexico	Narrow shelf fronted with sandy beaches trending toward volcanic sands in southern part; mixed marsh and mangrove shore with shallow rocky shelf
Campeche Bank	Punta Roca Partida– Cabo Catoche, Mexico	Wide shallow limestone shelves, scattered coral and coralline banks and atoll-like reefs offshore, inshore mangrove and seagrass shorelines, with numerous embayments and sandy beaches fronting barrier islands that enclose wide, muddy lagoons
Pinar del Rios Barrier Reef Coast	Cabo San Antonio– Havana, Cuba	Mangrove-fringed coastal embayments grading into sandy coral-studded shallows bordered offshore by barrier reef

Source: Extrapolated and modified from Odum, H. T., et al. (1974), Dr. K.L. Heck
(personal communication), and author's field notes.

RIVER DELTAS: LIFE IN THE STRESS LANE

River deltas are defined as alluvial (river-borne) deposits of sediments that appear roughly triangular or fingerlike in aerial view owing to the way the deposits are shaped by the river flow. Deltas have been classified into several subcategories (bird's-foot, bay, tidal) depending on their topography (the average high and low points connected by imaginary contour lines) and their morphology (the overall shape). Although deltas themselves are more or less permanent features, many are quite dynamic and undergo considerable change

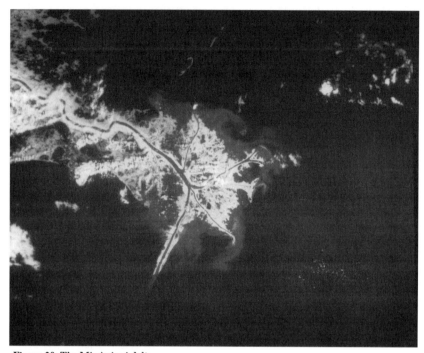

Figure 20. The Mississippi delta.
A classic example of a bird's foot delta, the Mississippi River splays out into the Gulf south of
Chandeleur Sound on the Louisiana coast. Five large distributary channels are easily seen. Less
visible are the numerous smaller dendritic branches of the main channels. Sediment deposition
(light gray) feathers outward from each channel. Lighter areas are marshes and mudflats, most of
which were deposited over the last century.The small fishhook-shaped landmass is Breton Island,
the coastal barrier that guards Breton Sound. [U.S. Geological Survey, EROS Data Center, Sioux
Falls, South Dakota]

depending on prevailing currents or over a given season (see Figure 20).

Deltas are another example of the interaction of rivers with the sea. The
occurrence of a delta simply means that sediments are being supplied by the
river more rapidly than the offshore tidal currents and wave action can remove
them. In general, rivers that discharge less than 500 cubic feet of water per
second do not form deltas; and only those rivers discharging greater than 50,000
cubic feet of water per second (such as the Mississippi River) form the great
deltas of the world. When such rivers reach the sea, they are no longer confined
to flowing within their previously defined stream banks. Consequently, the
velocity of flow decreases. As it does, the sediments previously carried by higher
velocity stream flow are dropped onto the seafloor. Such sediment depositional
areas can extend for tens of miles offshore, with riverine silt and mud traceable
to the edge of the continental shelf; they also often form large, submerged,

muddy or sandy mounds extending outward from the river mouth itself.

There are eight major river deltas that empty into the Gulf of Mexico. The most prominent, of course, is the Mississippi, more correctly called the Mississippi-Red Delta, followed by the Mobile Bay Delta. The Atchafalaya Delta in Louisiana forms the third important delta in the region. The Brazos-Colorado River Delta and the Rio Grande Delta in Texas, are together composed of drainages of 10 major rivers. Other large deltas include the Apalachicola in the Florida panhandle and a series of rivers along the inner Yucatán coast that empty into the Seco-Grijalva Delta on the west and the Grijalva-San Pedro y San Pablo Delta on the east.

Life on a Delta

The delta is a very special kind of estuarine environment. It is a region of continual shock, stress, and change in which only the most physiologically resilient organisms can survive. For example, the transition between fresh and salt water is substantially more abrupt than in a typical riverine estuary. In fact, the sharp salinity gradient in front of a delta is so great that massive salinity shocks may occur to organisms caught in the distributive channels of a delta. Moreover, organisms at the offshore bottom of a delta tend to remain exposed to nearly constant marine conditions, while those near the top of the sediment pile at the inshore edge may experience almost continual freshwater environments—a situation also seen in some classical riverine estuaries.

Temperature shock may also be a daily occurrence inasmuch as fresh river water is often colder than marine waters. This shock may be enhanced seasonally, for example when spring melt from upland snow layers rushes down a river and through the delta to the sea. Coupled with this may be constantly high turbulence as river flow meets incoming wave trains and tidal flows, so that the sediments remain almost continually disturbed.

Such turbulence has good and bad effects. Oxygen values may be high in surface waters owing to mixing, whereas low or even anoxic (no oxygen) conditions can develop in water layers just above sediments having high organic content and where decay is occurring. High turbulence also interdicts sunlight so that the potential for production of oxygen by photosynthesis is reduced or absent. In fact, many organisms on the delta floor exist in almost continual darkness.

Surface waters along a delta front are usually rich in nutrients brought downriver. Consequently, large standing crops of plankton are often found in this area. Because plankton form the basis of the marine food web, rich fishing grounds may also occur in front and along the side of deltas. On the debit side of the ledger, excessive nutrients may promote blooms of certain species of phytoplankton such as dinoflagellates, diatoms, or green, red, or brown algae. These organisms, through their life processes, may deplete dissolved oxygen at night. Zooplankton grazing on these plantlike organisms may show sudden population increases and tend to degrade existing water quality by increasing nitrates, nitrites and ammonia-based compounds. These aspects will be considered further in a later chapter.

Deltas and Distributions of Organisms

Many sessile organisms (bivalves, tubicolous polychaete worms) find the widely fluctuating salinities in the delta environment too hostile to tolerate, although the motile forms (crabs, shrimp, fish) can move up and down the deltaic estuary, each following its own particular estuarine or marine conditions. Farther offshore, as salinities climb and remain more stablized, the species diversity of both infauna (sediment-dwellers) and epifauna (organisms living on or above the sediments) increases.

In fact, it has been observed that both species richness and numbers of individuals may increase as one moves laterally away from a delta. In some instances one or more species may drop out, and be found only on one side of a delta instead of the other. Biogeographers call this disruption a "faunal or floral break." In other cases, the species may drop out inshore but still occur across the delta farther offshore on the continental shelf, thus effectively bridging deltaic influences and restrictions they impose on the shallower water counterparts. Whether the interdiction results in a partial or a complete faunal (or floral) break depends in large measure on the requirements and adaptability of the organisms being affected, as well as the extent of the deltaic influence in both the nearshore and offshore regions.

ESTUARIES AND THE WEALTH OF COASTAL NURSERIES

Although coastal rivers, bays, lagoons, and deltas may differ in geological structure, physiographic aspects, and hydrological regimes, they all share one feature: their receiving waters may undergo great fluctuations in salinity. In this sense they are all considered to be estuaries. Estuaries have been defined (albeit at times a little too broadly) as the place where the rivers meet the sea. But there is a great deal more to estuaries than just the simple intermixing of fresh and marine waters. Such mixing must occur on a regular basis and within a geographically delimited basin. Estuaries thus are as much a part of the marine environment as they are of the freshwater and terrestrial environmnent.

The one physical parameter that characterizess all estuaries is that their waters are polysaline, that is, they exhibit multiple salinities.[1] The mixing of marine waters (35+ ^{0}/oo) with fresh waters produces the "brackish" water (0.5-17 ^{0}/oo) commonly identified as estuarine, although salinities as high as 26 ^{0}/oo occur normally in many estuaries. This polysalinity gradient, from fresh to brackish to marine, is critical for the biology and ecology of the organisms occurring there.

Polysalinities: When the Rivers Meet the Sea

The estuaries in the Gulf of Mexico take many forms. Some, like the Mississippi, exhibit the classical long river-mouth topography with the associated depositional delta. Others, like Pensacola Bay and Santa Rosa Sound, lie behind barrier islands and are predominantly enclosed polysaline lagoons receiving freshwater input not from a single large river but rather from numerous smaller streams and tributaries. Still others, such as the Ten Thousand Islands area in southwestern Florida, are poorly defined in the geographical sense, and consist of vast saltmarshes and mangrove forests fed by rainwater, overland runoff, and numerous winding tidal creeks.

Typical riverine estuaries occur all around the Gulf of Mexico. From the Mexico-Texas coast to Louisiana, ten major rivers empty into the Gulf. Another seven rivers, beginning with the Mississippi at its delta, pour into the eastern Gulf from Alabama to Florida. The estuarine effects from the larger rivers often extend far out to sea. The fresh waters of the Mississippi River, for example, can be traced up to 40 miles offshore, and even farther in an east or west direction. In this instance the estuarine effects progressing offshore could be considered a case of the sea meeting the river (see Part Three Figure).

Salt Wedges and Tidal Mixing

In a typical estuary, the saltier (and therefore more dense) marine waters of an incoming tide enter a wide-mouthed river and flow upstream beneath the lighter, seaward-flowing fresh water. The parcel of heavier, more saline water appears wedge-shaped in lateral view and is therefore referred to as the "salt wedge."

However, some vertical mixing does occur, and the salt wedge formed by incoming marine waters becomes increasingly narrower and harder to delineate the farther up the river it progresses. When the tide reverses itself and flows back out to sea, the marine waters farthest upriver undergo still more mixing with the down-flowing fresh river water and the salt wedge becomes very much attenuated or destroyed.

Not all estuaries function in this classical manner. Many of the shallower tropical and subtropical estuaries that are not backed by major river systems (for example, southwestern Florida's Ten Thousand Islands) are mixed by the wind. These "meteorological tides" force estuarine waters into different parts of the basin. In some cases, a wind-forced tide may actually override a lunar tide. In others, large parcels of mixed waters, each with its own discrete salinity, may form large eddies and gyres as they progress slowly up or down the estuarine embayment.

Salinity Variations and Biotic Stress

These large-scale changes in salinity occur over tidal regimes in the Gulf that may be as short as 6 hours or as long as 24. The resulting polysaline environment induces stress in those organisms that cannot easily tolerate such drastic alterations. To adapt to these alternating high-low salinity regimes, estuarine organisms have evolved three strategies. They can abide, they can hide, or they can ride the tide .

Many species (sea squirts, free-living worms, and crustaceans, to name just a few) are able to control their internal salt and water content even though outside salinities may be higher or lower. In effect they prevent more saline water from "leaking in" or bodily fluids from "leaking out." They accomplish this by a variety of physiological processes collectively called *osmoregulation*. Others such as oysters, clams, and snails avoid a physiological response altogether by simply withdrawing into an impermeable body covering or shell to await more favorable external salinities.

Still other species (some tube-building worms) avoid salinity stress by burying or constructing burrows deep into the sediment where they retreat until the tidal situation and water salinity change for the better. The more motile organisms (many fish, shrimp, and crabs) escape the problems altogether by simply moving up and down the estuary, maintaining their position in water having the most favorable salinity for their lifestyle. And, of course, those having strict requirements for stable, high salinity water (for example, most sea stars, sea urchins, and brittle stars) simply avoid living in low-salinity estuaries or in those where salinity variations are of too great a magnitude for them to handle.

Estuarine Species: A Life of Constant Jeopardy

Although salinity regulation is important, it is not the only stress with which estuarine organisms have to contend. Turbidity in the water column can clog gills or prevent photosynthesis. Different-sized sediment particles can prevent feeding or cause burrows to collapse. Rapid temperature changes can alter physiological responses. Lowered oxygen levels usually inhibit most biological activities. Rapid tidal or river currents may dislodge or bury organisms in sediments. Tack on naturally occurring pathological microbes, and the ever-present predator, and living in an estuary becomes a continuous struggle for survival. When mankind's organic and inorganic pollution is added on top of all this, it is a wonder that so many organisms are able to survive at all.

APPLAUSE FOR AN ESTUARINE HERMAPHRODITE

One good example of an estuarine organism that has evolved a suite of adaptations not only to polysaline living, but to turbid estuarine conditions as well, is the common eastern oyster, *Crassostrea virginica*, so well known to gourmets. The eastern oyster is easily capable of living in low, and fluctuating salinity areas, and can seal its shell tightly when conditions become too unfavorable. Being a filter feeder, the species rarely goes hungry, because it literally inhales silty estuarine water with all its contained planktonic organisms through a siphonlike part in its fleshy mantle. The oyster then filters the food from the sediments, and ejects the sediments out another siphon.

Adaptations don't stop there. The left shell, the deeper one, is the valve that the oyster attaches to the substrate, be it shell hash, rock, dock pilings, concrete sea walls, or even other oysters. The bowl-like shape tends to keep the upper edge of the shell raised above the substrate so that sediment is less likely to enter and clog the oyster's gills. Should the latter happen, as it often must in high sedimentation areas, the oyster brings its powerful shell-closing (*adductor*) muscle into play. The strong muscular contraction claps both the valves shut, and the resulting internal pressure squirts the water inside the shell back out into the estuary. Anyone who has walked over an oyster bar on an outgoing tide has undoubtedly heard these tasty bivalves "applauding" and seen them spitting little squirts of water up into the air.

This same vigorous clapping is used by the female oyster to squirt her eggs out into the estuary so that they may be fertilized by the male oyster's sperm. The males, however, do not clap, but simply send their sperm out through the exhalant area, usually in the spring when the water temperature reaches about 20°C.[2] All it usually takes is for one male to begin to spawn. As the surrounding males and females inhale the sperm-filled water a mass spawning is triggered, with every mature male and female releasing its sexual products at approximately the same time. Once a male has shed his sperm he slowly changes into a female. The females, after releasing their eggs, may then revert to being males. This evolutionary adaptation, a form of *hermaphroditism*,[3] ensures that there will always be enough individuals in both sexes for reproduction.

Meanwhile, the fertilized eggs quickly develop into a planktonic larval stage called a *veliger* that spends the next several weeks at sea before returning to the estuaries. There, the young oyster, now called a *spat,* seeks the proper shelly, hard substrate on which to settle and set up housekeeping. Clumps of mature oysters release a soluble biological attractant that entices the spat to settle among the existing clumps. Commercial oyster growers turn this trick against the spat by spreading chopped-up empty oyster shells, called *cultch,* onto their culture areas, thereby increasing the "spatfall" and, it is hoped, the resulting harvestable crop. Applause, orgies, and trickery—as one grizzled oysterman said: "It's an old act, but it's a tough one to follow."

A net full of food.
Shrimpers spill the contents of a successful trawl onto deck. Each trawl, when set, may have a mouth width of 40 to 80 feet or more and can sample three to five linear miles of seafloor during a normal tow. Because the nets capture almost everything that gets in their way in addition to shrimp, a typical trawl will also collect benthic and epibenthic fishes and numerous invertebrates ranging from echinoderms and crustaceans to molluscs, corals, jellyfish, and sponges. Trawl fishing thus produces non-selective abundances and at the same time reveals the rich bounty of offshore waters. [Florida State Archives, Tallahassee, Florida.]

Part Four

Biological Resources

... there are skates, very fat and good; trout no more or less in color, speckles and taste, yet fatter and savory to eat; very fine bream, and sardines; also flounders, saw-fish, horse-mackerel, mojarra, and an infinite variety of other small fish. . . . There are also very fine oysters in the Champotón river. . . .

Diego de Landa, 1566
Relacion de las Cosas de Yucatán

Invertebrates

PILLARS OF THE MARINE COMMUNITY

U P TO NOW we have considered the environments of the Gulf of Mexico from a physical point of view, generally ignoring the animals and plants that inhabit these same areas. We now direct our attention to the animal species that constitute such a rich and varied fauna in the Gulf region. In later chapters we will assemble them, along with plants, into the biological and ecological components that make up the major coastal aquatic and maritime terrestrial communities that surround the Gulf of Mexico. Let's begin with the animals without backbones, the invertebrates.

AN ABUNDANCE OF RICHNESS AND DIVERSITY
Anyone who has strolled along a Gulf-side seashore or waded in a barrier-island lagoon has undoubtedly seen (and probably collected) bottom-dwelling marine animals at one time or another. Even the casual shell collector, picking over the debris and jetsam on sandy beaches, has brought home the remnant skeletons of bottom-dwelling species. These seafloor dwellers are collectively called "benthic" species *(benthos* = "depth of the sea"). Almost 99% of all benthic animals are invertebrates. The remaining 1% or so are vertebrates (animals with backbones) and are primarily fishes.

No better evidence of the marine origin or resultant diversity of life exists than in the invertebrates. Of the approximately 35 phyla (major categorical groupings) of invertebrates all but three are strictly marine or have sea-dwelling members (see Table 7). Two of these three are parasitic in terrestrial carnivores, and the third lives under logs in tropical rain forests.

The number and diversity of just the benthic invertebrates in the Gulf of Mexico and its associated waters is substantial. If the drifting animals of the plankton are included the numbers become dramatic indeed. Present estimates for some of the more prominent fauna include some 450–500 species of molluscs, about 1,500 crustacean species, approximately 600 species of polychaete worms, plus another 200 or so species of oligochaete (earthworm-like) annelid worms, perhaps 400 species of echinoderms (sea urchins, sea cucumbers, sea lilies, sea stars, brittle stars), at least 200 trematode (parasitic) worms, about another 200 worms in other smaller phyla, nearly 600 cnidarians (jellyfish, hydroids, corals, sea whips, and anemones), and perhaps 100 species of sponges. Unknown numbers of species in many of the smaller, less prominent or less studied phyla could conceivably add another 5,000–10,000 species, especially if the single-celled protozoans and bacteria are considered.

Who are all these organisms with the strange-sounding names? Many of the more abundant forms will prove familiar to most people, who know them by their common, rather than their scientific appellations. Others will be full of surprises and are not what they appear to be. Still others seem as bizarre and alien as any Hollywood-style creature from another world. All the invertebrates are classified in collective groups called phyla, in which all the organisms share structural and physiological similarities. Although there are about 35 such phyla in the world, just nine of these make up nearly 99% of all living animal species. Let's look briefly at a few examples, listed from the simple to the complex.

THE PROTOZOA: SINGLE-CELLED EXCELLENCE IN A MULTI-CELLED WORLD

If protozoans were not so small, they would be easily recognized by everyone. They are animal-like organisms composed of a single cell, without tissue or specialized organs, and are capable of movement. Unfortunately, the more than 30,000 species presently known are all microscopic, thus preventing a proper appreciation by most people for their diversity of form and function.

Because the protozoans (a category used here in the widest sense) are so diverse, space does not permit more than the most perfunctory consideration of their attributes. In general, five different types of protozoans are recognized: the flagellates, (distinguished by a whiplike thread, the *flagella,* at one end of the cell); the ciliates, (possessing small hairlike organs of locomotion called *cilia* all around the cell); the amoebas, more or less amorphous, but capable of assuming different shapes depending on the conditions they encounter; the sporozoans, also possessing cilia but lacking these in the main (usually infective) phase of their life cycle; and the opalinates, a curious group possessing both numerous cilia and central organizing bodies called *nuclei* within the cell.

It can safely be said that protozoans are everywhere in the Gulf, particularly since the majority of them prefer wet places. Moreover, numerous species are distributed worldwide, and their occurrence in the Gulf is often a consequence of the presence or absence of a host organism.

Flagellates are a widespread group found both on the seafloor and in the plankton. Commonly occurring animal flagellates are often parasitic (trypanosomes) or occur with little apparent harm (trichomonads) inside other animals, particularly fish. Dinoflagellates, once considered members in this group, are now separated as being more plant-like than animal-like.

Ciliates are a large, widespread, complex, and nomenclaturally unstable group. Many are found living internally in the guts of invertebrates; others grow on the body surfaces of fishes and invertebrates. They may be parasites, benign co-inhabitants, or simply opportunists.

The amoebas are among the best known of Gulf protozoans. Included in this broad grouping are the planktonic Formaminifera and Radiolaria both of which form small shells or tests, the former from calcium carbonate, the latter from silica. These two groups will be considered in greater detail in the chapter on plankton.

The sporozoans are an extremely important group in the Gulf, primarily because many of their members are pathogenically parasitic and cause diseases among shellfish, particularly oysters, shrimps, and crabs. Other important sporozoans include the organisms responsible for malaria.

The opalinates, composed of about 400 species worldwide, are one of the smaller groups of protozoans. Most occur in the digestive tracts of amphibians and fish where they appear to cause little harm.

THE PORIFERA: SPONGING OFF THE ENVIRONMENT

An easily recognized group of invertebrates, sponges occur worldwide from fresh water to the abyssal plains. Sponges are essentially sessile, hollow baskets of a horny material called *spongin*, in which are usually embedded microscopically small, often intricately formed, accretions of silica or calcium carbonate, called *spicules*. The sponge walls are perforated with numerous holes or pores (*pora* = "pore," *fera* = "bearing") connected to inhalant canals through which water containing their food is sucked in, before being flushed out at the top. Thus sponges are the only invertebrates to use the largest bodily opening not as a mouth, but as an excretory opening.

While many sponges look "spongy," there are other species that resemble more exotic forms, including long tubes, candelabra, cakes, vases, golf balls, and encrustations. The deep-sea glass sponges, so called because their skeletons are composed almost exclusively of silica, often resemble intricately carved Victorian glass vases.

In the Gulf of Mexico sponges are found almost everywhere in the marine environment, from estuarine mudflats to reeflike areas called sponge banks to the deepest sea. In addition to their own importance in marine ecosystems as animals capable of feeding by filtering large volumes of water, many species act as large apartment complexes. In one huge loggerhead sponge dissected at the Dry Tortugas, over 16,000 specimens of a small snapping shrimp were counted. Others act as homes for sea anemones, polychaete worms, brittle starfish, small snails and clams, and even fishes like gobies and blennies. The spiral worm shell, a marine snail, is found almost exclusively burrowed into sponges where, now firmly imprisoned, it spends the rest of its life feeding with its host on nearby food in the water column. Algae, sea grass, and corals may even become attached on the outer surfaces and near the base. With Nature it seems there is always some kind of housing shortage.

Commercial sponges were once more prevalent than today. Lacking spicules but rich in spongin, they were ideal absorbent and liquid-retaining material, from which the word sponge came. Overfishing, and the advent of artificial sponges made from cellulose, have rendered this industry archaic.

THE CNIDARIA: HOW TO SUCCEED WHILE REMAINING A JELLY

Jellyfish, man o' wars, by-the-wind-sailers, stony corals, soft corals, black corals, sea whips, sea fans, sea anemones, hydroids, sea wasps—probably no other invertebrate group has so many disparate common names attached to its different members than the cnidarians. Such an abundance of eponyms bespeaks a familiarity by the layman for these common organisms, even if the true relationships remain hidden.

Yet all cnidarians share a spate of common features, including a jellylike connective tissue, tentacles, and the possession of stinging cells called *nematocysts* (*nemato* = "thread," *cyst* = "cell") from which the phylum takes its name in a roundabout way. Cnidaria means "nettle" in classical Greek, and refers to these selfsame stinging cells. The cnidarians are the only phylum in the world to possess these. The tentacles, when expanded, give many cnidarians a flowerlike appearance, resulting in the scientific name of anthozoans (*anthos* = "flower," *zoa* = "animal") or flower animals for the sea anemones and corals. But these are deadly flowers that sting, kill, and eat their victims. This poisonous principle makes cnidarians the Lucretia Borgias of the marine environment. The venom shows chemical similarities to cobra venom and exhibits neurotoxic activity. Anyone who has ever been stung by a large sea anemone or a man-o'-war can attest to the potency of the toxin. Sea wasps, a type of offshore cube-shaped jellyfish, have an even more evil reputation, and some species can cause death in humans in 3 to 4 minutes.

Although a cnidarian is essentially a simple sac with a single opening that functions as mouth, anus, and genital aperture, it exhibits two different body forms. The *polyp* is an erect, cylindrical organism usually attached at its base, often forms large colonies, and may be naked (sea anemones, hydroids) or surrounded by a calcium carbonate or chitinous skeleton (corals, sea whips, sea fans). The *medusa,* on the other hand, is the familiar pulsating jellyfish, bell-shaped, free-swimming, always solitary, and never with any type of skeleton.

Cnidarians undergo a complex life cycle involving an alternation of generations, in which the egg that is produced from the adult polyp or medusa develops in the plankton into a larval stage called a *planula* that resembles a microscopic, inverted saucer with cilia around the edges. The planula either develops further into a type of larva specific for the organism, and this, in turn, eventually into another medusa (as in most jellyfish), or the planula (or subsequent larva) may settle to the seafloor where it undergoes a metamorphosis, changing into a polyp. In some cnidarians the polyp then produces a medusa (some hydroids); in others it produces an egg (corals). In either case the cycle starts over again. Imagine a jellyfish settling to the seafloor on the top of its bell and then growing a stalk and you get a good idea of how this metamorphosis takes place.

Ranging in size from microscopic hydroids lining seagrass blades or the pilings of a pier, to massive corals forming barrier reefs hundreds of miles long, the Cnidaria have truly carved out their place in the marine realm. Many other species (alcyonarian sea whips, actinarian sea anemones) attach to these reefs or other hard substrates and form vast sea gardens that wave and undulate in the currents. Still others prefer the nomadic life (moon jellyfish, man-o'-wars) and are permanently pelagic, found swimming or drifting far offshore where they continue their life cycles in the great empty regions of the sea.

Few cnidarians have commercial value. Black corals (antipatharians) are used in jewelry. Dried sea whips and sea fans used to be a common item in souvenir shops, as did brightly painted stony corals. Dried hydroids are still sometimes spray-painted green and sold as "evergreen houseplants," never needing water or fertilizer! With increasing environmental awareness it is now a crime to collect, damage, or otherwise remove most reef corals and sea whips and sea fans. Ecologists have pointed out that coral reefs and coral-bearing banks form valuable habitat for innumerable invertebrates and fishes. Even the swimming jellyfish can act as a refugium for larval fish including commercially valuable species such as hake, haddock, cod, and horse mackerel. Jelly they may be, but they're tough organisms and an even tougher evolutionary act to follow.

THE PLATYHELMINTHES: FLATWORMS OF THE WORLD—UNITED

For most people, flatworms are conspicuous by their apparent absence in their lives. Most, indeed, only vaguely recall platyhelminths (*platy* = "flat," *helminthes* = "worms") from high school or college biology courses as some little quarter-inch long bits of protoplasm that crawled and could be divided into two parts, each of which would produce another worm. Yet, if the other common names of "flukes" and "tapeworms" or the medical terms "schistosomiasis" or "sea bather's itch" are mentioned, then suddenly understanding dawns. Flatworms, as a heterogeneous group, become rather important.

For a group of creatures so simple, flatworms have evolved an extraordinarily complex series of attributes, behaviors, and life cycles. The simplest flatworms, in a general sense, are the planarians, those diaphanous creatures of the classical divide- and-reproduce experiments used in general biology classes. Skin divers may also recall seeing the brightly colored marine flatworms, termed polyclads, undulating like bits of brilliant and transparent tissue paper across coral reefs.

But the trematodes (flukes) and cestodes (tapeworms) are another matter. Both of these groups are parasites, either externally (rarely) or internally, and several species are thus of great medical importance. Both groups often go through a life cycle that requires development to a certain stage in one host and then transference to a second host to complete the development; they are thus of great biological interest. It is of additional interest that the first host is almost invariably an invertebrate, particularly molluscs and crustaceans, and the second host is usually a vertebrate, primarily fishes or reptiles, but also mammals, including man.

Trematode flatworms possess suckers that allow attachment to either the exterior or, more commonly, interior parts of their hosts. One of the most common, and most serious, of pests are the blood flukes that cause the medical disease *schistosomiasis*. It has been estimated that these worms relieve each of some 700 million people in other parts of the world of up to a quart of blood each day. This is equivalent to bleeding dry the entire population around the Gulf of Mexico every 24 hours! Fortunately for Gulf-side residents, the overwhelming majority of trematodes known from the region parasitize sea birds and fish. However, the trematode larvae released from certain marine snails found in estuarine regions along the Gulf, while searching for their final fish, bird, or reptile host, may instead burrow into the skin of sea bathers. This produces a condition called variously "sea lice" or "sea bather's itch," an allergic, but relatively harmless type of reaction that causes welts and itching similar to mosquito bites.

Cestodes, or tapeworms, are typically small, flat, ribbonlike worms that can attain phenomenal lengths; a species found in sperm whales reaches 30 meters or more (90 feet)! Cestodes are widespread, producing a variety of medical and veterinary conditions in people, livestock and pets, and in other wildlife. Among the more common species is the dog and cat tapeworm, whose larvae are carried by fleas. Many fishermen will also recognize cestodes as the "fish worms" they find buried deep in the tissues of sport and game fishes. Fortunately, the flesh of parasitized marine fishes, while appearing unsightly, is noninfective to man.

THE NEMATODA: PARASITES ORDINARY AND EXTRAORDINARY

Nematode worms, generally called roundworms, are mostly microscopic, transparent, usually smooth-bodied, cylindrical worms, tapered at both ends. They exhibit a characteristic whiplike thrashing motion when removed from the substrate they inhabit. Most species require two or more hosts to complete their life cycle and undergo four molts, enlarging at each stage and seeking another host (insects, molluscs, crustaceans are commonly sought) in the interim.

The nematodes are parasites extraordinaire and responsible for a number of serious medical and veterinary conditions. They are well known to anyone who has ever raised puppies or pigs. Both animals are commonly parasitized by roundworms. But these are among the largest of nematodes. Parents and school teachers will recognize the effects of other nematodes called hookworms,[1] whipworms, and pinworms, if not the actual microscopic worms themselves. The effects produced by these worms are often seen in poor or rural areas where hygiene is less rigorously maintained and many children go barefoot. The heartworm, another common nematode, is a serious threat to dogs, cats, and farm animals, producing a disease called by its generic term filariasis. The trichina worm, found in improperly processed, incompletely cooked, or raw pork, can produce the disease trichinosis. One ounce of an infected piece of pork sausage may contain over 100,000 worms, encapsulated (encysted) in the meat. In a less threatening situation, rural housewives will certainly know the vinegar eel, a nematode that feeds on the bacteria that turns wine into vinegar. Finally, home gardeners and farmers may be more familiar with the tiny and microscopic plant nematode species that disrupt their garden and agricultural crops.

In the marine environment nematodes parasitize many groups of plants and almost every major group of animals, from invertebrates to vertebrates. The largest nematode species occurs in whales and can reach 8 meters in length. Again, and fortunately for humans, no marine nematodes are known to be infective.

Nematodes are an enormously successful group of animals, found in almost every habitat in every part of the world. Their life histories rival any form of science fiction. Their adaptations to environments and hosts are nothing less than amazing. In the world's population there are an estimated 2 billion infestations, and there is not a person on earth who does not harbor one or more of these worms at one time or another.

THE ANNELIDA: WORMS TO KNOW AND LOVE

If one examines the general form (morphology) of all of the presently accepted phyla, one is struck by the fact that fully 17 of the 35 (nearly 50%) are wormlike. However, only the annelid worms (from *annulus* = "ringed") are segmented worms. This segmentation is usually rather obvious and is often reflected in the division of the body into four major regions: a head region, divided into two lobes, the first containing antennae and other sensory appendages, and the second containing the mouth and feeding appendages; the third region is the trunk that often contains appendages used in feeding or locomotion, and may differentiate during reproduction; the fourth is the tail region.

It may be generally said that the vast majority of worms encountered by Gulf residents on the seashore belong to the Polychaeta (*poly* = "many," *chaete* = "bristle"), one of the three major groupings within the annelids. Polychaete worms generally have noticeable locomotory appendages all along the body, and many species are rather colorful and bristly in appearance. The other two groups, the oligochaetes (earthworms) and hirudinoideans (leeches) have only a few marine members; the former lack head and locomotory appendages, and are primarily terrestrial; the latter have one or two distinct suckers on the body for attachment to their hosts and are primarily aquatic in fresh waters.

Polychaetes are further divided into two main groups: those that build and live in tubes (tubicolous) and those that are free-living and move actively through or over the substrate. The former build tubes of sand, shell, a leathery parchment, or mucous and inhabit every major substrate in the Gulf, from the shallowest to the deepest seafloor.

The free-living species can be found similarly, but draw most attention by their abundances, colorful forms, and behavior in the intertidal zone and on the reefs and banks of the Gulf. Fishermen will recognize clam worms, lugworms, parchment worms, and bloodworms. Scuba divers are familiar with featherduster worms, Christmas tree worms, fireworms, bristle worms, and scale worms, and a host of smaller worms lacking common names. Many of the more colorful forms wind up in home or schoolroom aquaria, where their habitats and their habits are visible to all. Indeed, in the Gulf of Mexico there are, at last count, nearly 600 polychaete species recognized by researchers, some 41% of which were new or previously unrecorded species for the Gulf region! Researchers conservatively estimate another 100 species will eventually be discovered as the less investigated areas along the Mexican shoreline and continental shelf are sampled.

THE CRUSTACEA: SUCCESS IS CHITIN AND JOINTS

Everyone thinks they know what a crustacean is, as long as it looks like a crab, shrimp, or lobster. Fair enough, but there is substantially more to this phylum than that. Containing nearly three times the number of species known in the molluscs and more being discovered and named each year, the crustaceans are a prominent example of evolutionary success. To see how and why all we need to do is look closely at one.

Crustaceans, like molluscs, are commonly called shellfish. And like molluscs, they are shelled exoskeletal animals. That is, they carry their skeleton, to which the muscles are attached, on the outside (*exo* = "outside"). Unlike in molluscs, however (where the shell is composed primarily of calcium carbonate), the exoskeleton in crustaceans is made up of chitin, a horny substance containing calcium salts and long-chain sugar molecules that biochemists call polysaccharides, rather than being composed of calcium carbonate. Not as dense as molluscan shell (for the most part) chitin nevertheless forms a hard, protective covering. Its one disadvantage is that, in order to grow, the animal must shed its old shell and form a new and larger one. Crustaceans (and all other arthropods for that matter) do so by molting.

But most people recognize crustaceans by another, and equally important, character. All crustaceans, somewhere in their life history, have jointed appendages, often with some form of claw at the tip. They were thus once classified in a larger, all inclusive group called the Arthropoda (*arthros* = "joint," *podos* = "legs"), a phylum that at one time encompassed the crustaceans, the spiders, scorpions, ticks and mites, and the insects, millipedes, and centipedes. Today, scientists recognize three separate phyla instead of one: the Crustacea, the Uniramia (insects, millipedes, centipedes), and the Chelicerata (spiders and their kin, and strangely enough, the horseshoe crab). But these all are still called arthropods for convenience.

Crustaceans are an extraordinarily diverse group of animals. Among the more familiar forms are brine or fairy shrimp (branchiopods) sometimes sold as "sea monkeys"; clam-shrimp (ostracods); fish lice (branchiurans); the primarily planktonic copepods; barnacles (cirripedes); mantis shrimp (stomatopods); pill bugs and sea roaches (isopods); beach fleas and sand hoppers (amphipods); possum shrimp (mysidaceans); krill (euphausiaceans); and the well-known shrimps, lobsters, and crabs (decapods). There are fully a dozen or more smaller, more cryptic groups that are seldom seen by the layperson. Many live between sand grains, in subterranean springs and wells, hot springs, cave pools, or are parasitic on other animals, including their crustacean relatives. Representatives from most of these groups are found from the cool, dank wetness of freshwater swamps to the sun-seared dryness of sandy beaches, and offshore from shallow seagrass beds and coral reefs to the water column above the near and far continental shelf and thence downward to the deepest and most stygian regions of the Gulf.

People recognize crustaceans for another important quality: some species are not only edible but extremely tasty to boot. Shrimp cocktail, camarones fritos, crawfish étoufée, lobster thermidor, langoustas diablo, chilled stone crab claws, and fried soft-shelled crab[2] are just a few of the gourmet items appearing on the menus of seafood restaurants around the Gulf.

But crustaceans can also be incredibly destructive. Parasitic copepods, amphipods, and isopods (often erroneously called fish worms because of their wormlike appearance) debilitate many species of sport and game fish. Gribbles, a type of wood-boring isopod, destroy wharf pilings; another isopod wreaks havoc on mangrove tree prop roots; a third even bores into concrete! Closer to home, pill bugs and sow bugs (not bugs but isopods) give home gardeners fits. Crayfish burrow in cotton fields in Mississippi and eat the sprouts. Land crabs devastate vegetable fields in Florida, burrowing and eating their way through a season's crop. Mud crabs and their tasty relative the stone crab destroy young oyster beds. And barnacles, growing over almost everything in the estuarine and marine environment, cause millions of dollars each year in fouling damages and their repair, and keep shipyards busy year-round.

THE MOLLUSCA: A PLETHORA OF SHELLY DIVERSITIES

To the average beach-goer, gastropods (*gastros* = "stomach," *podos* = "foot") and bivalves (*bi* = "two," *valvia* = "shells") are known more familiarly as snails and clams. Both are easily recognized as molluscs (phylum Mollusca), whether crawling on the beach, buried in the seagrass beds, or reposing in redolently steaming piles on a dinner plate. Shell collectors from the ancient Aztecs and Calusas to modern day conchologists avidly seek the colorful, the strange, and the rare. Thorny oysters, rainbow-hued scallops and tellins, pastel jewel box clams, speckled cowries, ornately spiny murexes, spotted trumpet shells, speckled olive shells, pearly wentletraps, and striped cone shells are just a few of the species that make up a richly diverse molluscan fauna in the Gulf. Whether collected as food specimens for scientific purposes, or just as souvenirs for the folks back home, molluscs provide an important natural resource.

Familiar edible forms include oysters, scallops, mussels, and conchs, and the less familiar but still eminently edible surf clams, coquinas, cancellated venus clams, and cockles. All have provided prized table fare since before the first Spaniards sailed along the shores of ancient Mexico.

Not so obviously molluscan are squids, octopus, and their long-armed relatives, known scientifically as cephalopods (*cephalos* = "head," *podos* = "feet"). All possess tentacles (actually modified feet) that project from the head region, and all have either dispensed with the typical molluscan shell or carry it reduced inside their bodies. Yet every canary or parakeet owner certainly knows about cuttlebones, which are not bones at all, but the internal shell of the cuttlefish, a close relative of squids. The rare paper nautilus, whose fragile, basketlike egg cases occasionally wash ashore, is another internal-shelled cephalopod, but one that lives far offshore in the open sea.

Closer at hand on the reefs, seagrass beds, and rock jetties are the numerous species of sea hares, sea slugs, and their relatives, who also hide their shells interiorly, but present a veritable mad painter's palette of brilliant colors to the world. Fringed, lobed, warty, smooth, speckled, banded, iridescent, jet black—no combination of intricate shapes and spectacular hues seems too bizarre or ostentatious to these little gastropods, who are certainly among the best examples of Nature's whimsy.

Even less obviously molluscan to the untrained eye are shipworms, which are not worms at all, but actually bivalve (clamlike) molluscs. The bane of every wooden boat or dock owner, these small clams bore into wood using the two shells as tiny scrapers, while the body of the mollusc secretes a thin, shelly lining along the burrow. Other members in the same general group as shipworms bore into coral rock, peat, and even other molluscan shells.[3]

More secretive are the tiny sand-dwelling scaphopods, commonly called tusk shells, because their shell resembles a small, highly polished ivory elephant's tusk. And clinging firmly to the wave-washed rocks with a large muscular foot are the furry, articulated chitons or coat-of-mail shells that appear more like roughened and raised prominences on the substrate rather than molluscs. Whatever their shape, size, style, or distributions, the molluscs of the Gulf of Mexico give proper emphasis to the meaning of the word diversity.

THE ECHINODERMATA: SPINY SHELLS AND PENTAGONAL RADIATION

The echinoderms (*echinos* = "hedgehog," *derma* = "skin") are among the easiest sea animals to recognize. Who has not strolled the beaches and seagrass-filled lagoons of the Gulf coast and seen sea stars (or starfish), serpent stars (or brittle starfish), sea urchins, and sea cucumbers? Less likely to have been seen or collected, owing to their distribution in deeper water, are the sea lilies. Although on the face of it all, these five different classes of echinoderms may seem to be only distantly related, if at all, they nevertheless share several features. They are all unequivocally marine or estuarine; have a unique hydraulically-controlled locomotory system involving hollow, tube feet (the water-vascular system); a body that incorporates calcareous stiffening rods, plates, or particles, termed *spicules*; and small, pincerlike defensive and preening organs (*pedicellariae*). But the most singular morphological feature shared among all echinoderms is that they are radially pentamerous. This is a fancy scientific term that means that the body is divided into five more or less equal portions. Whereas all other organisms have a clearly defined head and tail region, echinoderms approach the environment from all five sides. Think of sea stars or sea urchins moving along over the sand and the image becomes clear.

Perhaps the easiest way to understand how sea lilies, sea stars, serpent stars, sea urchins, and sea cucumbers are related one to another is to engage in a little imaginary game, but one based on evolutionary facts. Start with a stalked sea lily (crinoid), one firmly attached and with its mouth region pointed upward. Eliminate its stalk, give it the ability to move freely, and reduce the feeding arms to five. If this imaginary and now mobile five-armed sea lily is turned over so that the mouth region is oriented downward, the animal now resembles a serpent star (ophiuroid). If the arms are then made more fixed than movable, and the

Figure 21. Lilies of the field on the continental shelf.
Inappropriately named "live bottom," the continental shelf seafloor off southwestern Florida is paved with crinoid "sea lilies" and nodules of stony lithothamnioid algae. Looking like clumps of feathery grass, the crinoids raise their frilly arms upward to feed on the plankton in the swirling currents above them. Occurring most often in deeper water offshore, sea lilies are really animals related to sea urchins, sea stars, and sea cucumbers. The stony algae, appearing as white clumps around the crinoid bases, are marine plants that deposit calcium carbonate in their tissues. These specimens were photographed from a deep-diving research submarine in 124 meters of water (approximately 400 feet). [Courtesy Minerals Management Service OCS Gulf Region, New Orleans, Louisiana]

digestive canal is extended into the arms, the animal then has the general attributes of a sea star (asteroid). Now, eliminate the arms completely, let the bodily plates fuse solid, inflate the body, give it spines and place the entire digestive and reproductive systems within the enlarged test and the animal becomes a putative sea urchin (echinoid). Take this imaginary sea urchin and stretch it out into a sausage-shaped tube with leathery skin. Keep the mouth at one end and the anus at the other, reduce the spines to tubercles, and place a series of small tube feet along the length of the body. Presto! A sea cucumber (holothurian).

Crinoids (commonly called sea lilies for their very fanciful resemblance to flowers) are the most ancient of the echinoderms, tracing their origins to the Palaeozoic, over 500 million years ago. They are also the group least known to the common person, because most of the species are found below 10 meters, and the majority are found on the deeper parts of the continental shelf, slope and into the abyssal depths (see Figure 21). The animals are best visualized as a cuplike mouth surrounded by feathery tentacles (thus accounting for their other common name of feather stars) and mounted on a horny, flexible, segmented stalk. Most crinoids feed on plankton or small organic particles that become entrapped in their feathery arms. Although hidden from the view of most humans because of where they live, crinoids are among the most beautiful sea animals on earth.

Sea stars, often illogically called starfish, reflect their star-shaped body plan in their scientific name (Asteroidea; *astra* = "star"). Another ancient group, tracing ancestry back more than 400 million years, sea stars are easily recognized by nearly everyone, seashore dweller or not. Most species in the Gulf have just five arms, although in some of the deeper-living forms the arms are so reduced that the animal resembles a pentagon. One species, occurring mostly in warmer Gulf waters, may have nine or more arms. Nearly all sea stars are rather colorful, or at least attractively patterned (see Plate 9). They are common inhabitants of seagrass beds, coral reefs, sponge banks, and many other habitats on the continental shelf where they prey on molluscs and small invertebrates. The more bizarre forms are found in deeper waters on the continental slope and deep abyssal plains.

Serpent stars (or brittle stars) are another ancient group of "starfish," with fossils known from 400 million years ago. They differ from sea stars (asteroids) in that their five or six arms are very movable and undergo serpentine motion, hence the scientific name of ophiuroidea (*ophis* = "serpent," *oura* = "tail"). These same arms may be detached from the body by the animal during stress or as a defense mechanism, much like some lizards may detach their tails while making their escape from predators, hence the other common name for the group of brittle stars.

Serpent stars are rapidly moving predators capable of crawling or even running across the substrate in search of small invertebrates as prey. One group (the basket stars) is multi-armed and spreads the arms out like a loosely woven basket to entrap plankton from the water column. Serpent stars are widely distributed, found from shallow estuaries to coral reefs to the deepest parts of the Gulf, where they often occur in huge numbers on muddy substrates. Many are attractively banded and colored and have arms lined with glasslike spines, plates, and other ornamentation.

Sea urchins (echinoids) are yet another group that can trace its origins back more than 600 million years. Echinoids come in three types: the globose, coarsely spined sea urchins that resemble living pin cushions; the egg-shaped, fine-spined, burrowing heart urchins; and the very much flattened, fine-spined, burrowing sand dollars. Members of each of these groups differ outwardly, and often dramatically, from each other. But when the movable, covering spines are removed from their tests, some of the shared features become apparent. All have sutured tests, tube feet, and most distinctively (excepting heart urchins), the mouth placed on the underside of the body. Inside the mouth is a jaw apparatus called *Aristotle's lantern* because the five teeth coming to a point fancifully resemble a Greek lantern.

Most sea urchins are considered *herbivores,* eating mostly plant materials or organic particles from the substrate, including devastating attacks on seagrass beds in some instances. Commonly observed forms include the variably hued short-spined sea urchins of estuarine seagrass beds (see Plate 9B); the long-spined (and poisonous) black urchins of coral reefs; the dull gray, almost furry, burrowing heart urchins found living in muddy substrates; and the semi-inflated, burrowing sea biscuits and much flattened sand dollars found buried offshore of sandy beaches. On the deeper continental shelf occur more exotic forms, including urchins with paddle-shaped spines and the strange "panting urchins" in which the test, fixed and immovable in most echinoids, moves up and down during respiration (see Figure 22).

TABLE 7

The Complexity and Diversity of the Invertebrtates

Number of phyla presently recognized:	35*
Having marine members	32
Having 100 or fewer species	12
Having 20,000 or more species	5
Whose members constitute 99% of all living animals on earth	9
With members having "eyes"	7
With members having "ears"	0
With members having "feet"	7
With members that are permanently sessile	14
With members lacking a "mouth"	7
With members lacking a digestive system	4
With members lacking an anus	8
Reproducing other than by sex	9
Looking like "worms"	17
Having calcareous shells	3
Having chitinous exoskeletons	6
Appearing soft and jellylike	3
Appearing spongy	1
Having a leathery "tunic"	1
Microscopic or submicroscopic in size	16
Partially or entirely endosymbionts	6

*Zoologists are still not in agreement on where to place several one-celled and invertebrate groups. The awesome diversity of life and the forms it has assumed has never made invertebrate classification easy.

The data above are a synopsis from various sources.

The last group to be considered, holothurians, seems to resemble other echinoderms least of all. Anatomically, sea cucumbers have lost, or modified, many of the salient attributes of their other echinoderm relatives. Tube feet are much reduced and modified into tentacles around the mouth; the horny plates making up the test or body walls of other echinoderms are also much reduced and scattered throughout the leathery skin; and the radial plane has been changed from the top-bottom orientation of sea stars, brittle stars, and sea urchins to the front-back orientation we have come to expect in most other animals.

Holothurians might, in one sense, be thought of as analagous to surface earthworms. Their movement over the seafloor, eating the sediments, passing them through the gut and digesting out whatever organic particles might occur, and then eliminating the worked-over substrate, is exactly what earthworms do on the land.

Many holothurians superficially resemble cucumbers, thus accounting for their common name.[4] Others look more like giant multi-colored caterpillars stretched across the reefs. Still others, from the deep sea, swim rather than crawl. The more bizarre species look like nothing so much as flabby white footballs or black, roughened inner tubes. Clearly, seeing a "cucumber" requires as much latitude in one's viewpoint as holthurians exhibit in their lifestyle.

THE REMAINING PHYLA: THE IMPORTANCE OF BEING STRANGE

The invertebrates just discussed constitute approximately one fourth of all the recognized animal phyla. The remaining groups are made up of forms not easily recognized by laypersons. Among these are the microscopic rotifers (called "wheel animalcules") and tardigrades ("water bears"); some jellylike animals (ctenophores, known as "comb jellyfish") and bryozoans ("moss animals"); a multitude of worm and wormlike organisms called sipunculids, nemerteans, pogonophorans, nematomorphans (commonly called "peanut worms," "ribbon worms," "beard worms," and "horsehair worms," respectively); unusual shelled animals (brachiopods, or "lamp shells"); and numerous aberrant small phyla (phoronid, echiuroid, priapulid, and chaetognath "worms"), most of which are either not widely distributed, are composed of only 10 or 20 species worldwide, or can be determined only by specialists in invertebrate zoology.

Even though seemingly less important, all of these phyla have representatives living somewhere in the Gulf of Mexico. And it must not be forgotten that even though these invertebrates may not be as abundant or noticeable to the everyday beach-goer, they nevertheless have their own and very important place in the ecosystems of the Gulf. Nor should it be forgotten that ecology and evolution are intimately tied together and have been since the origin of life on earth, when Nature laid down one of her first laws: that the small, the nondescript, and the numerous will always support, in one way or the other, the few and the large. Any good text on invertebrates will provide more detail than can be given here and will point out the truth of a statement made by Louis Agassiz, one of the world's most distinguished zoologists, who said over 150 years ago: "The possibilities of existence run so deeply into the extravagant that there is scarcely any conception too extraordinary for Nature to realize."

Swimmers, Crawlers, and Flyers

THE MARINE VERTEBRATES

IN A GENERAL SENSE, the average person is probably more familiar with the vertebrates of the marine world than with the invertebrates. The vertebrates are usually large, often colorful, readily visible, easily recognized, and usually considered more "useful" to humans than the invertebrates. Members of each of the five classes of vertebrates—the fishes, amphibians, reptiles, birds, and mammals—can all be found in the Gulf of Mexico. Because of their very large numbers of individuals and species, fishes occupy a special place of prominence throughout the marine food web. They are, of course, the only totally aquatic class. The amphibians are the least abundant, being restricted to one species of marine toad and several small toads and tree frogs that occur on barrier islands. Other vertebrates, although less numerous than fishes, are also important. Two major, primarily terrestrial classes, the reptiles and the mammals, contain species that have abandoned their ties to the shore and returned to live in the sea. The third class of animals, the birds, have evolved a diversity of lifestyles that exploit numerous habitats, ranging from fully terrestrial to entirely aquatic. In the process the birds may exhibit habits ranging from being primarily walkers to being almost completely aerial. Some offshore species have all but abandoned the earth and spend most of their lives primarily in the air. In this chapter we shall look briefly at all of these vertebrates, the animals with backbones, that inhabit the Gulf of Mexico and its environs (See Plate 6).

FISHES: EXPLOITING HABITATS AQUATIC

Fishes are the most numerous of all the vertebrates. The dedicated fisherman, charterboat captain, or skindiver will probably be familiar with most of the more than 500 common species of sharks and bony fishes that have been recorded from the Gulf of Mexico (see Plate 6A). The shrimpboat captains, longliners, and deep sea anglers may, at one time or other, trawl or hook another 300 to 400 deep-living species — those rare, unique and often bizarre forms found on the offshore continental shelf, slope and down to the abyssal plains. An educated guess from ichthyologists (scientists who study fish) is that the Gulf has at least 800, perhaps 1,000, species of fish. Roughly 70% of these are either actually *benthic* (living on or within the bottom) or *epibenthic* (living near or associated with the bottom). Included in these very broad groupings are those non-benthic fishes called benthic-directed predators—fish that spend most of the time in the water column but feed on bottom-dwelling flora and fauna.

Many species of fish appear to be restricted to living on or above certain types of bottom habitats and are rarely found elsewhere. Others are more catholic in their requirements and will occupy or be associated with almost any seafloor protuberance, be it coral reef, mud pile, shipwreck, or oil platform. In these cases, the "sea bottom" is not necessarily horizontal but may consist of vertical platform supports, the sides of a sunken hull, or rock ledges.

Many commonly recognized benthic (or benthic-directed) fishes are also commercially valuable species, particularly the flatfish, groupers, drums, snappers, and mullet. These fishes gain part of their commercial value because they can be consistently collected on known "fishing grounds" or "fishing reefs."

Noncommercial truly benthic fishes are a diverse group. They include the gobies, blennies, clinids, toadfish, skates, rays, batfish, and stargazers of the estuaries and inshore waters, as well as the scorpion fish, sea robins, "eels" belonging to several different families, and other less familiar fishes of the estuaries, reefs and coastal shelf regions. Included herein are many tropical species such as the damselfish, angelfish, wrasses, parrotfish, and a host of other reefal and hard-substrate families, as well as a varied ichthyofauna living on and above the offshore sandy plains. Among the deep-sea bottom-dwellers are anglerfish, goosefish, brotulids, rattails, and other bizarre, rarely seen species from the bathyal (deeper than 2,000 meters) and abyssal regions (3,000 meters and deeper) (see Figure 22).

The open-sea, or *pelagic*, fish fauna is also rich in species. In this group are found the billfish (marlin, swordfish, sailfish), flying fish, the offshore game fish (cobia, dolphin, kingfish, wahoo), the jacks, mackerals (including bonita and tuna), and a host of cryptic forms that inhabit the water column and the floating seaweed patches (that fishermen refer to as weedlines) away from shore. All are familiar species to the offshore angler.

But if alien forms and terrible-toothed monsters are desired, the deep-water fishes of the Gulf can easily fill the bill. Here in the midnight water column live the jetblack gonostomatids, only six to eight inches long, but with mouths full of crystalline needles, and rows of tiny lights down their sides. Here, too, the giant-jawed gulper eels slither through the watery night seeking prey twice their own size to pack into distendable bellies, while tiny, bulbous-eyed hatchetfish dance away in schools of scaly silver and yellow-green bioluminescence. Glowing rows of yellow and green living lights signal a passing school of lanternfish on their way back from the surface. Deep, deep down on the seafloor, in the basement of the Gulf, lurk the rattails, brotulids, slickheads and other bizarre benthic forms. These heavy-bodied large-eyed fishes prowl the abyssal plains and nose about the knolls in a forever-dark land where scarlet shrimps pirouette, sightless lobsters crawl, and the sponges are carved from glass. Some, like the deepsea anglerfish (see Figure 23), use luminescent lures to light the way to ambush into their needle-toothed mouths. Others, like the tripod fish,

Figure 22. Life from the deep sea.
A sampling of fishes, crustaceans, an echinoderm, and a mollusc shows some of the great morphological variety of deep-living organisms. Elongate smooth-skinned fishes, large-eyed and flabby-bodied, with the unappetizing names of brotulid (upper right), rattail (center right) and slime-head (lower right) lie next to a pasiphaeid prawn (upper left) and a small armored glyphocrangonid shrimp (center left). At the bottom is a poisonous pancake sea urchin (left) and a glasslike deepsea scallop (right).

Figure 23. No exit.
The fearsome dentition of a deep sea angler fish dramatically illustrates a feeding axiom common to many bathyal fishes: "What goes in won't come out!" Yet for all its ferocious appearance this black-skinned benthic predator, a member in good standing of the lilliputian fauna, is less than six inches long.

Swimmers, Crawlers, and Flyers **155**

tiptoe across the oozy sediments, feeling for food while balanced on the stilts of their elongated pectoral fins and tail.

These deep sea ichthyofauna have been called "the illuminated minnows" because many have light organs (termed *photophores*; *photo* = "light," *phoros* = "carrier") along their sides, under their eyes and even on their tongues! They have also been called "the lilliputian fauna" because many are less than six inches long. Yet the common names of some of these species do ample justice to their rapaciousness: dragonfish, viperfish, giant swallower, gulper eel, bristlemouth. These are just a few of the carnivorous denizens in the realm of eternal night.

AMPHIBIANS: A DUALITY OF LIFESTYLES

The Amphibia (*amphi* = "on both sides"; *bios* = "life") as a vertebrate class are all those animals that exist in water—fresh, brackish, or marine—for one part of their life (usually as larvae or juveniles), and on land for another (mostly as adults). Typically, the larval stages breathe through gills, while the adults use lungs. Laypersons know the amphibians as the the frogs, toads, newts, salamanders, sirens and mud puppies. All these animals require water at least to lay their eggs, and allow their young (as tadpoles, for example) to mature. Some, like the sirens, mud puppies, and many frogs and salamanders, also spend their adult lives in water. Others (like many toads, some newts and salamanders) need only damp environments as adults, and can be found under wet leaves and rotting logs, along the banks of streams, marshes, and swamps. Nearly all the amphibians around the Gulf are terrestrial creatures, associated with freshwater habitats. But, as will be seen, many species can exist near marine habitats, particularly along estuaries and barrier islands, although they never actually enter saltwater, nor use it to raise their young.[1]

The ability to utilize both water and land in their life history gives amphibians several advantages, not the least of which is the opportunity to find food in both wet and dry areas. Their lifestyle also gives them at least two refugia, allowing escape from land predators into water, or from aquatic predators onto land. The ability to utilize wet and dry environments also gives them mobility to leave an area when conditions deteriorate and seek more favorable habitats elsewhere. But it is also a drawback in the sense that most amphibians (with the exception of some exotic tropical toads) require water for reproduction and maturing of young. Amphibians, more than most animals, are therefore creatures profoundly affected by drought, periodic dry seasons, the ephemerality of ponds, and fire in their habitats.

Amphibians are a truly ancient group, the first vertebrates to crawl out of the shallow seas and lagoons during the Devonian period more than 350 million years ago, and make a life on land. And for a long time they were eminently successful. But their star is descendant, and today the living amphibians "constitute a scanty and degenerate remnant of a once-dominant and abundant group."[2] Yet this primitive group of animals has been so successful that their common name, "amphibian," has been borrowed and applied to numerous other animal groups to succinctly describe their lifestyles. Thus, there are amphibious birds, mammals, and reptiles— all of which carry out some part of their life on land, and another in water. Scanty and degenerate the Amphibia may be, but their name lives on in higher life forms today.

The only truly marine amphibian occurring in the Gulf region certainly couldn't be overlooked! The marine toad, *Bufo marinus*, is a large (up to 9 inches), docile, insect-eating species found originally from southern Texas to Argentina. This toad, which can tolerate salt water and is often found near beaches, was introduced into Puerto Rico and Florida for insect control and now has spread through much of the lower part of the peninsula (see Figure 24). The only other amphibians that occur near Gulf shores are terrestrial or arboreal rather than marine. Several other species of toads and frogs are found around the Gulf, living in the pine and hardwood forests and coastal strands of the barrier islands and keys in the eastern Gulf of Mexico, and in the low scrub areas on the long barriers and coastal lowlands of the western and southwestern Gulf. The occurrence of these species is tied to the availability of suitable terrestrial vegetation rather than aquatic marine habitats. None are in any way marine.

MARINE REPTILES: INHABITANTS OF SEA AND SHORE

Reptiles are an ancient group, once dominating nearly all the lands and seas of earth. Today, they remain abundant and relatively widespread on land but are

Figure 24. A coastal giant.
The giant marine toad reaches nine inches or more in length, a truly princely size among amphibians. Known originally from south Texas and along the Mexican coast, the species was introduced into south Florida where it quickly found a happy home. Molesting one is ill advised. Although not agressive, milky secretions from its parotid glands, the large lumpy swellings just behind the eye, are toxic, causing skin irritation in susceptible humans and sickness and death in cats and dogs incautious enough to bite them.[Photo by Millicent Hampton-Shepherd]

very much restricted in the sea. Major seawater-dwellers include crocodiles and alligators, predominantly inhabitants of estuarine and shallow nearshore waters, some species of freshwater terrapins that occasionally wander into estuaries, and, of course, sea turtles that occur throughout the Gulf.[3]

Alligators and Crocodiles

The American alligator (see Figure 25) is a relatively widespread species. Usually found in fresh water, the species also frequents mangrove swamps and salt marshes around the shores of the Gulf from Texas to Florida. There are records of alligators swimming along open-sea beaches, and there is nothing to prevent them from making longer migrations along these shorelines if food or environmental conditions become unfavorable in freshwater areas.

The American crocodile, a more shy and retiring reptile than the alligator, was once widespread but is now very close to extinction. The last known remaining habitat for the crocodile in the continental United States lies in the mangrove swamps and desolate beaches along Cape Sable at the southern tip of Florida and in the Everglades National Park. Crocodiles may also have found refuge in the more remote portions of the Mexican coastline and along the

Figure 25. King of the swamps.
Surveying his kingdom with a baleful eye, the American alligator occupies a secure throne at the top of the freshwater foodweb in many places around the Gulf. This ancient carnivore, whose ancestors saw the dinosaurs go extinct, is also a critical element in many maritime ecosystems. "Gator holes" and "gator crawls" excavated in the muddy bottoms of streams, ponds, and lakes serve to trap receding water during the subtropical dry season. Fishes and other aquatic life concentrate within these small areas, where wading birds and other predators come to feed, thereby utilizing a food supply that might otherwise be wasted.

mangrove-covered shores of the Yucatán Peninsula. In the western Pacific Ocean, crocodiles have been recorded swimming over coral reefs in search of food, and their American counterparts may well be able to do the same.

Turtles and Terrapins

Several subspecies of diamondback terrapins are well-known saltwater inhabitants, including the southern diamondback, the Florida diamondback, the Mississippi diamondback, and the mangrove terrapin. All occur in brackish waters around the Gulf in salt marshes, estuarine lagoons, and mangrove-bordered waters. The mangrove terrapin not only occurs in the Florida Keys but is also found westward to the Marquesas Islands offshore. Diamondback terrapins are tasty items and are still hunted extensively for turtle stew and soup in some areas of the Gulf.

Other turtles known to inhabit brackish waters include at least two subspecies of the notoriously pugnacious snapping turtle, and the Mobile, Suwannee, and Florida redbellied turtles. Several other species, normally restricted in upland swamps and marshes, may occasionally wander into brackish water areas or swim across saltwater lagoons. The red-eared turtle, for example, is often seen on the flats

Figure 26. Slow and steady survivor of an ancient line.
The Florida gopher tortoise is an ancient reptile whose ancestors originated in the western part of the North American continent more than 60 million years ago. Two of the four remaining species in North America are found in the Gulf region. The Florida gopher is the only American tortoise found east of the Mississippi River, and occurs from Florida to Louisiana in the Gulf region. The species is supplanted by a Texican lookalike found in southern Texas and northeastern Mexico. A protected species throughout their range, gopher populations are nevertheless declining. Slow and steady often spells doom on high speed highways for these animals. But a more important factor in their decline is loss of habitat: the high pine woods, xeric oak scrub, and silica sand ridges that form such attractive sites for residential development in Florida and other Gulf-ring states. [Author]

behind Texas barrier islands. Even the slow-moving, terrestrial, Florida gopher tortoise of the sandy-scrub uplands has been observed swimming in the lagoons between the barrier islands in southwestern Florida (see Figure 26).

Sea turtles are the only truly pelagic reptile in the Gulf of Mexico. Five sea turtle species are recorded: the loggerhead, hawksbill, Kemp's Ridley, leatherback, and green turtle. Although sea turtles spend their entire lives at sea after hatching, they still remain tied to the shore by a single tenuous thread. The females must periodically crawl onto the beaches, dig a shallow nest, and lay their eggs (see Plate 6B).

Once in great abundance, sea turtles have suffered serious predation from a number of species, including humans. The life of a baby sea turtle is threatened from the moment the eggs are laid. Raccoons, opossums, and humans all consider fresh turtle eggs a delicacy. Ghost crabs, swimming crabs, and numerous shorebirds (particularly pelicans and seagulls) find the tiny new hatchlings a walking reptilian buffet on which they feed with great gusto. Nor is the surfzone and nearshore water a sanctuary. Waiting for the little swimmers may be dozens to hundreds of fish that are only too happy to feed on them as they struggle to make their way offshore and into the pelagic weedlines. Any turtles running this gauntlet still must contend with the usual environmental factors: predation, an adequate food supply, parasites, disease, and, of course, man, his nets, and all his refuse.

Those sea turtles that do survive may reach weights of several hundred pounds and lengths of 4 feet or more. By then, only the largest predators are a problem. Again, humans have inserted themselves into the food web by trapping turtles for their meat and to make products from their shells, and by inadvertently snagging them in shrimp trawl nets. Although these ancient and gentle reptiles are protected in the United States, other countries have no such restrictions and sea turtles, particularly the green and Kemp's Ridley, have been hunted almost to extinction.

Snakes, Lizards, and Skinks

There are, at this writing, no permanently marine snakes in the Gulf of Mexico. However, several species of snakes can be found from time to time in salt marshes, mangroves, and other brackish water areas. Among the most common are several subspecies of water snakes. In Florida, the mangrove water snake is truly aquatic (but not permanently so) and lives within the mangrove forests along the southern coast of the peninsula. The other species of water snakes are found in a variety of habitats ranging from saltmarshes to Gulfside beaches.

There is a rather extensive fauna of non-aquatic, maritime snakes and lizards that occur along Gulf coastal areas, on the barrier islands, and in the Florida Keys. These "coastal associates" can tolerate maritime conditions, and even immersion in salt water to some degree, although usually preferring a terrestrial existence. Rattlesnakes, for example, have been observed swimming between

COLOR PLATE 1. Wipe-out pipes

Not pipes stuck into the seafloor, but living animals, a nest of pogonophoran worms forms an erect clump on the gray sandy mud of a wipe-out zone several thousand feet down on the outer continental shelf of the Gulf of Mexico. Disturbed, if not dazzled by the probing spotlight of a deep-diving submersible, most of the sightless worms have retracted into their tubes, awaiting the submarine's departure and the return of their eternal night. [Courtesy Minerals Management Service, OCS Gulf Region]

(A) (above) Looking like deep-sea tumbleweeds, large bushy clumps of vestamentiferan worms form a ghostly underbrush on a hydrocarbon seep in the deep Gulf. In this hostile environment, where crude oil and methane gas oozes from seafloor cracks, and salt domes slowly dissolve into hot briny pools, chemosynthetic bacteria join with bizarre species of worms, molluscs, and crustaceans to form strange faunal assemblages that occur in no other habitat on earth. [Courtesy Minerals Management Service, OCS Gulf region]

(B) (right) Pale green lettuce corals and bright green algae make a salad garden fit for King Neptune more than 60 meters deep on the southwestern Florida shelf. Complex sessile plant and animal assemblages like these provide food, cover, and breeding space for numerous species, and a foraging ground for their predators. [Minerals Management Service, Gulf of Mexico OCS Region]

(A) Large oyster bars bake under a subtropical sun at low tide in southwestern Florida's Rookery Bay National Estuarine Research Reserve. Snaking out from the shoreline, oyster aggregations such as these provide a ready-made shallow water substrate for red mangrove propagules which quickly colonize the exposed reefs. [Courtesy Darryl L. Felder]

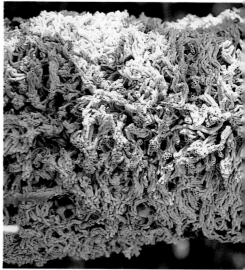

Brain coral mushrooms, starlet coral mountains, and sea anemones are some of the animal blooms found e Flower Garden Banks, the northernmost tract of corals in the Gulf of Mexico. The coral colonies ar green because of symbiotic algae called anthellae that live inside the otherwise transparent es of the coral polyps. Brilliant scarlet sponges and n bubbles of algae compete with one another for ing space among the corals. In the foreground, the orange feeding-fans of a polychaete "Christmas vorm" protrude from its limestone burrow. [Cour-Minerals Management Service, OCS Gulf Region]

(C) Reef-builders par excellence, wormlike vermetid snails join shell to shell, forming bioherms in the shallow estuaries of southwestern Florida. The millions of intertwined, calcareous tubules become a settling ground for other encrusting and fouling organisms such as barnacles, oysters, sponges, and sea squirts that will gradually cover most of their exposed surface. Eventually, mangroves will colonize the reef, stabilizing it still further. [Author]

(A) A fuselage from a derelict passenger plane prepares for its final approach off southwestern Florida, slipping into ten fathoms of water seven miles west of Naples. One of many different kinds of materials that were formerly considered waste and useful only for landfills, the once-sleek airliner will soon host a different kind of passenger among the rocky outcrops of the seafloor as the fuselage becomes colonized with marine life. [Courtesy Maura Krause, Natural Resources Management Department, Collier County, Florida]

(B) Full fathom five piles of old tires lie, now undergone a sea change into something rich and strange, and almost completely covered by marine growth. Cement-filled tires like these on an artificial reef off Marco Island, Florida, were an early attempt to recycle waste materials. [Courtesy Maura Krause, Natural Resources Management Department, Collier County, Florida]

(C) Dwarfing its towboat and assisting tugs, the 49,000-ton steel framework (or platform jacket) of the "Bullwinkle" petroleum drilling platform heads out to its final position on the Gulf continental shelf. Now in place, the jacket gridwork provides both structural support for its platform and ecological and topographical complexity in the water column, allowing the establishment of marine communities that would not normally occur in the area. [Courtesy Shell Offshore, Inc.]

COLOR PLATE 5. Barrier islands around the Gulf of Mexico

(A) (left) Going, going, and eventually gone, the Isles Dernieres off Louisiana's coast are slowly being reclaimed by the sea. A classic example of single beach ridge barrier islands, the curving sandy beach ridge and shallow wetlands behind are clearly visible on the barrier backshore. [Courtesy of Darryl L. Felder]

(B) (below) A prime example of a migrating barrier spit, Key Island (left) in southwestern Florida creeps southward toward its ultimate destination—union with Cannon Island on the right. Accreting layers of sand and shell hash are clearly marked by pioneer beach vegetation, forming concentric bands of green as the island shifts southward. Older semicircular tree lines of Australian pine mark previous shorelines. Offshore to the left, waves from the open Gulf wash over shoaling sands and are refracted across the tidal pass, telling mariners and coastal geologists alike that the island is still moving. [Collier County Natural Resources Management Department]

(C) (below) Known to mapmakers from the time of Ponce de Leon, and visited by indigenous coastal Indians for centuries before that, Cape Romano at the southwestern tip of Florida points its sandy arrowhead southward into the Gulf. Except for its accreting tip (where Australian pines dominate), the shallow-water interior of the Cape is filled with stabilizing mangrove forests. On the horizon, the hotels and condominiums of Marco Island rise in sprawling disarray along ancient parallel beach ridges and dunes once covered with coastal hardwood hammocks and mangrove swamps like those on Cape Romano, but now buried under haphazard development. The few eroding beaches that still remain must be continually renourished artificially. [Courtesy of Collier County Natural Resources Management Department]

(A) The merest hint of the wealth of Gulf estuaries is provided in the seven species of fishes collected in this short seine haul made along a southwestern Florida shore. The catch illustrates a feeding cross-section of carnivores (snook, barracuda, spot, silversides), plankton feeders (mojarra, anchovies), and herbivores (mullet). Dark clumps of drift algae hide numerous smaller species of invertebrates. [Author]

(B) Exhausted from her egg-laying travail, a loggerhead sea turtle pauses on a southwestern Florida beach to catch her breath before resuming her laborious trek back into the Gulf. If she survives she will return to this same beach next year and lay another 50 or more round, white, leathery-skinned eggs. [Courtesy Maura Krause, Collier County Natural Resources Management Department]

(C) (below, left) Pilot whales, a common marine mammal throughout the Gulf, are a species coming under increasing concern. Mass strandings such as this one in southwestern Florida invariably produce injury and death for many of the whales. The reasons for such suicidal beachings are unclear. Internal parasites have been postulated as a predisposing cause by affecting the whales' ability to echo-locate, so that they become disoriented and run aground. [Courtesy Gary Lytton, Florida Department of Natural Resources]

(D) "1 BR Gulf View." Ospreys or fish hawks are just one of an increasing number of species that have adapted to humans and our structures. Intracoastal Waterway channel markers make prime nesting sites, providing ready-made access and protection for rearing young. Often, the same nest will be used again and again by different couples, suggesting that housing shortages are not just a factor for humans. [Courtesy Theodore H. Below]

COLOR PLATE 7. Endangered species in the Gulf region

(A) (right) Although still allowed to be hunted in north Florida, the southern populations of the Florida Black Bear are listed as threatened, owing to encroaching civilization and loss of critical habitat. This large male, weighing approximately 200 pounds, was struck and killed by a truck just before dawn on a southwestern Florida highway. [Courtesy Darrel Land, Florida Game and Freshwater Fish Commission]

(B) (left) Another tragedy for a species already in decline, the Florida panther, a subspecies of the western cougar, is now thought to number less than 50 individuals throughout the entire state of Florida. Road signs advising motorists to use caution are often tragically ineffective—the large cats cannot read, and the speeding motorist remains heedless. This young male is one of several panthers killed in the last five years on Florida highways. [Courtesy Darrel Land, Florida Game and Freshwater Fish Commission]

(C) (below, right) Picking at a lead sinker flea that will never go away, a brown pelican illustrates the hazards of "gracious Florida living," particularly when it must share its coastal environment with humans. Although only a threatened species in Florida, the brown pelican is still considered endangered in the other Gulf states. Populations of this fish-eater once underwent serious decline owing to breakage or non-hatching of overly fragile eggs caused by DDT. This ungainly but loveable bird now must address another threat—drastic increases in human populations and concomitant loss of habitat within the most desirable coastal real estate of the Gulf. [Courtesy Theodore H. Below]

(D) (below) Manatees, the gentle giants of fresh and estuarine waters, are increasingly suffering injury and death caused by heedless or negligent boaters. This adult female and her young, both showing scars from previous encounters with powerboats, were lucky enough to survive. [Courtesy Florida Department of Natural Resources]

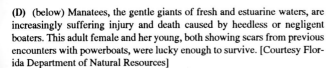

COLOR PLATE 8. The coastal zone interlock

COLOR PLATE 8. The coastal zone interlock

Like a system of capillaries, the hydrological networks that carry vital nutrients and freshwater runoff from the upland areas to the estuary are clearly seen in this false color infrared aerial photograph taken above the Ten Thousand Islands region in southwestern Florida. Wide, long freshwater hardwood swamps (red) are bordered by freshwater marshes and prairies (slate gray). Brackish marshes and marl prairies (grayish-white) are woven into the blue-gray reticulations of stream-fed salt marshes immediately below. These, in turn, mesh into the red-violet coastal mangrove forests, pierced by serpentine rivers and creeks, that border the deep blue waters of the marginal bays. The red-violet reticulated pattern of the Ten Thousand Islands mangroves is clearly seen across the lower portion of the picture and reaching upward toward the coastal mangrove system. The irregular white areas and thin straight lines indicate towns, highways, and manmade canals. Except for different upland and lowland vegetational species, the hydrological aspects of such systems are essentially similar throughout the eastern Gulf of Mexico. [Courtesy Natural Resources Management Department, Collier County, Florida]

COLOR PLATE 9. Meadows of plenty in the Gulf

(A) Sometimes Nature hides her works of art and magic in unlikely places. The beautifully brown-banded, fragile Medusa worm, a common polychaete of shallow estuaries, builds chitinous tubes under rocks or down into the substrate in seagrass beds and sends out its pale, blue, threadlike tentacles to feed on small organisms and detritus. When disturbed, the 1-2 feet long starlike net of blue threads is retracted into the tube so rapidly that they seem to disappear before one's eyes. [Author]

(B) Looking like multicolored pincushions, the variegated sea urchin lives up to its common name and takes on a variety of color forms in response to food and environmental conditions in its grassbed home. A favored food of small sharks that prowl the shallows, these herbivorous urchins grazing in large numbers can decimate shallow seagrass beds in the tropical and subtropical regions of the Gulf. [Author]

(C) Tropical shallow-water seagrass beds, such as those of Campeche, Yucatán, exhibit a wealth of invertebrates to the observant snorkler. Seen here are large cushion starfish, the spiral convolutions of a whelk eggcase, the pointed spire of a horse conch, the brown pinnacles of a demosponge, a large gaping cockle, a second molluscan eggcase, the bright red spiny fingers of another sponge, and a clump of drift algae. A large pen shell, a bivalve mollusc with a large scalloplike adductor muscle, lies opened at the feet of the red starfish. [Courtesy Betty E. Lemmon]

(A) (above) Warmed by the tropical sun, a rich organic soup stained brown by tannic acid simmers slowly among the prop roots of a summertime mangrove forest. Nutrients from decomposing leaf litter and detritus leaching into the clear, warm water mark the beginning step in the cycle of productivity—a complex nutritional pyramid that reaches from microbes at the base upward ultimately to mankind at the top. [Author]

(B) (above right) Clinging to a red mangrove branch, a mangrove tree crab patrols the arboreal high ground seeking its insect prey, with little algae and mangrove leaf salad on the side. The outgoing tide will find the little crustacean down at the tree base, picking its way carefully among the prop roots and pneumatophores, and hurrying to dine on the now-exposed small flora and fauna that cover these structures before the tide (and its own predators) returns. [Author]

(C) An apparent study in muddy confusion, three species of mangrove-dwelling snails go about the business of ridding the forest floor of stranded diatoms, detritus and leaf litter. Smooth and truncated banded coffee bean snails compete in the tidal puddles with corkscrew-shaped ladderform cerith snails, and the auger-shaped, multi-striped false ceriths. The snails, in turn, provide food for carnivorous large-clawed mud crabs that range throughout the mangrove forest whether the tide is in or out. [Author]

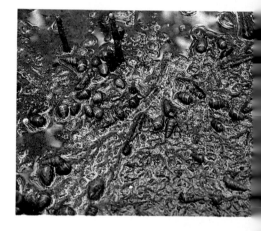

(D) The reticulated mangrove islets of the aptly named Ten Thousand Islands along the southwestern Florida coast are clearly seen in this aerial photograph. Small mangroves, growing on exposed shell heaps and living oyster bars, gradually coalesce with one another and snake across the shallow estuarine waters in a living green maze. The resulting labyrinth of trees and islands forms one of the most productive estuarine areas on earth. [Author]

COLOR PLATE 11. Life in the Gulfside salt marshes

(A) Large tidal channels exposed at low tide meander in great muddy loops through bright green saltgrass and cordgrass meadows in a northwest Florida salt marsh. Farther inland (left) and in the distance (far right) dark fields of spike rush form another station on the tidal commuter. The upland margins, marked by pine forests, provide the final link connecting the terrestrial flora and fauna with their estuarine counterparts, and the land—via the marsh—to the Gulf of Mexico. [Courtesy Darryl L. Felder]

(B) (left) In military precision, marsh periwinkle snails stand along a stalk of cordgrass in a Louisiana marsh awaiting the outgoing tide and a chance to forage on the mudflats. When the tide returns they will reclimb their grassy perch, withdraw into their shells and reseal the opening, protected against desiccation while awaiting the next tidal cycle. [Author]

(C) (right) Crowding in great pink and grey herds, thousands of fiddler crabs emerge from their burrows for a low-tide picnic of diatoms and detritus in a southwestern Florida salt marsh. Mating, reproduction and release of mature eggs can also occur during these food fests. [Author]

(D) Using fire as a management tool for snow geese and ground-nesting birds, biologists at Louisiana's Rockefeller Wildlife Refuge periodically burn the dry marsh wiregrass to set back its succession and encourage the growth of three-corner grass in its place. Such quick-burning, relatively "cool" fires consume the accumulated litter that could produce catastrophic wildfires, but leave the basal root clumps of the grasses, called culms, intact.[Courtesy Darryl L. Felder]

COLOR PLATE 12. Freshwater wetlands around the Gulf

(A) Looking like a gigantic bomb crater, a karst or solution hole lake reflects the blue southwestern Florida sky. Such ponds are formed when the shallow limestone substrate dissolves away, forming a depression that gradually becomes filled with water. In karst areas riddled with caverns the overlying pond can collapse downward forming large, circular sinkholes or *cenotes*. [Author]

(B) (left) Deep within Florida's famous Fakahatchee Strand a shallow freshwater lake, with floating algae and emergent vegetation, provides a serene glimpse of Eden. Lakes and ponds like this one form vital reservoirs of fresh water for plants and animals, and are among the earliest contributors of nutrients to the coastal zone interlock. The Fakahatchee Strand is one of several wetland systems that act as conduits to drain the southwestern Florida uplands directly into the Gulf. [Author]

(C) (below) A tributary of the Apalachicola River, with numerous smaller creeks branching off its main channel, meanders slowly Gulfward through freshwater marshlands. Water in the twisting channels and oxbows, carrying dissolved nutrients from upland areas and manmade pollutants from bordering farmfields, percolates through the marshes and is cleansed substantially of pollution and excess nutrients by the dense fields of grasses, sedges, and rushes. [Courtesy Collier County Natural Resources Management Department]

(A) Flying in crystalline elegance through the realm of eternal night, a small sea butterfly, in reality a planktonic pteropod mollusc, is illuminated briefly by a deep-sea camera as it searches with diaphanous grace for food in the aphotic zone of the deep sea. [Courtesy Dr. Marsh Youngbluth]

(B) More than 500 feet down in the epipelagic zone, the tiny glasslike barrel of a planktonic salp glides slowly through the pelagic night inhaling its microplanktonic prey. Scavenging copepods and other zooplankton swirl around the salp in glowing clouds.[Courtesy Dr. Marsh Youngbluth]

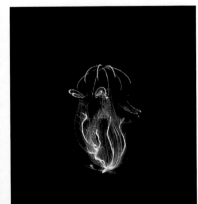

(C) Seemingly bedecked with strings of pearls and glowing with reflected light, a jewellike ctenophore, or comb jellyfish, hovers against the velvet blackness of the deep sea 2,000 feet down. In the background, pinpoint starlights from other planktonic animals are reflected in the spotlight of the deep-diving submersible from where this photograph was taken.[Courtesy Dr. Marsh Youngbluth]

(A) Deadly tentacles trailing up to 25 feet behind the violet and blue float of the Portuguese man o' war pose a continuing threat to the unwary, even when careened in a tidal pool. Confined mostly to the pelagic region, thousands of the gelatinous balloon-shaped colonies of this member of the pleuston occasionally blow ashore, causing pain and aggravation to Gulfside beachgoers. [Author]

(B) A dime-sized future trophy, this juvenile sailfish is but one of thousands of species of nekton that swim in the currents of the open sea feeding on planktonic invertebrates and small fish larvae. If it survives for several more years it may wind up dancing to a gamefisherman's tune played at the end of an outrigger line on an offshore charterboat. [Author]

(C) Hitchhiker through the world's oceans and perpetrator of a legend, the little square-bodied Columbus crab is a member in good standing of the pleuston. The crab that fooled Columbus spends its entire life offshore, first as a planktonic zoea larva, and then as an adult crab riding the floating seaweed and other drifting materials far out at sea. [Author]

COLOR PLATE 15. Oil fire at sea

Bathed in roaring flames, her decks awash, and settling by the stern, the oil tanker *Mega Borg* gasps out her final agony in roiling black smoke 50 miles south of Galveston in the open Gulf. Not evident is the petroleum pollution that resulted from this disaster—several million gallons of Angolan light crude oil that hemorrhaged from the tanker's hold. Leaking out around and behind the ship, and stretching for over 30 miles, the oil slick drifted for weeks on the Gulf's surface before being dispersed by wind and waves. [Patty Wood/Silver Image, by permission]

Like some alien spacecraft, a brightly lit oil drilling platform rises out of the dark waters of the Gulf of Mexico. In the ceaseless quest for black gold, today's roughneck conquistadores work day and night, fair weather or foul, to bring oil and natural gas up from the seabeds of the continental shelf. [Courtesy Robert M. Avent]

barrier islands in Florida, and at least two species are found on the Texas barriers as well. Water moccasins are known to occur in mangrove swamps, salt marshes and in the Louisiana bayous. Anoles (a type of lizard normally found in bushes and trees) are occasionally seen on floating debris in lagoons, and several other species of lizards, at least one species of gecko, and one skink species commonly inhabit barrier scrub and forests on the Florida Keys or scamper along the beaches of the coast and barrier islands from Florida to Yucatán. Although refusing to fit into our ecological pigeonholes as completely as we might desire, these species nonetheless illustrate how adaptation to existing conditions can aid in their survival and distribution around the Gulf.[4]

MARINE MAMMALS: LANDLUBBERS GONE TO SEA

Three major marine mammalian groups are still extant in the Gulf of Mexico: the sirenians (manatees), the cetaceans (whales and dolphins), and the pinnipeds (seals). All trace their origins (based on fossil evidence) back at least into the Miocene, an epoch that began about 25 million years ago. Their ancestors, in turn, evolved from terrestrial carnivores and elephantlike mammals, respectively, that lived in the Eocene, 55 million years ago. Today, with the probable extinction of the West Indian monk seal, the most abundant—and consequently the most noticeable—marine mammals in the Gulf are the manatees and cetaceans (see Table 8).[5]

Manatees

The West Indian Manatee is a coastal species occurring in waters of varying salinities, from fresh or slightly brackish to completely marine. They are commonly observed in the numerous tributaries and creeks that empty into the estuaries that ring the Gulf, in these same estuaries, and in the freshwater rivers, streams, and springs to the interior. Even though they are classified as primarily shallow freshwater and estuarine mammals, they often swim in nearshore marine waters off Gulf-side beaches. Feeding primarily on seagrass and other aquatic vegetation, manatees have been recorded along the Yucatán Peninsula northward to Vera Cruz, and along the western Florida peninsula from the Ten Thousand Islands north and westward around the Gulf to Texas. They are most numerous around the Florida and Yucatán peninsulas.[6]

Cetaceans

In the Gulf of Mexico at least 32 species of cetaceans occur. All these mammals, like their land-dwelling cousins (and manatees), are air-breathing. In general distribution, no part of the Gulf of Mexico would be denied them. The group is widely distributed; the whales are almost always found well offshore, whereas the dolphins and their relatives occur in both shallow and deep waters. The group can be divided into two categories: cetaceans having teeth in their jaws, and those having baleen or "whalebone" instead. The former are active predators; the latter are filter-feeders. As might be expected, owing to their large size and pelagic feeding habits, the larger toothed and baleen whales tend to remain well offshore in deeper water, but some species of dolphins are also primarily pelagic.

Eight species of great whales are on the federal endangered species list and six occur in the Gulf: the sperm, blue, finback, humpback, sei, and right whales.[7]

Toothed Whales

Sperm whales, the largest of the toothed whales, are the largest predatory mammals living on earth, feeding primarily on deep-sea fishes and squids.[8] Not uncommon at one time in the Gulf, sperm whales still occur mostly along the edges of the continental shelf. Large populations used to exist in the Atlantic Ocean southward to Antarctica, but these great sea mammals had their numbers decimated by whalers over a 150-year period beginning in 1761. An estimated 600 to more than a thousand sperm whales were killed worldwide during this time, mostly for their oil, termed *spermaceti*.[9] Today, except for very rare sightings offshore, sperm whales are known mostly by strandings of young animals.

Dolphins, also classified as toothed whales, have been widely reported from both inshore and offshore waters throughout the Gulf. Included in this general grouping are bottle-nosed dolphins (commonly, but improperly, called porpoises), long-snouted dolphins, rough-toothed dolphins, pygmy sperm whales, false killer whales, pilot whales, and true killer whales.

Specimens of most of these fish-eating species have been seen, either as isolated individuals or small groups feeding in shallow waters, or in large pods often numbering hundreds of individuals well offshore. Others have been recorded from numerous strandings along Gulf coast beaches (see Plate 6C). Captures, either in trawl nets of commercial fishermen or by commercial marine aquaria, provide further positive evidence of the widespread occurrence of these mammals.

The true killer whales (also called orcas) are, from a swimmer's point of view, fortunately rare, but may be expected to occur from time to time. Sightings off Port Aransas, Texas, and records from off Florida indicate the potential occurrence of this large, voracious predator. Lack of prey (seals, small whales) may be one reason for their rarity in the Gulf.

Other toothed whales recorded from Gulf waters include pygmy and dwarf sperm whales and three species of rare beaked whales known from offshore observations and Florida strandings.

Baleen or "Whalebone" Whales

The baleen whales differ from their toothed cousins by having large horny plates with greatly frayed edges lining the upper jaw. These plates ("whalebone") act in concert with the large fleshy tongue as filtering mechanisms to strain out plankton. Baleen whales may be more common than records indicate. Presently the finback whale is known primarily from stranding records in Texas, Louisiana, and Florida. The largest baleen whale (and also the largest mammal ever to live on earth), the blue whale (the sulfur-bottom whale of whalers), also occurs in the Gulf. The sei and the humpback whale, normally offshore species, have been sighted off Seahorse

Key and Tampa Bay on the central Florida coast, and the right whale[10] is also known in the Gulf.

West Indian Seals

One other marine mammal of interest, first noted in the Caribbean by Christopher Columbus, and later in the Gulf by Juan Ponce de León, is the West Indian monk seal. This small pinniped, presumably a fish-eater or perhaps feeding on crustaceans as well, occurred either singly or in small herds. At one time, like the whales, they were slaughtered by the early Spaniards and their fat was rendered into oil, which may have helped in their presumed extinction.[11] Obsolete records of sightings exist from the western Gulf in the vicinity of Galveston. Some anecdotal evidence of their presence on the Alacran Reef off northwest Yucatán suggests that they may not yet be extinct. But the picture remains bleak. Some vertebrae were collected on a small island off Campeche, but the last known live sighting was off Jamaica in 1952.

The California sea lion, a species normally restricted to the Pacific Ocean from California to Japan and Australia, has been recorded in the eastern and central Gulf but should be considered a stray or possibly an escapee.

Table 8
Marine Mammals Known to Occur in the Gulf of Mexico

CETACEANS

Baleen Whales and Rorquals

Right whale	*Eubalaena glacialis*
Blue whale	*Balaenoptera musculis*
Sei whale	*Balaenoptera borealis*
Finback whale	*Balaenoptera physalus*
Bryde's whale	*Balaenoptera edeni*
Minke whale	*Balaenoptera acutorostrata*
Humpback whale	*Megaptera novaeangliae*

Sperm Whales

Sperm whale*	*Physeter catodon*
Pygmy sperm whale	*Kogia breviceps*
Dwarf sperm whale	*Kogia simus*

Beaked Whales

Blainville's beaked whale*	*Mesoplodon densirostris*
Antillean beaked whale*	*Mesoplodon europaeus*
True's beaked whale*	*Mesoplodon mirus*
Cuvier's beaked whale	*Ziphius cavirostris*

Killer Whales

Killer whale	*Orcinus orca*
False killer whale	*Pseudorca crassidens*
Pygmy killer whale	*Feresa attenuata*

Pilot Whales or Blackfish

Atlantic pilot whale*	*Globicephala melaena*
Short-finned pilot whale	*Globicephala macrorhynchus*

Dolphins

Rough-toothed dolphin	*Steno bredanensis*
Fraser's dolphin	*Lagenodelphis hosei*
Saddleback dolphin	*Delphinus delphis*
Bottlenose dolphin*	*Tursiops truncatus*
Atlantic spotted dolphin	*Stenella frontalis*
Pantropical spotted dolphin	*Stenella attenuatus*
Striped dolphin	*Stenella coeruleoalba*
Spinner dolphin	*Stenella longirostris*
Clymene's dolphin*	*Stenella clymene*
Risso's dolphin*	*Grampidelphis griseus*

Manatees

West Indian manatee	*Trichechus manatus*

Seals and Sea Lions

West Indian monk seal	*Monachus tropicalis†*
California sea lion	*Zalophus californianus‡*

Source: U.S. Fish and Wildlife Service (1981) and Mullin et al. (1991).

* Known under other common names; presently accepted name given.

† Presumed extinct; bones from Campeche collected in 1984. (See O.Vidal, 1991. *Catalog of Osteological Collections of Aquatic Mammals from Mexico.* NOAA Technical Report NMFS 97. 36 pp.)

‡ Extralimital; otherwise known only from the Pacific Ocean.

BIRDS: FEATHERED SUCCESS IN THE VERTEBRATES

A noted ornithologist once stated that birds are different from all other verte-brates because they are the only chordates totally adapted to, and able to utilize, the three environmental media existing on earth: air, land, and water. Paradox-ically (with the exception of some flightless land birds), no bird is totally a creature of any of those media. They simply use each, alone or in combination, as the moment directs. In the Gulf, as elsewhere, birds might be totally dependent on the sea or the estuaries or the wetlands for their existence, yet no bird lives totally in the water (be it brackish or marine) in the same way that a crab, oyster, fish, or whale does.

Even those sea birds that spend the preponderance of their lives flying far out to sea must still return to land, to mother earth, for reproduction. This three-fold existence in the air, on or in the water, and on the land makes any general statement regarding the ecological classification of these winged ani-mals meaningless. Just as no diving or swimming bird can ever be classified as wholly pelagic, neither can any bird that is capable of flying ever be classified as totally terrestrial. And, as far as food resources are concerned, birds use them all. Birds are foragers for seeds and aquatic vegetation (many songbirds, ducks), ambush predators (hawks, owls), prey-stalkers (egrets, ibises and other wading birds), carrion-feeders (vultures, eagles), aerial robbers (frigate birds, ospreys, gulls), aquatic filter feeders (skimmers and shearwaters), and aerial "planktivores" (whip-poor-wills, chuck-will's-widows). Having evolved over the past 190 million years, birds have had ample time to exploit every aspect of their environment (see Plate 6D).

Compounding the problem of their ecological categorization is the fact that many inshore areas of the Gulf are inundated on a daily basis by tidal incursions. Boundaries between land and sea become vague; habitats are drowned or exposed; feeding or breeding areas shift at the vagaries of wind, weather, and water. Yet in these areas birds occur in a profusion of numbers and species, many following the tides in and out to feed, others roaming the upland dunes or skittering along the breaking wavelines searching for food.

THE AERIAL FAUNA OF THE GULF

Ornithologically speaking, the Gulf of Mexico is considered a tropical-subtropical sea, even though warm temperate conditions occur along its northern rim. Consequently, the avifauna found in the Gulf includes both tropical species that are at the northern limit of their range, as well as temperate forms that are at their southern limits. Overlying these distributions are the great seasonal migrations made by many temperate and even boreal (cold climate) land birds as they move to winter feeding grounds in the Caribbean and return home to spring breeding grounds in the northern regions of the North American continent. Nearly 75% of all migratory waterfowl in the United States use the coastal waters from Texas to Florida as stopover areas for resting or feeding.

Adding further complexity are the year-round residents of Caribbean origin, particularly those inhabiting warm areas such as Florida, southern Texas, tropical Mexico and Cuba. Finally, there are the occasional or "waif" species that may be blown ashore or out to sea, or that move in and out of the littoral and even offshore areas during their feeding or migrations. All of these factors make the enumeration of species in this very mobile fauna not only difficult but in some respects trivial.[12]

Offshore Birds

Offshore birds are so perfectly adapted to the open sea that they cannot survive without it. Their numbers are small, perhaps 25–30 species at most, and include the terns, shearwaters, petrels, boobies, and frigate birds, plus several other smaller groups. These birds feed in the offshore food webs, primarily on the open-sea fishes, and only rarely come close to shore. Their preferred breeding places are offshore islands, a landform in noticeably short supply in the Gulf. They are restricted for the most part to small coral islets such as the Dry Tortugas, Alacran Reef, and the Arcas and Triangle Keys, although even mainland beaches will suffice in a pinch. Least terns will even nest on sandy, heavily disturbed construction sites if other conditions are favorable.

Coastal-Associated Birds

This category is the richest of all in numbers of species and individuals. Over 90% of the approximately 500 bird species known from the eastern United

States have been recorded along the coastlines from Florida to Texas. Even though these numbers seem high, they are exceeded in the tropical areas of Mexico in the southwestern Gulf by the Caribbean-derived species. In this region the avifauna of the narrow, several-hundred-foot-wide coastal strip that extends back from the shores of the Gulf probably exceeds that of the entire United States in richness and diversity.

The number of species of tropical birds in lower Mexico, Yucatán, and southward into the Caribbean is immense. For example, Guatemala alone has more than 660 species, with some 300 species found in the tropical dry or moist forests of the Caribbean lowlands. Excluding these tropical forms, at least 125 species of birds characteristically occur over littoral waters and land. These are the birds of the intertidal zone feeding, roosting or passing through the great mangrove forests; wading in the vast salt marshes; overnighting on the wide bays; and wandering over the extensive salinas and mud flats.

Commonly recognized forms include herons, ibises, egrets, spoonbills, and other wading birds; pelicans, cormorants, and other diving birds; oystercatchers, gulls, sanderlings, and other seashore-dwellers; predatory birds such as the osprey and bald eagle; and numerous ducks and their relatives. Even birds normally considered upland-dwellers, such as sparrows, woodpeckers, flycatchers, vireos, cardinals, and mockingbirds can live or forage in the coastal saltwater bayous, creeks, and marshes.

Although these birds are generally thought of as coastal-associating forms, many undergo large-scale migrations and have been sighted far out to sea. More than 50 species fly directly over the open Gulf, including great blue and Louisiana herons, least bitterns, long-billed curlews, roseate spoonbills, and ruddy turnstones, all of which have been recorded from 30–180 miles offshore. Sandpipers and laughing gulls are also known from nesting sites on Alacran Reef some 80 miles off the Yucatán Peninsula.

Another group of some 64 species consists mostly of inland birds that have been recorded along the coast and open water but have no permanent ecological ties to those conditions. Included herein are hawks, swallows, robins, warblers, orioles, buntings, and a host of other forest and meadow species that populate the uplands.

Many of these species undergo wide-scale migrations southward into Central and South America. Although in some cases their observance over open sea may be a result of weather conditions (birds blown offshore, for example), many of the species make a consistent annual return migration northward from South America by crossing the Gulf from the Yucatán Peninsula. For these birds, the Gulf of Mexico becomes not so much a productive habitat to be exploited as a dangerous barrier to be crossed.

Endemic Coastal Birds

Endemic coastal birds are those species or subspecies apparently restricted to a limited geographical area and found nowhere else. Within the environs of the Gulf of Mexico north of Mexico at least 16 endemic subspecies are recognized. These include four seaside sparrows, three clapper rails, two long-billed marsh wrens, a heron, an egret, an insect hawk, a barn swallow, a Carolina wren, a horned lark, and a red wing blackbird.

Although these 16 species represent only a small portion of the total avifauna from the Gulf, it must be remembered that one of the reasons they are endemic is that they have not found conditions elsewhere particularly suitable to their survival. Their continued existence is thus more threatened by adverse environmental impacts than their more wide-ranging and tolerant counterparts. Quite often, habitat loss is a major cause of their demise. Seaside sparrows, for example, are essentially salt marsh birds that require specific biological conditions found only in certain marshes. When conditions are altered, populations may undergo decline or, as in the case of the dusky seaside sparrow, become extinct. The ivory-billed woodpecker is now extirpated in the continental U.S. The only known population is in Cuba. If it is able to survive, this species could now be considered an endemic or relict species restricted to its now-vanishing habitat.

Endangered Wildlife

LOSING OUR SPECIES

THE TOTAL NUMBER of species, animal and plant, found in the Gulf of Mexico and its environs is unknown. This is primarily because the largest group of organisms on earth, the insects, remains poorly investigated, with the exception of those species of economic, agricultural, or public health impact. Moreover, many of the "worms" in several different phyla are poorly known at best, and even the deep sea is yielding organisms heretofore unknown to science and often having obscure taxonomic relationships with known forms.

But among all this biota there are numerous species that have been given special status by government wildlife agencies. These species are deemed particularly vulnerable because they have been overcollected, extirpated as nuisance forms, had their populations reduced because pesticides have affected their reproductive physiology, or are in danger of extinction owing to habitat modification or destruction.

CATEGORIZING THE ROAD TO EXTINCTION

Several categories have been established by federal and state government agencies to focus attention on the species of special status. These are usually listed as follows:

Endangered—Species in danger of extinction or extirpation throughout all or a significant portion of their range as a consequence of natural or man-made factors that either affect the species populations directly, or act indirectly by reducing or eliminating critical habitats.

Threatened—Species likely to become endangered as a consequence of natural or man-made factors directly affecting resident populations, or indirectly by causing environmental deterioration to such an extent that such populations are rapidly reduced to the point of nonviability or recoverability.

Species of Special Concern[1]—Species that, by virtue of their isolated, disjunct, or small populations in Florida have become unique and/or significantly vulnerable to habitat modification, environmental alteration, human disturbance or exploitation such that they are likely to become threatened.

It is significant that one of the first criteria used in considering a population of species for assignment to any of the above categories is its rarity. Thus, any rare species has the *potential* to become threatened or endangered, although the *probability* as to whether it eventually will depends in large measure on a number of complex factors. It must be remembered that rarity in and of itself is not the overriding factor leading to endangerment. Many species are rare in one area because they are at the environmentally tolerable limits of their ranges. Others may be seasonally rare owing to migrations, naturally occurring fluctuations, or naturally deteriorating habitat.

Another complicating factor is that category definitions are not equivalent among the various federal and state agencies. Moreover, there is no agreement among the agencies as to which species should even be considered under any of the categories. Consequently, there is at present much confusion as to the "value" or the "rank" of species to be assigned. For example, the Indigo snake, *Drymarchon corais couperi,* is endangered in Florida but may be captured and sold in Georgia. Within Florida itself, gopher tortoises (*Gopherus polyphemus*) are threatened species in south Florida, but may be hunted and eaten in central and north Florida. Because endangerment is in the eyes of the bureaucratic beholder the result is often confusion for the layperson. The Florida black bear is considered threatened in south Florida but is allowed to be hunted in two north Florida counties (see Plate 7A). Petitions to have the Florida subspecies of black bear placed on the U.S. Fish and Wildlife Service's endangered species list have been denied owing to lack of manpower in the federal agency to determine whether the listing is warranted, and the more than 1,000 other species that are also being considered for the list. Yet the Louisiana black bear was placed "on the list."

ANIMALS HAVING SPECIAL STATUS

Within the Gulf of Mexico region at least 30 marine and freshwater aquatic invertebrates and a host of terrestrial insects are categorized as special status species by state or federal agencies. Numerous vertebrates have also been designated under categories of endangered, threatened, or species of special concern. Some of these are listed in Table 8.

Several of the vertebrates, such as freshwater fish or reptile species, may be of only regional special status by virtue of their known range. For example, about 10 freshwater fishes common in the Gulf coast drainages west of Florida reach their eastern limit of distribution in that state and so are classified under special-status criteria. Several others are listed that, owing to their exploitation or destruction of their habitat, are also regionally threatened.

PLANTS HAVING SPECIAL STATUS

Conservatively estimated, there are well over 4,000 species of plants in the Gulf of Mexico region. Approximately 10% of these have been studied sufficiently to allow them to be considered worthy of special-status categorization. Many of these species, like their animal counterparts, are easily recognized in a general sense by the public. For example, all of the native American orchids in Florida are on the list.[2] Others, because of special ecological features (slow growth, limited distribution, degrading habitat) are also included. Thus, diminutive epiphytic orchids no larger than 6 inches stand next to 50-foot tall royal palms on the endangered list.

In another example, the Fakahatchee Strand State Preserve in southwestern

Florida has 27 families and 106 species of plants on one endangered plant list or another within the state. This number constitutes 22% of all the plant species known to occur in the immediate vicinity. The Fakahatchee Strand has more endangered species than most areas in the United States east of Texas, and may have even more than that state. Yet the U.S. Fish and Wildlife Service lists only five plant species in Florida's Fakahatchee Strand State Preserve as threatened or endangered, and all five are still under review for suitability.[3] The Florida Committee on Rare and Endangered Plants and Animals, on the other hand, lists 124 species, plus another 46 considered rare or of special concern. More than 400 plant species in Florida alone have been designated under some type of special concern category by one government agency or another. Over 270 of these listed as endangered, threatened, or rare occur in the eight southwestern Florida Gulf counties alone. Of all the other Gulf states, only Texas has more threatened and endangered plant species than Florida.

THE "NOAH FACTOR": PROBLEMS WITH SAVING SPECIES

The federal government has provided guidelines and species listings, but state governments also define which species are deserving of preservation or conservation. Even county governments can pass ordinances mandating protection of plants and animals, particularly where development threatens the species or their habitats. Of course, such laws serve their purpose only if backed by vigorous enforcement.

An important aspect is that of public identification. It is often easier to work up public sympathy or concern for the well-publicized, or "star" species, than for others, because as humans we can identify more easily with those species and their plight (see Plate 7). For example, it is relatively easy to rally support to protect sea turtles, manatees, dolphins, pelicans, and eagles. Conversely, few people can identify with the palm polly orchid, the gopher tortoise, the least tern, the Everglades kite, or even the indigo snake. This dilemma can be aptly characterized the "Noah Factor" in reference to the obvious problems that biblical person must have encountered in deciding which of the lesser species were to be given room in the ark.

Another problem is how we perceive a species to fit into our scheme of things. Well-known species are often emphasized, even though they may form only a small, or apical, part of a given food web. But who pleads the case of the Okaloosa darter? The Key Largo rat? The Miami black-headed snake? The Enterprise Spring snail? Or the dusky-handed tailless whip scorpion?

Not only is it difficult for conservationists and regulatory agency personnel to bring these non-star species to the public's attention, it is even harder to convincingly show the layperson how each species fits into the general scheme of things, and therefore why it should be protected. No mean task when louseworts, club mosses, darters, rats, and snakes are involved.

Any listing of species under one form of protection or another must be viewed in its proper context. It should never be construed that such a listing implies that these species are considered "more desirable" than either their lesser known or their more common and less threatened counterparts. Here the general public must rely on the expertise of the wildlife scientists and trust the wisdom of the regulatory decision-makers—not always an easy thing to do.

A more insidious criterion that often sways decision-makers is the question often voiced by much of the general public, and even some so-called "conservationists": "What good is it?" This anthropocentric arrogance can no longer be accepted. Because the point overlooked here is that there is no rank in Nature. Indeed, as far as Nature is concerned, every species is "good" and therefore equally valuable. Otherwise such a species would not have survived, let alone evolved to become an integral part of the ecosystem in which it occurs. It is a wise person indeed who can look to the least as well as the great for conservation and preservation. Such an individual would know the simple and irrefutable ecological fact that the occupants at the top of the food web cannot survive without the support of all others beneath them. As the noted biogeographer G. Carleton Ray asked: "Are whales or plankton most worth saving?"[4]

THE BOTTOM LINE: SAVING THE "STARS"

Yet the realities of the "real world" of endangered species protection mandate that conservationists use every means at their disposal in terms of dollars, public outcry, and political power to protect these "star species" *and their habitats.* Then workable mechanisms to protect *all* species that are being severely depleted can be developed and implemented.

It is becoming increasingly clear that protection mechanisms focused on a few facets of a species' existence do not work well. Rather, a holistic approach, in which the species is protected from both direct harm (hunting, netting, pollution) and indirect harm (destruction of nesting or foraging habitat), is the only way to provide adequate protection. The mandate then becomes: Save not only species, but also habitats in which they live. If the habitat is preserved, then all the other "little species," the ones that lack the appreciation of the public, will fall under the "star species" umbrella. And, in a nice turnabout where the many support the few, the few may then save the many.

Two examples will suffice. In Florida, collisions with boats are the cause of about 25% of the total mortality of West Indian manatees.[5] As a viable first step, various laws and plans are being proffered to reduce or eliminate this mortality. But if the manatee's shallow-water habitat where it breeds and forages for aquatic plants is not protected from pollution or dredge-and-fill development, then we may ultimately be saving the species only for our zoos. Also lost in this failure will be a number of other threatened species such as the mangrove crab, starlet coral, and even important sport fish such as snook, redfish, and sea trout.[6]

Throughout the Gulf of Mexico, sea turtles are under continued survival pressure from habitat destruction of their nursery beaches, floating garbage and debris offshore, and shrimp trawling along their coastal habitat. The increasing build-up of coastal areas through resort and residential development permanently alters or destroys the beaches to which the female turtles must return to lay their eggs. Moreover, coastline lighting, an often concomitant consequence of resort development, can confuse the directional response of young hatchlings so that they turn toward the land instead of the sea and become victims of traffic, household pets, and desiccation. Reaching the sea is a mixed blessing. As the survivors grow up, they are subject to injury or death through ingestion of, or entanglement in, the floating plastic debris that has become so common in the world's oceans. Commercial fishery operations add one more hazard. According to the National Research Council more than 40,000 sea turtles are killed in shrimp trawls each year. Add that number to the natural pressures from predation and disease, and the stress on the overall sea turtle population is dire indeed.

Turtle Exclusion Devices (TEDs) on commercial nets are now mandated by law and should go a long way toward easing this artificial predation. Unfortunately, for the Kemp's Ridley turtle it may prove an academic exercise. Data from nesting beaches in Mexico suggest that the population has been reduced to less than 1% of its 1947 levels.

Make no mistake—special-status listings do serve a purpose, if only to alert us that yet one more species is on the verge of disappearing. But as conservation and preservation costs continue to rise, as the dollar value of preserved lands increases, as Third World nations readjust their priorities toward simply surviving, and as government budgets continue to function in a deficit mode, it will become increasingly costly and difficult to choose which species need protection the most. These factors will force us to make wrenching decisions: whom do we save, whom do we cast away? In the end, we will only attain ecological understanding and sophistication when our bumper stickers will read: "Help keep our ecosystems alive. Save all species!" Father Noah would have been completely familiar with the problem. . . .

Table 9
Some Vertebrate Species with Special Status in the Gulf of Mexico

Species	Status*	Habitat/Notes
FISH		
Key silverside fish	Endangered	Marine endemic
Okaloosa darter	Endangered	Freshwater coastal tributaries; NW Fla. endemic
Atlantic sturgeon	Endangered	Anadromous; habitat destruction common
River redhorse	Threatened	Clean freshwater; habitat declining
Grayfin redhorse	Threatened	As above
Cypress minnow	Threatened	Coastal freshwater rivers; restricted distribution
Blackmouth shiner	Threatened	NW Fla. endemic
Lake Eustis pupfish	Threatened	Central Fla. endemic habitat declining
Marbled rivulus	Threatened	Mangrove-salt marsh; hermaphrodite

Species	Status*	Habitat/Notes
Shoal bass	Threatened	Apalachicola River endemic; habitat declining
Mangrove mosquitofish	Special Concern	Mangroves, Fla. Keys; habitat declining
Spottail goby	Special Concern	Fla. Keys, shallow inshore waters

AMPHIBIA

Pine barrens tree frog	Endangered	Pine barrens endemic; Pleistocene relict?
Florida gopher frog	Threatened	Sand scrub; gopher tortoise burrows

REPTILES

Green sea turtle	Endangered	Marine, wide-ranging
Hawksbill sea turtle	Endangered	Marine, wide-ranging
Kemp's Ridley sea turtle	Endangered	Marine, wide-ranging
Leatherback sea turtle	Endangered	Marine, wide-ranging
American crocodile	Endangered	Estuarine wetlands; numbers declining
American alligator	Threatened	Freshwater swamps
Loggerhead sea turtle	Threatened	Marine, wide-ranging
Florida Keys mud turtle	Threatened	Fla. Keys freshwater endemic
Suwannee cooter	Threatened	Freshwater coastal-inland tributaries; population overexploited for food
Florida gopher tortoise	Threatened	Sand scrub endemic; habitat declining
Eastern indigo snake	Threatened	Inland sandy or wet lands; overcollected
Miami black-headed snake	Threatened	S. Fla endemic; habitat declining
Big Pine Key ringneck snake	Threatened	Big Pine Key endemic
Florida brown snake	Threatened	Restricted distribution; Fla. Keys
Florida ribbon snake	Threatened	Fla. Keys wetland endemic
Short-tailed snake	Threatened	Scrub oak endemic
Florida Keys mole skink	Threatened	Coastal sandy scrub
Florida Keys rat snake	Threatened	Fla. Keys endemic

BIRDS

Cuban snowy plover	Endangered	Nests on remote sandars
Wood stork	Endangered	Freshwater wetlands
Everglades kite	Endangered	Freshwater wetlands; specialized diet
Bald eagle	Endangered	Coastal areas; with specialized nesting
Peregrine falcon	Endangered	Coastal areas

Species	Status*	Habitat/Notes
Brown pelican	Endangered	Coastal bays
Kirtland's warbler	Endangered	Winter migrant; reduced populations
White-crowned pigeon	Endangered	Mangroves
Cape Sable seaside sparrow	Endangered	SW Fla. marshes
Red-cockaded woodpecker	Endangered	Old-growth pinelands
Least tern	Threatened	Nests on disturbed open sandy areas
Roseate tern	Threatened	Nests only in Fla. Keys
Piping plover	Threatened	Seashore dunes
Sandhill crane	Threatened	Inland marshes; restricted nesting
Audubon's caracara	Threatened	Dry coastal prairies central Fla.
Florida scrub jay	Threatened	Sand scrub endemic
Burrowing owl	Special concern	High sandy ground; habitat declining
Limpkin	Special concern	Freshwater wetlands
Marian's marsh wren	Special concern	Salt marsh endemic
American oystercatcher	Special concern	Bay island nesting
Little blue heron	Special concern	Fresh/salt marshes
Louisiana heron	Special concern	Estuarine; habitat declining
Snowy egret	Special concern	Fresh/saltwater wetlands
Reddish egret	Special concern	Coastal mangroves
Roseate spoonbill	Special concern	Coastal wetlands, particularly Florida Bay
Whooping crane	Special concern	Freshwater marshes
Ivory-billed woodpecker	Extinct?	Old growth hardwoods habitat lost
Bachman's warbler	Extirpated?	Winter migrant; woody lowlands
Dusky seaside sparrow	Extinct	Salt marsh habitat altered

MAMMALS

Species	Status*	Habitat/Notes
Finback whale	Endangered	Marine, pelagic
Sperm whale	Endangered	Marine, pelagic
Right whale	Endangered	Marine, pelagic
Sei whale	Endangered	Marine, pelagic
Humpback whale	Endangered	Marine, pelagic
West Indian manatee	Endangered	Fresh/salt waterways
Key deer	Endangered	Big Pine Key endemic
Key Largo wood rat	Endangered	Key Largo endemic
Key Largo cotton mouse	Endangered	Key Largo endemic
Alabama beach mouse	Endangered	E Ala-NW Fla. beaches
Perdido Key beach mouse	Endangered	E Ala-NW Fla. beaches
Choctawhatchee beach mouse	Endangered	E Ala-NW Fla. beaches
Silver rice rat	Endangered	Cudjoe Key endemic
Florida panther	Endangered	Big Cypress Swamp; restricted habitat
Gray bat	Endangered	NW Fla. caves

Species	Status*	Habitat/Notes
Indiana bat	Endangered	NW Fla. caves
Mangrove fox squirrel	Endangered	SW Fla pinelands
Red wolf (hybrids)[7]	Endangered	La. and Tex. coasts
Key Vaca raccoon	Threatened	Key Vaca-Grassy Key endemic; mangroves
Perdido Bay beach mouse	Threatened	NW Fla.coastal dunes
Florida mouse	Threatened	Scrub oak endemic
Lower Keys cotton rat	Threatened	Lower Keys endemic
Everglades mink	Threatened	Everglades system
Florida black bear	Threatened	Freshwater wetlands
Sherman's fox squirrel	Special concern	Scrub oak endemic
Round-tailed muskrat	Special concern	Freshwater marshes
Red wolf (nonhybrid)	Extirpated?	Wet and dry forests; extinct in Fla. Ala. Miss. (except Horn Island, Miss.)
West Indian monk seal	Extinct?	Coastal waters; last recent sight record off Jamaica, 1952

*May vary with state or federal agency; highest recent status listed.

Coastal Communities

THE LINK BETWEEN LAND AND SEA

HE VAST MAJORITY of animals, both invertebrates and vertebrates, live in close associations, forming large and distinctive communities that recur up and down the Gulf coasts. Such communities are often characterized by the occurrence of one or more species that dominate by size or abundance. There is usually a subsidiary group of other recurring forms existing on a particular substrate. Taken together they allow the community to be defined biologically, ecologically, and by area. Ecologists call this grouping a biotope (*bios* = "life," *topos* = "place").

Some easily recognized examples of coastal communities include (1) oyster bars on estuarine muddy bottoms, (2) serpulid worm reefs on sandy-muddy substrates, (3) sponge and soft coral banks on primarily sandy seafloor, (4) inshore and offshore coral reefs, (5) sandy beach and surf zone communities, (6) offshore sandy plain communities, and (7) even a jetty community of fouling and sessile organisms growing on permanent or semi-permanent artificial hard substrates such as jetties, wrecks and oil platforms (see Plates 2, 3 and 4). Some of these have been touched on briefly earlier.

Although each of these communities is composed primarily of benthic invertebrates, each also supports numerous epibenthic and true water-column species, both vertebrate and invertebrate, which come to feed, breed, or hide within the constructs of the community. Regular visitors also include birds and several species of land mammals.

WETLANDS: COMMUNITIES OF CRITICAL IMPORTANCE

Wetlands are those areas of seashore or upland that are daily or seasonally flooded by salt or fresh water for a variable but significant length of time. As a consequence, the type of soil and its ability to retain water is an important characteristic. More noticeable to the layman, however, is the fact that wetlands also tend to support definitive vegetational assemblages dependent on such floodings. Thus, wetlands are defined by plants rather than by animals, using characteristic plant species that dominate in terms of number, area occupied, or both. Easily recognized examples are mangrove forests, salt and freshwater marshlands, savannahs, and freshwater swamps and bayous (see Figure 27).

This definition is as much a matter of convenience as it is of observation. Even though these biotopes support their own, usually characteristic fauna, we do not define these areas by such. The primary reason is that much of the

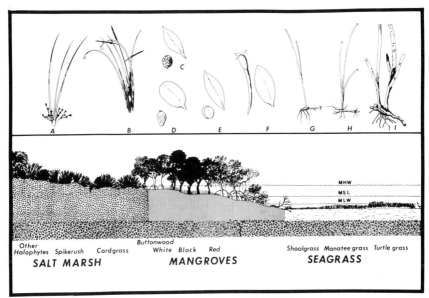

Figure 27. Plant zonation in a tropical estuary in the Gulf of Mexico.
Salt marshes, mangroves, and seagrass beds form an important wetland aggregate around the Gulf. Zonation is a result of tidal heights, frequencies, and durations. Mean high water (MHW), mean sea level (MSL), and mean low water (MLW) play a major role in determining plant occurrences and succession. In this schematic view (with vertical scale exaggerated), marshes grade into mangroves which, in turn, give way to seagrass beds. Leaves and fruits for the more common species are illustrated: (A) spikerush, (B) cordgrass, (C) buttonwood, (D) white mangrove, (E) black mangrove, (F) red mangrove, (G) shoal grass, (H) manatee grass, (I) turtle grass (not to scale).

associated fauna is more or less seasonally or tidally transient, may not be completely restricted to one biotope or another, and often is ephemerally present or sporadically visible. Plants are static, stable, and easily recognized; hence most biotopes are best characterized and circumscribed by their vegetation.[1]

This is not to downgrade the importance of the fauna, but rather to place it in its proper perspective. After all, a wetland may continue to exist for some time even if all the fauna is killed. Animals need plants more than plants need animals. Yet a wetland without animals would soon be an ecological desert and a dreary place indeed.

WETLAND COMMUNITIES: A PRIMER

Although all wetlands exhibit some similar physiographic features, no two anywhere in the world are ever exactly identical. Consequently, the fauna that may populate a salt marsh in the tropics is often substantially different from fauna in temperate-zone marshes. In addition, local and regional characteristics will affect the faunal species composition. Mudflats near the Mississippi River, for example, may support notably different communities from those found in

Tampa Bay. Faunal communities in the Laguna Madre grass beds differ in several respects from grass-bed species off the Dry Tortugas, and so on.

Even so, just as a wetland can indeed be characterized by the dominant vegetation, so there usually exists a typical fauna, assembled into animal communities that are more or less characteristic for each specific wetland. A good example is wetland birds. Many of the wading birds—the herons, ibises, and egrets—are found not only in marshes but also in savannahs, swamps, mangroves, and seagrass beds. They are adapted to the general conditions occurring in each of these biotopes. More importantly, they are able to feed and/or breed within them and are not restricted by any limiting factor except food.

A similar situation occurs with the invertebrates. Fiddler crabs, for example, are a ubiquitous member of the wetland fauna, being found from the shoreline margins of seagrass beds inshore to the muddy-sandy areas of savannahs and the fringes of freshwater swamps. They too are adapted to the variety of conditions that occur throughout these biotopes and are also able to feed and breed in them.

Other species are more selective. Again considering birds, redwing blackbirds are normally birds of salt and freshwater marshes and savannahs; they are rarely seen in mangrove forests. Although they are adapted to the marshland conditions, their breeding and feeding requirements preclude them from actively utilizing mangroves as a major habitat.

Turning again to the invertebrates, mangrove tree crabs are restricted by habitat solely to mangroves. Because their feeding and breeding requirements are tied so closely to the mangrove forest, they cannot survive even in the marshlands that often grade into the mangroves. Their respective "niche" is delimited by their physiological and ecological limitations.

It is easily seen, then, that species occurrence is more than simply availability of habitat. Numerous biological factors enter into the picture and each species that is able to exist within a given habitat must also be able to exist within the faunal communities that have developed within the same habitat. In other words, they must be able to fit into the "neighborhood" without undue stress to themselves or their neighboring species. Occurrence of a species in a wetland is thus a result of a combination of factors imposed by the environment, by the ecological requirements of the particular species, and by evolution.

THE COASTAL ZONE ECOLOGICAL INTERLOCK

The close relationships among biological conditions and the topography, drainage features, and soils in coastal areas have long been noted. A particularly important correspondence exists between the kinds of flora and fauna in an area and the existing hydrological-geological conditions. In this regard, then, wetlands are among the most critically important communities in the Gulf of Mexico.[2]

We now also know that individual ecosystems, while they may be isolated for purposes of study and characterization, can never be isolated from other systems adjacent to them. Coastal wetlands could not exist were it not for the overland runoff, the rivers and streams, and other hydrological components that carry not only fresh water, but the dissolved nutrients from upland areas down to the estuary. This holds true whether we are dealing with Florida mangrove forests, Louisiana bayous, or the shorelines of Texas coastal barrier lagoons or Mexican coastal embayments.

This interconnection of upland water sources with the coastal zone wetlands has been termed the coastal zone ecological interlock. In effect, freshwater and marine systems are interlocked in such a way that not only creates, but actually maintains the brackish water (that is, estuarine) systems that lie between the two (see Plate 8).

It can easily be seen that interruption or alteration of the upland portions of this interlock can have drastic and far-reaching effects on the lowland and estuarine portions. It is now recognized that coastal ecosystems invariably suffer when their upland connections are altered, for example, by residential or agricultural developments (see Figure 28).

When this occurs, important habitat and nursery grounds for many estuarine-dependent fish and shellfish, particularly those commercially exploited, suffer noticeable declines. Of even more importance, small upland perturbations often produce large-scale estuarine fluctuations both seasonally and over large areas.

Figure 28. The biopolitics of wetland development.
The realization in retrospect of what we had and either lost, gave away, or squandered is becoming increasingly coupled with a new environmental awareness of what still remains that we must protect. Conservation and preservation are now political issues as never before, and an informed public is making its voice heard at the polls. [Courtesy of Ed Stein, Rocky Mountain News]

Indeed, coastal ecologists have stated unequivocally that the maintenance and, more importantly, the overall productivity of the estuarine flora and fauna are dependent on upland waterflow into the lowlands. The estuaries rely on this flow not only for transfer of nutrients but also for the general lowering of salinities that takes place during its seasonal occurrence. Moreover, it is clear that the more these associated areas of water recharge and flow are damaged, from whatever cause, the greater will be the associated impact on coastal ecosystems.

And it's not only forested uplands that are being lost. Inland cypress swamps and coastal marshes around the Gulf are undergoing a decline, partially as a result of development and partially owing to the rampages of Mother Nature.[3] Outright physical destruction during land development for agricultural or commercial reasons is one factor. Intrusion of saline waters through alteration of land topography, storm tide overwash, or freshwater drawdown by wells is another major culprit. All these processes cause severe debilitation to freshwater systems or kill outright those vegetational species that cannot tolerate any salt in the water.

Of equal importance, insofar as management of coastal areas is concerned, is the maintenance of existing ecosystems. Old ecosystems are usually stable ecosystems, timed to the seasons and tuned to the ebb and flow of the tide. These old-growth systems persist not only because they have a great deal of built-in ecological resistance to change, but because they also exhibit ecological resilience, bending before breaking.

With rare exceptions, most of Nature's stresses imposed on ecosystems are long in application and slow in inducing response. Unfortunately, this is not the case with anthropogenic (human-induced) stresses. The consequence is ultimately injury, death, and the permanent loss of these vital areas. Although wetland loss is a very real concern, we should not lose sight of the fact that it will matter little whether we save any more wetlands if their associated uplands, an equally important link in the coastal ecosystem chain, are not also saved. The weakening or loss of any link in a chain renders the chain useless. Old ecosystems never become used up; they simply change. But old ecosystems can be destroyed. And their replacement, if it ever occurs, requires hundreds, if not thousands, of years. As Larry Harris, the noted ecologist and biogeographer, put it: "Natural resources are not given to us by our fathers; they are loaned to us by our children."

Seagrass Communities

INTERTIDAL ELYSIAN FIELDS

THE DOMINANT submerged vegetation in an estuary consists of sea grasses and algae. Sea grasses, which are true marine vascular plants with underwater flowers and seeds, grow in patches that can coalesce to form luxuriantly thick meadows. Within the Gulf at least seven species occur, with blades ranging in shape from wide and flat to long and cylindrical (Table 9; refer also to Figure 27 in previous chapter). Sea grasses can be found at one time or another along nearly every shoreline in the Gulf. But their abundances may differ depending on the existing environmental limitations to their settlement and growth.

WHY SEA GRASSES GROW WHERE THEY DO

Like their landlubber look-alikes,[1] sea grasses need sunlight, proper substrate and nutrients. Consequently, sea grasses are shallow-water plants that rarely occur deeper than about 30 feet except in waters of exceptional clarity. Turbid waters can limit or prevent their establishment and growth entirely, as can overly muddy sediments that do not encourage firm attachments by the rhizomes or underground rootstalks.

Sea grasses prefer relatively quiet, shallow, clear waters, particularly coastal embayments and lagoons. They cannot grow on high-energy beaches with persistent wave action because the substrate is constantly turned over, preventing the plants from becoming established. Although most species of marine grasses can withstand short periods of exposure during daily low tides, only the hardiest of sea grasses can survive in areas that undergo long exposure resulting from excessively low spring tides. Currents are also important for good seagrass growth, because they bring necessary dissolved nutrients into the area and can carry away smothering sediments.

Sea grasses by themselves play an important role in stabilizing substrates by binding soils with their rhizomes, and by acting as sediment traps that may eventually also stabilize and change the bottom topography in shallow estuarine waters. Moreover, seagrass productivity may exceed the total amount of all the benthic algae *and* all the plankton in the water column within the same general area.

MEADOWS OF RICHNESS AND DIVERSITY

Seagrass beds are usually areas of high plant and animal diversity. In fact, with the exception of coral reefs, seagrass communities are among the most speciose and diverse in the entire marine environment. For example, all three major bacterial phyla, probably all of the 23–25 protistan phyla (protozoans and

181

algae) and an undetermined number of fungal groups have been recorded.

TABLE 10
Common Seagrass Species in the Gulf of Mexico

Common Name	Description
Turtle grass (*Thalassia testudinum*)	Wide, flat, dark green blades. Most abundant sea grass in the Gulf. Limited exposure tolerance; 2–35 feet, rarely deeper, in clear sandy-bottom waters.
Manatee grass (*Syringodium filiforme*)	Thin, cylindrical, light green blades.Second most abundant grass in the Gulf. Often found mixed in with beds of turtle grass; occurs also in pure stands. Very common intertidal species, but may occur beyond 40-feet depth in places. Fair exposure tolerance.
Shoal grass* (*Halodule wrightii*)	Thin, flat light green blades. Most widely distributed of all seagrasses in the Gulf. Primarily intertidal, but to 30+ feet. High exposure tolerance; the most common species in estuaries and continually exposed tidal flats; never in same abundance as turtle grass.
Two-leafed seagrass (*Halophila decipiens*)	Paired, oval, bright green leaves arising on a slender stem from the whitish rhizome. Intertidal to about 90 feet in clear waters, quiet lagoons or brackish ponds. Poor exposure tolerance; essentially throughout the tropics.
Six-leafed seagrass (*Halophila englemanni*)	Thin, oval, serrated green blades in rosettes or whorls. Rare, occurring primarily offshore to 220+ feet, rarely intertidal. Usually intermixed with turtle grass.
Conshelf seagrass (*Halophila baillonis*)	Thin, oval, serrated green blades in pairs. Rare in estuaries, relatively common offshore, to 90 feet. May occur in pure stands in deeper water; intermixed with turtle grass in shallow subtidal regions. Limited tolerance.
Widgeon grass (*Ruppia maritima*)	Flat, thin, light green filamentlike leaves in whorls on thin, cylindrical stalk; rhizomes branch extensively. Fresh to brackish waters, often intermixed with turtle grass and shoal grass; intertidal and shallow subtidal. Limited exposure.

*Includes *Halodule beaudettii*.

Source: Synopsized from Dawes, 1974, Littler, et al., 1989, and Zieman and Zieman, 1989.

In addition to the main grass species, 20 or more species of large algae ("seaweed") may commonly occur. Upwards of 100 smaller algal species grow within the grass bed, either attached to the sea floor, or as epiphytic growth (*epi* = "upon," *phytos* = "plant") on the ribbonlike blades of the grass itself. At least two groups of trachaeophytes (higher plants) and members of at least 26 of the 33 marine invertebrate phyla are recorded from tropical and warm-temperate seagrass beds.

Tropical grass beds may contain over 300 species of invertebrates and more than 100 species of fishes. Their warm-temperate counterparts may have half that number. Yet what is seen is only one small part of the whole. The total number of species that compose a particular seagrass community will probably never be known. Many of the smaller, microscopic, parasitic, and endosymbiont (living inside other animals) species have yet to be described.

Every group from the primitive methanogenic (methane-gas-forming) bacteria and cyanophytes, or blue-green algae, to mammals utilize seagrass beds as a source of food, a refuge, and place for reproduction. Species may live in the sediments beneath the grass rhizomes, occur as epiphytic growth on the grass blades, or forage and hide on or within the grassy patches and clumps.

The invertebrates are both colorful and legion (see Plate 9). Typical and easily collected or observed seagrass "shellfish" include ornamented bivalves (cancellated venus and lucinid clams, bay scallops, arc shells, turkey wings, quahogs, and razor clams); a multitude of red- and brown-banded snails (tulip shells, conchs, whelks, ceriths, murexes); a wealth of small crustaceans (amphipods, isopods); bright red, green, or yellow stomatopods or "mantis shrimp"; and a living rainbow of decapods (including numerous species of swimming, mud, porcelain, and hermit crabs, grass, glass, and penaeidean shrimps, and even spiny lobsters).

The echinoderms are a prominent group in seagrass beds. Spiny pink sea urchins vainly try to cover themselves with shells, spotted and banded brittle stars wave from under every rock, reticulated sea stars tiptoe across the sandy areas, and sea cucumbers lie flaccidly like stolid gray sausages in the grass thickets.

Worms are everywhere. Diaphanous flatworms crawl and swim over the substrate, looking like fragile ivory-banded tissue paper. Brilliantly scarlet ribbon worms thread through the sand. Yellow, gray, and brown peanut worms (sipunculids) expand and contract from their rocky galleries. Multicolored polychaete worms weave their way through every bright green algal clump, while others send out pale blue tentacles in search of food from their leathery tubes buried in the bottom.

The sessile fauna is no less abundant and colorful. At least ten common species of sponges, colored brown, green, red, orange, and even blue, find attachments in the grass and on rocks and driftwood. Club and star corals form blunt, stony, brown thickets in the tropical areas while their yellow and purple sea whip and sea fan cousins wave in the currents farther offshore. Colonial tunicates, looking like bright red and orange galaxies, spread their starry gelatin across empty shells. A microscopic epiphytic fauna of hydroids, hydrozoans, and bryozoans clothes every blade of grass in yellow and green fur. And throughout the area the olive green grass provides a pleasing contrast to the golden and ivory sands and the porcelain blue coastal skies.

A distinct fish fauna is also associated with sea grasses and includes a second "commuter" group that migrates inshore from the reefs to overnight in the meadows before returning to the reefs at dawn. Among the fishes the bizarre, the strange, and the ridiculous are commonplace. Trunkfish and puffers bob like spotted and spiny clowns among the grass blades, dusky-colored gobies and clinids cling surreptitiously to the rhizomes, while juvenile porgies, spot, mojarras, and snappers race like silvery shadows among the grass tufts.

Skates, rays, and juvenile sharks patrol the verdant seafloor, fanning the sand into great white and gray clouds. There, at the base of an oyster clump, a mottled toadfish lies, dourly surveying his world. A short distance away a sergeant-major damselfish flashes his yellow and black stripes authoritatively while guarding his empty conch shell territory. A juvenile wrasse lazes under a vegetated ledge, watching the pipefish and needlefish skimming overhead just beneath the mirrored water surface. Off in the shadowed distance snook, sea trout, channel bass, and barracudas prowl, ever alert for the unwary, the careless, and the foolish. To the observer it seems a world of continual tension overlain by an affected insouciance, this continuing game of predator versus prey.

Let's not forget the out-of-water fauna: the more than 20 species of wading birds stalking their fishy and crustacean prey in the shallow grassy plots along the shoreline; the skimmers slicing the water with their scissorlike beaks; and the ospreys and pelicans circling high above, ready to plummet downward and capture their prey with a quick, slicing strike or in a foaming splash. These truly are marine elysian fields, and a paradise for hunter and hunted alike.

DRIFT ALGAE THICKETS: COMMUNITIES ON THE MOVE

If sea grasses form meadows, algae can form thickets. Because of storms or currents, several larger species of algae, particularly the reddish or brownish-red attached species (Rhodophyceae or Phaeophyceae), often break loose from the shallow estuary floor and form large, tangled floating thickets of seaweed. These thickets, called *drift algae*, become a floating habitat for *epiphytes* and *epizoa* that compose the fouling community that settles and grows on the blades and fronds of the grass and algae. They also quickly become the home and dinner table for numerous small invertebrate animals, particularly shrimp, amphipods, isopods, and snails, as well as some specially adapted fishes such as pipefish and gobies. More than 50 different types of small animals can be found in a large thicket, feeding and being fed upon. The clumps of drift algae thus form miniature floating microcosms that are carried by currents to and fro within the estuary.

GRASSY NURSERIES FOR WATER BABIES

An important but little noticed fauna are the juveniles and young of the many sport and game fishes that range over the seagrass beds and drift algae thickets searching for their larval and postlarval counterparts in the invertebrates. For a brief but critical period in their lives, the plant communities will act as a nursery to these fishes—the snook, croakers, drum, redfish, sea trout, snappers, groupers, and an ichthyological encyclopedia of others—providing food and shelter while they complete their pre-adult existence.

Let's not leave out the invertebrates. Juveniles of stone crabs, blue crabs, penaeidean shrimp, and spiny lobsters all must pass some time in the grass beds, feeding on the young of other invertebrates in preparation for their coming adulthood and ultimate migration back offshore. They will find the pantry well stocked. But so, of course, will their predators.

PASTURES OF PLENTY

All these species interact in one way or another and constitute the incredibly complex miniature ecosystems that make up much of the highly productive estuaries of the coastal zone. These systems are an intermeshing of invertebrates and vertebrates; wandering detrital feeders and sessile filter-feeders; herbivores, omnivores, and carnivores; prey and predators; the feeders and the food; a never-ending sequence of settlement, colonization, growth, maturity, migration, reproduction, death, and distribution of new young.

Yet the average observer sees only a minuscule time frame, a snapshot, of the great play of life that continually occurs in, on, and over these grass beds. Only a sea bird wading along the shore, a mullet jumping, a spider crab scurrying for cover provide any hint of the food webs and complexly structured communities lying at our feet.

It is not surprising that such a community fluctuates, changing with the days and the seasons, growing and reacting continually to climatic, tidal, sedimentary, and hydrological conditions. Animals come and go, are born and die, immigrate and emigrate, responding to their own innate cycles, the rhythms of the seasons, and to the ever-constant song of the sea.

Mangrove Forests

PRODUCTIVITY AND THE STENCH OF LIFE

MANGROVES HAVE BEEN CALLED "the trees that went to sea." These stilt-legged, tangled-root trees are more intimately tied to the sea throughout their entire life cycle than is any other tree. Beginning with their seeds, or *propagules*, dropped ready-to-sprout into the lagoons, the thousandfold return of seedlings that run aground in the tropical and subtropical bays and shores, and finally the full-fledged forests and swamps that flourish nearly everywhere around the Gulf of Mexico, mangroves truly have cast their "bread" upon the waters and been repaid. Indeed, mangrove saplings and trees are the most characteristic, as well as the most noticeable, vegetation of tropical and subtropical estuaries in the Gulf.

Four different species of trees are collectively called "mangroves": the red mangrove (*Rhizophora mangle*), the black mangrove (*Avicennia germinans*), the white mangrove (*Laguncularia racemosa*), and the buttonwood (*Conocarpus erectus*). The colors refer to the hue of the bark and can be used for field identification. The buttonwood has clusters of buttonlike seeds.

The four mangrove species grow quite well together and often form dense swamps or forests composed of their tangled aerial roots (red mangrove), prop roots (red, white mangrove), respiratory roots called *pneumatophores* (black, white mangrove), and low-growing twisted trunks (red mangrove, buttonwood). These same attributes help the different trees to become established and proliferate in the shallow, soft, muddy bottoms of estuaries.

MANGROVE ZONATION: MANY ISLANDS AND MINI-ISLANDS
Mangrove swamp forests are among the most clearly delimited of any wetland biotope. You are either in one or you are not. Although an *ecotone*, a transitional vegetational habitat between one major biotope and another, may sometimes occur, particularly where mangrove forest changes into salt or freshwater marsh, such a strip is quite narrow and rarely shows the diversity of plant species seen in other ecotones. In short, mangroves are gregarious.

In general, red mangroves are found the farthest seaward. And in many areas, such as offshore Florida Bay, the Ten Thousand Islands region, and off the shallow coastline of the Yucatán Peninsula, they form hundreds of miniature islands, with their long, flexible prop roots and aerial roots arcing out and downward into the water and the seafloor beneath (see Plate 10).

Immediately behind the red mangroves along the shore the black mangroves usually occur, their air-breathing pneumatophores projecting upward from the sticky black muck like so many flexible, respiratory pencils. Still farther up on shore the white mangrove, with its shorter, less-developed prop roots, forms the first landward phalanx of large maritime vegetation, while behind it and highest on shore grows the rough-barked buttonwood in gnarled and twisted coppices, or thickets.

Although the classic distribution occurs as just described, the actual zonation of mangroves in an estuary can be quite variable and is a function of the number and shape of the propagules, the depth of the water, and the available sediments. Red mangroves have long, cigar-shaped, green and brown propagules that usually drop directly into the water. Floating upright, they tend to "run aground" or become tidally stranded owing to their length (up to 10 inches or more). Thus, they normally germinate and grow in shallow water but farther from shore.

Black mangroves, on the other hand, also drop their small, green, purselike seeds into the water, but these are carried by tide and current along the estuary to be eventually recast directly onshore in great windrows where germination quickly occurs. White mangroves also have small, buoyant, flask-shaped seeds that must wash ashore before they can take root. The seeds of the buttonwood, the lightest of all, either germinate beneath the parent trees or are carried long distances by tides and currents to be thrown ashore far from their place of origin.

MUD, SALT, ROTTEN EGGS, AND HEAT: A POTPOURRI OF LIFE AND DEATH

Mangroves and mud go hand in hand. Mangroves and tropical heat are synonymous. Mangroves and hydrogen sulfide (with its characteristic odor of rotten eggs) are inseparable. With these three conditions—mud, heat, and hydrogen sulfide—the milieu of a mangrove swamp is succinctly summed up. Each, however, is interrelated to the other, and lacking any one, a large mangrove swamp cannot exist.

Mangroves invariably occur on muddy shores, particularly those with estuaries. The finely divided sediments offer an ideal substrate for settlement, rooting, and growth. As the tree itself grows, and sends out prop or aerial roots or pushes its pneumatophores up through the mud, these woody structures act as current baffles, causing more mud to be deposited around the tree bases. In effect, the mangrove acts as its own gardener, ensuring sufficient soils to maintain growth and nutrients.

Mangroves are tropical or subtropical trees. In the Gulf of Mexico they occur in Florida (where some 96% of all U. S. mangrove stands are found), along the southeastern coast of Mexico and the Yucatán Peninsula, and along the northwestern coastline of Cuba. Cold snaps of short duration (about 1-2 days, never longer if below freezing) are tolerated. Cold spells of longer duration and below freezing temperatures severely retard growth, kill back the upper branches, and may destroy the forest. The effects of such climatic pruning begin to be apparent above 28° north latitude in the Gulf. The most luxuriantly growing mangroves are usually found south of this latitude, though there are exceptions. Black mangroves, for example, are often found on the seaward side of Louisiana bayous and scattered in salt marshes along the northern Gulf from Mississippi to Texas (about 30° north). These trees, at the northern limit of their range, exist as stunted or dwarfed forms and are periodically killed back by intense cold fronts.[1]

The stench of hydrogen sulfide, often intermixed with methane (swamp gas), is a characteristic feature of the mangrove biotope. The smell of rottenness and decay, however, is really the bouquet of life and an indicator of proper functioning in one of the most complex biological systems in the world. For without the bacteria and fungi that act to break down the vegetational litter, and in the process release these odorous gases, the entire ecosystem would cease to function.

Most people think of saltwater when they think of mangroves. However, mangroves are more correctly known as salt-tolerating plants, or *halophytes*. Strictly speaking, they do not need saltwater as a physical requirement for growth or maintenance. In fact, most mangroves can grow quite well in freshwater, although they never form the large, biologically complex ecosystems so characteristic of estuarine and marine environments.

Adaptations to the highly saline environment in which mangroves occur include salt glands on the leaf stems and surfaces that excrete excess salt. Black mangroves, in particular, often carry a fine rime of salt on the undersides of their leaves. The tiny salt glands in the white mangrove are easily visible as two conical bumps, or papules, at the base of the leaf.

Mangroves are not a single community as once believed. Recent research has categorized mangrove forests into at least six different types, each responding to a complex mixture of soils, salinities, tidal flushing, water depth, land elevations, and available nutrients (see Table 11).

MANGROVES AND PRODUCTIVITY: A PERPETUAL PICNIC

The basis of the mangrove ecosystem is, of course, the tree—a tree that flourishes in an environment where temperatures, salinities, oxygen levels, and even the substrates fluctuate and shift, sometimes on a daily basis, and thus provide made-to-order habitat for many marine and estuarine organisms.

More important, however, are the leaves that the tree sheds throughout the year. This leaf litter forms the basis for the entire community food web. As the leaves fall they are quickly set upon by bacteria and fungi that begin to reduce them to their basic components. Carbon, nitrogen, phosphorus, and other elements are released or made available to higher organisms. Up to 50% of the weight lost by leaves through decomposition is made available as dissolved organic matter. The forest *microfauna*, composed predominantly of small crustaceans and molluscs, further break down the leaf litter to an insoluble component called *detritus*. As the tide floods through the forest, the detritus is flushed out into the estuary where it forms a basic energy source for other plants and animals. Meanwhile, birds roosting in the trees overhead add their own contri-

TABLE 11
Types of Mangrove Forest Systems in the Gulf of Mexico

Overwash Forests:	Occur on islands or mangrove-created banks or oyster bars that are frequently overwashed by tides. Red mangroves predominate, growing to about 23 feet. This community is commonly seen in the Ten Thousand Islands.
Fringe Forests:	Form a relatively thin strand growing along waterways that are infrequently inundated by tides. All species of mangroves may be found here, exhibiting the classically-defined zonation. This community often occurs along lagoons of barrier islands, with trees attaining 30 feet in height.
Riverine Forests:	Large strands growing along major streams, consequently flushed by daily tides. Growth is luxuriant, with red mangroves predominating. Tree heights may reach 65 feet. This forest is found associated with deltas along the Yucatán Peninsula, and in the Ten Thousand Islands.
Basin Forests:	Coastal strands associated with inland depressions that collect overland runoff. Tidal influence is prominent nearest the shore, decreasing farther landward. Consequently, a clearly defined zonation of red, followed by black, and then white mangroves usually occurs. Tree heights may exceed 50 feet. This type is found along the southwestern Florida coastline.
Hammock Forests:	Have Basin Forest attributes but the trees occur on slightly elevated (2-4 inches) ground relative to the surrounding substrate. Classical zonation may be present, but is restricted in abundance. Tree heights rarely reach 16 feet. This community often occurs intermixed with hardwood strands along previously drowned coasts, and along the lagoonal shores of barrier islands.
Scrub or Dwarf Forests:	Restricted to the area of Florida Bay, particularly near Cape Sable, and parts of the Ten Thousand Islands in Florida. Elsewhere in the Gulf of Mexico found primarily as frost-sensitive assemblages along northern Gulf lagoonal shorelines, and in south Texan and Mexican hypersaline lagoons. Red, black and white mangroves are usually present but rarely exceed 5 feet in height. Sometimes called a "bonsai mangrove forest," it may include trees 40 or more years old.

Source: Britton and Morton (1989); Myers and Ewel (1990); Snedaker (1989); and author's field data.

bution in the form of guano to the forest floor. All of these estuarine-based nutrients mix with upland freshwater runoff, which itself contains dissolved nutrients and other particulate organic matter. The entire richly organic soup trickles through the mangroves into the estuary, where thousands of mouths wait to sip.

Not all the energy utilized within the system comes directly from decomposition or detritus. Many animals, collectively called *grazers*, feed directly on the green leaves (insects, mangrove tree crabs, white-tailed deer). Some herbivores, like the mangrove tree snail and the coffee bean snail, scrape the microflora, including diatoms and other microalgae, from both the exposed and submerged tree roots. Other snails and hermit crabs browse on the various algae, fungi, and lichens growing on the trunks and roots.

Elsewhere, along the Yucatán coastline, for example, the mangrove systems differ dramatically from others in the Gulf. Here, where beach ridges and dune ridges form hypersaline lagoons, the mangroves are restricted to small hummocks usually consisting of a central red mangrove fringed by a hedge of black mangroves and salt-tolerant grasses. Animal species richness is reduced, with nest-building termites, tree snails, and fiddler crabs the predominant fauna partitioning the resources of this depauperate environment.

THE VIEW FROM WITHIN

The beauty and the complexity of a lush mangrove forest cannot truly be realized until one has walked, waded, or canoed through its depths. Here, in the quiet meandering tidal creeks and slowly moving backwaters, the deep green branches arc over the mirrored surface of the water, living reflections that ripple and melt one into the other. It is a quiet world, with only the distant yet incessant hum of insects mixing with the splash and gurgle of animals as they carry out their daily

Figure 29. The tangled mazes of productivity. Prop roots arc outward and aerial roots plunge downward to stake a claim in the soft muddy bottom of a tidal channel in a pristine Floridan mangrove forest. The roots provide places of attachment for some organisms and tidally-controlled dining areas for others. The nearly continual leaf fall from the surrounding trees will be actively worked over by life forms ranging from bacteria and fungi to snails, crabs, and fishes. The tannic acid leached from the dead leaves and detritus makes a nutrient-enriched tea that the turbid tidal waters and runoff from adjacent uplands will eventually carry out into the estuary.

incursions into the swamp (see Figure 29).

Yet in this quiet and apparently deserted forest, the great and continuing struggle of life is played out at one time or another by more than 100 species of larger invertebrates, 220 species of fishes, over 20 kinds of reptiles, at least 5 amphibian species, at least 200 species of birds[2] and some 20 mammals. These are probably conservative numbers.

A simple walk through a mangrove forest at low tide can reveal much to the casual observer. Along the tangled buttresses and ropy aerial roots evidence of animal life is abundant. Mangrove tree snails crawl slowly upward along the branches and twigs. In the still-liquid mud small groups of coffee bean snails wheel and circle as they graze on the dead leaves and litter carpeting the forest floor. Mud snails, seeking the injured and the newly dead, plow slowly along, tapping their sensitive siphons from side to side, like tiny blind men wielding their canes.

On the seaward red mangroves, out near the tidal channels, oysters grow in shelly layers from the highest water levels downward, sharing their prop-root homes with three species of barnacles. The swaying, woody aerial roots sometimes look frayed and chewed where a tiny isopod crustacean, looking very much like its common garden relative, the pillbug (also a crustacean), has hollowed out its home. Beneath the surface, waving gently in the quiet tea-brown waters, are numerous species of green and red algae, growing thickly on the roots and forming seemingly impenetrable mats along the tree trunks.

Small, green-striped hermit crabs ponderously portage their borrowed shells across the mud and around the pneumatophores. Other hermit crab species, bearing the tricolours of France on the tips of their legs, hobble and bump their way along the algal mats, searching for their lilliputian prey.

Stop and listen. That popping and snapping sound is made by pistol shrimp inhabiting the hundreds of burrows that speckle the muddy forest floor. Louder and more pervasive is the crackling and crunching sound of mangrove mud crabs dining on a continually movable feast of small snails and microcrustaceans. From overhead, the scuttling rustle of mangrove tree crabs sifts down as these truly arboreal crustaceans make their way up and down the trunk feeding on insects and the green mangrove leaves. Nearer the tree bases their mangrove wharf crab relatives share their provisions with each other and an ivory and orange-clawed land hermit crab.

A flash of red and orange in a burrow indicates another large mangrove crab, this one a true dweller on the mud. Its gaily colored *carapace* provides a startling contrast to the grays, browns, and blacks of its benthic habitat. Another movement, and a large brilliantly purple and blue land crab emerges, holding its gigantic claw like a shield in front of it. And underfoot, scurrying from hole to hole and constantly waving, waving, waving, the fiddler crabs party throughout the long day of tidal exposure, converting the slick, smooth, muddy surface into thousands of miniature pellet piles as they sort over the contained diatoms and other microflora.

Small, lithe, brown or green lizards sun themselves on the higher limbs or jump and chase each other up and down the trunk. Tiny green and brown tree frogs cling to the bark and peep and croak at the great golden orb-weaver spiders spinning their silken circles in preparation for their own twilight feasting. In the tea-stain shallows below, turtles paddle clumsily past alligators and warily eye water snakes that lie coiled and silent, with glittering eyes, awaiting their prey. Sunken among the prop roots, only his head showing, a dusky brownish mangrove snake bides his time, waiting patiently for the swirling tide to provide opportunities for another meal.

Where the trees and their roots remain submerged many fish hide. Schools of shiners, minnows, and killifish cluster and bump into each other, ready to break and run at a moment's notice. Pinfish, porgies, and mojarras dart nervously among the algal clumps while sheepshead browse on the fouling community. Gray and lane snappers move silently among the roots, sampling the slow and unlucky, both fish and invertebrates alike. Lurking deeper in the shadows and under fallen snags and rotting trunks are the silvery ghosts of snook, ladyfish, young barracuda, and tarpon. The abundant foraging fishes as well as blue crabs, shrimp, and other errant fauna constitute their prey.

Birds are strangely absent in the deep, shadowed interiors of the forest, although the hoarse chuckling call of the mangrove cuckoo can occasionally be heard. But along the tidal channels and the open bay margins it is another matter indeed. Here, prowling along the forest margins and estuarine shorelines, the wading birds—the herons, bitterns, ibises, and their relatives—probe and poke for their food, while the spoonbills carve the shallows into semicircles of foam. At day's end they will retire to their rookeries in the higher branches of the forest, joining the pelicans, cormorants, fish crows, and frigate birds already roosting or nesting there.

High overhead fish hawks and bald eagles mount an aerial patrol, riding the atmospheric gyres and searching for finned, feathered, or furry prey. Red-shouldered hawks scream imprecations from the treetops, while the vultures hunch quietly on dead limbs, waiting with the patience of undertakers for the inevitable remnants at the wake.

With the coming of twilight the mammals begin to line up at this stilt-legged smorgasbord. Raccoons lumber down to water's edge to snack on layers of coon oysters. Opossums creep among the tangled roots feeding on leftovers and whatever small prey they can find. Cotton rats forage among the leaf litter, stopping nervously and listening from time to time for the dreaded and deadly quiet footfall of the bobcat. Nearly submerged in a tidal channel an alligator takes it all in; she has seen it all before and knows her opportunities well.

And in the sporadic pools left by the retreating tide, strange, nearly microscopic, large-headed larvae gyrate and twist in rapid back-flips from the water's surface to the muddy floor and back. Their time of metamorphosis is near. Soon, with the descent of night, the petulantly insistent whine of saltmarsh mosquitoes will once again fill the air, a thousand times a thousand trilling aerial violins singing a song of warmth and blood and life.

MANGROVES AND MAN: A CONTINUING BATTLE

In spite of the acknowledged benefits that mangroves have for the estuarine systems in the Gulf, they are still little appreciated by many people. Too often this is a consequence of misunderstanding, lack of education, or outright and careless arrogance. Yet mangrove swamps are anything but wasteland; indeed, we are beginning to realize that mangroves, as a functioning part of an estuarine system, are among the most important habitats on earth.

In addition to their ecological value, mangroves and mangrove "swamps" as they are so pejoratively called, have been increasingly shown to benefit humans in numerous ways. First, the trees, their prop roots, and pneumatophores trap, hold, and stabilize sediments. Moreover, by collecting dead shelly material and other organic debris among the root system they aid in dispersing wave energy over a wider area of shoreline. Thus they act as natural seawalls in areas where shoreline erosion might prove detrimental to residential or commercial development.

Second, mangrove forests have a decided value in storm protection. Although even the best-developed mangrove forest cannot withstand the onslaught of a major hurricane, they still can mitigate flooding and wave damage. The amount of protection offered is a function of the width of the existing forest (the wider the better) and the direction and force of the storms.

Third, mangroves have a definite value to sport and commercial fisheries. Nearly every shallow-water, commercially valuable sport or game fish utilizes the mangrove-seagrass ecosystem in one way or another, whether it be as a foraging or breeding ground, or as a nursery area for their young. Commercial fisheries of oysters, blue crabs, stone crabs, pink shrimp, spiny lobsters, and numerous commercial and sport finfish, including mullet, menhaden, redfish, snapper, sea trout, snook, and even the naturally reef-dwelling jewfish and groupers, all depend on the mangrove-seagrass ecosystems for their health.

Fourth, mangrove ecosystems are critically important as habitat for native wildlife. A recent tabulation of species associated with or living within mangrove areas listed nearly 550 species of vertebrates. The invertebrate fauna has never been completely tallied, but indications suggest well over 200 species divided among sponges, cnidarians, various "worms," molluscs, crustaceans, and echinoderms. The total number of microflora and microbes is unknown.

Fifth, mangrove systems are of great importance to at least 12 endangered and three threatened species. Included among these are the American crocodile, hawksbill and Kemp's Ridley sea turtles, Florida manatee, bald eagle, peregrine falcon, Key deer, Florida panther, Barbados yellow warbler, and Atlantic saltmarsh and eastern indigo snakes. Species not presently threatened but which are partially or totally habitat-dependent on mangroves include numerous invertebrates (mangrove tree crab, red mangrove crab, mangrove tree snail, ladderform cerith snail), at least one species of mangrove water snake, and the mangrove cuckoo.

Sixth, contrary to the image all-too-often proffered by some people, mangroves do have an aesthetic value. This value is quickly translatable into dollars, whether it be an adjunct to real estate sales where the uninterrupted forests provide pleasing vistas for the homeowner, or to the local sport fishermen or pleasure boater who wends his way down a meandering mangrove-lined tidal channel, or the natural history buff who visits the swamps in the hopes of adding to her life list of birds, or even the winter visitor or tourist who just wants to see what a mangrove swamp is all about.

Seventh, mangroves have been recently shown to have value in assimilating wastewater nutrients, not only from municipal sewage plant discharges, but also from everyday urban runoff.

Finally, mangrove forests have provided valuable economic products. The charcoal industry once flourished in Florida using black mangrove and buttonwood to produce the fuel. Today, black mangrove flowers contribute directly to the Florida honey industry, presently valued at nearly $3.5 million dollars per year.

The values accruing from these benefits, however, are too often decreased or negated by the destruction of mangrove forests. Of the approximately 460,000 acres of mangroves remaining in Florida, nearly 90% occur in the four southernmost counties, where some 20,000 or more acres have been destroyed. Fortunately, much of the remaining acreage is either undevelopable (owing to state laws), inaccessible (Ten Thousand Islands area), or owned or held by government or private agencies (National Park Service, National Audubon Society). Unfortunately, elsewhere in the Gulf, legislation is weak or nonexistent. The mangrove forests of Cuba and the strands and hummocks of Yucatán and the lower Mexican coast are presently unprotected. The ramifications their removal may have for shore stability and ecosystem alteration remain largely unknown at present.[3]

Salt Marsh Communities

RIDING THE TIDAL COMMUTER

S ALT MARSH. The very words conjure up desolate vistas of rushes and cordgrasses spreading away to the horizon while a cold winter wind soughs and sighs across the land. Remembering our Old World traditions, we tend to think of marshlands as heaths or bogs, in the British sense, and thus we envision them as wastelands filled with muck, mud, and cold sea fogs—places to be seen from a distance, and certainly no place in which to be stranded, or worse, lost.

This picture is pretty close to the truth, at least insofar as a general view of any marshlands will reveal. But marshlands are like a distantly viewed oil painting filled with somber grays, greens, and browns. The smaller, brighter details can only be seen upon close approach. Close up, a marsh reveals secrets that, at best, could only be suspected from a distance.

Consider the tidal channels. An observer looking over a typical marsh sees these meandering narrow pathways crisscrossing the great expanses of grassland. A closer look and the channels become stratified waterways, bordered by rushes and grasses at their upper levels, pockmarked with burrows and cavities at their midlines, and carrying the gray, sluggish, tidal waters at their bottoms.

These tidal channels are Nature's own irrigation ditches. In them the salt water from the sea, now diluted and mixed by the freshwater runoff from the uplands, is carried up into the high marsh and then back out through the low marsh on every tidal cycle. And, like a system of highways, the periodically flooded tidal channels carry both detritus and a mobile epifauna, the commerce and the commuters of the salt marsh; they arrive with the incoming tide and depart with it as it drains.

A question that immediately springs to mind is: Why would estuarine animals travel inland? The answer, of course, is the simple dichotomy stipulated by Nature: to feed and to breed. Like some neritic regions above the continental shelf, salt marshes are areas of high *primary production*, where large amounts of living tissue are produced each day. However, unlike the neritic regions, where the major producers are the phytoplankton in the water column, in a salt marsh the benthic vegetation assumes this role. Here, production comes from the very grasses, rushes, sedges, and attached and drifting algae that comprise most of what a casual observer sees when viewing the system. Production also comes from the diatoms and other microorganisms that the viewer doesn't see.

195

All produce detritus and larger particulate organic matter, up to 98% of which is exported to the estuary. There, a very large group of invertebrate and vertebrate organisms finds this exported material nutritionally quite attractive.

THE VEGETATIVE CONNECTION

If estuaries are the places where the rivers meet the sea, then salt marshes can be characterized as the meeting places for freshwater and marine biota. Because many salt marsh organisms cannot escape the changing salinities brought about by incoming tides, they have no other alternative but to adapt. Consequently, physiological abilities to tolerate drastic changes in salinity are often highly developed in salt marsh plants and animals. In addition, salt marsh organisms also tend to show greater temperature tolerances, as well as the ability to adapt to a number of other changing variables, including pH, dissolved oxygen, light, water turbidity, and the like.

Marshes are essentially fields of reeds, rushes, and grasses laced with natural irrigation canals. The most common salt marsh plants are spikerush (*Juncus*), saltmarsh cordgrass (*Spartina*), saltgrass (*Distichlis*) and four or five other species of reeds and rushes that often intermix with the first three. Regional marshes often support characteristically dominant vegetation: cattails and bullrushes in the secondary bays of Texas, cordgrasses and spikerushes in the Gulf-front Louisiana and Florida marshes, and glassworts and saltworts in the hypersaline lagunas.These plants are able to exist in an area where the soils are salt-saturated, oxygen-deficient, low-lying, and periodically inundated. They thus avoid competition from those plants that cannot tolerate these adverse conditions. An immediately noticeable consequence is that in a typical salt marsh there is often a uniformity of plant species, with thousands of individuals occurring across a broad coastal band (see Plate 11A).

But marshes are rarely isolated. Instead, they almost always intergrade into another ecosystem, whether it be upland into the freshwater coastal zone, or downshore and into the estuary itself. In fact, the chief difference between a freshwater marsh and a salt marsh is the proximity and accessibility of the sea. Over a normal period, estimated to take about 1,000 years, a freshwater marsh can be transformed into salt marsh by seawater influx.

Along the Gulf of Mexico salt marshes in the south may intergrade seaward with mangrove forests (Florida, Mexico), or may actually replace mangroves in more northern latitudes. Salt marshes can also form waterside vegetational complexes on the back of barrier islands (Louisiana), on delta channels and bayous (Mississippi), or actually wade out into the estuary as small islets of marsh grass and rushes (Mississipi, Texas, Mexico). Their physiographic distribution often rivals their vegetational complexity.

Progressing landward, salt marshes may be replaced by fresh water marshes (Louisiana, Mississippi), coastal hardwood hammocks (Florida, Mexico), rainforest (Mexico), salt pans and desert areas (Texas, Mexico), or grassy meadows and coastal plains (Mississippi, Louisiana). However or wherever they occur, salt marshes are the interface between one vegetational system and another, and between one hydrological regime (the marine and estuarine) and another (the estuarine and fresh water).

Broadly speaking, the vegetational distribution of salt marshes is mostly a result of tidal zonation. In general, salt marshes can be divided into two main zones: the low zone, where the land is flooded by more than 360 tidal inundations each year; and the high zone, where less than 360 inundations occur per year. Within these two zones are further subdivisions. Marshland biologists now recognize the *high marsh*, an area nearly completely removed from tidal influences; the *mid marsh*, an area reached by all spring tides; and finally the *low marsh*, which is inundated by spring and high neap tides. Needless to say, the distribution of both freshwater and saltwater plants and animals is critically affected by the number, extent, and duration of such floodings. At the opposite end of the salinity scale, the amounts and timing of freshwater input also determine the vertical distribution of the flora and fauna *(zonation of the biota)* throughout the marsh. Thus, in one sense, salt marshes can be thought of as merely drier estuaries, but ones in which zonation is not so much influenced by *total* inudations as by *periodic* flooding.

WHERE DO THEY COME FROM? WHERE DO THEY GO?

It may be surprising to learn that salt marshes are not old features along a shoreline. Most tidal marshes can measure their life span in thousands of years at most. Thus, compared to ancient rocky shores and coral reefs whose ages are often measured in hundreds of thousands or even millions of years, salt marshes are relatively young. Many marshy areas have undergone so many periodic, long-term flooding and emergences as sea levels rose and fell that their ages, let alone their existence, are discontinuous. Still others have had long, albeit intermittent, associations with drowned river valleys. In these places the new marsh is growing on the peat foundations of its ancestor but may have experienced a hiatus of thousands of years between its earlier state and the one that exists today.

Much of the subsidence of coastal land is a result of the weight of sediments deposited by rivers. Around the Gulf, land subsidence caused by sediment loading may be as much as 1 centimeter (about 0.4 inches) per year. As the land slowly sinks, the sea transgresses farther inland, providing conditions that eventually can lead to formation of a salt marsh. This subsidence is therefore partially responsible for all that will eventually transpire in the marsh, as well as for the eventual change in conditions from fresh to saline.

A good example of such fluctuations is the Mississippi River marshlands. This mighty river is responsible for at least 40% of all the coastal wetlands in the United States. The Mississippi delta fan, with its millions of cubic yards of sediment deposits, has been the birthing place for many of these wetlands. And the cemetery for many more. As the fan continues to expand outward and into the deeper Gulf, it causes these same wetlands to become permanently flooded (refer again to Figure 20).

SALT MARSH PRODUCTIVITY: FOOD OF MANY KINDS IN MANY PLACES

One important consequence of this interpositioning between purely marine and purely freshwater zones is that salt marshes are the recipients of freshwater flow, with its concomitant land-borne sediments and nutrients. And because salt marshes are almost invariably adjacent to terrestrial uplands or freshwater wetlands, the nutrient flux between these biotopes also invariably proceeds down the gradient seaward—that is, toward the estuary. There, the upland sediments and nutrients mix with seawater and its contained sediments and nutrients. The end result is an area of extremely high biological productivity, among the highest (along with sea grasses) of any ecosystem on earth. Productivity of a salt marsh is comparable to, or actually can outweigh, that of agriculturally-tilled lands, resulting in a *biomass* (the total weight of dry tissue) that exceeds five tons per acre on an annual basis. Only cultivated sugar cane lands exceed salt marshes in the production of organic nutrients.

Because of their complex ecological interactions and the various food webs that exist within their milieu, salt marshes are one of the most valuable biological resources in any coastal zone of the world. This value is reflected in the commercial and sport fisheries they support; the recreational, educational, and aesthetic aspects associated with marsh wildlife; and the numerous "free" services that marshes provide. For example, nearly all of the commercial finfish and invertebrate fisheries in the northern Gulf are built on marshland ecosystems. Either the larval and postlarval (subadult) stages of these animals use the marshes as a nursery ground, or the adults use the marshlands as feeding and breeding areas. Recent studies have shown that it is the area of marsh in the shrimp nurseries that determines the quantities of shrimp caught, and not the size of the estuary or offshore fishing grounds. Salt marshes thus share in productive importance with sea grasses and mangroves in more southerly regions.

It is also necessary to consider the many physical services marshes provide, including sediment entrapment, purification of overland runoff, storm surge buffer zones, and dry season reservoirs—all factors that are beneficial to humans as well as to marshland wildlife.

DEPRODUCTIVITY: A HUMAN SPECIALITY

It has been estimated that salt marshes and associated wetlands are disappearing at a rate of about 0.5% per year. This translates into over a million acres already lost, and another million acres ready to go by the year 2000. The litany is long, persistent, and dismayingly familiar. We are destroying our wetlands with a profligacy unmatched in any previous century.

The problem is nowhere better illustrated than in Louisiana, a state containing 41% of the nation's total coastal wetlands, and where nearly 16% of its total area is coastal marsh. Each year, from 40 to 60 square miles of marshland disappear owing to a multitude of natural and man-made impacts. To date nearly three quarters of a million acres of wetlands have been sacrificed to residential, agricultural and industrial development. When coupled with previous losses of over half a million acres caused by subsidence, sea-level rise, barrier island degradation, and river delta configurational changes, the amount of land forever gone becomes truly alarming. The U.S. Army Corps of Engineers estimates that by the year 2040, just 50 years from now, an area larger than the state of Rhode Island will have disappeared from Louisiana's coastal margin.

Even supposedly simple and beneficial modifications, such as levee construction to contain the Mississippi River, produce a net wetland loss of over 10,000 acres per year. For example, oil-barge and oil-well access channels in the Calcasieu Basin in Louisiana have allowed more saline Gulf waters to move into previously fresh or slightly brackish water areas. The result has been loss of critical vegetation, particularly those species that stabilize marsh banks and prevent erosion.

The outlook is not good, yet it is also not all bad. One consequence of riverine sediment deposition is that the Atchafalaya Delta has already created 10,000 acres of land. By the year 2030, if depositional rates do not change, over 80 square miles of land are projected to be created, most of which will be marshlands. It is doubtful, however, that this natural "mitigation" will be sufficient to offset the continuing losses elsewhere.

Nor is Louisiana alone in its problems. In Texas, blockage of sediments to the Sabine River estuary by hydrological power dams has not only accelerated wetland loss but has altered the migratory patterns of shrimp into the estuary. In Florida, loss of marshes and other wetlands has been blamed for the decline of several sport fisheries. And development continues mostly unimpeded.

The paradox of deproductivity, however, is that wetland values rarely, if ever, accrue directly to the owner of marshland. Rather, the commercial fisherman, the oysterman, the ornithologist, the amateur birder, and the combined human populations in areas miles away and downstream are the direct recipients, even though no actual monies are exchanged. And although an undisturbed marshland remains a continually renewable resource, it usually generates little or no revenue by itself; yet the downstream revenue from a marsh turned into a real estate development is irretrievably lost.

A WALK ON THE WILD SIDE

To be a member in good standing of the salt marsh community, the species must be able to withstand stress. Stress comes in a variety of guises and challenges the organism's ability to regulate internal salinity, temperature, oxygen dependency, hydrogen-ion concentrations (pH), desiccation (drying-out), insolation (exposure to the sun), and several other physical or physiological factors. Thus, as noted earlier, we may expect saltmarsh species to adhere to the dictates of estuarine living: abide, hide, or ride the tide (see Figure 30).

Salt marshes are not only grassy and reedy areas; they are muddy areas as well. Thus, the animals that would walk or crawl or swim in a salt marsh must be able to tolerate muddy-water and muddy-bottom situations. Let's begin our journey inland by stopping on a typical sandy-muddy beach fronting a salt marsh and opening onto an estuary.

Figure 30. Awaiting the tidal commuter.
A large white egret stalks fishes and invertebrates along a tidal channel in Louisiana's Rockefeller Wildlife Refuge east of Cameron. Wading birds share the apex of saltmarsh food webs with several other predators, including raptors such as hawks, ospreys, and eagles, reptiles like alligators and crocodiles, and carnivorous terrestrial mammals such as bobcats, panthers, bears, and raccoons—and even, eventually, with mankind. [Courtesy of Jennifer Felder]

Around our feet, in phalanxes of hundreds if not thousands, are fiddler crabs (see Plate 11). These small crustaceans dig burrows above the tidemark but follow the tide downshore to feed on the stranded diatoms and other detritus. Temporary burrows may be constructed—vacation holes, if you will—which function as refugia when the numerous shorebirds and wading birds come calling. They can also function as boudoirs for the seemingly perpetually amorous males who, by waving their "fiddling" claw, seek to attract females into the hole for mating.

Fiddler crabs give new meaning to the old adage of "between the devil and the deep blue sea" because they form a mobile but very desirable food item for a number of vertebrates. Raccoons and many species of wading birds find them a tasty addition to their fish-filled diet. And the water is no sanctuary either. Crabs that wade too far out into the estuary to escape being eaten by wetland birds may be picked off by any of several species of estuarine predatory fishes. Even blue crabs have no compunctions about dining on their semiterrestrial, big-clawed relatives. Most of the true marsh fish fauna, however, consists of killifish, sailfin mollies, minnows, and other small fish, so only the juveniles and the smallest of adult fiddlers are at risk.

Farther up on shore, crawling through the wrack and debris of the weedline, several species of square-bodied, small-clawed wharf crabs pick over the organic litter, eating the best and discarding the rest. Just offshore, juvenile blue crabs scuttle across the bottom searching for small polychaete worms and carelessly slow fish. The horseshoe (or king) crab is also seen, bulldozing through the substrate just as it has done for 300 million years, seeking the clams and other buried sea life that form its prey.[1] Occasionally, a daisy-chain of a large female with two or more smaller males blunders by, all intent on a single purpose: reproduction.

Still farther offshore, glass and grass shrimp fidget and dance across the bottom, waiting for the tide to carry them farther up into the marsh and their feeding grounds. Here they will partition the environment, one species feeding near the bottom, another higher up in the tidal channels. The bits and pieces of partially decayed marsh-plant matter form much of their food, but they are not adverse to taking living material if the opportunity arises. Amphipods and isopods beware! But the shrimp must eat quickly, for there is but one tidal commuter train that will return them to the estuary, and it is almost always on time. Missing it means stranding—and death.

The grass and glass shrimp will be joined on the incoming tide by male blue crabs hurrying to join the females already waiting in the far upland brackish and freshwater tributaries.[2] They, too, have reproduction on the mind. The male will remain in low-salinity waters, an intermittent bachelor as is his wont, while the female waits for the tens of thousands of eggs she has deposited under her abdomen to ripen. In only a few weeks she will return downstream to the mouth of the estuary, and there shake the fully developed eggs loose from her abdomen. In a few short seconds some thousands will hatch into a cloud of microscopic, swimming larvae called *zoeae*, that will be carried out to sea to find their destiny in the offshore plankton. The young that survive will return one day, riding the tidal currents back home into the estuary where they will live for a while, until hormones and seasons say it is time to swim again upstream.

Small gray mud snails plow meandering furrows in the flocculent mud, searching for detritus and decay. Buried beneath them several families of clams poke their siphons up through the sticky, black sediments, sampling the incoming waters for plankton. Nearby, like children practicing gymnastics, oysters have built a large and unsteady clump. They gape slightly, filter-feed briefly, and then snap shut, with irascible spits and spurts of tidal water. When the tide ebbs, the oysters will shut down completely, even going so far as to slow their respiration and shift into an anaerobic mode using only the oxygen in their tissues.

Around the oyster bases small mud crabs play, sparring and jousting while they attempt to catch the many small green polychaete worms living among the shelly interstices. Over the edge of the oyster bar several dark brown snails appear, materializing like Indians on a ragged western ridge top. The oyster drills and rock shells have arrived and come to demand their due. Many of the younger, thin-shelled oysters will soon feel their feeding sting. But the colony will survive.

Along the edge of the beach and inland, the marsh grasses grow, forming tufts and thickets of spiky greenish-gray and brown blades. From a distance the cordgrasses and black rushes look like perpetually frozen explosions of vegetation. Scattered in crackly green mats, saltwort and glasswort spread across the areas disdained by the grasses and rushes. The worts taste almost briny, revealing their physiological mechanisms that concentrate internal salts for excretion via specialized glands in the rhizomes and leaves.

This saltiness is of no concern to the small gray marsh periwinkles. These snails will spend the duration of the incoming tidal cycle in a type of hibernation, clinging in militarily precise rows on the blades of the rushes (see Plate 11). As soon as the tide changes and the last of the ebbing waters have drained away in rivulets at the plant base, they will revive and begin their slow, probing journey down to the marsh floor. Here they will join the numerous other animals taking advantage of the cornucopia spilled by the departing waters. Primarily herbivores, they search for algae on the rocks, driftwood, and debris lodged in the mud.

Ask any hunter about marshes and he will tell you about wildfowl. Marshes are well known as habitat for mergansers, wigeons, and other ducks, brant, and geese. But other birds find habitat and home here as well. Redwings, sparrows, wrens, and warblers flit among the cordgrass tufts, some staying to build nests and raise families. Wading birds stalk their fish, frog, and crawfish prey along the shorelines, leaving three-toed tracks as their calling cards. Several species of hawks range over high and low marsh, seeking small rodents, reptiles, or birds. Larger raptors such as the osprey and bald eagle sample the offshore fish population. They too must follow the tidal commuters, if primarily from a distance.

Several species of mud-dwelling turtles can be found in the tidal channels and wandering among the reeds. The diamondback terrapin is among the most common. Other reptiles are neither so common nor so harmless. Cottonmouth moccasins visit, searching for unwary fish. And even alligators are found from time to time.

The mammals are not to be left out, either. Raccoons going oystering leave their tiny hand- and foot-prints in the mud, arriving and leaving with the tide. Nutria, a South American rodent immigrant, and muskrats move less than quietly among the grassy tussocks. Bobcats prowl the upland edges looking for them and the numerous other rodents and rabbits that commute into the marsh on falling tides. Gray foxes often leave their upland dens to make periodic forays into the marshlands. Otters and mink slip through the reeds in search of their prey, and even black bears and panthers may occasionally roam into the near edges of the marsh.

And above all, always above all, comes the sound of insects: the keening of mosquitoes, the rasping buzz of horseflies and blackflies, the swift and certain whine of deerflies. Even worse are the silent, tiny sand flies or "no-see-ums," an insect that is guaranteed to make marsh-walking an exercise in tribulation and penance, no matter what the mammal, bird, or reptile. All these insects are searching for blood; nearly all will find it in one animal or another.

As the tide withdraws and twilight approaches, the lethargy and solitude of the seemingly dormant marshlands drains away with the waning afternoon. Birds flutter and call from among the reeds; others croak noisily along the shore. High overhead a gaggle of geese, searching for overnight accommodations, breaks V-formation to circle warily before splashing down heavily in the open water ponds. A bevy of wood ducks, angry at the disturbances, quacks and complains noisily before settling down again to feed. Fish crows sprinkle themselves across the reddening sunset like drops of ink, caw-awing to one another about the upcoming night. Swallows peep and chirp incessantly as they settle in for the evening. A group of wrens scolds an approaching water snake with marsh sparrow omelet on his mind. The noise soon draws the attention of a solitary osprey circling on hunger-patrol, and she swoops in for a closer look.

Onshore, the great pinkish gray legions of fiddler crabs have emerged again from their sandy burrows and roam in huge chitinous waves across the exposed tidal flats, feeding between the times they are being fed upon. Isolated pools, left partially drained by the tide, smack and splash as minnows and killifish pop at the evening-active insects.

From a dead snag a marsh hawk glares down on his domain searching for the timorous field mice squeaking and chittering among the rushes. The marsh grows silent; now is the time of the carnivore—owls from above, bobcats from without, snakes from within. As twilight turns into evening, a harvest moon rises bright yellow-orange in the east, hanging like a Japanese lantern on a hook of dark cloud. Far, far above in the darkness a lone nighthawk ascends ever upward, his high-pitched feeding cry echoing across the dark sky, reverberating down the star-studded corridors of night toward the far horizon.

Freshwater Communities

LIVING ON A SALT-RESTRICTED DIET

FRESHWATER WETLANDS share many of the vegetational and physiographic characteristics of salt marshes, except that salty soils and salt waters are only occasionally a problem. Most freshwater wetlands are found well above the highest tidemark, and if they receive any saltwater influence it is only through storm tides or the very highest of spring tides.

Even so, freshwater wetlands are not completely isolated from saltwater wetlands. Often, the freshwater wetland is the transitional area between the relatively dry terrestrial uplands and the lowlying coastal lands. Fresh water seeping or flowing into these bogs, freshwater marshes, swamps, and savannahs often overflows to run further downgradient and eventually mix with the brackish or saline waters of saltmarshes, mangroves, salinas, and barrier island lagoons (refer again to Plate 8).

Vegetation in freshwater wetlands has lost (or never gained) the ability to excrete excess salt; indeed, if salty waters do intrude (for example, during hurricane or other storm surges), most of these plants suffer severe trauma or are killed outright. Hence, freshwater vegetational systems are literally on a salt-free diet. In contrast, saltmarsh vegetation can not only excrete excess salt via their roots directly into the soil, but can also withstand repeated exposures to fresh waters. Consequently, one often sees "typical" saltwater wetland vegetation (mangroves, cordgrasses, black rush, glassworts) mixed in with the "typical" freshwater wetland species of sedges, bullrushes, cattails, sawgrasses, southern wild rice and maidencane.

Another immediately noticeable feature of most freshwater wetlands—and one lacking in saltwater wetlands—is the large number of floating and emergent plants. These include arrowhead, pickerelweed, water lilies, alligator flag, and several open-pond submerged grasses. Trees and large woody shrubs, never a prominent feature within salt marshes (unless they be mangroves), also grow scattered throughout freshwater wetlands. Carolina willow, pop ash, pond apple, swamp bay, tupelo, and cypress are able to exist, often in numbers sufficient to categorize the wetland by their presence (willow head, cypress swamp, pond apple slough, bay head) (see Figure 31).

PROBLEMS IN FRESHWATER LIVING

The invertebrates living in fresh water differ from their marine counterparts in three main features: (1) they are subject to a nearly continuous inflow of fresh

Figure 31. A forest under water.
Majestic and venerable in its towering silence and cloaking of Spanish moss, a cypress and mixed hardwood swamp rises around its central freshwater pond in Florida. Wet forests such as these that are periodically or constantly inundated by freshwater inflow occur around the Gulf from Mexico to Florida. Differing mainly in the species of trees found within them, these swamps may support hundreds of species of plants and vertebrate animals, and probably thousands of species of invertebrates. Temperate zone swamps, such as those in Louisiana, may show less diversity but exhibit taller and older trees. Once considered as just so much worthless land to be filled by developers, freshwater swamps are being increasingly recognized for what they really are, complex vegetational assemblages rich both in species and aesthetic beauty.

water into their bodies, requiring constant excretion of dilute urine; (2) their eggs are usually large and few; and (3) their larvae, if any, develop rapidly in situ and do not enter the plankton. In fact, many freshwater invertebrates (e.g., crawfish) bypass the usual planktonic, develomental stages seen in their marine relatives, and produce instead young that resemble, in miniature, their parents. Others (e.g., freshwater clams and snails) pass their equivalent planktonic stage within a miniaturized "ocean," while still safely ensconced inside the egg. These features are all adaptations that have taken place over thousands, if not millions, of years as the freshwater species gradually severed their evolutionary ties with their saltwater ancestors.

Even though maintenance of internal salts and water concentrations is a continuing problem for both freshwater and marine aquatic forms, the problems associated with the process, known as osmoregulation, are neatly sidestepped by many species, particularly those that are semiterrestrial or terrestrial. These species have, in effect, exchanged a permeable body covering (and thus one subject to "swelling" or "leakage") for one relatively or completely impermeable. By containing internal fluids at a specific or only slightly variable concentration of salinity, they are able to cut the ties to both the marine and freshwater environments. These terrestrial forms and many aquatic species compose the fauna associated with freshwater wetlands.

THE FAUNA OF FRESHWATER WETLANDS

Sweep a dip net through a freshwater marsh or pond and the immediate impression the observer gets is a multitude of "buglike" forms. And indeed, on close examination, the majority of animals prove to be either insects or crustaceans. However, some other phyla are also abundant; but because most of these forms are extremely small or microscopic they are rarely seen by the layperson. Yet just a hand-held magnifying glass quickly reveals these species and their microcosm when a sample of pond water is poured into a dish.

Here are the rotifers, tiny "wheel animalcules," spinning through the water and then landing on their almost prehensile "foot." There, a long, transparent horsehair worm whips itself across the bowl. Tiny clam shrimp furiously pedal their way along the glassy bottom. Bright red water mites, looking like tiny swimming spiders, gyrate here, there, and everywhere.

Larger animals are, of course, more easily noticeable. The vertebrates are better represented and certainly better seen in fresh waters. Many fishes, nearly all amphibians, and several groups of reptiles are strictly freshwater-dwellers. Certain birds and mammals are also solely freshwater-associating or -dwelling species. It is a curious fact, in spite of this, that even though colonization of fresh waters probably began over 300 million years ago, the total number of freshwater species is still several orders of magnitude smaller than marine and estuarine groups.

As might be expected, the faunal communities living in freshwater wetlands are determined in part by the overall vegetational characteristic of the wetland itself. Redwing blackbirds, for example, prefer open freshwater marshes and savannahs, where the brilliant red "shoulder patch" of the male flashes against the green rushes. Here their repetitive "conkla-reee!" emanates from the reeds and cattails along shore. They are almost never seen in cypress swamps or willow heads.

On the other hand, cardinals, vireos, and flycatchers are birds of both dry and inundated forests, but are uncommon on the more open canebrakes of the savannahs. Their chatter and chirping on a summer morning can rouse the soundest sleeper. Yet, like their redwing relatives, they are where they are because food—and cover—play such an important role in their lives.

Other species seem less selective about habitat but more selective about food. Herons, egrets, and ibises, for example, stalk their prey in shallow waters, fresh or saline. These long-legged, long-billed predators are not only birds of the open seagrass beds, marshes, and mangrove shores, but can also be found in old-growth cypress swamps. Because their food items are abundant in either area (fish and crabs or fish and frogs), and because the birds have less need for cover, they can utilize the best of both worlds.

As anyone will tell you who has spent a night in the swamps listening to the Batrachian Serenade in Croak-sharp Major, much of the smaller fauna in freshwater wetlands belongs to the amphibians, the frogs and toads. These ancient animals (along with the salamanders) were among the first to permanently forsake the sea and take up a terrestrial and freshwater existence. Frogs and toads are widely distributed in all types of freshwater habitats, but they remain dependent on availability of their insect food as well as the continuing existence of freshwater or damp environments.

By day they are shy and retiring. Look for them deep in the bullrushes along a savannah pond, or clinging in almost perfect camouflage-green and brown to the branches of a cypress or a mangrove. Listen for their piglike grunting as they taunt you from a sawgrass marsh. Turn over a rotting log and they leap away into the forest. Usually the only indication they are around is the liquid kerplunk! as they dive into the nearest water. Yet at night their eyes shine like glowing coals in the light reflected from a flashlight, and they seem to be everywhere, watching the nocturnal visitor to their realm like souls trapped in purgatory.

Crayfish, on the other hand, can live in savannahs, freshwater marshes, or even cypress swamps—anyplace where the bottom sediments are adequate for feeding, burrowing, and reproducing. Look for them scooting across muddy bottoms, darting among the flocculent green algae and leaving a "smoke screen" of disturbed sediments and debris in their wake. They are more nocturnal (night-living) than diurnal (day-lovers) but can almost always be found in clean, clear waters, particularly if rocks and other shelter are abundant.

Living in shallow ponds and ditches is not without its dangers, particularly for the very edible. Crayfish must constantly avoid predation from within (the fishes) and from without (birds, frogs, raccoons). They must also be ready when the dry season arrives and their ponds evaporate. If the habitat goes dry, they burrow into the substrate and plug the hole with mud, leaving a kind of muddy chimney to mark their abode. Here they *estivate* (enter a sort of suspended animation) until the waters return.

At least three species of large freshwater shrimp (sometimes called prawns) also occur in savannahs and tributarial streams. Curiously, they have retained a planktonic larva that requires the adult females to enter brackish or estuarine waters where the eggs are hatched and the larvae released. After a time in the marine plankton, the larvae metamorphose and remigrate back into fresh waters.

Although the *marine* land crabs are widely distributed in saltwater wetlands, they too remain firmly tied to the sea by virtue of their larval development in the plankton. However, all of the subtropical and tropical *terrestrial-freshwater* land crabs undergo direct development, the young hatching fully formed from the eggs, with no need to spend time in the plankton. Most freshwater land crabs are mountain-dwellers, inhabiting the dark, wet, fern-strewn interiors of Mexican cloudforests. But they often descend to the coastal savannahs via the numerous upland streams and tributaries.

Of all the terrestrial invertebrates, only the insects (the largest phylum on earth) and the nematode worms have an abundance of strictly freshwater representatives. In fact, the insects are the only phylum that is now almost totally without marine representatives. But their freshwater-loving species make up for this lack by vying with the nematodes in both number and distribution.

Whirligig beetles, looking like little black whirling dervishes on the surface of any quiet pond, are commonly seen. Related to these are the spindly-legged water striders, whose only marine cousin walks the waves far offshore. Lurking below the surface lie giant predatory water beetles, waiting to snatch fish, frog, or even other insect prey with their rapacious forelegs.

Many other insect species are partially tied to fresh waters, spending their larval life in ponds, streams, and ditches. Dragonfly larvae are major predators on freshwater invertebrates before they shed their swimsuits and take to the air. Mayflies, aptly named the Ephemera by entomologists, often emerge suddenly from fresh waters in astounding numbers. They do not feed, because their adult life is so brief—about one day—that they must concentrate solely on reproduction. And, of course, there are always the familiar mosquitoes of which all species must spend their larval stages in water, whether fresh or brackish, before emerging to complete their sanguinophilic life history on land.

VISITORS TO THE WETLANDS

While there is a fauna definitely restricted within the freshwater wetlands, there is also a large transient fauna that occurs in these areas. In fact, with the obvious exception of marine or estuarine species such as fiddler crabs and saltwater fishes, there are many species that not only visit or live in saltwater wetlands but may also be found in freshwater wetlands at one time or another during the year.

Many wildfowl, for example, can be observed on the open ponds of a salt marsh, as well as on open lakes deep within a freshwater cypress swamp. Polysaline fish such as the sheepshead minnow, sailfin molly, and mosquito fish do equally well in fresh and salt waters. Blue crabs move into fresh water to mate, eels come upstream to forage before returning to the sea to reproduce, and several small species of "saltmarsh crabs," plus at least one allegedly marine snapping shrimp, can live quite happily for varying lengths of time in fresh water.

SIMILAR SITUATIONS, DIFFERENT PROBLEMS

Yet for all their differences, freshwater wetlands still share some commonalities with their estuarine and marine counterparts. Food webs are invariably detrital-based, or depend on uptake of dissolved nutrients by freshwater algae and vascular plants or by resident microbiota. Freshwater plankton (primarily diatoms, and crustacean larvae like their marine counterparts) is a major component, as is a large and motile epifauna consisting of insects, frogs, toads and salamanders, turtles, and snakes. At the top of the aquatic food web fishes or wading birds usually dominate, with the exception of those systems where large carnivores such as alligators occur. Preying upon smaller organisms are a multitude of birds, amphibians, reptiles, and mammals, more so than in the marine environment, where the carnivorous fish species far outweigh their freshwater relatives in numbers of species and importance. Thus, what fresh waters lack in species abundance they make up for in species diversity.

Freshwater wetlands are among the most diverse and complex of all biotopes (see Plate 12). At least 13 different types of swamps, 8 types of marshlands, plus numerous variants of each associated with rivers, lakes, and springs have been categorized. East of the Mississippi nearly 50 rivers and their associated wetlands empty directly into the Gulf of Mexico, 28 of these occuring in Florida.

But many freshwater wetlands are under siege. Because they often occur adjacent to higher, drier ground, these areas are subject to development. Many developers simply fill them in, seeing a necessity to add to developable land area while eliminating a noxious "swamp." In Florida alone an estimated 56% of the state's historic wetlands have been lost to draining and filling.

A report to Florida's governor, covering the period 1985-1990, indicated that the Florida Department of Environmental Regulation issued 1,262 permits requiring creation, enhancement, or preservation of wetlands, or about two permits every three days. And these were only a third the number of all the permits authorizing dredge-and-fill activities during the same period!

ONLY GOD (AND DEVELOPERS?) CAN MAKE A TREE

President George Bush's Wetlands Policy advocates no net loss of wetlands—an admirable policy in and of itself, but one subject to numerous interpretational loopholes, not the least of which are the requisite legal consensus as to what defines a wetland, which governmental agency has highest and final protective jurisdiction, and the uncritical acceptance of a prevailing but totally mistaken mitigational notion that wetlands can be "created" to replace those destroyed.

Implicit in the euphemism "created wetlands" is the unproved idea that, by grading an area into a depression, establishing a series of topographical contours from higher ground to lower, revegetating the denuded area with marshland plants, and then filling the depression with water, one can thereby create a wetland.

This concept of "creating wetlands" has been criticized by ecologists as being too simplistic, if not downright impossible. True wetlands require decades, if not centuries, to develop. Although altered or destroyed wetland areas may, indeed, be revegetated with wetland plants, the results seem to be more cosmetic than ecologically "real."

Success is usually trumpeted by the number of observed wading birds or the species of foraging fishes that appear. This limited ecological viewpoint, focusing as it does on the higher order carnivores, fails to take into account all the hydrological, chemical, and biological factors that, over a period of tens to hundreds of years, have acted in concert to produce a viable, self-sustaining wetland. It completely overlooks the algae and lower plants that form the primary producers in such a system. Nor does it consider the thousands of microscopic and larger invertebrate species, from insect larvae to crayfish, from rotifers to snails, the multitude of "worms" in several phyla, and a host of other components (detritus, decay) that form the cogs and gears of *any* viable, complex ecosystem.[1]

Serious doubts remain as to whether such systems will actually become functioning or self-supporting wetlands, maintaining all the attendant microbial, invertebrate, and vertebrate species that normally occur within a mature ecosystem.

Add to this government bureaucratic ignorance, ineptitude, inconsistency, and insufficiency in regard to monitoring, evaluation, enforcement and ensuring adherence to stipulations, and the magnitude of the problem becomes almost overwhelming. In fact, lack of long-term monitoring and failure to take remedial action was blamed for the overall poor success of wetlands created in Florida under U.S. Army Corps of Engineers permits.

Yet the blame cannot all be placed on bureaucracies. The major problem—lack of adequate assessment of wetlands, *before* any mitigation or "creation" takes place—is neither new nor restricted to the regulatory agencies. Often, there are few or no data available for the ecological or biological requirements of "lesser" wetland species, animals or plants. Rarely do permit applications stipulate complete sets of baseline data on *all* the plants and animals, the water chemistry, hydrology, soil characteristics, and other environmental factors existing in an area to be altered. Few county and state agencies have the broadly-based expertise to foresee every problem before it occurs, recognize insufficient or outright false data, or have enough money to recruit the necessary personnel to ask the proper questions or, more importantly, obtain the complete answers. Even more rarely are complete plans submitted during the permitting process that detail how the new wetlands will be "created" or maintained in subsequent years. And, in a "robbing-Peter-to-pay-Paul" activity, many of the plants used for "creation" or mitigation of one wetland are collected or stolen from other wetlands! Finally, owing to the high cost of providing complete assessments, and the time lost in monitoring programs before the first spade of earth can be turned, most developers are content to satisfy the letter, rather than the spirit, of the law. They base their compliance goals directly on satisfying exactly and only what the environmental impact statement (EIS) or permit application requires. Thus, the regulatory agency's hands become tied to the EIS or stipulations in the permit itself.

However, more enlightened developers have begun to realize that existing freshwater wetlands can serve a variety of human needs while remaining a valuable biological, ecological, and aesthetic resource. Long-term studies by the Center for Wetlands at the University of Florida, for example, have repeatedly shown that cypress swamps and flooded prairies can function admirably as water cachement basins and even sewage scouring ponds. As coastal populations continue to grow and developable land continues to shrink, innovative uses will continue to gain importance. Freshwater wetlands, like all other wetlands, are too critical a resource to squander any more.

PONDERABLES FOR OUR FUTURE

Fact: From January 1, 1985 through December 6, 1990 the Florida Department of Environmental Regulation (FDER) issued 1,262 permits for wetland mitigation and restoration.

Fact: Some 3,345 acres of wetlands were to be "created" to compensate for the destruction of 3,305 acres.

Fact: FDER reviewed for effectiveness 63 such permits (5% of the total number of permits issued) for 119 wetland "creation" sites.

Fact: In 21 (34%) of the permits, no mitigation had been attempted.

Fact: By implication, another 38 sites were not in complete compliance with the stipulated conditions.

Fact: Of the 63 permits, only 4 (6%) were in compliance with the required mitigation!

Fact: The ecological success rate for "created" wetlands was 12% for freshwater areas and 15% for tidal areas.

Fact: In another study by the South Florida Water Management District (SFWMD) which has jurisdiction in 13 southern Florida counties, 4,439 acres of wetlands received permission for destruction since 1987.

Fact: Mitigation had been attempted in only 40% of the wetland "creation" projects.

Fact: Of the projects that had been attempted, 63% suffered from hydrological problems, including improper water levels and insufficient hydroperiods.

Fact: In 80% of the projects invasion by undesirable plant species (including the notorious melaleuca or cajeput tree, a "weed tree" introduced from Australia) was common; untreated stormwater was discharged from parking lots, industrial sites, citrus groves and residential areas directly into the other wetlands.

Fact: Only 4 projects met the goals stipulated in the SFWMD permits!

Source: S.T. Bacchus (1991). Can wetlands be successfully created? *The Palmetto*, Fall 1991, pp. 3-6.

Other Maritime Wetland Systems

EVERAL LESSER-KNOWN maritime wetland systems also occur around the Gulf of Mexico. These systems are often built on a complex infrastructure of marshes, seagrass beds, and variable inputs of fresh and highly saline water, and they are additionally influenced by arid deserts or humid montane areas lying behind the wetlands (see Figure 32).

HYPERSALINE LAGOONS

At the opposite extreme to freshwater wetlands, and possessing their own unique set of conditions and associated problems for the biota, are hypersaline lagoons. Along the arid coastlines of southern Texas and northern Mexico occurs a great barrier island system. The low, sandy offshore barriers front a barren region of salt pans and saline flats that intergrade onto the desert-backed shoreline. Extending between the shore and the barrier islands is the largest hypersaline lagoon system in North America, a polysaline estuary that extends for over 260 miles from the vicinity of Port Aransas, Texas, southward to Carvajal and Bahia Salada, Mexico. This is the Laguna Madre.

A second, but much smaller, hypersaline lagoon system is found along the northern shores of the Yucatán Peninsula. Longitudinal beach ridges paralleling the coastline isolate inshore basins which contain trapped seawater that through evaporation can exceed 55 parts of salt by weight per thousand parts of water by weight (or $55^0/00$ salinity). Appearing more like inundated salinas, these lagoons support a depauperate fauna, and a flora more distinctively tropical, that ranges from the previously discussed mangrove hummocks to salt marshes that eventually grade into tropical xeric (drought-tolerant) forests.

The Laguna Madre is really two lagoons: (1) the nominative Texan component, which includes Baffin Bay, and (2) the Mexican portion called Laguna Madre de Tamaulipas. Although separated from each other by the Rio Grande estuary at Brownsville, Texas, the two lagoons are physiographically and hydrologically similar. Both share low rainfall, high evaporation rates, shallow bay configurations, and limited exchange of seawater through widely dispersed tidal passes.

Water conditions in these lagoons may undergo extreme fluctuations. Temperatures may reach 100° F and higher, and salinities may vary from nearly fresh to over $70^0/00$, twice normal seawater strength. In the Laguna Tamaulipas,

LAGO LICRON

LAGO JESUS MARIA

Figure 32. The land where the sea meets the desert.
This view from space shows the Laguna Madre de Tamaulipas below Matamoros, Mexico.
Narrowing rapidly southward, the Laguna passes Lago Licron and the Rio San Fernando
to the left before spilling out westward in the large Lago Jesus Maria midway down its
length. From Matamoros south to Lago Jesus Maria the barrier island is cut by numerous
passes and several washover fans indicative of storm-tide breaching into the Laguna
immediately behind. Farther south, as it approaches the Rio Soto La Marina near the bottom
of the photograph, the Laguna becomes less distinct. In a region rife with Spanish history,
the conquistadores of Cortes would today be amazed at the extensive agricultural development in the area, faintly visible to the left of the Laguna. [U.S. Geological Survey, EROS
Data Center, Sioux Falls, South Dakota]

owing to hurricane closure of tidal passes, completely saturated brines eight times as concentrated as normal seawater (290 ^{0}/oo) have been recorded. A further consequence of the high evaporation rate is the precipitation of many chemical salts, notably calcium carbonate (mostly limestone) and inorganic and organic nutrients (phosphorus).

Such extremes in physical and chemical conditions make life in these lagoons a continuing trial. In addition to physical stress, osmoregulatory abilities are tested to their limits. Biological productivity is consequently low, as are *species richness* (the number of species measured per unit area) and *species diversity* (the number of individuals in each species per unit area). Food webs therefore tend to be rather simple. In some shallow areas the dominant life is composed of mats of blue-green "algae," pink, purple, and sulfur-producing bacteria, and some other related microflora.

In general, variably hypersaline areas contain few species and individuals, whereas in stable hypersaline areas, although species richness still remains low, the numbers of individuals per species may become extremely high. As salinities decrease toward more typically marine conditions, species richness increases while numbers of individuals/species decrease. The system is thus constantly undergoing checks and balances as hydrological conditions change.

This is not to say that well-developed and relatively speciose systems do not occur. In the Texan Laguna Madre, for example, vast beds of sea grasses (*Halodule, Thalassia*) provide the necessary topographical and biological complexity to allow development of complex food webs. Many of the fishes and crustaceans are migratory feeders, moving in and out of the bay and the seagrass beds over tidal cycles.

As might be expected, any disturbance within the lagoons can have more serious consequences than in less-stressed systems. Biological energy drains resulting from the constant need to adapt to temperature-salinity shocks place many organisms on the cutting edge between survival and extinction. A simple introduction of one more toxin, even if detrimental to just a single species, could cause drastic realignment or total collapse of the food web.

The results of such stress can be far-reaching. In one instance, organic overload from sewage pollution in a section of the Mexican Laguna Madre depleted the entire oxygen content in the waters, killed the existing benthic algal community, and dropped the productivity and species diversity of the entire system to almost zero. Clearly, these systems are less resilient to imposed stress, whether it be natural or human-induced. The contained biological communities often have no refugia and the ecosystem crashes or becomes severely modified.

DESERTS AND XERIC LANDS

To most people, deserts are not normally associated with wetlands. Yet even though deserts are arid for much of the year, they are still subject to seasonally heavy rainfall. And although much of the rainwater is immediately absorbed in the parched soils, much also runs off down dry *arroyos* and ravines. These erosional features are responsible in large part for the well-known flash floods.

Figure 33 A & B. La tierra de los moscaitos.

(A) Ecologists classify as "Southern Lowland" the region along the inner coast of Yucatán around the state of Tabasco. Much of this area supports thick, tropical jungles, where every square inch of ground is covered with plants, and warm rains continually drip from the dank vegetation to form pools teeming with life on the forest floor. Parts of this lush, tree-choked landscape are little changed from the days of first Spanish contact and still keen with the songs of a million biting insects that the Spaniards called little flies, or "moscaitos."

(B) Freshwater rivers such as this stream in Yucatán continually add sediments and nutrients to the lagoons and bays that pockmark the southwestern shoreline of the Gulf. In these areas, the fauna and flora must be adapted to sudden, large pulses of fresh water from tropical rains rushing down from the mountains, as well as to the ceaseless change in salinities brought by the incoming and outgoing tides.

An important consequence of these excessive runoff events is that large amounts of sediments and nutrients are carried toward the coastal estuaries, either by the flooding activity itself or as part of a larger and more continuing flow in the rivers and streams that empty into the estuaries. Such events are a major source of sediments that fill in and destroy the coastal lagoons when the land reclaims its acreage stolen by the sea.

Another important consequence of cloudbursts and flash flooding in these desert lands is that large pulses of fresh water are injected into the coastal lagoons. These rainwater pulses can lower the salinity drastically, from a norm of about 40 ^{0}/oo down to only 2 ^{0}/oo. While a surprising number of estuarine organisms (nearly 50 species) can tolerate hypersaline conditions, few can withstand the osmotic shock produced by such drastic and rapid changes in salinity.

Good examples of this type of system are seen around the Rio Grande deltaic plain, and southward into the Mexican state of Tamaulipas. Portions of the Texan Laguna Madre also exhibit these conditions.[1]

MOUNTAIN-RIMMED PLAINS AND RAIN-FORESTED VALLEYS

Along parts of the Yucatán Peninsula and Bay of Campeche occur a series of lagoons backed by mountain-rimmed plains and rain-forested valleys (see Figure 33).

The Yucatán Peninsula, in fact, is a complex montage of vegetational ecosystems, beginning with fringing mangrove forests or strands along most of its coastline and then grading into thorn forest, and tropical deciduous (leaf-dropping) and evergreen forests farther inland and up into the mountains. Along the Bay of Campeche the evergreen forests separate mangroves from the montane tropical moist forests.

Although these may seem to be the antithesis of desert-backed lagoons, the stress factors are similar in many ways. The one major difference is that here freshwater input imposes a continuing stress, particularly during the rainy seasons when lagoonal salinities may drop to 3–5 ^{0}/oo and remain so for weeks or months at a time.

Sediment loading is also important as the many rain-fed tributaries empty their erosional products from the mountains into the larger rivers for eventual deposition in the lagoon. At such times the rivers become roaring, turbid masses of washed-down sediments, rich in nutrients but also heavy with sands and muds. Tidal regimes, current patterns, ecological habitats, and biological activities in the lagoons can all be severely altered. Recovery may require weeks or may not occur until the wet season ends. Animals and plants in these systems thus live on a continual teeter-totter of excess freshwater input on the one hand and salinity shock on the other. Here, as elsewhere, acclimation and adaptation is the name of the game.

Plankton

WANDERERS AND DRIFTERS IN THE GULF

THE GULF OF MEXICO, like other major seas of the world, supports a vast population of microscopic organisms that drift or occasionally swim from the surface layers to just above the seafloor. This miniature flora and fauna is called *plankton*, from the Greek word meaning "wanderer." The plankton that occurs in nearshore areas and over the continental shelf is called *neritic* plankton (*nereidos* = a sea nymph). That which is found in the far reaches of the open sea, beyond the continental shelf, is called *pelagic* plankton (*pelagios* = "of the sea") (see Color Plate 13.)

Because plankton (or plankters, as the individual organisms are called) are so small, few people know they exist until oceanic conditions become right to allow massive explosions of growth in numbers, termed *blooms*. Then, some species of these tiny drifters may color the water for hundreds of miles, produce scintillating phosphorescence, or cause fish kills and release airborne toxins that cause human respiratory and eye irritation.

There are two major types of plankton in the world's oceans, plantlike drifters that use photosynthesis to make their own food from the dissolved nutrients in the sea, and animal or animallike drifters that feed upon the plant drifters. The former, called *phytoplankton* (*phyto* = "plant"), are responsible for the basic or primary productivity that forms the basis for every single food web in the Gulf of Mexico.

The second group, termed *zooplankton* (*zoon* = "animal") are the browsers and grazers on the phytoplankton, or predators on their zooplanktonic counterparts. Within the second group are other zooplankton known as *meroplankton* (*meros* = "in part"). These miniature organisms may be *carnivores* (*carnis* = "flesh"; *voro* = "to eat"), that is, meat-eaters; *herbivores* (*herba* = vegetation) or plant eaters; or be nonselective *omnivores* (*omnis* = "all"), eating almost anything that comes their way. The meroplankton, usually composed of the larval stages of the numerous marine invertebrates found in shallow and deep waters of the Gulf, in turn form at least part of the diet of still other predators ranging in size from larval fish to the great blue whales.

Some idea of the abundances of these minuscule marine organisms can be gained when it is realized that the great blue whale (the largest mammal) and the giant whale shark (the largest known fish) feed only on plankton. It is a curious fact, but one indicative of the nutrient sources available in the sea, that

217

the largest animals in the world subsist entirely on some of the smallest.

PHYTOPLANKTON: THE GRASS OF THE SEA

The tiny floating plants of the sea are made up of four main groups: diatoms, dinoflagellates, coccolithophores, and cyanophytes (at one time known as blue-green algae). All are microscopic—some so small that they are placed in a separate general group called *nannoplankton* (*nano* = "dwarf").[1] Other larger floating algae, such as Gulfweed (*Sargassum* sp.) and the previously discussed drift algae of the estuaries, also drift in the surface waters at the mercy of winds and currents, but are not called plankton. They will be considered later.

Diatoms

Excluding, for the moment, the nannoplankton, the diatoms are by far the most numerous of all the larger phytoplankton organisms, both in numbers of individuals and number of species. Together with the dinoflagellates, considered next, they are the "grass of the sea." These one-celled plants are unique in being composed of a capsule made of two valves, one nested inside the other, and each made of pectin (the same substance found in apples and other fruits) and silica, a component of glass and one of the rarest minerals in the sea. The protoplasm that forms the plant body is contained within the capsule. Here also are found the *chromatoplasts*, the tiny green bodies colored with chlorophyll that enable the diatoms (and other floating plants as well) to conduct photosynthesis.

Diatoms, like nearly all other phytoplankton, are considered to be *autotrophs* (*auto* = "self," *trophos* = "feeding"), that is, they manufacture their own food via photosynthetic activities (*photos* = "light," *synthesis* = "assembly"). Thus, most species are found in the upper layers of the open sea, or even in the thin films of water that cover estuarine mudflats on low tides. It is safe to say that no matter where one looks in the Gulf of Mexico, diatoms will be found.

Owing to their siliceous (silicon-containing) skeleton the diatoms often assume fantastic shapes ranging from tiny sculptured boatlike forms to miniature perforated Victorian pillboxes. Many species occur in long chains of individuals, connected in a series of squares, ovals, oblong ellipses, or in radiating starlike patterns. Curling spines, thorns, or spears made of almost pure silica ornament many of these forms (see Figure 34A).

Although diatoms may occur in huge numbers, they rarely produce "blooms" that are occasionally seen in some other phytoplankton. In some instances, however, large concentrations of certain diatoms may collect at the sea surface and produce noticeable oil slicks from the organic oils and fatty acids stored in their capsules as a by-product of photosynthesis.

Dinoflagellates

Dinoflagellates are the second major component of phytoplankton. Unlike diatoms, which passively drift to and fro, the dinoflagellates can swim, although they are capable of moving only weakly in any direction. Most possess two whiplike threads, called *flagella*, by which they propel themselves through the water (*dinos* = "whirling," *flagella* = "whip"). In general, a dinoflagellate looks

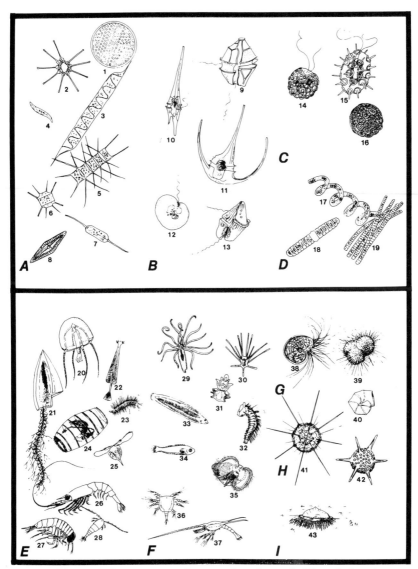

Figure 34. Marine plankton. Representative types of nearshore and offshore plankton (composites drawn from living or preserved specimens, not to scale).

Phytoplankton: (A) Diatoms, 1-8. (B) Dinoflagellates, 9-13. (C) Coccolithophores, 14-16. (D) Cyanophyta or Blue-Green Algae, 17-19. *Zooplankton:* (E) Holoplanktonic invertebrates, 20. Pelagic medusa, 21. Siphonophore (a type of jellyfish), 22. Arrow-worm (Chaetognatha), 23. Pelagic polychaete worm, 24. Salp (Urochordata), 25. Sea butterfly (Pteropod mollusc), 26. Krill (Euphausiacean crustacea), 27. Amphipod (crustacea), 28. Copepod (crustacea). (F) Meroplankton (larval stages of invertebrates and vertebrates). 29. Arachnactis (sea anemone), 30. Pluteus (sea urchin), 31. Bipinnaria (sea star), 32. Polychaete worm larva, 33. Leptocephalus (eel), 34. Fishlarva, 35. Veliger (snail), 36. Nauplius (barnacle), 37. Zoea (crab). Holoplanktonic protozoans—(G) Foraminifera (carbonate-shelled), 38-40, (H) Actinopoda or Radiolaria (silica-shelled), 41-42. (I.) Pleuston (sea surface drifters). 43. By-the-wind-sailor (adult stage of a type of jellyfish).

like a microscopic ornamental chicken egg with a thread at one end and a second thread wrapped in a groove around the middle. Inside the shell are the usual complement of chromatoplasts, in this case colored brown, yellow, or red, allowing photosynthesis to take place.

Dinoflagellates also exhibit a variety of shapes, ranging from the so-called naked forms that look like little transparent apples or barrels, to the armored forms that carry a series of interlocking plates on the body. These are often highly sculptured or perforated by pores. Some species resemble Japanese Samurai helmets, others the horned helms of Vikings, and still others appear almost alien in their configurations (see Figure 34B).

Dinoflagellates are unusual in another respect. Although most are considered plantlike and produce their own food by photosynthesis, some species are also able to absorb organic substances or assimilate microscopic particles of dead animal matter, in a process called *heterotrophy* (*heteros* = "alternate"; *trophos* = "feeding"). Still other species utilize the best of both nutritional modes, photosynthesizing when light conditions are appropriate and absorbing organic materials when light conditions are too low. As a consequence, dinoflagellates are one of several protistan groups that bridge the gap between strictly plant and strictly animal nutritional modes.

Two ways in which most people come to know dinoflagellates are during outbreaks of either "phosphorescence" or "red tide." Many species of dinoflagellates are *bioluminescent* (*bios* = "life," *luminosos* = "full of light"); that is, they are able to produce "cold light" as a by-product of their metabolism. When huge windrows of these bioluminescent species occur offshore, or wash onto the beach, the entire sea surface or the onshore driftweed line may glow with an eerie blue or yellowish-green light. Travelers tell tales of boat wakes stretching like luminous pathways to the horizon and swimming fish outlined in fiery shadows as they race through the water disturbing the tiny light-producers. At night, the average beachcomber can usually see a small bioluminescent display in the driftweed by simply picking up and shaking fresh stranded seaweed.

The second event is less aesthetically pleasing. Red tide, which is not a tidal phenomenon at all, occurs when environmental conditions offshore allow massive dinoflagellate reproduction to occur. The resulting "bloom" appears reddish or brownish in color owing to the color of the chromatoplasts in each dinoflagellate individual. Toxic by-products released into the sea may cause large-scale mortalities of fishes and invertebrates. This phenomenon will be discussed in the next chapter.

Coccolithophores

The coccolithophores are among the smallest of the phytoplankton, none visible without high-powered microscopes. These tiny plantlike cells have two apical whiplike flagella which propel them through the water. Some forms may have a third small, usually coiled, thread between the flagella called a *haptonema* (*haptos* = "[responding] to touch"; *nema* = "thread"). The common name of coccolithophores (*coccus* = "grape," *lithophorus* = "stone carrier") refers to the fact that many species have the cell completely covered and ornamented with plates of calcium carbonate, termed *coccoliths*. The various species have many shapes, but some resemble miniature globes covered with tiny rings, circles, or saucers (see Figure 34C).

Coccolithophores are primarily tropical phytoplankton, occurring in the warm surface waters. Because of their extremely small size they are often overshadowed by the larger and more abundant diatoms and dinoflagellates. Nevertheless, coccolithophores are an important component of the pelagic (open-sea) plankton because they provide a food supply of very small particles that many of the smaller invertebrate larvae can utilize. It is regrettable that for a great number of species the life history is either poorly known, or completely obscure.

Cyanophytes

Cyanophytes (*cyanos* = "blue"; *phytos* = "plant") are among the most primitive of all plantlike organisms. At one time called "blue-green algae," this ancient group of chlorophyll-bearing organisms shows many more similarities to bacteria; thus, they are often referred to as *cyanobacteria*. Their ancestry is not only traceable to bacteria, but well back in to the pre-Cambrian geological era, at least 650 million years ago, and perhaps as much as 3.5 billion years ago—in short, some 500 million years after the formation of the earth itself!

Cyanophytes form an important component of the plankton, especially in the tropical areas of the Gulf of Mexico. Although never found in the abundances of diatoms or dinoflagellates, the cyanophytes can occur from time to time in numbers large enough to discolor the water dirty-yellow.[2]

Although the cyanophytes are true passive phytoplankton, drifting from place to place, some species exhibit a curious and unexplained forward-backward motion. All species are microscopic, but on occasion they may occur in long, threadlike filaments or strands, making them visible to the naked eye (see Figure 34D).

Not all species are planktonic, however. In some cases the cyanophytes may grow on wave-sprayed rocky areas. Other species contain calcium carbonate crystals deposited between and around the "algal" filaments and are important in the actual production of this mineral, or aid in its precipitation from overlying waters. Together with the green and red algae, these blue-green organisms are responsible for the formation of many limestone deposits. Along quiet estuarine shores they may occur in such numbers that they form layered rocky deposits called stromatolites.[3] On land they produce much of the calcitic muds that compose the marls of the Everglades region in southern Florida.[4] They are also found in large numbers in alkaline lakes and marshes in Louisiana.

ZOOPLANKTON: THE BROWSERS, GRAZERS, AND PREDATORS

The zooplankton are the animal forms that drift or swim weakly in the sea. These animals are divided into two major categories, the *holoplankton* (*holos* =

"entirely"), which spend their entire life cycle in the open waters of the sea, and the *meroplankton* (*meros* = "in part"), which spend only a portion of their life cycle, usually their larval stages, in the open sea. Both groups, however, are extremely important components of the marine food web.

Holoplankton

The holoplankton is dominated by copepods, by far the most numerous group of multicelled invertebrate animals in the sea. Copepods are minute crustaceans that possess extremely elongate antennae, and shorter antennules, which they use to propel or "row" themselves through the water (*kope* = "oar," *podos* = "foot"). Copepods may be herbivorous, grazing only on the abundant phytoplankton, or they may be carnivorous, feeding on other zooplankton or each other. Some are omnivorous and will eat plant or animal if they can catch it. Their main competitors are "jellyfish," ranging from microscopic, transparent, bell-shaped medusae to larger siphonophores looking like glassy bishop's miters, up to the lion's mane jellyfish, an offshore species that can grow to nearly three feet in width (see Figure 34E).

Other members of the multicelled holoplankton are larger and thus more familiar in appearance. Besides the previously mentioned jellyfish, they include pelagic (open-sea) marine molluscs such as the pteropods (*pteros* = "wing," *podos* = "foot") or sea butterflies that swim by using their greatly modified feet (see Plate 13A); several strictly pelagic polychaete worms; a totally marine group called arrowworms (Chaetognatha) that possess fearsome looking, grasping spines on the head (*chaetos* = "bristle," *gnathos* = "jaw"); several forms of crustaceans including amphipods, isopods, shrimp, and even some totally pelagic crabs;[5] and salps (see Plate 13B), primitive barrel-shaped organisms whose tadpolelike larvae possess a structure called a *notochord*, and are thus distant relatives of our own phylum, Chordata.[6]

Many holoplankters have rather bizarre forms or pass through unusual life cycles before attaining their final adult morphology. But all are carnivorous to some degree, some completely so. Many (for example, euphausiid crustaceans, called "krill") employ a specialized feeding apparatus to filter phytoplankton and other zooplankton from the water. Others, such as the arrowworms, are ambush predators, darting forward to seize their prey with claws, spines and other armaments. Still others, like the jellyfish, are more passive predators, trailing long deadly tentacles behind them and reeling in the stunned or dead plankton that become entangled therein. Some pteropod molluscs produce a filmy mucous net which they drag through the water and entrap their prey. The *ctenophores* or comb jellyfish (*ctenos* = "comb," *phoros* = "bearer") use highly specialized, sticky cells on their tentacles, fancifully called *lasso cells* because the animals appear to "rope in" their prey (see Plate 13C). In short, Mother Nature has provided numerous ways for planktonic predators to feed.

Two other extremely important, as well as numerous, groups in the holoplankton include single-celled protozoans belonging to the orders

Foraminiferida (*foramin* = "opening," *fero* = "bearer") and Actinopoda (*actinos* = "ray"; *poda* = "foot," in reference to their radiating spines and protoplasmic feet. The Foraminiferida, usually called "forams," are microscopic plankters that construct minute skeletons of calcium carbonate. They are so abundant that when they die their skeletons often form thick layers of limey ooze on the seafloor, called *globigerina ooze* in reference to a dominant genus in the group (see Figure 34G).

The actinopods, which include the radiolarians (*radios* = "radiating," again referring to their spines), are also exceedingly abundant and construct highly intricate and ornamented skeletons made of glass (silicon dioxide).[7] Many species look like miniature crystalline sunbursts. Their skeletons also may carpet the deep seafloor in some areas with layers of radiolarian ooze hundreds to thousands of feet thick (see Figure 34H).

MEROPLANKTON

If the holoplankton are diverse and bizarre, the meroplankton are even more so. In this group are included all the larvae of marine invertebrates and vertebrates, many of which show little or no resemblance to the final adult form they will eventually attain. An individual's life cycle may be made additionally complex if the species must undergo one or more metamorphoses (molts and changes in body forms) before reaching the postlarval or subadult stage.

The crustaceans are changelings par excellence, many beginning as a primitive larval stage called a *nauplius* and then undergoing a series of molts (up to 30 or more in some species) before beginning to look like the final adult. Other animal groups such as the echinoderms (the sea urchins, sea cucumbers, and sea stars) are even more bizarre and produce larvae that on first appearance do not seem to be even remotely related to the adult form (see Figure 34F). Indeed, the larval stages of some of the less diverse phyla have names as strange as their forms. Included are the *pilidium* larva of nemertine worms, the *actinotrocha* larvae of a phoronid worm, and the *cyphonautes* larva of bryozoans or moss animals; none resemble their respective adults in any way. Here, under the microscope, are forms fascinating, beautiful, and alien, rivaling anything that could be produced by science fiction.

The meroplankton are, for the most part, carnivores or omnivores, although many are quite capable of subsisting on phytoplankton for long periods of time. Some species cannot metamorphose into the subsequent stage without assimilating the necessary vitamins or other growth-enhancing substances found mainly in the marine plants. But all have one thing in common: eventually each will metamorphose one final time and leave the plankton to take up its preadult or adult existence either directly on the seafloor or swimming in the water column above.

THE PLEUSTON: FLOATS IN THE PELAGIC PARADE

There is another group of open sea organisms that does not quite fit any of the definitions so far considered. These are the *pleuston* (*pleustes* = "sailing or floating"), the animals and plants that drift on or just below the sea surface.

These wanderers travel the sea lanes propelled by both currents and winds. Familiar examples include the blue Portuguese man o' war, a virulently venomous siphonophore animal colony related to true jellyfish (see Plate 14A); two small harmless, rounded colonial jellyfish—*Velella*, the pale blue by-the-wind-sailer, and *Porpita*, called blue buttons; two genera of brilliantly colored snails, one of which is shell-less (*Glaucus*) and resembles a fanciful blue and silver worm, and the other (*Janthina*), with a deep violet shell, that makes floats of mucous bubbles. Gooseneck barnacles on driftwood can also be considered pleuston. *Sargassum*, the well-known raggedy brown Gulfweed that often washes ashore in great windrows, is a plant member of the pleuston.

While none of these organisms, with the exception of *Glaucus,* can actively swim, most can alter their direction of drift. The man o' war changes its sailing direction by twisting its gas-filled float, allowing it to tack before the wind. *Velella*'s float is fixed but functions similarly. *Porpita, Janthina,* and *Sargassum* are more truly drifters. Both blue buttons and the snail remain at the sea surface, the latter clinging to its precarious raft of manufactured bubbles. Gulfweed is buoyed up by the numerous gas-filled floats that look like tiny, yellowish-brown beach balls scattered among its fronds. All these organisms, and some other floating algae, are essentially at the mercy not only of sea surface currents but also of surface winds that can push the algal clumps into long, aggregated weedlines far out at sea, or blow them *en masse* into great windrows on shore.

THE NEUSTON: PLANKTON OF THE SEA SURFACE MICROLAYERS
But an even more important component of the plankton is well-nigh invisible and includes the numerous species of bacteria and protozoans and other single-celled organisms that adhere to the fine film of proteinaceous matter at the sea's surface and live, feed, and reproduce on or in it. Scientists call these organisms *neuston* (*neuster* = "swimmer") and the film they live on or in is named the *sea surface microlayer*. It is truly the dividing line between the sea and the sky.[8]

Scientists now know that this sea surface microlayer has important ramifications not only for the organisms that live in the sea, but also for those on the rest of the planet. As a consequence of human industrial and technological advances many of the pollutants produced by such activity are carried into the sea, either via the atmosphere or through runoff, where they become concentrated in the microlayer. As the concentrations of pollutants increase they can adversely affect both the composition and the viability of the organisms within the microlayer. The phytoplankton and zooplankton, next step up the nutrient ladder, may then become affected. They, in turn, may poison their predators, and the dominoes begin to fall. Thus, a polluted microlayer may become a deadly soup capable of poisoning everything from invertebrates to fish to whales to sea birds.

Moreover, chemical interactions between phytoplankton, bacteria in the microlayer, and the atmosphere can result in increased emissions of sulfide gases. These gases carry particles of sulfur into the atmosphere and water droplets form around them. High water vapor in the atmosphere can produce increased cloud cover. Greater cloudiness means a reduction of sunlight, resultant decreases in photosynthesis, including reduced production of oxygen, and a general lowering of atmospheric and sea surface temperatures. In a sense, then, the sea surface microlayer and its associated plankton act much like a thermostat, regulating the amount of sunlight hitting the earth, and thus governing the ambient temperature of the planet.

PONDERABLES FOR OUR FUTURE

Fact: The ubiquitous and astronomical numbers of plankton, through their life processes and their disintegration after death, produce tons of amino acids, proteins, fatty acids, oils, and cellular particles each day.

Fact: This organic debris accumulates in the sea surface microlayer, forming thin invisible films that can develop into visible "surface slicks."

Fact: Toxins—including copper, lead, zinc, and cadmium—bind to naturally occurring organic molecules and become concentrated in such slicks from 10 to 100 times greater than in the immediately subsurface waters.

Fact: Pesticides in sea surface slicks have been measured in concentrations up to several million times that found in the rest of the water column.

Fact: Combustion-derived hydrocarbons from motor vehicles, aircraft, watercraft, and refuse incinerator and power plant fallout form a chronic and continually measurable input of pollution in the sea surface microlayer.

Fact: Sunlight acting on microlayer pollutants can break down many of them into more toxic forms; others disintegrate into less harmful compounds.

Fact: A complex interchange between pollutants in the microlayer and ambient phytoplankton is hypothesized to be part of a global thermostatic system that regulates the amount of incoming solar energy warming the earth.

Fact: Natural emissions (primarily sulfides) from phytoplankton produce nuclei around which water droplets condense to form clouds. By their presence, extent of surface area, volume, and longevity, these clouds regulate the amount of sunlight, and thus heat, reaching to, or reflected back from, the earth's surface.

THUS: What happens between the sea and the sky has momentous importance for life on earth. The activities of some of the least of earth's organisms (plankton and bacteria), coupled with the wastes, pollution and contaminants produced by earth's allegedly highest life form (mankind), may well determine the future quality and continuance of life over the entire planet.

Source: J.T. Hardy (1991).

Researchers now look at the upper three feet of the ocean's surface much as if it were a multilayered cake. Within the first two thousandths of an inch, for example, occurs an incredibly dense accumulation of minerals, chemicals, and microorganisms, and nanoplankton. The next several inches are populated by the larger (or macro-) plankton discussed earlier. Following this is a layer of other organisms such as jellyfish, bony fish, juvenile sea turtles, and a host of other swimming creatures termed "nekton." It is to these last organisms that we turn next.

THE NEKTON: PELAGIC MOVERS AND SHAKERS

One other pelagic, but nonplanktonic, group must be considered. These animals, large and small, have the ability, albeit sometimes quite limited, to direct their own motion through the sea, either by swimming or pulsing water in some manner. Called nekton (*nektos* = "swimmer"), they are never fully at the mercy of sea currents and winds like their planktonic and pleustonic brethren. The nekton include organisms as diverse as large jellyfish, squid, larval and postlarval fishes, crustacean postlarvae and adults (prawns) and, of course, all the actively swimming marine vertebrates. Included herein are all the fishes, from the tiny silversides to the huge whale sharks, the reptiles such as marine turtles and sea snakes, and mammals of the sea from the seals and sea lions to the great blue whales (see Plate 14B).

All can be classified as either carnivores or omnivores, and most occupy the highest levels of the far offshore food webs. Thus, the nekton are predators, not only on other nektonic species (dolphins eat flying fish), but on the pleuston and plankton as well (sea turtles eat man o' wars; whales eat plankton). But the tables are always easily turned. The pleuston and plankton can also be predators on the nekton (man o' wars eat dolphin postlarvae; crab postlarvae eat small pelagic snails). It's a complicated world out there in the pelagic regions, and as an old marine ecologist once said: There ain't no sanctuary!

WEEDLINES: ALGAL OASES IN A BLUE DESERT

Although the far offshore waters of the open Gulf contain thousands of species and millions of individual organisms, these numbers are lost in the cubic miles of water beyond the continental shelves. Here, far from land-based runoff and coastal nutrients, the sea water changes from green to a deep and abiding blue. Here too is a watery kingdom of such crystalline clarity that sunbeams dance and flicker in dazzling vertical shafts, piercing downward hundreds of feet before disappearing into the cobalt-shadowed depths of the sea. To the casual observer,the overall impression is that of an azure and empty oceanic wilderness.

Yet life, teeming and in vast numbers, exists, although most of it is either diaphanous or completely transparent, or much too small to be seen with the naked eye. And except for an occasional flash of silver and gold as a patrolling dolphin takes her prey, or the shimmering iridescence of a jellyfish commuting from nowhere near to somewhere far, the subsurface waters appear devoid of animals and plants.

But appearances in the open ocean are always deceiving. Above the deceptively empty waters the drifting weedlines form a floating canopy—a living brown, yellow, and green oasis populated by the pelagic microfauna, plankton, pleuston and nekton, and fellow sojourners of the macrofauna seeking both respite and refuge from the open sea.[9]

Blue-water fishermen know these "weedlines" to be a prime haven for many sport fish (such as dolphin, wahoo, cobia, and kingfish) which patrol the weedy thickets and feed on the numerous invertebrates (snails, crabs, shrimps) and vertebrates (small pelagic fishes, sea turtles) that have sought refuge in the floating clumps.

In addition, the floating thickets support a complex and speciose community in and of themselves, consisting of many invertebrates (snails, polychaete worms, small crabs, shrimps) and vertebrates (Sargassum frogfish, Gulfweed pipefish, and sea horses). The latter spend nearly their entire life climbing on, over, or through the Gulfweed fronds, hiding their fishy forms under a disguise of frondlike filaments, and preying and being preyed upon.

The *Sargassum* community is a circumscribed world of microscopic clutter, where the familiar morphologies that distinguish plant from animal become blurred, and things are not always what they seem. Numerous sessile, epiphytic forms, including the miniature, encrusting bryozoans or moss animals, and the jellyfish-related hydrozoans, attach themselves to floats and fronds and sweep the surrounding seawater clean of microplankton. In turn, a tiny species of pycnogonid (sea spider) clambers about with much arm-waving while nibbling on the larger epiphytes. A diminutive brown sea anemone, colored to resemble the fronds, waves its tiny tentacles into the pelagic currents, seeking hapless plankton. Nearby, a raggedy-edged clump of Gulfweed suddenly begins to move and magically transforms into an impeccably camouflaged Sargassum nudibranch. This shell-less snail, an omnivore and world traveler, is forever confined to its floating Gulfweed home. Near the mirrored water's surface a feisty, speckled brown and yellow Gulfweed crab spars with a small, reddish, square-bodied Columbus crab (see Plate 14C) over the mottled remains of a Gulfweed shrimp, both oblivious to lurking danger. Hanging motionless in the water off to one side, a juvenile silvery-gray kingfish awaits the outcome, and the victor, with hungry eyes.

Darting in and out under the floating algal clumps are dozens of tiny, silvery, yellow or blue fish—the juveniles of the great pelagic predators—now spending their kindergarten months in a school where predation is exquisitely defined and its lessons reinforced daily, particularly for the survivors. Sun-silvered flashes signal a phalanx of kingfish and mackerels searching the weedline borders, seeking guests and residents alike. A squadron of silver-blue flying fish wheels nervously near the surface before leaping upward to skitter and glide across the cobalt waves and out of submerged harm's way. Most land safely. But circling overhead, and then diving from out of the sun, several large petrels pick off stragglers before climbing quickly skyward again, each mewling a victory cry to its mates. Farther below, drifting between the shimmering shafts of sunlight, blue-gray shadows with sickle-shaped tails and long dark fins pirouette and turn in a slow and continuous ballet of searching, predation, and death.

Sun diamonds sparkle across the tops of the slowly heaving thickets—high noon on the weedline. The gentle lap and splash of the waves is broken from time to time as one life yet again escapes another—or comes to an end. In this pelagic arena the gladiators are always hungry and the food webs are as tangled as the Gulfweed itself. Life begets life and life destroys life, making it a commodity that is neither cheap nor expensive, but simply one both abundant and without value. And there will always be vacancies among the weeds. Miniature microcosms all, these pelagic communities live and die in an oceanic timelessness, tied forever to the ragged and undulating weedlines that snake across the vast, blue, watery deserts of the distant open sea.

The Cycle of Life

PLANKTON, PRODUCTIVITY, AND THE SUN

THE BASIS FOR ALL LIFE in the sea, and indirectly all life on earth, is the ability of marine plants, particularly the phytoplankton, to photosynthesize.[1] In this process plants use sunlight as an energy source to convert carbon dioxide(CO_2) and water (H_2O) and inorganic materials into energy-rich organic compounds (carbohydrates), while at the same time releasing oxygen (O_2) as a by-product. The simplified equation is:

Plants + Inorganic Matter + Carbon Dioxide + Water → Carbohydrates + Oxygen + Water

The rate of formation of these energy-rich organic compounds from the inorganic nutrient materials is termed *primary productivity*. Nearly all the primary productivity on earth, with the exception of some chemical syntheses by bacteria, is a consequence of plants.

Related to the rate of formation, of course, is the total amount of organic materials produced, which is called *gross primary production*. Quite simply, primary production means what is produced, and primary productivity refers to how fast it is made. Scientists usually express primary production as the number of grams of carbon (C) made in a given area or volume of seawater, over a particular period of time. This may be stated in units as small as grams of carbon per square centimeter per day (gms C/sq cm/day) to larger units of weight, area, and time as in kilograms per square kilometer per year (kg C/sq km/year).

Similarly, *secondary production* is defined as the production of carbon that occurs when secondary producer organisms (that is, most zooplankton) feed on the primary producers—the plantlike phytoplankters and their products. *Tertiary production* is simply the consumption of secondary producers by still other predators (for example, other zooplankton, fish, whales) and so on up the line. The connection of primary, secondary, and tertiary producers is called a *food chain*, and will be discussed below.

In order to produce this carbon, there must be a given amount of plants in an area. The total plant *biomass* (the weight of the living plants, and in this case phytoplankton) in a specified area or volume of seawater at a specified time is called the *standing crop*. Putting it all together—the standing crop of plants (phytoplankton) existing in a circumscribed part of the ocean, the amount of carbon the plants produce, and how fast they can produce it over a period of time—illustrates the interrelationship of primary productivity, primary production, and standing crop. The potential for some standing crop figures is enormous (see Table 11) and dramatically illustrates the almost profligate plentitude of Nature.

However, because animals (for example, the zooplankton), are continually grazing or browsing on the phytoplankton, they may also be part of the standing crop. These secondary consumers feed on the primary producers and so maintain their populations. The tertiary consumers are those animals that feed on the browsers and grazers and include the carnivores and omnivores of both the plankton and the nekton. All are connected in food chains that, taken together, form the great marine food web (see Figure 35).

SUNLIGHT AND THE WEB OF LIFE

Simple food chains rarely exist in nature;[2] instead, food chains form *food webs* by connecting and disconnecting, reticulating and disentangling, throughout an ecosystem as the number of species and the individuals involved increase, decrease or disappear. To illustrate simply: diatom Species A (primary producer) photosynthesizes using CO_2 and water, and then reproduces to make two diatoms. Along comes copepod Species B (secondary producer) and eats one of the diatoms, and then reproduces. Salp Species C (tertiary producer) filter-drifts through the area and feeds on both the diatom and the copepod. A sea turtle spies the salp and eats it. A shark then preys on the turtle. And on the sea surface in his boat a Mexican fisherman catches the shark on a longline and takes it home to feed his family. It is easily seen that this food chain is just one part of an immensely complex food web. And there are many food webs throughout the Gulf of Mexico.

From its relatively simple beginnings the food web becomes increasingly complex the higher up the ladder one ascends. Eventually, the top rung of the ladder is reached and is found to be occupied by just a few carnivores such as the predatory fish, seabirds, and marine mammals. Yet for all their grandeur being at the "top of things," these species could not exist without the lowliest of phytoplankton, the primary producers of the sea. So do all things in the sea, and concomitantly on land as well, become interrelated from the least to the greatest.

The relationship of the sun to this cycle of productivity is that of a constant source of light energy. The seven seas of the world have been called Nature's greatest hydroponic tanks, and the metaphor is very apt. Seawater contains every essential nutrient for plant growth. Yet, with but a few exceptions, no plant growth on the earth's surface is possible without light energy; furthermore, no productivity is possible without plants. No animals could exist without plants; indeed, oxygen-dependent life on earth would cease without plants.

The sun may shine on the sea, but not all the sunlight enters the water. The amount depends on several factors, including the latitude of earth being observed, and how high above the horizon the sun appears. In general, less sunlight

TABLE 12
How Many Diatoms Does It Take to Make a Copepod?

Diatoms—Standing Crop

Number of diatoms estimated to make 1 gram (1/32 oz) dry weight organic matter	675 million
Number of diatoms estimated to occur in 1 cubic yard of seawater	10 million–6 trillion
Estimated dry weight of diatoms occurring in 1 cubic yard of seawater	9 grams (0.28 oz)
Number of diatoms estimated to occur in the Gulf of Mexico	20 sextillion
Estimated dry weight of diatoms occurring in the Gulf of Mexico	33 quadrillion tons

Copepods—Standing Crop

Number of copepods estimated to make 1 gram (1/32 oz) dry weight organic matter	300,000–500,000
Number of copepods estimated to occur in 1 cubic yard of seawater	80,000–1 million
Estimated dry weight of copepods occurring in 1 cubic yard of seawater	2 grams (0.06 oz)
Number of copepods estimated to occur in the Gulf of Mexico	3 quintillion
Estimated dry weight of copepods occurring in the Gulf of Mexico	8 quadrillion tons

The Bottom Line

Number of diatoms needed to make the equivalent of 1 copepod	About 1,800
Number of copepods supportable by diatoms occurring in 1 cubic yard of seawater	About 1 per 4 diatoms

Source: Extrapolated from W. S. Schmitt (1947).

enters the sea in northern latitudes at dawn than at tropical latitudes at high noon. Approximately 44% of the incoming solar radiation is scattered by dust particles and molecules in the atmosphere. This scattering accounts in part for the blue color of the sky. Another 6% of solar radiation is reflected off the sea surface. Of the sunlight that is absorbed into the sea, approximately 2% is scattered by particles and molecules in the water column. Oceanographers call this scattering *underlight*, and it produces, in part, the deep cobalt blue color of the open sea.[3] The depth of water in which light penetrates in amounts sufficient to allow photosynthesis corresponds roughly to the *epipelagic zone*, the highest level of the pelagic region. Below this zone occurs the *mesopelagic* and *bathypelagic* zones, the middle and the deep portions of the pelagic region. These are shadowed and lightless depths, where sea creatures exist on the borders of perpetual twilight or swim and drift deep in the realms of eternal night (see Figure 35).

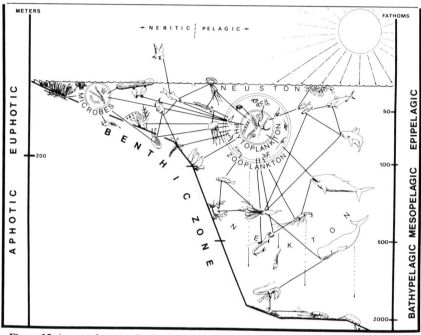

Figure 35. A general marine food web.
The basis of most marine food webs are the microscopic bacteria and fungi (the *Microbes*), and the bacteria, algae, and protozoans of the sea surface microlayer (the *Neuston*), that break down organic matter and release dissolved nutrients for use by plants ranging from *Benthic Zone* sea grasses and algae to *Neritic* (continental shelf) and *Pelagic* (oceanic) phytoplankton. *Phytoplankton* in the *Euphotic Zone*, the light-filled upper water levels of the sea, use energy from sunlight to incorporate these organic nutrients into their cellular components, producing oxygen and/or carbon dioxide as by-products. The phytoplankton are consumed by *Zooplankton* herbivores living in the water column, and these, in turn, are eaten by *Zooplankton* and *Nekton* carnivores. The food web gains complexity as the organisms increase in size, terminating with the huge baleen and sperm whales, sharks, and other carnivorous fishes found in the offshore *Epipelagic, Mesopelagic, and Bathypelagic Zone*. Along the seafloor various *Benthic Zone* animals (invertebrates to fishes) also feed on *Phytoplankton, Zooplankton*, or on each other, as do other carnivores on other herbivores throughout the water column. The fecal material from all these organisms falls in a continuous rain, along with the remains of other animals and plants, through the *Euphotic* and the lightless *Aphotic Zone* to the sea floor where it is either eaten by scavengers or is ultimately attacked by *Microbes*, thus completing the cycle. The food chains and resulting webs shown here are diagrammatic and illustrate only a small portion of the relationships among thousands of species from the surface waters to the deepest seas.

How far sunlight penetrates into the sea also depends in large part on the clarity of the water. Water clarity determines the depth of the *euphotic zone* (*eu* = "true," *photos* = "light"). Far offshore, where little dissolved substances occur, the water may be exceptionally clear and sunlight can penetrate as deep as 600 feet or more, although at that depth the light is very much attenuated. An observer hovering at the bottom of the euphotic zone at 600 feet would see only an empty, but pervasive deep blueness fading rapidly to black. At these depths— the beginning of the *aphotic zone* (*a* = "without," *photos* = "light")—so little light is available that almost no plants (with the exception of some primitive algae and diatoms) can photosynthesize.

THE GREEN TIDES OF PRODUCTIVITY

In spite of the abundances and wide distribution of phytoplankton in the open waters of the Gulf, it is generally conceded that the productivity of sea grasses, associated algae, and epiphytes in the shallow nearshore areas and estuaries exceeds that produced by the plankton in the open sea. Several factors that account for or enhance such productivity are upland runoff, rates and amounts of tidal exchanges, tidal and current flushing throughout the area, basin configurations, turbulence, and general nutrient enrichment. In effect, general plant productivity is exposed to more and greater perturbations in the shallow nearshore areas than in the open areas of the Gulf, where many conditions of the surface and shallow pelagic environment may be nearly constant.

In the Gulf, as elsewhere, the estuaries are considered the most fertile in regard to productivity, followed by the nearshore and offshore continental shelf areas, and finally by the open (pelagic) Gulf.

Upwelling is another aspect of fertility that must be considered. In addition to storm-induced vertical mixing, certain regions (such as the Mississippi Delta, the Campeche Bank, and the northeastern Gulf of Mexico) exhibit higher primary production owing to a multiplicity of factors caused by river discharge and simple nutrient overturn from deep-sea waters along the continental shelf that occurs during upwelling events.

Another factor that accounts for variations in productivity is that many phytoplankton species are seasonally abundant. In some areas, heavy blooms of nontoxic dinoflagellates, for example, may remove enough oxygen from the water column to precipitate fish kills. In other cases, population blooms and resultant large standing crops can increase the fertility and overall biological productivity of coastal waters.

All in all, the coastal waters of the Gulf of Mexico are populated by numerous widely distributed, but essentially coastal species that form a resident population. However, intrusions by "foreign" species may occur from time to time as a result of surface currents, upwelling, and other factors. If these intruders become abundant, the resident populations shift, grow, or decline. The resident productivity in the associated waters may also change. Inasmuch as the phytoplankton forms the basis of the extant food webs in these waters, introduction of "foreign" species can eventually affect the upper levels of the food web on which so many secondary and tertiary consumers depend by altering the overall productivity.

RED TIDES: THE DEADLINESS OF EXCESS

Red tides, as noted earlier, are not really tidal events at all but the occurrence of large population explosions and/or aggregations of dinoflagellates that, because of their numerical abundance, produce vast areas of discolored seawater. Red tides occur in areas of heavy land runoff or where offshore upwelling exists. The resultant input of nutrients produces unbridled growth and reproduction. Winds, surface currents, and tidal action may act in concert to further concentrate the populations. Within the Gulf of Mexico such "blooms" are a periodic phenomenon along the west and northwest coasts of Florida, the east coast of Texas, and in the Bay of Campeche, Mexico.

Red tides commonly produce fish kills. The dinoflagellates themselves, in the course of normal life activities, produce a substance that is simply a waste product to them, but unfortunately is neurotoxic to vertebrates and many invertebrates. In low populational numbers the toxin is either diluted or has only incidental effects on other sea life. In large outbreaks, however, the toxin becomes concentrated in seawater and can paralyze or kill a number of fish species. A synergistic factor is that high dinoflagellate populations also lower dissolved oxygen levels, so that the fish, already stressed from oxygen lack, die either from the effects of the neurotoxin, or depleted oxygen, or both (see Figure 36).

Several common dinoflagellate genera have been implicated in red tides, but only two have been associated with mass mortalities. The most notorious species belong to the genera *Gymnodinium* and *Alexandrium* and their relatives. These dinoflagellates, reaching concentrations of 200,000 to 75 million cells/liter of seawater, produce *saxitoxin*, one of the deadliest toxins on earth, and one without a known antidote at present.

In addition to the observable fish kills, red tides produce hidden and potentially lethal effects for humans. The toxin may become concentrated in several species of commercially-fished invertebrates, including clams, mussels, and oysters. The poisoning occurs when shellfish that have fed on dinoflagellates incorporate the odorless, tasteless saxitoxin into their tissues, and then are eaten by humans. The resulting intoxication is called "paralytic shellfish poisoning." In addition, saxitoxin can produce several other nonlethal but medically dangerous effects. One chronic effect occurs when a person breathes saxitoxin- containing aerosols, the minute water droplets produced by breaking waves and carried onshore by prevailing winds. Respiratory and eye irritation and allergic effects are common and can make beaches and seashores uninhabitable for weeks at a time.

Nor are the effects felt just by people. Offshore reefs may be so depopulated of the fish fauna that it may require months or years to reestablish their biota. Oysters and clams on inshore bars and beds may be rendered unfit for human consumption. The potential for biological magnification of toxin from one species to another remains an additionally serious but enigmatic factor

Although red tides can do great damage to marine biota, and produce economic hardships for commercial fisheries as well as for the tourist industry in areas where the tides are common, their effects are, for the most part, restricted to short time frames and localized areas. Eventual control of red tides is presently unfeasible, but the ability to forecast their occurrence is being studied. Like the weather, red tide may never be controlled, but may eventually prove to be partially predictable.

In summary, productivity, like every other biological and physical phenomenon in the Gulf, is never simple, either in its action or its effects.[4] Yet this very complexity reflects on the awesome ability of Nature to not only create and provide food for her own, but in some cases to produce devastating effects on these same populations. Humans, relatively late players in this ancient scenario, might do well to learn these lessons, particularly when the fragile food webs can be so easily disturbed by our thoughtless activities.

Figure 36. Death on the sands.
Hundreds of thousands of dead or dying fish wash ashore along a Florida Gulfcoast beach, the hapless victims of a red tide bloom. When an excess of nutrients occurs in the nearshore waters Nature responds with her own superabundances, a population explosion of billions of tiny dinoflagellate plankters. The byproducts of their life processes, merely waste to the dinoflagellates, are unfortunately toxic to many higher marine organisms and produce death either directly through intoxication, or secondarily through depletion of oxygen in the water column. When the victims wash ashore the result for humans is discomfort at best and a hazard to health at worst. [Florida State Archives, Tallahassee, Florida]

A tower into the deep.
The "Bullwinkle" platform, currently the tallest fixed offshore oil drilling platform in the world, stands in 1,350 feet of water on the continental shelf about 150 miles southwest of New Orleans. Taking more than three years in construction and final emplacement, "Bullwinkle" is projected to produce some 44,000 barrels of oil and 100 million cubic feet of natural gas per day in 1992. [Courtesy Shell Offshore, Inc.]

Part Five

Economic Resources in the Gulf of Mexico

This people at first sight seems to be a company of traders come together for purposes of business, and . . . one finds that their one test of the value of everything in this world depends on the answer to this single question: "How much money does it bring in?"

Alexis de Tocqueville, 1831
Letter to Chabrol

I cannot express my thoughts better than by saying that the Americans put something heroic into their way of trading.

Alexis de Tocqueville, 1835
Democracy in America

Working the American Mediterranean

T HE ECONOMIC RESOURCES of any region are a complex combination of the kind of items available; their abundance and ease of exploitation; the need for them as perceived by the buying public; their collection, distribution, merchandising, advertising, and sale. Such resources may be local, regional, or international in scope depending on whether the item is produced and consumed in the immediate vicinity, produced locally and exported to other parts of the world, or produced elsewhere and shipped into, or out of, a given region.

In cases where one company or a conglomerate controls a certain resource, the factors listed above become additionally subject to monopolistic or oligopolistic controls that can result in artificially induced abundances or rarities. A prime example of this is the petroleum industry, whose economy fluctuates with, and is often completely controlled by, pricing established by OPEC nations and other cartels.

The regional factor is also important. A given item may be locally abundant and provide a major impetus to the local or even regional economy. The phosphate mining industry in Florida is a good example of this situation: the product (fertilizer) is used regionally but is also exported overseas.

But regionality may also work against a local economy. For example, an item may be locally abundant but not as financially exploitable (owing, say, to labor costs) as it may be in an area where labor is cheaper. The fisheries industry epitomizes this situation, particularly in Mexico and Cuba, where market prices reflect abundant, available, and relatively cheaper labor than in the United States.

Geographic factors also influence the economic resources of a region. Deep-water ports, for example, are restricted to certain areas where hydrographic and topographic conditions are favorable. An immediate demographic influence is thus linked to this type of situation as employees of local companies, service personnel, and other infrastructure and municipal populations expand around the port. In many cases, the local economy is tied so tightly to port or harbor that its closing or failure can result in both economic and demographic collapse.

Economic resources may also be seasonal (for example, agriculture and citrus industries), perennial (such as food processing industries), or tied to some other short- or long-term fluctuating economic factors (construction and associated industries). Perhaps most importantly, the viability of any economic resource depends on its ability to avoid product obsolescence and financial non-competitiveness, whether resulting from the product itself or induced by marketing trends, labor costs, or availability.

Finally, economic resources in any region invariably fall under some aspect of government control, including such things as local or state taxes and surcharges, many complex government policies for leasing and permitting, and the nuts and bolts of the Treasury chest, international import duties and tariffs. Whether a resource from one region will be available in another very often depends on whether these governmental criteria are met.

The economics of the coastal zone are not simple. International agreements, for example, also impact regional economics. In 1982, after several years of negotiation, the United Nations Conference on Law of the Sea Treaty (UNCLOS) was signed in Caracas, Venezuela. The treaty was passed by a vote of 130 to 4, with 17 nations abstaining. The treaty provided for a 12-mile coastal sovereignty zone, a 200-mile offshore economic zone, encouragement to limit offshore pollution, regulation of deep-sea mining, and the right of marine vessels to free and unimpeded passage through straits controlled by countries. Not lost on the treaty signers was the fact that 95% of the harvestable living resources, 98% of petroleum resources, and large amounts of mineral wealth lie within 200-mile economic zones—that is, on or above the continental shelf. The economic ramifications for the Gulf of Mexico, with two narrow straits, wide continental shelves, massive petroleum explorations, and a burgeoning population are apparent. [1]

The economic resources in the Gulf of Mexico are varied, ranging from heavy industry, petroleum, and chemical manufacturing to wide-scale agricultural activities, an abundance of fresh and saltwater fisheries, and tourism and recreational industries (see Table 13). They therefore have a multitrillion dollar impact on the economy of the region. With these thoughts in mind, let us briefly examine the more important of these resources in the American Mediterranean.

TABLE 13
Summary of Economic Resources in the Gulf of Mexico

Industry	Product Amount per Annum	Dollar Value	Percent U.S. by Item
Fisheries	2.3 billion lbs	$585 million	38% (1985)
Export trade	608 million tons	$ 70 billion*	45% (1986)
Petroleum	2.4 billion bbls	$ 50 billion	72% oil (1987)
	14.3 trillion cu ft	$100 billion	97% gas (1987)
Manufacturing	100 billion items*	$ 99 billion	14% (1986)
Agriculture	Variable†	$ 25 billion	38% (1985)
Tourism	10 million people	$ 10 billion	50% (1985)

* Variable; estimated from annual meristic sources.
† Includes crops, livestock and poultry, forestry and fisheries.

Data extrapolated from U. S. meristic yearbooks; Mexican and Cuban commerce probably adds another 10–20% to the overall totals.

The Petroleum Industry

OIL FROM TROUBLED WATERS

BELOW THE PLACID, turquoise waters of the continental shelf, deep beneath the overlying muds, sediments, and rocks of the ancient sea floor, lies a buried treasure. A treasure that formed hundreds of millions of years ago when the Gulf shorelines were steaming, vegetation-choked swamps and savannahs. A treasure of such recent and inordinate value that it is now schemed for, bargained over, and sought by the modern technological conquistadores of the twentieth century. Euphemistically called "black gold," this treasure lies in great pools of oil and extensive pockets of natural gas. Teasingly out of sight, yet pinpointed with all the high-technology accuracy of magnetometers, seismic reflection apparatus, side-scan sonar, and a host of other modern electronic devices, these vast pockets of oil and natural gas are ending their hundred-million-year old wait and calling out to industry to explore, expand, and exploit.

These petroleum deposits, the grease sumps of the Jurassic some 135 million years ago or greater, have attracted the attention of modern petroleum companies for more than 50 years. Since the discovery of oil on the outer continental shelf (OCS) of the Gulf, petroleum exploration and removal has become a very big industry indeed. The first successful offshore oil venture in the United States took place in 1938 off the Louisiana coast. Expansion came rapidly. From 1954 to 1986 the U. S. government offered for lease more than 420 million offshore acres, took leases on 41 million and permitted establishment of more than 5,000 drilling sites on the outer continental shelf of the United States. Some 4,200 of these, forming 83% of the national offshore total, were in the Gulf of Mexico, primarily off Texas and Louisiana. The more than 26,000 wells that were drilled yielded, until recently, about 95% of the oil (7 billion barrels) and 99% of the natural gas (71 trillion cubic feet) from all the OCS lease sites combined.

LOOKING FOR PETROLEUM NEEDLES IN A SEAFLOOR HAYSTACK
Offshore oil is produced using 4 types of platforms. The *fixed platform*, firmly attached by long legs to the seafloor in depths of 1,500 feet or less, is the one most people visualize when oil platforms are mentioned. A second type, called a *compliant tower*, is also fixed to the seafloor by legs but is resilient enough to bend when struck by lateral current or wave forces. Its operational depth ranges from 1,200 to 3,000 feet. *Tension leg platforms* are floating structures fastened to the seafloor by steel tubes (called "tendons") held under tension, and by lateral

Figure 37. How to dig for black gold in the Gulf.

wire ropes and chains. Although floating, its vertical motion is restricted by its anchoring tendons. They are operational to depths of 7,000 feet and more. *Floating production systems* is a fourth type of platform that consists of a semisubmersible structure anchored by wire rope and chain to the seafloor. Such a platform undergoes both lateral and vertical motion owing to wave action. In addition to sea surface platforms, subsea wells may be connected by single pipeline or manifolds and multipipeline systems. thereby extending both the lateral and the vertical production range (3,000–7,000 feet) of surface systems. There are a lot of ways to tap those black gold pools and natural gas pockets (see Figure 37).

The magnitude of petroleum exploration operations is financially enormous even though the area of OCS that actually undergoes final drilling is relatively negligible. Data provided by the Minerals Management Service (MMS), the federal agency in charge of all OCS operations, showed that in September 1991, more than $42.8 billion was paid to lease 10,383 tracts located on 52.6 million acres of seafloor. Although this may seem like a large amount of land, consider the following. Over 124,000 tracts on 680 million acres were offered for lease! That's over 1 million square miles of seafloor![1] In 1990, nearly 261,000 tracts were delineated in the entire OCS, which includes the Atlantic, Pacific and Alaskan continental shelves as well as the Gulf of Mexico. Of these, over 161,000 (62%) were never offered for lease. Of the remaining 99,000 tracts (38%), only 12,000 (4.7%) were actually leased, and a little more than 4,400 such tracts (1.7%) were finally drilled. The bottom line was that less than 1,500 of these tracts (0.6%) wound up with production platforms. There's an awful lot of seafloor out there covering those pools of petroleum![2]

Although the major concentrations of drilling rigs and stations are found off Louisiana and Texas, additionally important exploratory and production activity occurs off the Mexican coast. In 1985, for example, Mexico produced nearly 143 million tons of crude oil, almost 27 million cubic meters of natural gas, and more than 60 million tons of petroleum products. Elsewhere, Cuba produced 788,000 tons of crude petroleum and nearly 8 million tons of petroleum-related products in her refineries.[3]

Figure 37. How to dig for black gold in the Gulf.
Mobile offshore drilling units (called MODUs) come in several varieties but all float and are capable of being moved from site to site. The familiar bottom-supported MODUs include jack-up rigs (A), so called because once the unit is towed into place the three or four support legs are "jacked down" until seafloor contact is made, and then the drilling platform is "jacked up" until it is well above the highest waves. The rig of the tension-leg platform (B) floats, but is anchored to the seafloor and held under tension by steel tubes. The drillship (C) is self-propelled and carries a derrick amidships above a "moonpool," a walled enclosure through the center of the ship's deck and hull that opens at the water's surface. Once on site drillships are anchores, or maintained in position using propellers called thrusters, or both. [Courtesy Minerals Management Service, OCS Gulf Region]

Today, more than 95% of all the offshore oil and gas in the United States comes from the Gulf of Mexico.[4] Coupled with land-based sites in the states of Texas, Louisiana, and Florida—all of which have active, though smaller, fields producing both petroleum and natural gas—the Gulf of Mexico becomes a very rich service station indeed (see Figure 38).

Not all oil in the Gulf originates from the Gulf. The Louisiana Offshore Oil Port (LOOP) transfers petroleum imports, particularly crude oil from Venezuela, the North Sea, and the Middle East, via pipeline some 19 miles to shore for refining and other industrial uses. Seven ports in the Gulf, with major facilities located at Houston, New Orleans, Corpus Christi, Baton Rouge, and Tampa, also handle substantial amounts of petroleum and petroleum-based products from both home and abroad. Lightering operations, or the transfer of petroleum products from large vessels to smaller ships, occurs on a regular basis off Texas and Louisiana.

THE BLACK AND WHITE OF BLACK GOLD

As might be expected, the products of offshore oil leases provide a substantial amount of income to U.S. oil companies. But the leases themselves bring revenue to the federal treasury as well, because the oil companies pay large amounts of money at competitive auctions for the leases and the right to search for petroleum. For example, the Minerals Management Service reports that more than 67,000 lease tracts, totaling some 366 million seafloor acres, have been offered since 1954. Slightly less than half of the total offering of $92 trillion,

Figure 38. Supertanker.
A Very Large Crude Carrier (VLCC) plows through the cobalt waters of the Gulf. Capable of carrying millions of gallons of oil, supertankers such as this one are a cost-effective way to transport large amounts of petroleum around the Gulf or around the world. [Courtesy Minerals Management Service, OCS Gulf Region]

some $40 trillion, was accepted as bonus leased tracts—that is, tracts that were sold to the highest bidder.[5] More than 21 million acres are under federal lease and nearly 7 million acres of these are in active production.

The figures in Table 14 illustrate clearly why oil companies (and some branches of the federal government) continue to look toward offshore oil drilling in the Gulf. They also help explain the characteristic unwillingness of some sectors of government to "just say no" to oil development. First year rentals on leased sites in the Gulf of Mexico OCS since 1954 total over $161 million. Through 1986 the federal government had received over $1.5 billion in bonuses and over $10 million in lease revenues just from sites off Florida![6] Who takes in more money for the U.S. government? Only the United States Treasury Department.

Yet the magnitude of oil leasing and development in Florida pales into insignificance when compared to that taking place off Texas and Louisiana. In fact, the Mississippi-Alabama-Florida area plus Louisiana-Texas supports 57 refineries with an aggregate production capacity of nearly 7 million barrels of oil a day. Moreover, the same area contains 112 oil and gas pipeline landfalls from state coastal waters, and another 129 from OCS waters. Over 82% of these pipeline landfalls are found in Louisiana. Add to that the nearly 50 oilfield supply bases, the 19 platform fabrication yards, and 11 major shipyards, and petroleum exploration in that "Sportsman's Paradise" becomes a very big business indeed.

TABLE 14
Projected Values of Gas and Oil Deposits in the Gulf of Mexico

Western Gulf (Texas)	$35,953 billion
Central Gulf (Louisiana-Mississippi)	$37,194 billion
Eastern Gulf (Alabama-Florida)	$ 2,454 billion
All Other OCS Areas Combined	$19,996 billion

(Inflation would add about 5% to the values each year; changing world oil prices could add 100% or more.)

Source: U.S. Department of the Interior, Minerals Management Service Report, 1987.

OILING THE SQUEAKING WHEELS OF EXPLORATION

We are a petroleum-dependent civilization, from the automobiles we drive to the plastics with which we wrap our food. In the United States, with the highest per capita ownership of motor vehicles in the world, there are enough motor vehicles today to allow every American man, woman, and child to drive his or her own car at the same instant—with no back-seat drivers! Oil, and natural gas, truly make our wheels and our world go around.

And it's easy to see why. Oil and its by-products are geologically accessible, economically exploitable, commercially convertible from gas to liquid to solid, and demographically desirable, particularly as transportation fuels. Yet since the beginning of the twentieth century, we have already used more than 62% of our domestic reserves. And at 14 million barrels of oil a day (our current rate of consumption), even the discovery and exploitation of a giant oil field (holding 100 million barrels of oil) would give us at most one week's supply.

As long as this remains true there will be continuing economic and social pressures to find and develop new sources of oil and natural gas. Concomitant with exploration comes expansion of facilities for refining and transporting these fossil fuels. But because the Gulf of Mexico contains unspecified but seemingly large amounts of oil,[7] the emphasis has shifted from older continental-based wellfields in east Texas and California to exploration and development of the offshore continental shelf (OCS) in the Gulf of Mexico, off California, Oregon, Alaska, and the Atlantic coast.

Make no mistake. Petroleum exploration and exploitation are good for the economy, both locally and regionally. The economic equation itself resembles the six-sided benzene ring of petroleum chemistry. Energy sources produce jobs, job activities make energy demands, energy demands require fulfillment, fulfillment requires exploration, exploration finds energy sources, energy sources produce jobs. In the United States we too often take this situation for granted. For less fortunate, or developing countries it is usually a matter of survival. In Mexico, with a per capita income of $1,990 per year, it is becoming increasingly clear that not only must the existing abundances of oil and natural gas be exploited, but that pressure will continue to seek and develop new reserves in the Gulf. Mexico has already looked to the future in building a pipeline for transferring liquid natural gas to the United States. But we should not take this as an indication that our petroleum needs are thereby satisfied. As one Cajun roughneck noted, "We okay until mama hog cut off our milk." Meanwhile, our society continues to hitch its modern chariots to fossil fuels.

PONDERABLES FOR OUR FUTURE

Fact: Burning 1 ton of carbon in fossil fuel creates more than 3.5 tons of carbon dioxide.

Fact: One tank of gasoline can produce up to 400 pounds of carbon dioxide (CO_2), a "greenhouse gas" now believed responsible in large part for an overall increase in world temperature (global warming).

Fact: It is estimated that in order to avoid major climate change, up to 80% of all CO_2 produced through the burning of fossil fuels and forests will have to be eliminated.

Fact: Motor vehicles produce large amounts of three other major emissions affecting our environment today: carbon monoxide (which binds to red blood cells and displaces life-giving oxygen); nitrogen oxides (which react with water, especially rain, to create nitric acid); and hydrocarbons (which can react with nitrogen oxides in sunlight to produce ozone, a chemical irritant but also an important compound in the upper atmosphere that shields harmful ultraviolet rays coming from the sun).

Fact: Nearly 50% of all sulfur dioxide emissions, and some 30% of nitrogen oxides, come from burning of coal. In the United States, coal-fired electrical plants consume some 85% of all the coal burned.

Fact: Natural gas, from deep inside the earth and composed primarily of methane, produces up to 70% more energy for each unit of CO_2 produced than does coal.

Fact: Coal reserves, based on current world rates of consumption, are estimated to last about 1,500 years. Natural gas reserves are estimated to last about 120 years; U.S. supplies would last about 18 years if natural gas was substituted for coal as an energy source. Oil reserves are estimated to last about 60 more years.

Source: W. Fulkerson, et al. (1990). Energy from fossil fuels. Scientific American, volume 263, number 3: 129-135.

Commercial Fisheries

FEEDING A HUNGRY WORLD

THE GULF PORTION of the American Mediterranean is an exceptionally productive sea. Annual production of finfish (fin-bearing fish) and shell-fish (molluscs, crustaceans) is variable but can exceed 2.3 billion pounds in a good year (see Table 14). Commercial fishery landings in the Gulf are among the most financially productive of any fishing industry in the United States, often exceeding $600 million dollars a year. Gulf fisheries landings compose 38% of the entire national total by weight, and 26% by value. Four of the top five commercial fishery ports in the United States (based on fishery weights) and six of the top ten (based on actual economic value) exist in the Gulf (see Figure 39).

The Gulf of Mexico also supports an outstanding recreational fishery. On a good year some 4 million fishermen make over 25 million fishing trips in the Gulf region, and these anglers constitute approximately 33% of the total recreational fisheries in the entire nation. But finfish are not the only "fish" in the sea. In the Dry Tortugas and Yucatán Peninsula spiny lobster are number one on the fun-and-games agenda. Along the coastal areas of Florida, the pink shrimp "running" out the passes at night form one of the most riotous, seasonal and regional, recreational fisheries, with gear ranging from seine nets and dip nets to plastic buckets and bare hands. No matter when or where, whether for fun or profit, the Gulf of Mexico is a good place to fish.

The magnitude of these fisheries notwithstanding, data indicate that in spite of the total U.S. fishery effort, at least 70% of all finfish and shellfish consumed in the nation are imported! Per capita consumption of seafood in the United States is more than 15 pounds a year. As one state agency analyst put it, "We are considered a nation of beef eaters, but seafood is also important."

CATCHING THE REGIONAL DOLLARS

Total landings and their realized dollar values fluctuate from year to year in response to both ecological and economic factors (see Tables 14 and 15). Interestingly, Louisiana consistently leads all the Gulf-bordering United States both in weight of landings (more than 1.8 billion pounds in 1985) and dollar value (exceeding $230 million dollars) per year, and accounts for nearly 70% of all finfish and shellfish landings in the Gulf by weight and nearly 40% of the total dollar value in the region. And, the nation's top fishery port (Cameron) is located in this most productive Gulf coastal state. This shouldn't be surprising

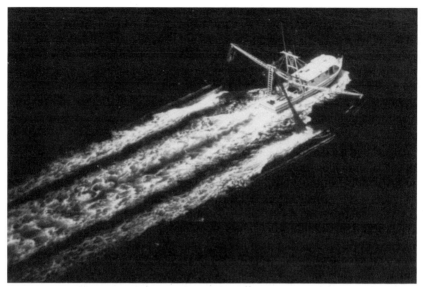

Figure 39A. Commercial fishing in the Gulf.
Booms outboard to port and starboard, a Gulf shrimper cleans its trawls on its way to the next shrimp station. Shrimp boats such as this one ply the shallow offshore waters around the Gulf from Florida to Mexico seeking pink, white, and brown shrimp for the fishmarkets, dining tables, and baitboxes of the world. [Florida Department of Commerce, Division of Tourism, Tallahassee, Florida]

Figure 39B. "Picking the trash."
A crew member on a shrimp boat sorts pink, white, and brown shrimp into wire baskets and shunts the remaining haul of bottom fish and benthic invertebrates out the scuppers behind him. At one time all of these organisms were considered "trash," and were routinely shovelled back overboard. Today, in many parts of the Gulf, trashfish are being kept and form an important part of the economy in the Gulf of Mexico. [Florida Department of Commerce, Division of Tourism, Tallahassee, Florida]

Figure 39C. Putting treasure in the purse.
A commercial fishing boat closes the loop on a shallow water net, encircling the bounty in nylon or cotton netting. Purse seining and gill netting are two methods that incorporate encirclement in a specific area to capture fish, particularly menhaden, mackerel, and mullet. [Florida Department of Commerce, Division of Tourism, Tallahassee, Florida]

Figure 39D. Mobile trash.
Batfish, weird-looking flattened creatures with lobelike fins that they use to crawl across the seafloor, are a common element in many areas of the Gulf and are often taken in large numbers during trawling operations for shrimp. Batfish are among several species of so-called trashfish that are being utilized today in a variety of ways ranging from pet foods to people foods.[Author]

given the richness and abundances of Louisiana's estuarine habitats.

Although Mississippi ranked second in finfish in 1985 (418 million pounds), Texas landings of 59 million pounds, bolstered primarily by the more valuable commercial shellfish, easily exceeded Mississippi's total dollar value ($193 million vs only $38 million). Still, Mississippi's total landings by weight accounted for nearly 20% of all fin and shellfish in the Gulf, although comprising only about 7% of the total regional value.

Florida fisheries at 62 million pounds accounted for only 3% of the total regional volume but, owing to the more valuable shellfish, ranked (like Texas) third in regional value (17%), behind Texas (30%) and Louisiana (39%). Alabama landings of nearly 27 million pounds is the lowest of all the states although the dollar value of nearly $40 million exceeds that of Mississippi. These 1985 values are summarized in Table 15 and may be compared with those of 1987 listed in Table 16.

TABLE 15
Ranked Fisheries and Fishery Values in Gulf Coast States, 1985

	In-state Ranking in lb, $	Pounds	Dollars
Louisiana			
Fish	(1,2)	1.6 billion	$ 63.9 million
Shrimp	(2,1)	116.5 million	$135.0 million
Other shellfish	(3,3)	44.3 million	$ 32.3 million
Texas			
Fish	(3,2)	1.8 million	$ 23.2 million
Shrimp	(1,1)	52.5 million	$161.3 million
Other shellfish	(2,3)	5.1 million	$ 8.8 million
Florida			
Fish	(1,3)	29.6 million	$ 24.6 million
Shrimp	(2,1)	27.5 million	$ 49.9 million
Other shellfish	(3,2)	5.4 million	$ 26.2 million
Alabama			
Fish	(2,3)	4.1 million	$ 1.5 million
Shrimp	(1,1)	19.2 million	$ 35.6 million
Other shellfish	(3,2)	3.7 million	$ 2.6 million
Mississippi			
Fish	(1,2)	418.6 million	$ 13.1 million
Shrimp	(2,1)	16.6 million	$ 22.5 million
Other shellfish	(3,3)	2.8 million	$ 2.1 million

Source: U.S. Department of the Interior, Minerals Management Service (1987).

But the Gulf states should not rest too smugly on their laurels. Mexican fisheries in 1987 produced 2.3 billion pounds, with an export value exceeding $150 million in U.S. dollars. And even the 436 million pounds caught by Cuba is not unimportant in a country with a per capita income of $1,600 per year, particularly when much of it is consumed internally. In fact, fisheries exports constitute the third most important industry in this island country after sugar (first) and nickel (second). However, the influence of regional economics is also clearly seen. In 1987, Mexico and Cuba landed 2.71 billion pounds of fish, or over 300 million pounds more than all the Gulf fisheries in the United States combined (2.4 billion pounds), yet the final realized value was $181 million less that that in the United States.

The preeminent fisheries in the Gulf can be summed up in two words: menhaden and shrimp. Menhaden form the largest commercial fishery by weight in the United States, while the three commonly collected species of shrimp, the brown, white, and pink, plus the regionally important rock shrimp and royal red shrimp constitute the most valuable fishery in terms of dollars.

Menhaden are found throughout the Gulf of Mexico, but the predominant fishery occurs from Mississippi to Texas. In addition to being a source of food, menhaden are processed into numerous other products ranging from animal food to lubricating oils and fertilizers, as well as being incorporated into such unexpected items as cosmetics, margarines, and paints and varnishes.

TABLE 16
Ranked Fishery Values by State in Gulf Coast States, 1987

State	Total Fishery (lb)	Total Value
Louisiana	1,700,000,000	$312,000,000
Mississippi	418,000,000	$ 46,000,000
Florida	120,000,000	$113,000,000
Texas	116,000,000	$246,000,000
Alabama	37,000,000	$ 64,000,000
Mexico	2,269,000,000	$150,000,000
Cuba	436,000,000	$450,000,000*

*Estimated; statistical data varies depending on government sources used.

Source: A. D. Blume. and S. Iudicello (1987); *The Economist* (1988).

SHELLFISHERIES: FEEDING THE WORLD'S GOURMANDS

Invertebrates, primarily crustaceans, form a major money crop in the Gulf. The commercially valuable species include shrimp and crabs. The shrimp fishing industry is both local and international, with trawlers and processing and packaging plants located throughout the Gulf of Mexico region. The major fishing grounds, however, are localized. Pink shrimp grounds, for example, are more or less restricted to the eastern Gulf and to the Campeche Banks off Yucatán. Although pink shrimp are the most commonly trawled species in these areas, white and brown shrimp are also taken.

Elsewhere in the Gulf, the situation is reversed and both brown and white shrimp exceed pink shrimp in relative abundance and commercial value. In fact, considering the entire Gulf, brown shrimp rank second behind menhaden in yield, followed by white shrimp. These species are most common in the northern and western Gulf, particularly off Louisiana and Texas where the shrimp fishery in total tons taken and value received is second only to that of Alaska.

Blue crabs vie with industrial bottom fish (see below) to form the third largest fishery in the Gulf, both commercially and recreationally. Over 10 million pounds of these delectable crustaceans were taken on Florida's Gulf coast alone in 1974, and despite recent major population fluctuations the fishery remains a multimillion dollar industry. Several species constitute the "blue crab" and are variably abundant both locally and seasonally. Research has shown that entire populations of blue crabs will migrate along coastal regions, thus accounting in part for the observed fluctuations in numbers.

In spite of its third-place ranking by size, the blue crab fishery is not as valuable as the Eastern oyster fishery, which ranks third in dollar value and accounts for 60% of all the oysters taken in the United States. This fishery is also a recreational as well as commercial industry, with major activity concentrated from Apalachicola Bay in northwest Florida westward to Aransas Bay in Texas. The Pass Christian Tonging and Dredging Oyster Reefs off Mississippi are among the largest, nearly continuous oyster reefs in the world, and constitute a prime fishery resource in the northern Gulf. Again, Louisiana leads the Gulf in oyster production, as anyone who has ever eaten these salty morsels on Basin Street in New Orleans can attest.

The fishery ranked fourth in value might prove a surprise to anyone but Louisianans. Two species of freshwater crayfish constitute a commercial and recreational industry worth over $8 million dollars a year, with sales and distribution no longer confined locally, but exported around the world. Along with catfish, crayfish form a major freshwater aquaculture industry in the Gulf region.

As the above synopsis suggests, some areas are more dependent on invertebrate fisheries than others. For example, crustaceans are a Florida bread-and-butter fishery, with pink shrimp the most important fishery both in yield and value, followed closely by the spiny lobster, and then the regionally important rock shrimp and stone crab fisheries. Spiny lobster are also an important fishery in Mexican waters off the northeastern and northwestern Yucatán Peninsula, and around the Alacran Reef where trapping provides seasonal income.

But Poseidon's cornucopia is not limitless. Blue crabs were once a valued resource in Florida with annual landings exceeding 3 million pounds. The fishery has declined substantially in both value and abundance in recent years because of pesticide contamination and over-fishing. The fishery itself has proven to be unpredictably seasonal, owing in part to the previously noted penchant the crabs have for migrating along the Florida coastline. Recovery has been slow.

Stone crabs provide another example. The largest commercial fishery for stone crabs occurs in southwestern Florida where nearly 80% of all annual U.S. landings takes place. After catastrophic declines from a 10 million pound per year high, and subsequent near-extinction of the fishery in the late 1970s, trapping was regulated, and a closed season was established between May and

October to allow breeding and aid in recruitment and recovery of existing stocks. Other crustacean fisheries, however, are more dependable. Shrimp, for example, are fished throughout the year. In the United States, the commercial lobster season in Floridian waters extends from the end of July through March, with a three-month hiatus to allow spawning and stock recovery. On the other hand, rock shrimp, an offshore group of species, are under no such restrictions and are fished throughout the year.

Other shellfish of local or seasonal importance include calico and bay scallops, squid, and some tentative explorations into the feasibility of harvesting deep sea red crabs and royal red shrimp. While their value is not inconsiderable, these fisheries have not yet approached the monetary yields of the well-researched, well-orchestrated shallow-water shrimp and crab fisheries. Major commercial areas are concentrated along Florida's central and northwestern coast from Tampa westward to off Louisiana and Texas.

Several other invertebrates also play a role. Sponges form a small, somewhat esoteric, but commercially valuable market on Florida's west coast. Queen conchs, and several other molluscan species (scallops, oysters, quahogs) constitute both recreational and commercial fisheries of regional importance in the same area. While not actually a fishery, commercial products from the seashell and sea curio trade are of some value to the tourist market, not only in Florida but all along the Gulf coast of the United States, and in parts of Mexico as well.

In Alabama, invertebrate fisheries are also important, with shrimp, crabs, and oysters predominating. With some 2,500 shrimp trawlers registered in the state, and Mobile Bay and Mississippi Sound acting as important nursery areas for brown, white, and pink shrimp, it's not surprising that Alabamans can identify with the old Tin Pan Alley song "Shrimp boats are a' comin'." And as far as many coastal residents are concerned, with the Mobile Bay estuary rich in finfishes including sea trout, redfish, southern flounder, and mullet (to name just a few), a "Gone Fishin'" sign for the front door is de rigueur.

Mississippi goes her neighbor Alabama one better by having a longer estuarine coastline, although she shares with her the waters of both Mobile Bay and Mississippi Sound and all their finned and shelled bounty. Boasting over 5,000 acres of state-managed public oyster beds, and the world famous Pass Christian reefs just offshore, Mississippians do enjoy their oysters. But brown and white shrimp and blue crabs also grace their dinner plates and form important invertebrate fisheries.

Louisiana, with some 64% of all the tidal marshes along the Gulf coast, is the shrimper's mecca. But the waters of the Terrebonne-Barataria Bay and Lake Borgne–Breton Sound estuaries also provide prolific oystering. Indeed, over 230,000 acres of private oyster leases are found along the Louisiana coastline; another 690,000 acres of public oyster grounds also exist, mostly east of the Mississippi River. And to top off this fishermen's platter, blue crabs are Louisiana's fourth most valuable fishery.

Texas does everything in a big way. Over 1.5 million acres of estuaries produce everything from shrimp, to oysters, to blue crabs, with brown and white shrimp forming the most important invertebrate fishery. The critical importance of pollution effects on Galveston Bay becomes immediately apparent when it is realized that some 80% of Texas oysters come from this bay and its nearby estuaries. Not surprisingly, commercial crab operations also find this system and others down even into the Laguna Madre important crab harvesting areas.

FINFISHERIES: COMMERCE AND RECREATION COMBINED

Like shellfish, finfish form an important commercial product in the Gulf. With more than 600 common species recorded from fresh and salt waters, and perhaps another 400 not yet sought commercially, it is safe to say that almost any of the larger freshwater or saltwater fishes constitute some part of the overall fishery economy throughout the region. Most are taken using methods as diverse as the fishes themselves. Anglers make an average of 20 million saltwater fishing trips per year into the Gulf of Mexico for food and sport. Whether the gear is pork rinds and cane pole, speargun, rod and reel, or roller rig, the resulting catch (over 145 million marine fishes alone in 1985) makes up a market that is conservatively valued in tens of millions of dollars per year. Add in the associated values of boats, tackle, fuel, marine equipment, supplies, and accessories and the figures quickly soar into the billions of dollars per year. As a bait shop owner once said: "Fishin' ain't only fun, it's profitable!"

Excluding the menhaden fishery already discussed, most of the other commercially valuable species in the Gulf can be grouped into five main categories: the bank fishes (such as snappers and groupers) which are found on the sponge banks; the tropical reef fishes (grunts and other species) restricted by temperature to the warmest waters in the southeastern and southwestern Gulf; the bay and estuarine species (e.g., redfish or channel bass, mullet, spotted seatrout) which depend on ecological conditions in the shallow inshore waters; the anadromous species (snook, sea catfish, rock bass) that enter freshwater at certain times; and the strictly offshore species (dolphin, mackerel, tuna, tilefish) which require the relatively consistent marine conditions of the nearshore continental shelf. Fishes that overlap into one or more of these categories include the surfzone pompano, seabass, and bluefish, nearshore Spanish mackerel and mullet, reef and jetty-associating drums, porgies, sailor's choice, parrotfish, and a dozen other species beloved of onshore and offshore angler alike.

The finfish market is itself restricted to neither amateur nor professional. It too can be divided between species taken in commercial quantities and used for food and those comprising the sport and offshore game fisheries and used primarily for recreation. And although finfisheries are nothing if not diverse, many are often of merely local or regional importance. Tilefish, swordfish, and several other offshore species are found in deeper continental shelf waters around the Gulf, but their availability is limited to anglers with the appropriate gear. On the other hand, redfish, snapper, grouper, pompano, snook, seatrout, members of the mackerel family, flatfishes (flounders, soles), several species of sharks, mullet, and reef- or rock-dwelling forms are taken throughout the Gulf and provide both an economic and recreational base for many coastal areas. These, in turn, compete with a bewildering and diverse array of locally esteemed freshwater varieties for the family dollar.

ONE MAN'S TRASH, ANOTHER MAN'S TREASURE

Tourists, American and otherwise, are often amazed at the diversity and abundance of fish for sale in Mexican and Cuban markets, and in many ethnic seafood shops in the Gulf's larger cities. Many of these same species are either not recognized for their food value or are considered to be inedible or less desirable species—at least until they taste them. Yet even back home this diversity is becoming a commonplace. As tastes become more sophisticated, and prices of the standard gourmet varieties continue to rise, more and more varieties of fishes previously considered to be "trash" or bizarre species are appearing in fishmarket and supermarket display cases. Recent examples include monkfish, a deep water anglerfish from U.S. waters, and orange roughy from the deep sea off New Zealand.[1]

Reversing a previous trend, several species of "trash fishes," species such as cusk eels, snake eels, batfish, tongue soles, and other smaller bottom-dwelling species once thrown back overboard, are also being increasingly utilized in other markets.[2] For example, the industrial bottom-fish fishery seeks trash fish and is geared toward using many of these species as pet food. Averaging close to 100 million pounds per year and nearly $2 million in value, the industry is concentrated in the nearshore shallow waters of the north-central Gulf. Fish meal for food, and fish and fish byproducts for fertilizer are other products resulting from this effort. In summary, it can be safely said that, in the Gulf of Mexico, if it swims it is probably sought, caught, and bought.

As important as these fisheries are it should not be forgotten that 90% of the commercially valuable species and 10% of the recreationally valuable catch all depend in one way or another on the breeding, feeding and nursery areas in the thousands of acres of estuaries, salt marshes, mangrove forests, and seagrass beds that line the shallow-water rim of the Gulf. Their continued functioning is essential for continuance of these fisheries.

TERRITORIAL WATERS AND FISHERY JURISDICTIONS

In 1983, a presidential proclamation established a 200-mile-wide Exclusive Economic Zone around the continental United States. Extending from the seaward limit of state jurisdictional boundaries (see below) this zone was placed under federal jurisdiction in order to protect, conserve, and regulate the marine resources (fisheries, minerals) contained within it. The U. S. also claimed fishery jurisdiction to 200 miles offshore under the precepts of the Magnuson Fishery Conservation and Management Act. This act was in line with agreements established by the United Nations Conference on the Law of the Sea which held that any maritime nation could claim economic jurisdiction over marine resources for up to 320 kilometers (200 miles) off its coastlines.

By act of Congress, state boundaries of jurisdiction (state territorial waters) extend 3 miles out to sea for all maritime states, including those around the Gulf of Mexico. Florida and Texas are the only exceptions. Florida filed suit against the United States to extend her jurisdiction, and in 1960 the U.S. Supreme Court held that Florida's jurisdiction extended 3 nautical leagues (9 nautical miles) into the Gulf of Mexico. Thus, not only do intertidal and submerged shallow subtidal lands belong to the people of Florida and Texas (as they also do in the other Gulf states), but critical continental shelf lands do as well. The ramifications of this jurisdiction extend from OCS leases to fishing rights, law enforcement, and environmental protection.

Individual states have also established their own regional fishery councils and legislative bodies to oversee fishing in their territorial waters. These commissions interact with federal agencies, such as the National Marine Fisheries Service, or the U.S. Fish and Wildlife Service, in an attempt to manage the impacts of commercial and recreational fishing on the Gulf ichthyofauna. Yet owing to the complexity of the fisheries involved, the lack of funding necessary to hire fishery investigators (and enforcement personnel), and the paucity of data on fish populations, some fisheries are exploited beyond the maximum sustainable yield and then collapse. Recent examples in the Gulf include redfish, king mackerel, and the aforementioned blue and stone crab fisheries.

The problems are exacerbated in several ways. Offshore territorial boundaries may be definable by LORAN, radar, and satellite navigation, but the fish populations respect none of them. And the fisherman must follow the fish to make the catch. In some instances, offshore fishing violations become reminiscent of Old West claim-jumping and fence-busting, and laws are often enforced down the barrel of a rifle.[3] In other cases, the scientific data, tediously obtained over several years, flies in the face of local or traditional fishing methods, and contradicts anecdotal evidence or "good ole boy" knowledge, thereby creating rancour and mistrust among the very people the agencies are trying to protect. In still other cases, local fishermen find that they cannot compete against foreign fleets and offshore factory ships that are literally poaching in their territorial waters. The situation is clearly complex, and no easy solutions are foreseen.

With starvation and famines on the increase in many parts of the world, careful management of existing fishery resources becomes all the more important. And the Gulf of Mexico will certainly play a major role in the future.

Tourism

PLAYING IN THE AMERICAN MEDITERRANEAN

THE EXTENSIVE and easily accessible coastlines of the Gulf of Mexico act as natural topographical and geographical magnets for tourism, a $50-billion-per-year industry. Responding to what many consider an almost primitive urge, tens of millions of people migrate seasonally to the coastal areas of the Gulf. State bureaus of tourism and local chambers of commerce have been quick to recognize the economic potential of these migrations and have exploited local attractions in an effort to separate the tourist from his or her dollar.

WHERE THEY GO, WHAT THEY DO

Not surprisingly, the saltwater beaches of the Gulf in the United States are the region's major recreational tourist attraction, providing an easily accessible shoreline exceeding 1,800 miles in length from Florida through Texas. Scattered along or near this coast are one national park, three national seashores, two national monuments, one national memorial, 15 national wildlife refuges, six national natural landmarks, two national estuarine reserves, two national wild and scenic rivers, 12 national wilderness areas, and nearly 200 sites that are on the national historic register. At the state level there are more than 100 state parks, preserves, reserves, and wilderness areas (Florida alone has 37 state parks, and Alabama ten, Mississippi three, Louisiana nine and Texas 12, located on the Gulf coast or within an hour's drive from it).[1] In the private sector are 18 national Audubon sanctuaries, and at least 60 other federal, state or private conservation areas. So for the nature lover, history buff, camper, hiker, or those just wanting to "get away from it all," there's plenty to see and do along the Gulf.

South of the border there is even more. Beaches crown the major Mexican recreational areas, nine *parques naturalas* and *parques nacionales* (natural and national parks) occur on or within an hour's drive of the coast, and numerous historic sites can be visited along some 1,200 miles of often nearly pristine coastline. Here, many of Mexico's 6.3 million tourists spread a portion of the $3.1 billion they spend each year.

While information is sparse, even in socialism Cuba clings to her pre-Castro image as a Caribbean mecca for tourists. More than 240,000 visitors spend an estimated $48 million a year in the Pearl of the Antilles, with emphasis, of course, on harder currencies (dollars, marks, yen), rather than socialistic rubles. Sadly, an economic apartheid seems to exist, with tourists (and their currencies) taking precedence in services and accomodations over the local populace.

258

All these activities are, of course, a major source of recreation and income for local inhabitants as well, particularly in the United States. Added to this, however, are the increasing numbers of international tourists, primarily from Latin America (Venezuela is a leading exporter of tourists), Canada, and Europe (where Great Britain leads all other nations in tourist export), who come for their share of fun and sun in the Gulf.

Major cruise ship lines commonly use ports in Florida, Louisiana, and Texas on their international itineraries to other areas of the Gulf, particularly the Mexican coastline and the island of Cozumel off the eastern Yucatán Peninsula, just below the boundary between the Gulf of Mexico and the Caribbean Sea.

SEASIDE RESORTS

As noted above, seaside resorts and recreation are among the major attractions for tourists along the Gulf coastline (see Figure 40). Florida (with nearly 600 miles of recreational beaches) and Texas (with over 100 miles) lead the Gulf region in seaside tourist activity. Major areas include central and southwestern Florida from Pinellas and Hillsborough Counties south through Collier County; northwestern Florida, particularly in the Pensacola-

Figure 40. Playing with danger on La Playa.
Mile after mile of condominiums and resort hotels crowd the beaches around the Gulf of Mexico enticing the winter visitor or tourist to come and play. Yet in many such areas, playing on La Playa will eventually become a catastrophic experience. The narrow shorelines, constantly eroding owing to existing longshore currents and being continually degraded by helter-skelter construction, must be periodically restabilized using groins, bulkheads, and other "shore-hardening" methods. Passes and inlets must also be prevented from closing, often through the use of sand-stealing rip-rap jetties, as seen here on Naples beach in southwestern Florida. Yet coastal construction continues to creep dangerously close to the sea. With the frontal onslaught of a fullblown Gulf hurricane many of these residents may wind up playing on a different beach. [Courtesy of Collier County Natural Resources Management Department]

Escambia Bay region; Alabama, along the shores of Mobile Bay; the Mississippi coast in the Biloxi area; and much of the Texas coastline, with emphasis along the barrier islands and Padre Island seashores. The larger Mexican cities of Tampico, Vera Cruz, and parts of the Yucatán Peninsula also support seaside tourism.

SPORT AND GAME FISHING

Closely associated with seaside activities are sport and game fishing, ranging from low-cost individual boating to the more expensive offshore party boats and deep-sea charter fleets. While the glory days of offshore big game fishing may be gone from Cuba, Mexico has picked up the slack. The Yucatán remains a game fisherman's paradise, with plenty of marlin, sailfish, and swordfish awaiting the lucky angler. Inshore, the mangrove tidal creeks, salt marsh tributaries, coastal barrier lagoons, and cypress-lined bayous from Florida around the Gulf to Mexico to Padre Island and beyond provide numerous recreational opportunities for the dedicated inshore sportsman.

SNORKELING AND SCUBA DIVING

According to the United States Department of the Interior, there are over 3,800 square miles (10,000 square kilometers) of seagrass areas in the Gulf, with over 3,200 square miles (8,500 square kilometers) of these found in the eastern Gulf. All but about 200 square miles occur along the Florida Gulf coastline. Thus, this area is a wader's, snorkeler's (and angler's) delight.

The reef and reeflike areas are so extensive and so widely distributed around the Gulf that no estimate of area would be meaningful. Suffice it to say that snorkeling on the shallower reefs gives way to scuba diving on the deeper ones, where a self-contained air supply allows longer time on the bottom, thereby providing a greater appreciation for aesthetics, exploration, or spearfishing, all of which feeds the coffers of this $100-million-a-year business.

Locally popular reefs off southwestern Florida at Dry Tortugas, the Flower Garden Banks off Texas, and the pristine waters around the Yucatán Peninsula beckon snorkelers and scuba divers. South of Tampico, Mexico, and about four miles offshore of Cabo Rojo lies the Arrecife Lobos system, a nearshore coral reef, lagoon, and sandy islet complex that attracts divers because of its proximity to, and accessibility from, the nearby shore.

Modern-day sea hunters also seek the permanent fish havens of offshore oil platforms where spearfishing and scuba diving activities often exceed those in shallower and more nearshore areas. A related, but admittedly more dangerous activity of recent origin is cave-diving in the freshwater springs and sinkholes of in the Big Bend area of Florida east of Apalachicola and in some of the circular cenotes (deep sinkhole wells) in the Yucatán Peninsula. More recently, palaeontological and archaeological diving, and exploring for lost treasure and artifacts, have caught the public's fancy. Historical disaster areas along the Texas coast and the west central and southern coastlines of Florida are being probed for the remains and booty of Spanish galleons, British men o' war,

Confederate gunboats, and nineteenth and twentieth-century commercial vessels lost on account of weather, war, or accident. [2]

HUNTING, CAMPING, AND BOATING

Hunting, camping, and boating are also major money industries all along the Gulf coast. The extent of just a portion of this industry can be grasped when it is realized that the U.S. Minerals Management Service estimates that there is at least one motorboat for every 21 people living in the Gulf region of the United States!

Moreover, with nearly 250 special land-use areas—20% of which are lands under federal ownership or administration and another 70% under state jurisdiction—there are plenty of opportunities to see the great outdoors in the Gulf region. In addition to the parks, seashores, preserves, and other recreational areas noted earlier, these lands also include 13 national forests located near the coast, comprising over 3.6 million acres, where hunting, fishing, camping, and hiking are prominent activities. In addition, a multitude of private resorts, campgrounds, and recreational theme parks can also be found. Most of the public lands, and all of the privately owned commercial enterprises, are easily accessible by land or water vehicles. The vacationer along the United States coastline of the Gulf of Mexico is never more than about an hour's drive away from one kind of recreational area or another, be it public lands or private resorts.

Those seeking less crowded areas journey to the Mexican shore, where modern resorts are often less than an hour's drive from the ancient temples of the Aztecs and Mayans. Many of these relatively unpopulated areas offer vistas of unspoiled natural beauty and an escape from the hurly-burly of the modern Gulf. All in all, if you can't find a vacation spot to your liking around the Gulf, you aren't looking very hard.

Agricultural Resources

FARMING THE LAND AND THE SEA

T HE AGRICULTURAL and agriculturally related resources in the Gulf region are farmed crops, livestock and poultry, and fruit. The major farmed crops include rice, corn, cotton, sugarcane, sorghum, soybeans, tobacco, wheat, and several other cereal staples. Also in this category are vegetable crops, including tomatoes, beans, lettuces, peppers, onions, and other garden produce.

In the United States the major Gulf farming areas occur in Florida, which ranks second only to North Carolina among all the southeastern states in overall farm sales, and which, in the total production of fresh market vegetables, is exceeded only by California (see Table 17). Louisiana and Texas also support a large vegetable market. Louisiana's sweet potato crop is the largest in the nation, but rice and cotton are also important. Texas concentrates on cereal grains, sorghum, and peanuts, and harvested more corn and wheat than Alabama, Louisiana, Mississippi, and Florida in 1987. Cotton is number one in Mississippi, followed by soybeans and rice, while in neighboring Alabama soybeans have supplanted cotton as the number one cash crop, followed by peanuts and cereal grains. In fact, soybeans are an increasingly big business crop in the Gulf states, and Mississippi and Louisiana have taken the lead in the number of acres harvested of this legume.

TABLE 17
Valuation of Farming Industries in the Gulf States

	Number of Farms (1988)	Livestock Value (1987)	Crop Value (1987)
Florida	40,000 (1.8%)*	$1.10 billion	$4.12 billion
Alabama	49,000 (2.3%)	$1.56 billion	$588 million
Mississippi	43,000 (1.9%)	$1.04 billion	$939 million
Louisiana	35,000 (1.6%)	$521 million	$899 million
Texas	156,000 (7.2%)	$6.06 billion	$3.03 billion

* Percent of U. S. total number of farms.

Source: *The Europa World Book* (1990).

Another important crop is sugarcane, which rose to both regional and international importance after trade relations were severed between the United States and Cuba. One third of all U.S. sugarcane in the nation is produced in Florida, where it forms the leading dollar-value product in farm sales. Texas and Louisiana are also important sugarcane-producing states (see Figure 41).

Citrus and fruit-growing industries rank second in overall monetary value, with oranges and grapefruit forming much of the economic base. As might be expected, Florida ranks first in citrus economy, with over 30% of its total agricultural economy devoted to this crop. In fact, over 95% of all the orange-juice concentrate used in the United States is processed in Florida. Texas has also invested in citrus, though its total production does not approach that of Florida (or its west coast competitor, California). But there is plenty of market to be shared. Citrus is sold locally, regionally, and internationally, with the primary importer of U.S. citrus being Japan. Other fruit crops include local or regionalized species such as peaches, watermelons, cantaloupes and a variety of other melons, strawberries, pineapples, and grapes. Other fruits, such as guavas and sapodillas, form a small portion of the markets in Florida and Texas and vie with other local ethnic produce in Mexico. On the other hand, most of

Figure 41. Shucking for sugar.
Sugarcane continues to be a major industry in the Gulf of Mexico, with Florida and Cuba leading producers. Sugarcane agriculture is a labor-intensive industry, and the fields in the incredibly rich mucklands around Lake Okeechobee in Florida have produced immense crops which are quickly utilized by a sugar-hungry world. Unfortunately, pesticide, herbicide, and fertilizer runoff has been implicated in the continuing eutrophication of Lake Okeechobee, as well as in the disastrous decline in the quality of sheetflow water that supports the Everglades National Park and its adjacent ecosystems. Federal and state agencies are presently working on solving the problems, but there are no easy or quick fixes. [Florida State Archives, Tallahassee, Florida]

the citrus that Cuba grows apparently remains within that country.[1]

Livestock and poultry are third in rank to agriculture, and Texas and Florida are both important beef and dairy cattle-ranching states. In a different use of available lands, Louisianan cattle ranchers graze their livestock on some of the extensive coastal marshlands of that state. Surprisingly, however, Tennessee and Kentucky exceed all three Gulf coast states in dollar values of cattle ranching. In the poultry markets, Texas and Alabama lead the other Gulf states in numbers of chickens sold in 1987 (10.9 and 10.0 million, respectively), followed by Mississippi (8.1 million), Florida (4.6 million), and Louisiana (1.1 million).

Forestry, including lumber and wood by-products, is a major industry along the Gulf coast. Alabama ranks first in total acreage of land held in corporate tree farms, followed by Florida. Pine forests, once the standby for turpentine and similar products, have now assumed a new role as major producers of wood pulp for the paper and cardboard industries. Large pulp mills are found in northwestern Florida and parts of Mississippi, where portions of the national forests are managed for this product.

Aquaculture, the commercial cultivation of aquatic organisms, is becoming increasingly important throughout the Gulf region. Catfish farms form both a staple and a stable industry in all the Gulf states. Although much of the product is sold within the United States, particularly to fast food chains and local supermarkets, large-scale catfish farmers in Louisiana are attempting to tap an apparently receptive overseas market. Their efforts are aimed particularly toward Europe, where catfish is marketed as a high-priced delicacy under the trade pseudonym "topper." That's a long way from the cane pole and breadball activities that kept several generations of youngsters amused on warm country-summer days.

Not all fish aquaculture is confined to the rearing pens. Recent advances in controlling the spawning period of redfish in Texas have allowed the young to be reared in captivity and then released into the estuaries to enhance the local fishery. This came about through a tripartite effort in which the Gulf Coast Conservation Association donated the money to build the hatchery, the Central Power and Light Company donated the land, and the Texas legislature appropriated the operating expenses. Farsighted cooperative ventures such as this point the way to the future for some fisheries, particularly estuarine species.

Other aquacultural efforts have been directed toward saltwater shrimp farming, a difficult and costly process that has so far been commercially marginal; freshwater shrimp aquaculture, with more encouraging results; and the culture of a variety of imported fishes of the family Cichlidae (*Tilapia* species),which are marketed under euphemistic trade names such as "vermilion snapper" or "butterfly bass."

In Louisiana, and to a lesser degree in Texas, freshwater crayfish farming has become an important local industry. Originally restricted primarily to the restaurant and fish-market trade, the product is now exported to a number of other neighboring states where "crawdads" are considered a trendy and very tasty gourmet item. Cajuns can only shake their heads and smile. They knew that all along.

Outside the United States, both Mexico and Cuba share an important part of the world agricultural market (see Table 18). Mexican agriculture is a $10-billion-a-year industry. Although the country is a relative newcomer to world vegetable markets, Mexico is rapidly approaching international status as a major agricultural crop producer, at least in the Gulf region, where her corn, sorghum, and wheat form important exportable assets.

But Mexico's major crop is sugar, which in 1987 totaled more than 42.5 million tons, well over the 34 million ton total of all her other vegetable and grain crops. Mexico gives Cuba a solid run for her money where the 81 million tons of sugar forms the primary export crop of that island country, bringing in approximately $5 billion in 1988.

Mexico makes her mark in world markets in other agricultural products as well, with some 31 million head of cattle, 17 million pigs, and 10.5 million goats contributing beef, veal, pork, and goat meat for sale. Dairy products including milk and eggs are also important. In fact, viewed overall, almost every common fruit, vegetable, nut, livestock and dairy product forms a substantial part of Mexico's economy, showing that she is a force to be reckoned with in the coming decades.

Cuba is no slouch in agricultural markets either, producing over 11 million tons of agricultural products (tomatoes, bananas, cassava flour, rice, sweet potatoes) in a country about one sixth the size of Mexico. The nearly 1.1 million tons of citrus and 1.7 million tons of beef and veal, milk, eggs, poultry and pork are other staples of the Cuban economy.

TABLE 18
Comparison of Selected Agricultural Economies in Mexico and Cuba
(in millions of tons per year)

	Mexico	Cuba
Sugarcane	45.6	81.1
Milk	8.4	1.2
Beef/veal	1.4	0.1
Eggs	1.1	0.1

Source: *The Europa World Book* (1990).

Although sugar is the major export money crop, of greater interest is Cuba's second ranked agricultural monetary crop, milk. Much of the 1.2 million tons produced annually is presumably consumed at home.[2] In that island worker's paradise much of what is produced apparently is used by the existing population, so that Cuba must rely on imports to sustain her citizens. In 1988 Cuba's major trading partners were the Soviet Union, East Germany, and Czechoslovakia (some $4.7 billion dollars). With the collapse of both communism and the economies of the U.S.S.R and East Germany, the waters of international trade around Cuba become muddy indeed. It remains to be seen whether relying on such specialized industries will allow Cuba to continue to compete among the increasingly competitive Third World nations both in the New World and abroad.

A Diversity of Other Economies

T HERE ARE, OF COURSE, numerous other industries, both local and national, utilizing the wealth of the Gulf of Mexico both on land and at sea. As technological advances and exploratory activities open up new frontiers, it is a safe bet that new treasures will continue to be found and exploited. Some of these economies are briefly examined below.

MINERAL MINING

In the Gulf coastal region of the United States, Florida leads all of the southeastern states and ranks sixth in the nation in dollar value for nonpetroleum minerals. Florida's "white gold" is phosphate rock, a fossiliferous legacy from Florida's past (see figure 42). The major mining deposits today are located in a four-county area east of Tampa Bay. A smaller area is found west of Jacksonville in the state's northeastern corner. Phosphate rock is used in a multitude of ways, but its major use is in fertilizers for both agri-business and home gardening. With one of the largest commercial phosphate ventures in the eastern Gulf located in Florida, it is not surprising that over 85% of the entire supply of phosphate for the United States is produced in that state. South of the border, Mexico also digs for phosphates, taking nearly 700,000 tons from her quarries in 1987.

If phosphates are Florida's white gold, plain old table salt (or halite) helps to fill the coffers of Louisiana and Texas and the salt shakers of the world.[1] Large deposits, often miles thick, are mined in both states. Louisiana produced more than 11 million tons of halite in 1987.[2] Texas also uses her salt domes as storage areas for the U. S. Strategic Petroleum Reserves. Cuba, on the other hand, does it another way—evaporating sea salt in shallow estuarine flats to the tune of 220,000 tons a year.[3] Although usually considered a seasoning, halite has a multitude of other uses in tanning, fertilizers, manufacturing of chlorine gas, metallic sodium, and hydrochloric acid, and in melting snow on icy highways and sidewalks.

Even mundane deposits like sand, clay, and gravel are money-makers. Alabama and Mississippi mine limestone and calcareous sands for cement, and Texas mines clays for drilling muds to be used in deep-well oil rigs. Louisiana is currently exploring large sand deposits offshore with a view toward utilizing them in beach renourishment by replacing shoreline sediments washed away by tides, currents, or storms. Similar deposits of quartz sand off Mississippi and Alabama have potential use in glass making. Cuba in 1988 produced over 6.5 million tons of silica sand and nearly 14 million tons of crushed stone for a

Figure 42. Mining Florida's white gold.
Artificial mountains of phosphate rock dug from Florida's ancient shores and valleys by huge
dredges are pushed into storage mounds preparatory to their being loaded on conveyor belts for
transport to agrochemical factories. Phosphates are an important industry in Florida and provide
some 85% of all the phosphate rock mined in the United States. Similar operations take place in
Mexico. [Courtesy Florida Department of Commerce, Division of Tourism, Tallahassee, Florida]

variety of uses ranging from concretes to mosaics.

Sulfur is another important mineral in the Gulf, occurring in large deposits
associated with salt domes on both the mainland and the continental shelf.[4] First
discovered in 1949 during oil exploration activities, this mine contained an
estimated 45 million tons of sulfur. Louisiana's Caminada and Grand Isle mines
are also important; the latter has been in operation since 1960 and has produced
more than 27 million tons of sulfur. Yet production is often disparate. For
example, in 1986 Louisiana mined 576,000 tons, while Mexico produced more
than 2.5 million tons in 1987.[5] This disparity may be expected to change very
soon. The Main Pass sulfur mine, located in 210 feet of water east of the
Mississippi River, is projected to produce more sulfur than the Grand Isle and
Caminada mines put together. The mine itself is considered the largest sulfur
reserve in North America, and (concomitantly) is one of the largest natural gas
and oil discovery sites in the entire Gulf.

The commercial potential of sulfur deposits on the continental shelf around
the Gulf, although quite variable, is extremely important. Elemental sulfur, for
example, is used to produce most sulfuric acid, one of the most important

industrial reagents in the world. Sulfur is also important in the manufacturing of fertilizers, particularly phosphate-based compounds. As an example of this importance, demand for sulfur in the United States has always exceeded both its supply and production.

But the mineral is not overly abundant. Current estimates are that only one salt dome in ten contains workable supplies, and less than one in 100 have deposits exceeding 20 million tons. The Minerals Management Service of the U.S. Department of the Interior currently administers the sales of offshore sulfur leases; the dozen or so existing leases are presently restricted to small areas off Texas and Louisiana.

Mexico has a well-developed onshore mining industry, producing nearly 14 million tons of ores ranging from gold and silver to copper, iron, nickel, mercury, manganese, uranium, coal, and numerous other mineral compounds such as barites (a component of drilling muds) and fluorites (used in glass manufacturing, steel making, and as an ornamental material in vases and bowls). The value of Mexico's mining industry fluctuates depending on world pricing but certainly exceeds $11 billion dollars a year by the most conservative estimates.

Cuba's mining industry is also important, with nickel (second only to sugar in export value), chromium, and vast iron deposits totaling more than 244,000 tons per year and bringing in the equivalent of several million U.S. dollars a year.

CHEMICAL MANUFACTURING

Because of the preponderance of petroleum products available around the Gulf, it was a natural result to locate chemical manufacturing plants there. Major sites of development include the Galveston-Houston area, Corpus Christi-Brownsville, the corridor from New Orleans to Baton Rouge, and the Tampico-Vera Cruz-Coatzoacoalcos area in Mexico. In the United States, more than 50% of all the chemicals sold are produced or refined at plants in the vicinity of Galveston Bay. And at least 30% of the entire U. S. petroleum industry operates in the same area.

Most of these plants produce petrochemicals, products derived from the chemical fractionating (distilling) of crude oil. One primary component is methane, commonly known as swamp gas when it occurs naturally. Methane produces methylene compounds, important chemicals in many plastic manufacturing processes. Another, called ethane, is broken down to make ethylene. Ethylene and its related products form the basis for the synthesis of nearly all other organic chemicals. Still others include the more familiar butane and propane, the major components of natural gases used in everything from gas heaters to barbecue grills. From these come butylene and propylene, chemicals used in manufacturing plastics, rubber products, anti-freeze liquids, food preservatives, anti-knock compounds in gasoline and numerous other day-to-day products. Benzenes form another "starting point" compound similar to ethylene, for making more complex petrochemicals including phenol, which is used in perfumes, dyes, pharmaceuticals, and explosives. The list goes on with hexanes, heptanes, octanes, and so forth, that are incorporated into everything from high-grade aviation fuel to artificial sweeteners. It has been said that the number of compounds that a good petrochemical engineer can make is limited by only two things: imagination and money. And in the petrochemical industry there is an abundance of both.

PONDERABLES FOR OUR FUTURE

Fact: World reserves of sulfur are estimated at 1.45 billion tons.

Fact: Sulphur reserves in the United States were estimated at some 171 million tons in 1984, or about 12% of the world's supply.

Fact: Sulfur reserves from all known resources in the United States are estimated at about 364 million tons.

Fact: United States' cumulative demand for sulfur projected from 1983 to the year 2000 is estimated at nearly 287 million tons, or 80% of its reserves.

Fact: World demand for sulfur and its byproducts continues to exceed output. For example, Canada's inventories were reduced from about 24 million tons in 1980 to about 10 million tons in 1985.

Fact: Projected cumulative demand for sulfur and its byproducts by the rest of the world from 1983 to 2000 is 1.1 billion tons.

Fact: If current and projected rates of use by the United States and the rest of the world continue (estimated at 1.36 billion tons by the turn of the century), world inventories of sulfur will be severely depleted by the year 2000.

Source: Anonymous (1989) *Sulfur & Salt Leasing: Summary of Issues*. OCS MMS 87-0036.

OTHER ECONOMIC ACTIVITIES

Important smaller industries along the Gulf coast include food processing (much of which is associated directly with the agricultural and fishing industries in Alabama and Mississippi); textiles (Alabama); timber, lumber, construction, and supporting industries (Mississippi); manufacturing, including electronics, machinery, steelmaking, and general wholesale and retail products (every state); and transportation (Texas). The latter industry, although smaller in size than many of the others, is often critical in both dollar value produced and its importance to the economy of the traveling public. This economy is often directly reflected in the success or failure of tourist-oriented regions around the Gulf. One other industry is of some importance to Louisianians—the fur industry. The Sportsman's Paradise produces more fur than any other state in the nation.

Mexico and Cuba also have their share of smaller industries. For example, in 1987 Mexico produced nearly 22 million tons of cement and more than 14 million tons of tires, manufactured 16.5 million tons of gasoline, made 7.6 million tons of steel, brewed nearly 700 million gallons of beer, and produced nearly 50 million cigarettes. Much of these products went to Mexico's three main trading partners: the United States ($7.9 billion), Japan ($795 million), and Germany ($835 million). Cuba, in the following year, manufactured 286 million tons of textiles, nearly 15 million tons of leather goods, nearly 4 million tons of cement, made over 1 million tons of gasoline, and produced almost 17 million cigarettes. Most of this went to Eastern bloc nations or the Soviet Union.

From these few examples it can easily be seen that the Gulf of Mexico is one of the most important industrial regions in the western hemisphere. The additional value it retains is due in no small part to the availability of seaports and airports which allow direct connection to the large markets of South America and to the trade routes of the world. The relatively close proximity of the Panama Canal also makes the Gulf a natural conduit for access to the Pacific Ocean and the nations of the Far East.

Were the early Spanish explorer-merchants aboard those four commercial vessels that fateful day in June 1497 able to come back today, they would be dumbstruck at the bounty of the area and its consequent exploitation by all of the old enemies of Castile. Without a doubt they would also be more than a little dismayed at the loss of the sea they once so smugly considered their own Spanish lake.

"Hanged by the neck until dead."
In a continuing and deadly harvest, a kingfisher hangs entangled in castoff monofilament nylon fishing line, strangled by the careless litter of an unthinking angler. These, and other fisheating birds, such as pelicans, gulls, and terns, suffer painful injuries and an often slow and agonizing death when they become entrapped in our improperly discarded plastic products. Through a macabre twist of fate—and the negligence of mankind—the fishers have too often become the fished. [Courtesy Theodore H. Below]

PART SIX

Pollution: Mankind's Continuing Input

It is easier to discover another such a new world as Columbus did, than to go within one fold of this which we appear to know so well; the land is lost sight of, the compass varies, and mankind mutiny; and still history accumulates like rubbish before the portals of Nature.

Henry David Thoreau, 1845
A Week on the Concord and Merrimack Rivers

Fouling our Nests
with a Vengeance

IT HAS BEEN ARGUED that every living organism on earth is some form of polluter. In the great cycle of life, animals pollute through respiratory and digestive activities; the prey pollutes with their decaying carcasses; the predators pollute with their fecal material; plants pollute by dropping leaves and releasing carbon dioxide during nighttime respiration; algae pollute through explosive blooms in over-enriched lakes; bacteria pollute with their breakdown of organisms and release of noxious gases; and every organism pollutes an otherwise pristine environment simply by existing in it, and thereby exerting some type of change. The ineluctable conclusion is that life itself, in order to continue, requires constant, continuing, and often major changes in the physical and biological environments. What is lost in this simplistic statement, however, is that before mankind learned how to so effectively manipulate, and thus sidestep, his evolutionary heritage, the environments of earth were generally able to tolerate such changes, primarily because these same changes occurred so slowly or at such low levels of intensity that the ecosystems which were affected were still able to adjust.

Ecologists have long known that ecosystems can adjust to changes by resisting adverse impacts (that is, by overcoming them) or by adapting to such impacts (that is, by absorbing them). Such ecosystems exhibit either "resistance" or "resilience," in much the same way that an oak tree resists strong winds, whereas the more supple willow tree bends with them. In any case, the ultimate result is the survival or persistence of the system. When any parts of an ecosystem are lost or permanently altered, the system itself usually changes. These changes may be subtle (perhaps the extirpation of one or two species or the gradual decline of a species population) or overt (the rapid decline of populations and loss of numerous species). How severely a system will be affected depends on a multitude of factors including the magniturde of its biological diversity (the numbers of species and individuals within each), the adaptability of these same species to the altered ecological conditions, the restructuring of food webs to replace the species that are lost, and so on. Any system that cannot restructure itself along these and other lines either undergoes population crashes, or in the worst case, disappears. The extinction of any species is bad enough—the extinction of an ecosystem can be catastrophic.

RENDERING THE UNACCEPTABLE COMMONPLACE

Today we are seeing increasing evidence of ecosystem alteration by loss of species through extinction, extirpation, or destruction of habitat. Much more insidious, however, is the environmental destruction resulting from pollution. Through the mechanism of a million minor pollution events, mankind, like an insatiable colony of termites, is slowly nibbling the world ecosystems to death. No better example exists than in the Gulf of Mexico, where more than 800,000 acres of shellfish beds have been reclassified in terms of harvestability since 1971 as a direct consequence of point source (direct) and non-point source (diffuse) pollution. Some 720,000 of these acres are now partially or completely off-limits for shellfishing. As noted in the House and Senate Merchant Marine Report for 1988: "The prevalence of contaminants in our coastal waters is rendering the unacceptable commonplace."

Just how bad could it be? Consider these facts. According to information provided by the Florida Department of Environmental Regulation, the waters of the Gulf of Mexico presently cover two inactive radioactive waste sites, 10 explosives and toxic chemical ammunition sites, 16 inactive industrial waste sites, one inactive ocean incineration site, over 35 dredged-material disposal sites, and over 20,000 oil and gas wells. And this doesn't even include debris and pollution from shipwrecks and other environmental accidents.

PEOPLE + POPULATION = PROBLEMS

We cannot escape the fact that mankind has exerted a distinct and profound impact on the environment. Whether by bulldozing rain forests, dumping domestic and industrial wastes into rivers and estuaries, poisoning the atmosphere with toxic and acid-producing chemicals, or just by "being there," mankind makes an impact. These negative influences often occur in direct proportion to the size and growth rate of a population, a fact long recognized by ecologists as operating in lower organisms. And the coastal areas of the Gulf of Mexico are a prime example of this.

For example, two of the five fastest growing coastal states in the United States are Florida and Texas, both with extensive Gulf-front lands. Along the Texas Gulf coast five metropolitan areas have assumed major proportions in development and population. These are Beaumont-Port Arthur, Galveston-Texas City, Corpus Christi, Brownsville-Harlingen, and Houston (the largest city in the southeastern U. S.). Population densities average 160 persons per square mile.[1] But other states are not lagging behind, and the population growth rates over a 30-year period are nothing short of explosive (see Table 19).

The Gulf coast of Florida is by far the most rapidly growing part in the eastern region. With important large cities (Pensacola, Tampa, St. Petersburg) and major resort and retirement areas (Pinellas, Sarasota, and Collier counties), the "Sun Coast" beckons to more and more who seek the good life. Overall, the population increase on Florida's Gulf coast is projected to exceed 1.5 million in the next 20 years. Coastal Texas will be a close second with a projected increase of 1.1 million people in the same time period.

Demographers may dismiss these figures out of hand, pointing out that they do not compare to population densities of the northeastern corridor or the coastlands of middle and lower California. But the projected figures do suggest a trend that, without proper growth management and planning, could enhance what many environmentalists, regional planners, and demographers see as an accelerating decline in environmental quality and natural resources all along the maritime Gulf. Population means pollution, be it sewage, automobile emissions, garbage, industrial or municipal utility exhausts, or even just the hundreds of everyday problems that go along with bigger-city living. The specter is already present in smog in Mobile; degradation of existing water quality in Galveston; pulp mill effluents in the Florida panhandle; phosphatic-acid waters in Tampa; and sick or dying lakes, rivers, and streams from Naples to Brownsville.

POLLUTION VERSUS WASTE: A DICHOTOMOUS DILEMMA

There is, nevertheless, a dichotomy between pollution and waste, just as there is a dichotomy between nonhazardous and hazardous waste. If it is a given that pollution is the inevitable consequence of life on earth, then it is also a given that before humans altered the cycles, pollution and waste were not only tolerated, but actually integrated into the environment. The difference, of course, is that the waste produced before historic man entered the scene was not necessarily hazardous to the environment. Today, with our abilities to create substances and even elements totally foreign to earth, the problem has grown into a crisis. Yet the crisis need not be either permanent or unmanageable. With the proper and timely application of education and technology it can be overcome. It may require something as simple as reexamining our previous and long-held concepts about pollution. As one researcher summed it up, "Pollution is a waste of resources, and waste is pollution of resources."

Making the rules that we like, and breaking those we don't, we have attempted to alter the environment to suit only ourselves. In so doing, we have produced contaminants and pollution events detrimental not only to ourselves, but also to many of the species with whom we share this water planet.

What are the major types of pollution? In the Gulf they can be broadly summed up in five categories: (1) excess nutrients (including sewage); (2) industrial wastes and contaminants (including petroleum and its by-products, heavy metals, municipal runoff, and a host of inorganic and organic chemical compounds); (3) biocides (pesticides and herbicides); (4) man-made trash and debris (plastics, paper and cardboard, glass, and other insoluble refuse); and (5) twentieth-century impacts, a broad category which includes thermal, radioactive, and other uncommon forms of pollution. We will look briefly at each category in the following chapters.

TABLE 19
Population Growth in Gulf Coast States, 1960–1990

State	Coastal Land Area (sq. mi.)	Thousands of People/Sq. Mi.		
		1960	1990	% Increase
Florida	36,943	2,207	5,668	156
Alabama	2,827	363	484	33
Mississippi	1,790	189	344	82
Louisiana	6,535	1,912	2,821	48
Texas	20,784	2,681	5,409	101
TOTAL:	78,879	7,353	14,726	100

State	*Total State Populations in Millions of People		*U.S. Ranking	
	1988	2000	1988	2000
Florida	12.3 (5%)†	15.4 (5.8%)	4	4
Alabama	4.1 (1.7%)	4.4 (1.7%)	22	23
Mississippi	2.6 (1.1%)	2.9 (1.1%)	31	29
Louisiana	4.4 (1.8%)	4.5 (1.7%)	20	21
Texas	16.8 (6.7%)	20.2 (7.6%)	3	2

Source: Morgan, K. et al. (1990) and U. S. Department of Commerce,
Bureau of the Census (1989).
* = estimated
† ( ) = Percent of total U.S. population

Nutrients

AN EXCESS OF BENEFITS

E VERY LIVING ORGANISM on earth attempts to do three things: obtain nutrients, process them and eliminate the waste, and replicate itself. From the smallest bacterium to the greatest of blue whales, life is a continuum of ingestion, digestion, and reproduction. As a consequence, a species' waste products are returned to the environment, often in a state not usable by other species until changed in some way, either by physical, chemical, or biological processes.

In many cases one species' wastes are often another species' nutrients. The cyclical interaction of respirational activities between plants and animals provides a good example of how this occurs. Put simply, plants utilize carbon dioxide and produce oxygen during photosynthesis—animals breathe oxygen and exhale carbon dioxide during respiration. But there's a lot more to it than just that. During the long, involved process of evolution, certain chemical entities have become particularly important as nutrients to plants—some produced by animals, some made, or altered from other materials, by microbes as part of their own life processes. Among these are the inorganic salts of nitrogen (nitrates, nitrites), phosphorus (phosphates), sulfur (sulfides and sulfates), and a series of nitrogen-bound compounds based on ammonia (NH_3). All can be found in animal wastes or decay.

Equally important are other metallic elements that occur in small amounts (traces) and are required by all living organisms for their complete health. These trace elements are all soluble to varying degrees in fresh and salt water. Consequently, they appear in aquatic systems either as a direct result of cycling by the organisms that exist within a system or as a result of being transported into it via runoff, rain, rivers, or artificial input.

The production of these nutrient elements, and their cycling through the environment and the living organisms within it, will determine the "ecological health" of a system. If the biological entities within a system are able to use either nutrients occurring within a system, or entering from without (the ambient or the entrained nutrients), the system can maintain itself over a long period of time. Conversely, a scarcity of the ambient or the entrained nutrients often results in populational decreases or loss of one or more species. When this happens it produces a perturbation in the system that may eventually lead to its decline.

EUTROPHICATION: OVERDOING A GOOD THING

On the other hand, excess nutrients that enhance populational growth beyond the capacity of a system to support it can also produce an imbalance. These imbalanced systems are said to be undergoing *eutrophication,* a process of nutrient over-enrichment. Eutrophication, which has been defined as a form of aging that occurs in any water body, will eventually occur in any system. Slow and natural, or accelerated and artificial, it indicates that the aquatic system is approaching or has attained senescence—in effect, it has grown old.

It must not be thought, however, that eutrophication is always the result of human activity. It is not; in fact, the process has been taking place for thousands of years and, in nature, is part of the total ecological picture. No ecosystem is forever. And the fossil and recent geological record provides chapter after chapter of the growth, maturity, and eventual senescence and death of such systems. As a naturally occurring event, eutrophication is part and parcel of the life history of any ecological system.

However, the picture changes when mankind enters the scene. Such simple events as soil erosion (through poor agricultural, silvicultural, or land development practices), urban runoff, and dumping of industrial, agricultural, and human-associated wastes can greatly accelerate the eutrophication of a body of water. The speed at which such eutrophication occurs is directly related to the area, volume, and depth of the water body, its ability to process the unnaturally occurring enrichment, and its resistance or resilience to changes imposed as a consequence of eutrophication.

Eutrophication is often seen in ponds, lakes, lagoons, and other enclosed water bodies in which excess nutrient input is prevented from being flushed through the system. As a consequence, plants undergo rapid populational increases, either as algal blooms or as benthic overgrowth. This begins a slow but inexorable cycle of massive growth, death, decomposition (via bacteria), and deoxygenization (as a consequence of decay), that eventually leads to deterioration of the ambient water quality.

Because rivers and streams have long been the traditional sewers of mankind, they are the most prone to eutrophication. More importantly, and less obviously, these same flowing waterways carry their excess nutrient loads into other water bodies downstream. The resultant effect is often cumulative, with downstream areas undergoing more rapid eutrophication owing to the pulsed input of nitrates, nitrites, sulfates, phosphates and a multitude of trace nutrients. And where rivers empty into the sea, in the estuaries, the effects of eutrophication often become glaringly apparent.

The classic indicators of eutrophication are usually large, dense mats of algae (usually blue-green cyanophytes, although green and red algae also form blooms) and fish kills. The one process inevitably leads to the other; and as oxygen continues to be depleted through respiration and decay processes, even the plants begin to die. As the dead and dying plant and animal matter sinks to the bottom, the decay process robs the water column of even more oxygen, and eventually a thick, sticky, black goo laden with hydrogen sulfide, methane, and ammonia carpets the bottom.

WHERE DOES IT COME FROM? WHERE DOES IT GO?

There are probably as many sources of excess nutrients that can act as pollutants as there are cities, towns, and villages on earth. When it is realized that the Mississippi River alone drains nearly 1.25 million square miles, or approximately 41% of the entire land area of the United States, some idea of the magnitude of the problem can be gained. Pollutants from as far west as Bozeman, Montana, or as far north as Jamestown, New York, may eventually find their way into coastal Gulf waters. In fact, nearly ten times more nutrients are introduced from upstream sources than occur in coastal areas. Yet most of these inland-generated pollutants are so diluted in the freshwater rivers, absorbed onto sediment particles or absorbed by plants, animals or directly into the sediments that by the time they reach the Gulf they are of little significance in and of themselves.

It is often quite a different story along the Gulf coastal margin, that area extending from the beaches to approximately 50 miles inland. Within this coastal zone sewage is a major pollution source, even that treated to secondary levels.[1] Coastal zone treatment plants often dump secondarily treated waste water directly into the rivers and lagoons that empty into the Gulf, hoping that dilution is the solution to pollution. But it doesn't always work. In Galveston Bay, for example, over 51% of the area has been permanently closed for harvesting of shellfish owing to pollution by coliform bacteria.[2]

Although treated sewage waste is 99.9% water, it is the nutrients dissolved in this water that create one set of problems. One consequence is that nitrates, nitrites, and ammonia-based compounds are flushed into local waterways, and eventually add an artificially enriched nutrient supply to estuaries and the nearshore Gulf waters.

Many of these nutrients are greedily scavenged by plants. When benthic algae or floating phytoplankton assimilate these nutrients, a population explosion often results. The final result may be as benign as soupy green water and suspiciously fat oysters and clams, to more drastic effects such as periodic die-offs of fish and red or brown tides.

Another important nutrient entering aquatic ecosystems is phosphorus. Again, incompletely treated sewage is a major culprit. It has been estimated that nearly 50% of the phosphorus compounds in sewage originates from detergents. Whether from homes, restaurants, laundromats, or car washes, high-phosphorus waste water is a fact of life. Modern sewage treatment plants may remove only about 30% of all phosphorus and 10% or less of all nitrogen compounds.

Urbanized areas are guilty of another nutrient pollution source: urban runoff. Storm-water runoff is often high in nitrogen and phosphorus compounds, a result of rainwater washing the streets, golf courses, and lawn-covered yards of the city clean of fertilizers, leaf litter, animal fecal material, offal and other anthropogenic (human-created) wastes.

But urban areas stand not alone in guilt. Poorly managed agricultural lands often are responsible for excessive amounts of nitrates and phosphates, a result of heavy or indiscriminate overfertilization of food and forage crops. Feedlots and pasturelands add their own burden, primarily in manure-formed nitrates and nitrites. A hidden danger in these types of nutrient pollution is that in many cases not only is surface water contaminated, but subsurficial groundwater and aquifers may be affected as well as the contaminants percolate downward.

Even industrial operations can add excess nutrients. A prime polluter in the form of phosphorus is Florida's phosphate mining industry. In addition to causing ordinary eutrophication, phosphates have also been implicated as one of several predisposing factors in the outbreaks of the notorious red tides that occur along Florida's west coast.

Nor can we ignore the remaining 0.1% of sewage, because this portion is composed of the solids that are also a prime source of pollution. These solids contain the pathogenic bacteria and viruses that threaten human health either directly through drinking water or bodily contact by swimming, or indirectly via ingestion of contaminated seafoods, principally shellfish such as oysters, clams, and mussels.

The organic solids can also impose a biochemical oxygen demand on the water causing aerobic (oxygen-using) organisms (fish, invertebrates) to suffocate. The resulting putrefaction from their decay further lowers the ambient water quality and can tip the system over into partial or total ecological collapse. Combined with these effects are the aesthetically displeasing sights of floating sewage refuse and indigestible particles on the seafloor.[3]

In the United States the decline, or abolition, of oceanic sewage outfalls has alleviated much of the immediate problem of nearshore eutrophication. However, storm and general urban runoff continue to be a major problem. In the less developed areas of countries like Mexico, particularly the rural areas away from major population centers, there is still incomplete pollution control. Coastal villages may depend on the outgoing tide to flush away raw sewage. Even in the United States, with our vaunted technological advancements in sewage treatment, there are still coastal areas where septic tank drainfields percolate their effluvia into the estuary.[4] And while the overall size of the Gulf of Mexico suggests that (for these areas at least) dilution may indeed continue to remain a partial solution to this form of pollution, it should not be complacently accepted as the only solution. If nothing else it should be realized that mankind is wasting valuable nutrients by pouring them into waters that have been functioning quite well without such excesses for millions of years. Until sea treatment and nutrient recovery becomes economically feasible, ecologically critical, and legislatively mandated, these nutrients will continue to be lost—and our coastal environment will continue to pay the price.

Offshore Oil

OPENING PANDORA'S BOX

O N JUNE 9, 1990, the *Mega Borg*, an 886-foot supertanker of Norwegian registry, rolled slowly in a calm sea 57 miles southeast of Galveston, Texas. Carrying a cargo of Angolan light crude taken on at Palanca, Angola, half a world away, she was in the process of "lightering," transferring oil to a smaller vessel, before continuing on to Galveston, Texas City, and eventually the island of Aruba in the Dutch West Indies off the north coast of South America. Suddenly a series of explosions shook the pumping and engine rooms, blowing huge metal hatches hundreds of feet down the deck and raising flames to above the level of her bridge. The fire emergency alarms began to clang, and in just minutes the entire stern compartment area became a roaring inferno. Built in Sweden in 1976, the single-hulled, 141,000-metric-ton *Mega Borg* was by no means an obsolete vessel. But her captain, knowing the explosive volatility of her cargo, immediately saw the danger and gave the order to abandon ship. The *Mega Borg*, dead in the water, was soon almost completely afire and began to settle at the stern (see Plate 15).

Dying, but not soon dead, the ship's agony would continue for more than a week. From her ruptured cargo tanks thousands of gallons of light crude oil spilled into the Gulf where, floating on the deep blue sea surface, they ignited, adding their own swirling pall of thick black smoke to that belching from the stricken vessel. As the ragged black cloud rose into the pale blue sky, the cobalt waters around the tanker began to reflect rainbows of oily iridescence. Slowly the sheen spread outward, eventually extending for 30 square miles behind the ship as the offshore currents carried the pollutants shoreward, toward Galveston, Corpus Christi, and the beaches of the east Texas and the Louisiana coastlines.

The fires burned for more than a week, in spite of the best efforts of local and foreign fire-fighters to control the blaze. They, and the U.S. Coast Guard, knew all too well the catastrophe that would happen if the fire-twisted hull broke apart and all of the 38 million gallons of unrefined oil spilled into the Gulf. But before the conflagration was extinguished, an estimated four million gallons of light crude oil had leaked from *Mega Borg's* ruptured hull, two of her crew were dead, two more, trapped in the petroleum-fueled hell of her pump room, were missing and presumed dead, and another 17 were injured. The environmental damage today remains unassessed but could still be bleak. Apparently no floating pools of unburned oil, volatilized by the sun, have yet washed ashore on the tourist-thronged beaches of the northern or eastern Gulf. But the hidden cost in environmental degradation of pelagic organisms, disrupted offshore food webs, and the larvae, the juveniles, and subadults of fishes and invertebrates will never be known. There is no one to tally their decline. Some would call it the luck of the draw.

SPILLED OIL—PETROLEUM POLLUTION

It can be expected that as oil supplies and prices continue to be controlled by foreign cartels and politically unfriendly nations, increased emphasis on locally available petroleum exploration and exploitation will be demanded by both the U.S. government and the American people. So much oil exploration and transportation activity inevitably leads to spills, blowouts, and carrier accidents. Between 1964 and 1980, more than 30 major oil spills or leaks occurred on the U.S. continental shelf, resulting in losses ranging from 100 barrels or approximately 4,200 gallons, to 160,639 barrels, or nearly 6.75 million gallons of oil.[1]

More recent statistics are a black litany indeed. Galveston Bay, November 1979: the tanker *Burmah Agate* collides with another vessel; 10.7 million gallons of oil spilled. Pilottown, Louisiana, November 1980: the tanker *Georgia* leaks 1.3 million gallons of oil. Montz, Louisiana, March 1982: the tanker *Arkas* collides with another vessel, spilling 1.5 million gallons of oil. Cameron, Louisiana, July 1984: the tanker *Alvenus*, hard aground, spills 2.8 million gallons.

Accidents involving VLCC (Very Large Crude Carriers) can be vastly more serious. Many of these carriers are among the largest seagoing vessels on earth, with lengths approaching a quarter mile and beams the size of a football field. Spills such as those from the ill-fated *Amoco Cadiz* (60 million gallons), *Torrey Canyon* (36 million gallons), and *Exxon Valdez* (11.2 million gallons) release substantially more crude oil in a relatively shorter time than blowouts (the uncontrolled, catastrophic eruption of gas, oil, or water under pressure from a petroleum-bearing formation).

Not all spills take place offshore. In Galveston Bay, Texas, ship collisions, groundings, and outright spillage in 1987 emptied over 80,000 gallons of oil, hydrocarbons and hazardous materials into the environment. About 30% of the spillage occurred in the Houston Ship Channel alone. A recent incident in June 1989, involving a spill of 250,000 gallons of oil in Galveston Bay and the Houston Ship Channel, emphasizes this potential for disaster. And still it continues. On July 28, 1990, two oil barges collided with a Greek tanker, spilling 500,000 gallons of heavy crude into the Galveston estuary. In September 1991, a 10-inch pipeline transferring oil from an onshore storage facility to a barge ruptured and spilled 40,000 gallons of light crude oil into Galveston Bay, creating a slick more than four miles long and threatening a wildlife refuge. These "pulses" of oil often produce long-lasting or permanent effects on the shallow-water or nearshore continental shelf ecosystems.

But shipping is not always the culprit. The dubious honor for the world's largest accidental oil spill is held by offshore petroleum exploration operations in the Gulf of Mexico. A major oil well blowout at the IXTOC-1 platform occurred in June 1979, in the Bay of Campeche off Yucatán. This disaster continued to release an estimated 20,000 to 40,000 barrels (0.8 to 1.7 million gallons) of oil per day for nearly ten months. Before IXTOC-1 was capped in March 1980, an estimated 140 million gallons of oil had been emptied into the Gulf. Much of this oil eventually threatened shallow-water marine life along the Mexican and Texas coastline some 200 miles to the north, reducing intertidal and subtidal populations of marine organisms 30%-80% and forming asphaltlike "reefs" up to 18 feet wide and 300 feet long!

By contrast, the blowout of the Ranger exploratory well in November, 1985, was relatively paltry, adding another 6.3 million gallons to the Gulf. Before that, according to statistics from the Environmental Protection Agency, between 1980 and 1984 alone more than 26 million gallons of oil were spilled into the Gulf of Mexico. As one research scientist noted wryly, "It all boils down to whether you want your pollution to be acute or chronic."

The National Academy of Sciences estimates that fully 50% of all oil pollution in the oceans originates from production and distribution operations—specifically, transportation (32%), accidental spills (13%), and offshore production and refining operations (5%). Continued contamination increases the potential for wide-ranging and often permanent environmental destruction. A shallow-water oil spill of the magnitude of the VLCC *Exxon Valdez* disaster, if entrained in existing coastal current systems, could permanently alter or destroy many of the shallow-water ecosystems around the entire Gulf of Mexico.[2]

RUINING A DAY AT THE BEACH

Some lesser impacts of petroleum pollution are felt all the way down to the individual level. Illegal washouts of tanker bilges offshore produce oil slicks often tens of miles long. As the volatile components in these slicks are evaporated by the sun, the remaining "sludge" forms black, gooey patches of floating "tar." Indeed, the composition of these patches closely approaches the consistency and makeup of fresh asphalt. Rolled around by waves and winds, the patches form tar-balls that soon wash ashore to create sticky and annoying nuisances for the holiday beach-goer. Ironically, the simplest solvent for removing beach tar is mineral spirits, itself a product of the petroleum industry.

Recent research now makes it possible to identify the polluting vessel by matching the chemical "signature" of the oil slick to that found in the ship's tanks or at the loading port. Stiff fines and jail sentences are prescribed for convicted violators, but insufficient enforcement personnel (primarily the U.S. Coast Guard) and support funding have made this program substantially less effective than it could be. So don't put away those mineral spirits just yet.

CATASTROPHES WAITING TO HAPPEN?

To anyone who has ever stood on a Louisiana barrier island beach, the strange, stilt-legged oil platforms rising like alien spaceships against the sea horizon are a startling sight (see Plate 16). At night, they appear as brightly lit cities, lending an eerie and other-worldly ambience to the dark offshore waters. Flickering across miles of sea, the great gas lamps of the petroleum giants mark the continual exploitation of one of the Gulf of Mexico's most valuable—and non-renewable—treasures. Not even Aladdin's lamp yielded so much wealth. Or raised the potential for so much ecological destruction if carelessly used.

In a report assessing the impacts of proposed outer continental shelf oil and gas lease sales in 1988, the Minerals Management Service projected a total of nearly 123 million acres for lease, nearly 50% of which were located in the eastern Gulf.[3] Recent plans to lease and drill on the southwestern Florida continental shelf generated extensive controversy and brought under scrutiny the entire suite of problems associated with petroleum exploration and development. Moreover, the tragic, yet ironically timely, oil spill in March 1989 by the VLCC *Exxon Valdez*, the groundings of three large commercial ships on the reefs in the Florida Keys in the fall of 1989, and the recent *Mega Borg* disaster have increased public awareness of the dangers involved. State and federal attention has been directed toward initiating measures for protecting fragile coastal ecosystems in the Gulf, from the salt marshes, bayous, and beaches of Texas, Louisiana, Mississippi, and Alabama, to the coral reef tracts in the Florida Keys and the extensive mangrove-lined estuaries of the Ten Thousand Islands.

Could another *Exxon Valdez* or *Mega Borg* catastrophe ever happen? Oil companies pooh-pooh the notion, citing their generally good tanker-safety records. They point out that between 1973 and 1984, offshore oil spills totaled approximately 0.1% of offshore oil produced during the same period. They also emphasize that natural oil seeps contributed nearly 1000 times as much oil to the world's seas as did accidental spills. But oil spills are like airplane crashes. They may be few and far between, but when they occur they are unmitigated disasters. Indeed, the *Exxon Valdez* tragedy by itself has shown that however "nearly perfect" the spill record is, it still isn't good enough.[4]

Moreover, the nearness of conventional shipping lanes to many coastal areas is a continuing threat. For example, ship traffic inbound to the Gulf passes within 20 miles of the shores of Florida and Cuba. A VLCC supertanker is so large, and has such a long directional response time (usually several miles), that an error in navigation that pointed such a vessel toward shore probably could not be corrected before impact, even if it was detected immediately. Consider this. Had the *Mega Borg* been outbound through the Yucatán Channel or the Straits of Florida toward her final destination of Aruba when she caught fire, the spilled oil could easily have been carried in currents running along the Yucatán coast, or into Florida Bay, and along the Florida Keys.

No one knows the actual probability of a grounding and spill event. But every year, nearly 60,000 tankers and barges bring oil into or carry it out from the major U.S. Gulf ports of Tampa, Mobile, Pascagoula, New Orleans, Sabine-Natchez, Houston, and Corpus Christi. In Mexico's corner of the Gulf, the ports of Tampico, Vera Cruz, Coatzacoalcos, and Progreso load Mexican crude from the large fields offshoreof Vera Cruz, Tabasco, and Campeche States. Some 2,500–5,000 tankers pass through the Straits of Florida annually. How much oil do they carry? An average tanker cargo may be nearly 11 million gallons of oil. In terms of foreign oil imports alone, these Gulf coast ports handle more than 106 million tons a year.

ECOSYSTEM VALUES, ECONOMIC REALITIES

How bad would a major oil spill be? A 2.1-million-gallon spill (50,000 barrels) off Caribbean Panama in 1986 provides a potent scenario of what could happen. The Panamanian spill affected about 2,000 acres of coral and 4,000 acres of mangroves, painting a sheen of death over the shallow tropical waters, the sea grasses, oyster bars, and any living organism unable to escape its path. Recovery has been slower than originally projected and is now estimated to take at least 20 years. Even then, the total magnitude of the spill's destructive effects will probably never be known.

Although a large oil spill is visibly disastrous, much of the damage is insidious. Tar from the IXTOC-1 blowout was buried in tons of sand when Hurricane Allen thrashed Padre Island, Texas, in 1980. Ten years later the millions of tiny tar blobs still in the sand are an enduring legacy of the IXTOC-1 catastrophe.

The costs of such spills can quickly become astronomical, not only in cleanup expenses, but in the continuing degradation of the environment as well. Actual economic losses, of course, are in part subjective. Dollar values of coral reefs range from $800 (Florida Department of Natural Resources) to more than $2,800 per square meter (independent economic analysis). An acre of coral reef is thus valued at $3.2 million minimum DNR value.

Mangroves are less valuable (at least according to a recent court decision in Puerto Rico), but still occupy their own regal realm, with a value of $100,000 per acre. If these values are applied to the Panamanian oil spill, it is easily seen that the estimated loss of 2,000 acres of coral and 4,000 acres of mangroves would cost nearly $7 billion dollars. Whether the state or federal courts would assess a similar value to Gulf reefs, mangroves, and other areas remains moot. How do you value the loss of the Flower Garden Banks? The Marquesas reefs? The Alacran Reef? Bayou Lafourche? The oyster bars of Pass Christian?

The most critical point is that the monetary loss of these ecosystems cannot be simply assessed primarily because ecological time cannot be valued. It is priceless. Once a system that has taken hundreds to thousands of years to reach development is destroyed, the interim recovery period (assuming one exists) becomes impossible to price. Our great-grandchildren will be served that invoice.

The similarities are, nonetheless, alarming. As in Panama, many areas along the Gulf coast support old-growth ecosystems. Like Panama, many are relatively remote or inaccessible by land- based cleanup operations. Moreover, water too shallow or too dangerously shoaled to allow access by cleanup vessels is a common feature of Gulf and Panamanian shorelines.

While cleanup vessels might conceivably be able to work close inshore along much of the west coast of Florida, an oil spill washing into the mangrove-studded

Ten Thousand Islands area, or Florida Bay, where nearshore water depths are often measured in inches even at high tide, would pose insurmountable problems.

Even cleanup could prove devastating. The spreading of detergents, chemical dispersants, and high-pressure blast cleaning could be more damaging to many habitats (oyster bars, vermetid and sabellariid reefs, seagrass beds) than the actual oil spill. Even more alarming is the fact that the best cleanup efforts recover no more than 10%-15% of any spill. The rest continues to volatilize, coat, form residues, and kill. Studies on the IXTOC-1 residues, and research conducted on a Massachusetts salt marsh oil spill, show that oil residue still exists 20 years after these accidents occurred. These results clearly indicate the fallacy of relying on *any* contingency plan for oil spills in any shallow-water systems in the Gulf.

How much would cleanup cost? It depends on the amount spilled, the conditions at the site, and its accessibility. The cost for cleaning up mangroves and beaches damaged by an accidental oil spill from the tanker *Howard Starr* off Tampa in 1978 was nearly $1 million. That's small potatoes. The Exxon Corporation estimates that the cleanup of the *Exxon Valdez* has so far cost more than $2 billion, and it isn't over yet. Not included in these direct costs, of course, are both immediate and long-term damages incurred to shallow subtidal and intertidal ecosystems, not only by oil but by the physical grounding of the ship itself. No one knows what the effects will be on the rich Alaskan fisheries. But the lawyers, judges, and insurance underwriters will be gathering for years to come.

Prince William Sound, Alaska, is a long way from the Gulf of Mexico, as well as several orders of magnitude less populated. Had such a spill occurred in Gulf coastal waters, the cleanup costs and continuing environmental degradation could conceivably reach figures in the tens of billions of dollars or more. In addition, long-term impacts on marshes and other wetlands, as well as the potential destruction of coral reefs, seagrass beds, and mangrove forests, would have serious and perhaps fatal effects on regionally important fisheries such as mullet, shrimp, blue crabs, stone crabs, spiny lobsters, and crawfish. The effects on more widespread "international" fisheries such as menhaden would be difficult to assess owing to the complexity of their food chains. Closer to home, the short-term impacts of a major coastal spill on development and tourism in just the Florida Keys, for example, would be monumental.

WHAT TO DO, WHEN TO DO IT?

Government estimates indicate that the amount of oil and gas potentially extractable from new leases on the OCS may be trivial (less than one week's supply for the United States) compared to other sources. Given this, some may question whether new wells should be permitted. Others ask why stronger regulations aren't put in place to govern any type of spill, be it blowout, pipeline break, or tanker disaster. The answers don't come easily. Regulations may function effectively, but they have to be enforced. And the courts must impose suitable punishments for the infractions. As lawyers on both sides of the case will tell you, there are always mitigating circumstances to be considered.

There are numerous regulations that govern oil spills, petroleum effluents, and other discharges, beginning with the Federal Water Pollution Control Act of 1972 (33 U.S.C. 1231, et seq.), the Outer Continental Shelf Lands Act (OCSLA), and the Comprehensive Environmental Response Compensation and Liability Act, or "Superfund," to name just a few. The EPA of Regions IV and VI regulate petroleum exploration, development, and production operations in the Gulf, and issues National Pollution Discharge Elimination Systems permits on the amounts of discharges, listing prohibitions, and providing requirements for reporting during OCS operations. Ocean dumping is regulated by the Marine Protection, Research, and Sanctuaries Act of 1972 (33 U.S.C. 1401, as amended). In addition, the MMS requires annual inspection reports from pipeline operatores, and the U.S. Coast Guard conducts perriodic surveillance overflights from 10 to 50 miles offshore to monitor potential pollution events. Title III of OCSLA provides for a liability fund administered by both the Department of Transportation and the U.S. Treasury Department. The fund covers spills and accidents from any OCS facility, as well as any tanker, barge, or other watercraft carrying petroleum from an OCS facility. In addition, criminal and civil liabilities may also apply, ranging from $10,000 a day in civil actions to fines of up to $100,000 and imprisonment for up to 10 years, or both.

But there has already been some reaction. On June 11, 1990, two days after the *Mega Borg* incident, then Florida governor Bob Martinez signed a bill prohibiting oil exploration on the Florida continental shelf. By month's end President George Bush had also signed a federal bill suspending OCS oil exploration on new leases until after the turn of the century.

Some other steps have been taken. Both the Senate (August 1989) and the House of Representatives (November 1989) passed bills aimed at alleviating the problem. Among some of the stipulations are a mandate for double-hulled vessels and authorization for the Coast Guard to take charge of any oil-spill disaster. Up to now, commercial companies have directed the operations, simply because they are more knowledgeable, have the necessary equipment, and are often (but not always) in the vicinity.

Yet even this best-of-intentions legislation walks the long road toward an oil-fired hell. Single-hulled vessels are "grandfathered" in until after the turn of the century.[6] Shipping and oil companies balk at levied assessments beyond current insurance values, and at the potential for liabilities imposed long after a spill has occurred. And no one wants to do anything (let alone be held liable) until Congress makes up its collective mind. That may be a long time coming. Both the shipping and oil industries have powerful lobbies. Some Washington observers estimate that it will take at least two years before everything can be put in place, *after* everyone agrees on the legislated stipulations.

Other suggestions include ironclad legislation requiring posting of performance bonds by any tanker or oil-carrying vessel proposing to enter a state's jurisdictional waters. Although many shipping lines carry multimillion-dollar insurance on their vessels, these monies are primarily replacement costs for the cargoes. The final damages often exceed these values. Thus, fines, assessment of all cleanup costs, and revocation of master's (and other ship's officers) licenses should be considered where negligence resulting in a spill can clearly be demonstrated. Civil suits for both punitive and mitigational damages should also be part of such legislation, with private citizens, municipalities, local governments, affected businesses and industries, and other aggrieved parties granted standing to initiate appropriate legal action.

Looking toward another aspect, VLCC lanes should be immediately restricted to the outer edge of the continental shelf, regardless of current flows that may slow a ship's progress. Increased surveillance by the U.S. Coast Guard offshore and by state marine patrols in jurisdictional coastal waters should be implemented. Vessel inspections for oil tight integrity, particularly in storage and transfer operations, should be mandated every year for newer ships (10 years old and under) and every six months for older ships. Tankers older than 25 years should be severely restricted from carrying any hazardous liquids. Coastal lighters and smaller coastal tankers should fall under individual state jurisdictions as they enter each state's waters. Federal funding (produced from loading fees on all carriers) for analysis and identification of trace oil slicks from offending vessels, coupled with a vigorous enforcement and prosecution program, would go a long way toward eliminating illegal offshore bilge-pumping and leaking holds. And, as always, education becomes both a tool and a weapon for an aroused public.

Won't all this produce yet another federal bureaucracy? Possibly. More paperwork? Probably. And won't the costs be passed on to the general public by the oil companies? Most assuredly. But the benefits accruing to the environment in the Gulf of Mexico would be both priceless and shared by all. Yet, until Congress finally moves, and these or similar recommendations are implemented, there is presently only one solution: keep your fingers crossed—and your mineral spirits handy.

Industrial Wastes

A DEADLY ALPHABET SOUP

THE UNITED STATES OF AMERICA is properly considered one of the greatest industrial societies on earth. Yet in acknowledging this greatness we must also accept much of the blame for the resultant pollution in the Gulf of Mexico that has been caused by our industries. A major portion of this environmental contamination is a consequence of several pathways, including runoff from landfills; municipal sewage; legal and illegal industrial discharges; and long-distance transport by wind, rain, and snow.

Although the coastal margin of the Gulf of Mexico is not nearly as heavily industrialized as are parts of the Great Lakes region or the northeastern United States, there are major industrial areas to be found. The cities of Tampa, Birmingham, and Mobile come immediately to mind, as do the Baton Rouge-New Orleans corridor in Louisiana and the Galveston–Houston area in Texas. Taking Texas as just one example, over 50% of all the chemicals made in the United States are produced or refined in the vicinity of Galveston Bay. At least 30% of the entire US petroleum industry also operates here. And where there is industry there is also pollution (see Table 20) .

Smaller, regional industrial areas are also found in northwest Florida (primarily pulp mills and chemicals manufacturers), Mississippi (agrochemical manufacturing), and in southeastern Mexico (petrochemical industries). All produce organic and inorganic industrial wastes. In the Gulf coastal region, nearly 48% of the total wastewaters discharged from point sources comes from petrochemical and chemical industries. How these industries treat such waters or dispose of them not only directly affects the receiving waterways but eventually has impacts on the Gulf of Mexico itself.

Many organic wastes—for example those produced through sugar refineries, pulp wood or paper-making processes, and food processing factories—deplete oxygen in water bodies more drastically than even untreated sewage does. Because of the complex chemical structure of many of these pollutants, they require a longer time to be broken down into less toxic components. Moreover, many of these pollutants, particularly the organo-halides (composed of chlorine, bromine, and fluorine-attached benzene rings) are not only extremely slow and difficult to break down under natural conditions, but are extremely toxic as well. Thus they remain poisonous even as they slowly disintegrate.

TABLE 20

The Potential for Pollution around the Gulf of Mexico

Category	Potential for Pollution
Shipping	Gulf ports handle 45% of U.S. import and export shipping tonnage.
Chemicals	More than 500 chemicals are produced in industrial plants along the Gulf coast. From 82%-92% of all plastics or plastic-related chemicals are made in Gulf states.
Hazardous Wastes	Four of the five Gulf coast states lead the nation in release of toxic materials to the environment.
Toxic Air Pollution	Of 52 industrial facilities listed by the EPA as highest potential cancer risks, 24 (48%) are located on the Gulf coast.
Petroleum	44% of the total U. S. refining capacity occurs on the Gulf coast. 58% of the total U.S. gas processing plants (418) are located in the five Gulf coast states.

Source: Data synopsized from several EPA sources.

Two examples indicate the potential for disaster in coastal ecosystems. Along a 90-mile stretch of Interstate 10 between Baton Rouge and New Orleans, 126 petrochemical plants and seven oil refineries are located, attracted there in part by navigational access to the Mississippi River that also flows through the region. Once called "the Chemical Corridor," the area was recently renamed "Cancer Alley" by its residents, because nearly 87,000 tons per year of pollutants and toxins are washed, dumped, or leached into the aquifers, tributaries, and streams that eventually feed the Mississippi. Add that load to the already existing 4.5 billion gallons of raw sewage daily, plus the 30 tons of pesticides and herbicides, 5 tons of cadmium, and the 175,000 tons of fertilizers the river carries annually from draining nearly 41% of the U.S. mainland, and the figures become mind-numbing indeed. The EPA has already designated 21 Superfund Waste Sites along the Mississippi above Louisiana.[1] Table 21 lists other Superfund sites in Gulf states presently undergoing assessment or cleanup.

Organic and inorganic pollutants can have economic as well as environmental ramifications. The National Oceanic and Atmospheric Administration (NOAA), in a 1987 report, summarized selected data on chemical contaminants measured in fish and bivalve mollusc tissues for three years.[2] Of 145 coastal sites throughout the United States tested for 12 chemical contaminants, 41 localities were listed as most contaminated. Of these, nine were found in the Gulf region. In another study, the U.S. Fish and Wildlife Service reported that many contaminants entering Galveston Bay become tied up in the sediments. Dredging or other disturbances stir the sediments up and re-release many of the toxins into the water column. Species as disparate as crabs and cormorants were found to be contaminated with petrochemical compounds. Even worse, some crab fisheries were shut down when mercury contamination was discovered.

Table 21

Superfund Sites Presently Undergoing Assessment or Cleanup

Location	Total Sites	Sites in Gulfside Counties*	Total Cleanups Started	Total Cleanups Completed
Alabama	12	4	5	1
Florida	54	14	10	4
Louisiana	11	3	4	0
Mississippi	3	0	1	1
Texas	29	4	10	1
Totals:	109†	25	30	7†

*Counties actually fronting the Gulf of Mexico. Many sites in other counties may drain through surface or groundwater directly or indirectly into the Gulf.
†Total Superfund sites in the U.S. = 1,207; total permanently cleaned up outside Gulf of Mexico = 311; Average time of cleanup from first assessment to completion = 6-8 years.

Source: EPA Documents 540/4-90/002, /010, /019, /025, /043; 540/8-90/009, /010.

PCBS AND PAHS: UBIQUITOUS AND PERMANENT

Some of the most notorious organo-chemical pollutants are the polychlorinated biphenyls (PCBs); polycyclic aromatic hydrocarbons (PAHs); and a witch's brew of other synthetic organic substances originating from coal tar products and by-products, petroleum catalytic-cracking plants, asphalt manufacturing, dry-cleaning industries, and even from compounds produced as toxic by-products in the chlorination of drinking water. Also included are dioxins and several other deadly compounds representing some of the most virulently carcinogenic chemicals ever created by man.[3]

Urban runoff is yet another major source of PAHs, particularly from rain-washed asphalt and macadam roadways. Petroleum spillage from filling stations, oil-recovery stations, petrochemical disposal areas and repositories and marinas also account for much if not most of the PAHs in aquatic environments.

It gets worse. Although PAHs are degraded by light, the photo-oxidation process that removes much of these compounds from the atmosphere is itself dangerous, producing carcinogenic (cancer-inducing) or mutagenic (chromosome-altering) reaction products. In aquatic systems PAHs may degrade only slowly, if at all, and thus remain actively toxic for years. Toxic effects of different PAHs may be exhibited in estuarine organisms at concentrations ranging from 300 to 2,500 parts per billion. Uptake by sediment- or deposit-feeders may biologically magnify the occurrence of PAHs throughout the food chain. Some organisms may concentrate, rather than expel, these products. The resulting bioconcentration factors for selected estuarine organisms can range from a low of less than 100 times the ambient concentration to more than 11,000 times ambient values. It is clear that whether naturally occurring or man-made, PAHs are of tremendous concern today.

Yet with all of this being said, it may come as a surprise that not all of these organic contaminants are directly man-made. Forest fires, for example, release greater amounts of PAHs into the environment than does burning of fossil fuels. Factors as diverse as volcanic eruptions and synthesis by microorganisms also account for production of PAHs. In other instances, PAHs formed in one place may be carried by rain clouds to another, contaminating relatively pollution-free areas.

On the other hand, PCBs are totally anthropogenic and their occurrence anywhere on earth is a consequence of man's pollution. These compounds have been found in both the Arctic and Antarctic, in the Pacific and Atlantic Oceans, and on every continent on earth. Up to 91% of the adult human population in the United States have measurable concentrations of these chemicals in their tissues.

Major sources of PCBs in aquatic systems are shipyards and marinas where, during maintenance operations, fuel and oil transfer, and machinery operations, PCB-containing fluids are either spilled or wash into the water.

Because PCBs are stored in fatty tissue and lipids, the vertebrates show higher concentration and greater susceptibility to contamination. These include fish (codfish, salmon, trout, flounder), reptiles (sea and freshwater turtles), birds (primarily wildfowl, seabirds, and migratory species like robins and starlings), and mammals (sperm whales, manatees, otters). In fact, according to the U.S. Fish and Wildlife Service, "Trace concentrations of the more persistent, more highly chlorinated PCBs are detected in fish from almost every major river in the United States."[4] One out of every six bluefish harvested may contain PCBs in excess of federal standards. Researchers at Woods Hole Oceanographic Institution have noted that PCBs cannot be completely flushed from an organism's system (e.g., shellfish), but apparently remain in the tissues permanently.

And this is only what has been measured. Hidden but not inactive are the various chemical pollutants—the slugs of used biocides, industrial wastes, detergents, agrochemicals, industrial solvents and lubricants, and a plethora of other inorganic and organic chemical products—that form gelatins, colloidal suspensions, emulsified contaminants, and precipitates that swirl, ooze, and foam in our waves, currents, and tides and are eventually cast ashore on our beaches.

These compounds can clog the gills and other respiratory organs of fish and sessile and motile invertebrates; act as systemic or contact poisons to any living organism; interfere with physiological, behavioral, and reproductive processes; or simply coat the seafloor and suffocate the existing flora and fauna while preventing recolonization by other species. Perhaps the most serious consequence is that these compounds may severely affect or kill the larval stages of benthic and epibenthic species. This one-two punch, whereby the adults are killed or forced out and the larvae are killed or prevented from settling, can lead to precipitous declines in both animal and plant communities.

HEAVY METALS: SHORT-TERM INPUT, LONG-TERM STORAGE

Heavy metals represent another important type of industrial pollution. Contamination of drinking water with certain chemical forms of these otherwise naturally-occurring elements has serious medical consequences. Heavy metals are known to cause, or have been implicated in, neurological, cardiac, and urological damage; cancer; respiratory problems; and even death in susceptible individuals.

The litany of environmental and toxicological effects caused by arsenic, cadmium, chromium, copper, lead, mercury, nickel, selenium, silver, thallium, vanadium, and zinc is long, repetitive, and continues to grow. Prime sources of input include outfalls (sewage and industrial); marinas and ship yards; urban runoff; landfills; slagheaps from foundries and steel mills; talus piles from ore mines; waste dumps; inadvertent or deliberate spills of industrial solvents, petroleum and petrochemicals and their by-products; and the vast variety of trash and toxic debris that accumulates as the regrettable consequence of modern living.

Because heavy metals are *metals,* they cannot be broken down further into nontoxic forms, although many of their compounds exhibit varying degrees of toxicity depending on a multitude of environmental and chemical factors. In general, however, once an aquatic system is contaminated with heavy metals, it remains so for years if not decades. Thus, heavy metal contamination may lie hidden and unobtrusive, slowly accumulating until it explodes onto public awareness with a deadly and immutable vengeance.

Lead and mercury poisoning are two recent examples involving widely divergent species: freshwater bass in Florida lakes and swordfish and sharks from continental shelf waters. Raccoons in the Big Cypress Swamp contain such high levels of mercury that they have been implicated in the mercury-poisoning death of at least three Florida panthers, including the last two breeding female cats in Everglades National Park.

In other instances, the potential consequences of heavy-metal contamination remain clouded by lack of standardized testing procedures, or even agreement as to what constitutes minimum acceptable values for acute or chronic toxicities. Often one form of a metal is more toxic than another. And toxicity may also be tied to existing environmental conditions. In other instances, biological magnification that does occur may take place over such long periods that test organisms show little contamination when first examined. Ironically, with the advent of more sensitive testing apparatus, many metals previously thought absent are now being detected, or are being measured at higher levels of accuracy.[5]

A good example of increased detectability are the organic tin complexes, whose toxic effects are now able to be measured in parts per billion. Organotin compounds commonly are found in harbors and marinas where the use of anti-fouling paints on watercraft is common. These compounds are considered generally more toxic to aquatic organisms, particularly those living in the microlayer of the uppermost sediments, than even chlorinated insecticides,

PAHs and PCBs. Of greater import, zooplankton may rapidly take up some organotin compounds from the water column and thus act as biological magnifiers by passing it on to their predators. Accumulation of organotin compounds on sediment particles, and their subsequent ingestion in sublethal amounts by benthic organisms (bivalve molluscs, polychaete worms) over long periods of time may bioconcentrate the toxins, again magnifying their occurrence in predators higher up the food chain, such as fish, birds, and humans. In our zeal to kill the organisms that foul our boat hulls we may be poisoning ourselves.

THE SIMPLE INORGANICS: TOXICITY VIA REPRISAL

Even "simple" inorganic acids (hydrochloric, sulfuric, nitric), caustics (hydroxides of sodium and postassium), halides (bromine, chlorine, and fluorine gas), cyanides (potassium and sodium), and common ammonia can cause pollution problems if not properly contained or disposed. For example, sulfuric acid spills from phosphate manufacturing have been a major contaminant in Tampa Bay. Another and more insidious source is municipal solid waste incinerators which produce tons of sulfuric acid mist (among numerous other toxic components) as a byproduct of their combustion activities. Such mists can form a major component of acid rains. Motor vehicle exhaust also contains sulfur dioxide and related compounds that can unite with atmospheric water in a complex chemical reaction in which the end result is sulfuric acid.

All these chemicals are essential to one kind of manufacturing process or another and so they can only be regulated, not eliminated. If anything positive at all can be said about their input into aquatic systems, it is that most of these compounds are quickly diluted to low or negligible levels of toxicity. Moreover, few organisms can survive in, let alone directly take up and bioaccumulate, toxic levels of these relatively simple inorganic compounds. Thus, transference up the food web is unlikely. The danger in their introduction comes more from the continued effects on plants, alteration of sediments, disruption of planktonic and benthic food chains, and degradation of oxygen levels in the receiving water body. Many of the long-term effects are so subtle as to be nearly undetectable and are manifest finally in alteration of behavior in wildlife as well as lowered rates of reproduction, growth, and survival.

POLLUTION AND PERMANENCE: A CONTINUING PROBLEM

Industry has produced "the good life" and raised the standard of living for many. Yet the concept of "better things for better living through chemistry" is a simplistic equation in which the pollution factor was never weighed. It makes no sense to maintain a high standard of living if the environment in which we live becomes irretrievably degraded in the process. The air we breathe, the water we drink, the foodstuffs we eat, and the very land that we walk on does not exist in unlimited quantities.

Although recent pollution events such as Love Canal in New York; Times Beach, Missouri; and Bhopal, India have raised the environmental consciousness of much of the world, spills, introductions, and misuse of toxic substances continue to occur. And the invoice for environmental degradation continues to increase. Pristine waters, once polluted, may never be made wholly clean again. Poisoned land will remain uninhabitable for decades. And there is no sanctuary from toxic atmosphere, as the inhabitants of Los Angeles have long ago discovered and the people of Tampa and Mobile are finding out.

Is there hope? Yes and maybe. Although strong laws exist, their enforcement is often sporadic or tangled in bureaucratic red tape. And enforcement means having not only the necessary personnel to detect violations but the necessary resources in time and money to bring violators to court. It goes without saying that the willingness to do so must first exist. Sadly, there is evidence that this vital first step is lacking. The General Accounting Office recently castigated both the U.S. Army Corps of Engineers and the EPA because neither agency employed sufficient surveillance to detect unauthorized activities. In fact, the Corps did not inspect many sites to ensure that permittees were adhering to permit conditions. Some environmental groups have charged that the Corps has intentionally limited its own jurisdiction over discharges into wetlands, avoided permit review, and ignored unauthorized dredged and fill activity. In rebuttal, the Corps cites lack of manpower and conflicting assessments as to where its jurisdiction should be directed.

While pressing for changes that would eliminate bureaucratic apathy and mismanagement, the citizen should also take matters into his or her own financial hands. The ordinary consumer can wield an effective stick. As far as industry is concerned, financial feasibility is the bottom line for production. It is only when consumers boycott the products that industry sits up and listens. The U.S. consumer spends over $3.5 trillion a year on goods and services, and that's a very big stick indeed. Even more encouraging is the fact that nearly 78% of these market-goers would be willing to pay more for environmentally safe products, *produced in an environmentally safe manner.* In a market poll of 1,000 consumers, 77% said that their decision to purchase a product was affected by the environmental reputation of the company involved.[6] It is precisely this type of "green" revolution that will provide a necessary first step towards eliminating contamination in the air, land, estuaries, and marine environment within our own American Mediterranean.

Biocides

SPEAKING CHEMISTRY'S DEADLY LANGUAGES

L
ETS PLAY WITH ANAGRAMS. What do Azinphos-methyl, Chlorpyrifos, Demeton, Diazinon, Dichrotophos, Disulfoton, Fonofos, Glyphosate, Malathion, Parathion, Phosalone, and Terbufos have in common? These are simply a few of the organophosphorus pesticides applied at an average rate of more than 22 million pounds yearly within the coastal zone of the Gulf of Mexico. Parathion, Terbufos, Fonofos, and Azinphos-methyl are among the most toxic organophosphorus pesticides ever created.

Want to try again? What do Aldicarb, Benomyl, Butylate, Carbaryl, Carbofuran, Mancozeb, Maneb, Methomyl, Molinate, and Thiobencarb share in common? These are carbamate pesticides of choice in the states bordering the Gulf of Mexico. Of the three most commonly used field chemicals (Butylate, Carbofuran, and Methomyl), Carbofuran and Methomyl are the most toxic.

Still interested? What's the relationship among Malathion, Fenthion, Naled, and Temephos? These are mosquito-abatement pesticides used in the majority of mosquito-control programs in the Gulf of Mexico coastal zone. An estimated 13 million acre-treatments using Malathion, 4-7 million acre-treatments using Naled, and 1-2 million acre-treatments using Temephos are made each year.[1] Approximately 20% of all acre-treatments of all organophosphorus or carbamate pesticides in the entire United States consist of mosquito-control applications.[2]

NONSELECTIVE CHEMICAL KILLERS

Just what are organophosphorus and carbamate pesticides? Put simply, these are formulations of organic chemicals and compounds of phosphorus or carbamic acid (a nitrogen-bearing organic acid). Many of these formulations are extremely toxic manmade chemicals. According to a study by the U.S. Fish and Wildlife Service: "Of the organophosphorus and carbamate pesticides contributing to more than 50% of the total use [in the entire United States], all but one. . . . are classified as highly toxic." The study goes on to make the following deadly point: "Therefore, most of the potential hazard to non-target species [i.e., those not intended to be killed] is produced by only a few widely used and highly toxic chemicals" (see Figure 43).[3]

What does "highly toxic" mean? In this case, the phrase describes *neurotoxins*. Most organophosphorus and carbamate pesticides block the action of a natural body chemical called acetylcholine-esterase. Acetylcholine-esterase acts like an "on-off switch" by breaking down an electrical transmitting sub-

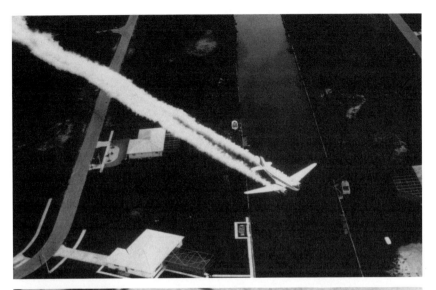

Figure 43. Casualties of "friendly fire."
(A) Spreading death the old-fashioned way, a DC-3 from a southwestern Florida mosquito control agency lays down a toxic fog of organophosphate insecticide and vaporized diesel fuel over residential areas in a Sisyphean effort to control the hordes of saltmarsh mosquitoes that breed in the marshes and mangroves of the Ten Thousand Islands. Although millions of mosquitoes will be killed, still more millions will escape, protected by the surrounding dense mangrove forests and marshlands. [Dr. Scott Ritchie, Collier Mosquito Control District]
(B) An unwanted result—numerous species of nontargeted organisms, including the dragonfly shown here, are often unintended victims of such flights. Ironically, many of these organisms feed voraciously on the same mosquitoes being killed.

stance (acetylcholine) between nerves so that the nerves don't remain continually active. When this "on-off switch" is destroyed by an organophosphorus or carbamate chemical, acetylcholine causes the nerve endings to degenerate into a runaway firing mode. Then, like a downed power line, the nerve fires continuously and aimlessly, triggering violently uncontrolled muscular spasms. The spasms increase in number and violence until, like a runaway clockspring, the nerves or muscles break down completely. The consequences for the organism are then both immediate and fatal.

PESTICIDES AND BIOCIDES: KILLING NOW AND LATER

In 1982, nearly 8 million pounds of Chlorpyrifos, a major organophosphorus agricultural pesticide, were spread across croplands and wetlands in the United States. Of this amount, more than 330,000 pounds were sprayed on wetlands to control mosquitoes, and another 100,000 pounds were used on golf courses to destroy mole crickets and other turf-eating insects.

This acutely toxic pesticide can kill aquatic organisms in doses as low as 1 part per billion, create sublethal effects in other wetland species, and become bioconcentrated (accumulated in large, nonlethal doses) by some fishes from 400 to 1,000 times its local concentration. Even when applied at recommended dosages of less than 7 ounces/acre, mortality, deleterious sublethal effects (alteration of behavior, reduced reproductive capability), and bioaccumulation have been produced in aquatic plants, zooplankton, nontargeted insects, small invertebrates, crustaceans, waterfowl, and fish.

Moreover, Chlorpyrifos may continue killing indiscrimately for weeks after application. It may require two or more weeks to be completely degraded in seawater, and up to 24 weeks, or almost half a year, before breaking down in soils. In fact, Chlorpyrifos is so toxic that the U.S. Fish and Wildlife Service has recommended that its use as an insecticide (specifically for mosquito control) be restricted in wetlands, estuaries, and waterfowl-breeding areas, and that its agricultural applications be curtailed in watersheds. The agency has also recommended that the average four-day concentration in saltwater should not exceed five parts/trillion more than once every three years.[4]

Carbofuran is a broad-spectrum carbamate insecticide registered for use on alfalfa, peanuts, corn, rice, and sugarcane. This compound has been implicated in wildlife kills including ducks, geese, red-shouldered hawks, sandpipers, red-winged blackbirds, frogs, crawfish, fish, and even earthworms. Degradation time of the pesticide in water varies dramatically depending on pH, ranging from as short as one week in alkaline waters (pH 8.0) to over 13 years in acidic waters (pH 5-6). Thus, slightly acidic soils, waters, and acid-rain effluents may prolong the persistence of carbofuran in the environment.

Pentachlorophenol (PCP), an organochlorine compound, is a fungicide and wood preservative that has also been used as an insecticide, herbicide, algicide, disinfectant, and even as an ingredient in anti-fouling marine paint. It is the third most heavily used pesticide after the herbicides Alachlor and Atrazine. PCP is the preservative of choice for wood to prevent damage by fungus, bacteria, and wood-eating insects such as termites and powder post beetles. Its use in lumber, telephone poles, and other wood products is matched by a multitude of other applications including paper, cable-coverings, textiles, leathers, rope, rubber, and ink. Some uses are incredible. PCP has been employed as a woodpecker repellent and was even added as an illegal preservative in a Japanese soy sauce!

PCP is ubiquitous. Most people living in industrialized societies carry detectable levels in their bodies. It has been found in natural food chains, in marine fishes and invertebrates, in drinking water, human blood and fatty tissue, and even in the milk of nursing mothers. PCP can be absorbed through the skin, ingested with food, or inhaled. It can also be bioconcentrated by wildlife.

But the news isn't all bad, is it? One of the most deadly and long-lasting insecticides that ever affected the Gulf of Mexico region was Mirex, a chlorinated hydrocarbon directed against fire ants. Florida, Alabama, Mississippi, Louisiana, and Texas employed it extensively, spreading it over nearly 80 million acres of land. As death rates from nontargeted organisms escalated, and an increasing incidence of birth defects and tumors appeared in humans, the EPA finally banned its use in 1978.

Unfortunately, according to data presented by the U.S. Fish and Wildlife Service, Mirex and its metabolites have been shown to be among the most stable and persistent organochlorine compounds ever created by man, resisting chemical, photolytic, microbial, metabolic, and thermal degradation.[5] Thus, owing to its low level of degradability Mirex will continue to remain available as a systemic and incredibly toxic pesticide well into the 1990s. In other areas of the United States, such as the Great Lakes region, Mirex is estimated to remain potentially toxic for as much as 600 years! Here is a deadly legacy, one which will be passed to our children and our grandchildren yet unborn.

Mirex has yet another level of deadliness. Even as it degrades, its by-products themselves are acutely toxic. Nor is it safe to destroy it by incineration. For example, when heated to 700°C (1,300°F) Mirex decomposes into another notoriously toxic compound, one that was responsible for massive fish and invertebrate kills in the York River estuary of Virginia. Its name is now infamous: Kepone.

GONE BUT NOT FORGOTTEN

Dr. Bernie Yokel, president of the Florida Audubon Society, once ruefully noted: "I have always been impressed by our ability to kind of set traps for ourselves—and then spring them!" Some pesticides and their usage in the United States shows that we are still setting and springing those traps. Even though some pesticides have been banned in the United States (e.g., DDT, Dieldrin) the residues continue to break down into equally, or even more toxic, compounds. One study in Florida conducted for an 11-year period on eagles, ospreys, hawks, and owls found DDT or its metabolic breakdown products in 100% of all analyzed muscular tissue and in 77% of all brain tissue. Residues of Dieldrin, another chlorinated hydrocarbon pesticide were found in concentrations from 78% to 91% of fatty, organ, and muscular tissues. Because many of these birds feed on fish and aquatic animals, the suspicion is that a lower level of the food chain may be seriously contaminated. For example, studies on fiddler crabs exposed to DDT, and its breakdown product DDE, showed behavioral anomalies (reduced escape or hiding responses) that made them more vulnerable to predators.

Even more alarming is the fact that although DDT may be banned for sale in the United States it is still being used, legally and illegally, on many farm products. Mexico, which still allows controlled use of DDT, exports many vegetable crops into the United States. Agricultural runoff into the Gulf may contain residues of this long-term pesticide. Moreover, even in the United States many legal pesticides are allowed to contain up to 15% by weight DDT because the Federal Insecticide, Fungicide and Rodenticide Act (FIFRA) passed in 1972 allows the compound as "an unintentional impurity." Again, agricultural runoff containing these residues offers the potential for continuing pollution of the Gulf.

And just because certain pesticides are illegal for sale in the United States does not preclude their continued manufacture inside the U.S. for sale to other countries. These ecologically arrogant chickens all come home to roost when the same countries then export back to the United States their coffee, bananas and other fruits and fruit juices, vegetables, cotton and other clothing fibers—all grown or treated with varying amounts of banned substances.

HERBICIDES: KILLING OUR OXYGEN SUPPLY

With the advent of chemically based farming and urban gardening, plant biocides have come to the fore. Herbicides are now used for a multitude of situations, ranging from elimination of weeds in farm fields, to control of roadside and canal weeds by municipalities, to maintenance of that most desirable of all suburban merit badges, a perfect green lawn.

The killing mechanisms are relatively simple. Contact herbicides kill foliage by interfering with photosynthesis, thus interrupting a major oxygen-producing pathway. Soil sterilizers indiscriminately kill soil microorganisms, many of which are essential for plant growth. The systemic herbicides kill by creating runaway growth: the plants literally starve to death while undergoing accelerated growth.

Many herbicides are selectively applied to certain crops, so their effects might seem to be restricted. But because many of these same compounds are relatively long-lived, they may continue to affect both targeted and nontargeted plants for weeks or months. Many other herbicides are nonselective and can kill *any* plant. Thus, their indiscriminate use poses a serious threat for parts of our environment, particularly where waterways can carry the toxins into estuaries or the Gulf itself. Because phytoplankton, marine algae, and sea grasses have similar energy pathways and general physiological mechanisms, they may be as severely affected by inadvertent spills as they would by purposeful applications. Green plants, on land and in the sea, are the only major source of oxygen on earth; consequently, their indiscriminate destruction will have ramifications for all life forms.

Numerous organic and inorganic herbicides (for example, Aquathol-K, Cutrine or copper sulfate, and even 2, 4-D) are also applied directly to canals, lakes, and ponds by government agencies to control algal blooms, reduce unwanted floating and bottom-growing plants, or eradicate exotic plant species. The rationale is that plant-choked waterways are not only the bane of boaters, they may also exacerbate flooding of adjacent lands during storm events by impeding drainage. But indiscriminate applications of herbicides to these water bodies may have a double whammy, first by killing the targeted plants which then sink and decay, and then secondly when plant decomposition drastically lowers dissolved oxygen levels, producing large-scale fish kills. In either situation the aquatic ecosystem is altered for a period of time.

TOXIC TRACES—HIDDEN DEATH

The deadly litany doesn't stop here. There are other equally insidious killers lurking in some herbicides and pesticides. Appearing as legally acceptable by-products or impurities, these chemicals may be as toxic or even more so than their parent compounds. For example, commercially produced PCP is not pure, but heavily contaminated with a multitude of other organochlorine and phenol-based products including chlorophenol, dibenzofuran, hexachlorobenzene, and the most toxic substance every produced by man, dioxin. According to the U.S. Fish and Wildlife Report cited earlier, ". . .the relative toxicities and accumulation potentials of some of these contaminants may exceed those of PCP by several orders of magnitude."

One particular group of substances, with the mouthfilling name of polychlorinated dibenzo-*para*-dioxin (abbreviated PCDD), masquerades innocently in our garden and pet supply stores and lies in wait on our lawns, swales, and farm fields. This family of compounds is present as trace impurities in several industrial chemicals and particularly in some herbicides. Of the 75 or so PCDD isomers (chemical compounds having a similar molecular structure), only a few are deadly. But those that are, are violently efficient. One, named 2,3,7,8-TCDD, has been called the most toxic synthetic compound ever tested under laboratory conditions. As one of the PCDD-dioxins, it ranks as the most virulently poisonous chemical compound ever created by man. Toxicity levels are measured in parts per trillion and can produce cancer, fetal abnormalities, genetic disruption, cellular breakdown, destruction of immunological systems, and alteration of reproduction.[6] The Centers for Disease Control considers concentrations of one part per billion in the soil as hazardous to human health. Yet, according to the U.S. Fish and Wildlife Service report, "No regulations governing PCDD contamination exist at present [1986]."[7]

PCDD's first sprang upon the public's consciousness with the reports on use of Agent Orange defoliant during the Vietnam War. Following that debacle, scattered reports of poisonings on farm workers, migrant laborers and even suburban gardeners who had used 2,4,-D and 2,4,5-T herbicides began to appear. Further misapplication and misuse of herbicides containing traces of dioxin have resulted in PCDD's accidentally contaminating the environment resulting in deaths not only of wildlife but domestic animals as well. [8]

AN ENVIRONMENT IN PERIL?

With more than 100 different organophosphorus and carbamate chemicals registered for use, and thousands of different pesticide products currently available in the United States, the killing of species in our environment has taken on a single-mindedness that almost approaches genocide. Organochemical compounds are now available to kill almost anything that lives. Their use includes applications as insecticides, herbicides, nematicides, acaricides, fungicides, rodenticides, canicides, and even as bird repellents.

It matters not whether the toxicant input occurs through aerial spraying of wetlands for mosquitoes, or citrus groves for medfly in Florida; or whether it washes into our rivers and streams via agricultural runoff from our vegetable, cotton, and tobacco fields in Alabama and Mississippi, or enters the ecosystem as urban runoff or industrial waste outflows from the chemical, pulp, and fertilizer plants in Louisiana or Texas. The end point is the inshore lagoons, bayous, and bays, and the nearshore waters of the Gulf of Mexico. From there the contaminants enter the food web in a variety of ways, becoming bioconcentrated or biomagnified upward in those organisms that survive. [9]

Pithy epigrams to the contrary, dilution is not always the solution to pollution. Even greatly diluted pesticides may wreak havoc on a species. Because many of the pesticides are at least partially water soluble they can freely enter the water column of rivers, lagoons, estuaries and even the open Gulf. Also usually overlooked is the fact that many pesticides were explicitly developed to interrupt or interfere with physiological and neurological mechanisms common to all arthropods (insects, mites, spiders, crabs, shrimps, and lobsters). They are more correctly classed as arthropodicides. The third and most important point is that the larval stages of many of our commercial shellfish (shrimps, crabs, lobsters, in particular) are more susceptible to even the minute, diluted doses than are the adult stages.

What does all this mean for these aquatic species? Three consequences. First, they will be exposed to debilitating or fatal dosages as planktonic larvae; second, they will suffer additional debilitating or fatal exposure during the benthonic or nektonic postlarval and juvenile stages of their life cycles, most of which must be carried out in our estuaries; and third, even as bottom-dwelling or swimming adults they may not find sanctuary, because of direct effects on their physiological systems from remnant toxicants in the immediate environment, or indirect effects that occur when they eat other contaminated prey. Thus, for many of these commercially valuable species, it's one, two, three strikes and they're out.

The magnitude of the problem extends beyond just the hapless commercial arthropods. Researchers from the University of Miami's Rosenstiel School of Marine and Atmospheric Sciences found a veritable supermarket of pesticides in hermatypic reef corals and octocorals in the Florida Keys. Among the compounds were Chlordane, Heptachlor and its derivatives, Lindane, Aldrin,

Dieldrin, Mirex, Methoxychlor, DDT, DDE, and several others. Chlordane, a known carcinogen, was long used to treat subterranean termite infestations, particularly in Florida. It has been banned for sale in the United States since 1987, but is still manufactured here and exported to Central America. DDT has been banned in the United States for more than 20 years. The sources of these toxins have not been positively identified, but leaching from contaminated ground in Florida, advection on agricultural sediments transported down the Mississippi River and eventually around the Gulf in the Loop Current, and runoff from agricultural operations in Cuba and South America entrained in the Florida Current, are all suspected.[10]

ARE BIOCIDES NECESSARY?

So why are biocides used? The reasons are primarily economic. The total loss of agricultural products due to pests and disease is estimated at 42% of the total yearly production. Almost half of every item grown in our farm fields may not reach our tables, pantries, or closets. For every $3 invested in pesticides and herbicides a $12 yield in food crops is produced. This 1:4 ratio allows food prices in the United States to remain from 30% to 50% lower than they otherwise would be and reduces the pressure to convert forests, wildlife preserves, parks, and preserves into agricultural units.

Contrasted against these benefits are the unassailable facts that *less than 1%* of any particular application ever reaches the targeted organisms. Moreover, many of the targeted species are becoming resistant to biocides. Some entomologists estimate that by the year 2000 virtually all insect pests will show some degree of resistance. The circle seems vicious and unending.

Is there a choice or solution? As with all important questions, the answer is equivocal. If we mandate use of fewer, less toxic pesticides are we willing to accept the concomitant increases in prices we would pay for our food, clothing, and lumber? Can we be satisfied with less mosquito control in our marshes and estuaries? Will we be happy with slightly bug-blemished vegetables, fruits, and grains? Can we live without totally green lawns, roadside swales, and golf courses? How many roaches, moths, flys, wasps, ants, silverfish, crickets, fleas, ticks, and that most fanciful of all aerosol-bomb insects, the ubiquitous "crawling bug," are we willing to tolerate in our homes, schools, restaurants, hospitals, and places of business? And if we are willing to accept all of this, can we impose our mandate on the rest of the world? And then enforce it?

Clearly we are rapidly approaching a dilemma. And it is a dilemma that will encompass not only the farm fields and city lawns, the forests and the roadside swales, but our estuaries and fishing grounds, and eventually entire ecosystems. It must never be forgotten that the incredible complexity of living organisms is matched only by the even greater complexity of the ecosystems that they compose. Indiscriminate use of biocides not only kills the individuals, but may also destroy the ecosystem itself. It's our environment we are talking about. And it's our choice to make.

Garbage and Debris

CHOKING IN OUR OWN WASTE

IN 1920 DR. HERMANN STAUDINGER looked at the material he had just created. Using a complicated series of acidifications he had shown that small molecules, through chemical interactions, can join together to form long chains, called *polymers*. He also realized that he had made, from previously existing materials, a substance which had never before existed on earth. The material forever after would be called by its generic term—plastic.

AN ETERNITY OF POLYMERS

Beginning with the first crude malleable substances, the chemical compounds called plastics have undergone a virtual explosion of development. In 1933 British chemists created polyethylene. By 1937 polystyrene had been developed; nylon appeared in 1938, teflon in 1944 and orlon in 1948. As development continued, the uses for plastics seemed endless, ranging from the aesthetic to the pragmatic, the esoteric to the indispensable. By 1987, more than 55 billion tons of plastics were produced by U.S. industries. Of these, U.S. consumers discarded more than 22 billion tons, or 40%.

Today we need only look around us to see plastics in a multitude of different forms, ranging from food wraps and garbage bags to drinking glasses, fast-food containers, and soft-drink holders. Space-age implementation includes automobile dashboards and bodies, automatic weapons, artificial heart valves, computer and electronic industry parts and software, and as part of the interior structural components in aircraft and spacecraft. Plastic (polypropylene) would eventually be used to contain and soak up another pollutant: oil and hazardous waste spills in the sea. From land, to sea, mankind has now even reached out into space with plastics, in components of orbiting satellites, discharged waste from Apollo missions, and on the moon and Mars where landed vehicles remain after missions were accomplished. Unless they are disassembled, they will remain there for eons.

It can truly be said that plastics are not only an integral part of twentieth-century life, but they are here to stay. Lightweight, easily manufactured, and with a multiplicity of uses limited only by their tolerances to high temperatures and their malleability and brittleness, plastics have moved into industry, science, and technology with a vengeance. In the process they have bumped aside such tried-and-true, but now old-fashioned, usages once monopolized by steel, rubber, and glass.

There is one other characteristic of plastics that makes them so desirable for industrial and technological applications. Most plastics are alien compounds, never before seen on earth, so they are only rarely subject to weathering, degradation, and breakdown. Their best features are also their worst. In short, they are durable. Plastics are here, now and forever. Nothing makes plastics but man[1], nothing uses plastics but man. Nothing biologically degrades plastics. We may be litterbugs, but there are no "bugs" that eat our plastic litter.

GARBAGE IN—GARBAGE OUT

Mariners since before the Spanish conquistadores have been dumping refuse into the Gulf. But the majority of that waste was food waste (garbage), wood, or metal, and either recyclable or degradable. Today, however, most of the estimated 115 tons of debris dumped daily into the Gulf is plastics.[2]

And plastics are everywhere. Floating far out at sea, resting on the sands of the most remote islands, bobbing in nearshore waters and in the lagoons, rolling on condominium-lined beaches, blowing onto the uplands—everywhere. How bad is it? Plastic containers (as well as aluminum beer cans and glass condiment bottles) have been found in the deepest parts of the Gulf of Mexico, in waters nearly 3 miles deep. How ironic that in places where man has not yet ventured, his litter precedes him. The statistics are staggering. From 60% to 80% of all floating anthropogenic debris in the world's oceans is plastic. An estimated 639,000 plastic containers may be thrown overboard by merchant vessels every day. That's more than 233 million a year. In Florida alone, in 1988, more than 60% of the nearly half a million items picked up on a voluteer beach cleanup were plastics. Over 65% of the 195 tons of beach litter in a 1987 Louisiana clean-up were plastic. A three-hour beach cleanup along 122 miles of Texas shoreline in 1988 collected 124 tons of garbage and debris, the majority of which was plastic. National averages in beach clean-ups ranged from 47% to 74% plastic.

Plastic wastes form a large part, but by no means all, of our beach-littered environment. Walk any beach along the Gulf of Mexico and the amount of glass (bottles, jars, light bulbs), wood (crates, decking, cargo stakes), rubber (tires, machine or engine belts, gaskets, condoms), paper products (cardboard boxes, filters, magazines, newspapers and other media publications), metal (tin cans, aerosol containers, aluminum items), plant fiber materials (cloth, rope, netting), and petroleum by-products (tars, oil slicks, petrochemical sludge, congealed grease) is mind-boggling (see Table 17). The surface waters of the sea have become a vast conduit for all of the manufactured waste produced by man on earth.

Where does it come from? Webster's Dictionary defines *flotsam* as "floating wreckage of a ship or its cargo." *Jetsam*, its counterpart, is defined as "cargo thrown overboard to lighten a ship in danger." There should be a third term, *purgamentsam*, (purgamentum = "garbage, rubbish, filth") which is here defined as "refuse, garbage, or filth thrown overboard." In each case the items, if buoyant, may float for long periods of time and eventually wash ashore. How much? A Gulf-wide beach cleanup in 1988 collected over 545 tons of washed-ashore debris in a single day!

Our modern society is a waste generator. An estimated 7 million tons of ocean-floating waste are dumped each year. By whom? Merchant shipping (6 million tons), commercial fishing boats (375 thousand tons), recreational boating (114 thousand tons), military vessels (82 thousand tons), passenger vessels (31 thousand tons), oil platform operations (4 thousand tons), and shipping accidents and storms (110 thousand tons). The merchant fleets of the world throw overboard nearly three-quarters of a million glass, plastic, and metal containers every day! Passenger ships add another 170,000 pounds each day. Mom, Pop and the kids are worse. On a typical recreational outing they throw more than 312 tons of refuse overboard each day. And then complain about how dirty the waters, the beaches, and the shores are!

PEOPLE PROBLEMS FOR NONPEOPLE

All this may seem to have implications only for landfills and human society, but the ramifications are much more widespread. In addition to the widespread contamination problems caused by the low or nonexistent biodegradability of plastics, there is another series of crises that directly involve other organisms on earth. Humans may only be subject to the annoyance of plastic litter clogging the street gutters, blowing across the landscape, or washing ashore on the beaches, but the remainder of the vertebrate and invertebrate world must contend with it on a more fundamental level.

Seabirds and sea mammals have been strangled by plastic six-pack holders and monofilament nets and fishing line (see Part Five Figure). In Florida, animal deaths resulting from entanglement in monofilament line was recorded in 16% of all the sites involved in cleanups. Sea turtles eat plastic packs and other floating plastic refuse, mistaking it for the jellyfish which form a large portion of their diet. Marine fish ingest floating plastic items that clog their digestive tracts and kill them. Marine shrimp get degraded styrofoam pellets caught under their carapaces and die. Even benthic fauna such as oysters suffer plastic contamination inside their shells.[3]

Yet not all the blame should be put on polluters at sea. In many cases, land-based polluters also contaminate Gulf shores via discharge through storm drains and sewers. The plastic tampon applicators, sanitary pad liners, and disposable diapers flushed down our toilets are neither less identifiable nor more degradable than the galley offal and head wastes, dumped or flushed from ships far offshore.

What is most tragic is that mankind is beginning to accept beach litter as a "natural" part of the seashore. On shores where once only seaweed and spindrift were found now occurs refuse that will never biodegrade. No better example of this litter problem exists than that of Padre Island, Texas, the long barrier island fronting the Laguna Madre (see Table 22).[4]

WASTE NOT, WANT NOT: WHAT CAN WE DO ABOUT IT?

In a recent conference on Environmental Quality in the Gulf of Mexico at Galveston, Texas, participants were asked to indicate the most pressing problems. Of the 44 categories listed, ranging from habitat degradation, population congestion, and private property rights versus public interest, the one topic receiving most mention and thus perceived as most important was debris and garbage in the sea and on the shore. Although it is among the simplest forms of pollution, is the easiest to observe, and has the simplest and most obvious of solutions, it has nevertheless proven to be among the hardest to clean up.

As with any litter, the simplest way to prevent it is to discard it in an acceptable manner. None of the five major litter components (paper, glass, metal, plastics, or biological materials) are incapable of being recycled. The benefits are both apparent and hidden. For example, recycling a ton of paper saves 17 trees. But it also frees up 3.3 cubic yards of landfill space. The same holds for glass. The energy used to create one new aluminum can from raw materials can be applied to creating 20 cans from recycled materials. Recycled plastic resins are one-third cheaper than fresh resins. The space saved in landfills could just as easily be occupied by the litter that is presently nonrecyclable and which washes ashore or contaminates our beaches. It has been said, and rightly, that recycling requires a fundamental change in thinking: it means caring about things once considered to be garbage.

TABLE 22
Flotsam, Jetsam and Purgamentsam from Padre Island Texas in 1986

Non-Styrofoam plastics:	95,662 items
Styrofoam plastics:	19,280 items
Glass:	20,042 items
Metal:	22,098 items
Paper:	10,337 items
Wood:	4,157 items
Rubber:	20 items
Total pieces of debris:	171,596 items
Total area of collection:	122 linear miles
Average number of items/mile:	1407; about 1 every 4 linear feet

Data from: Report to Texas General Land Office, Center for Marine Conservation, 1987.

Some waste items pose vexing problems. The 16 billion disposable diapers used every year may take as long as 500 years to decompose. Six-pack rings may take 450 years to break down. The one billion pounds of fast-food plastic containers may never break down completely. They form a continually accumulating portion of our landfills, some of which, at 150+ feet in height and over 50 acres at their base, approach the size of the plaza and temples at Testihuacán. As one waste-management slogan reads: "Everybody wants us to pick it up, but nobody wants us to put it down."

What else can be done? Scientists, resource managers, and politicians are equivocal on this point. Local governments, such as those administering Padre

Island, spend in excess of $14 million/year on beach cleanup alone. These are tax dollars from citizens' pocketbooks. Education, of course, is the common element in the solution: informing every segment of society—consumers, producers, packagers, regulators, waste haulers and disposers, and, of course, politicians—that garbage and waste simply do not go away by themselves.

Recycling is always a good solution. Technology today has advanced to the point that even polystyrene food containers, soft drink bottles, and milk jugs are being recycled, first being cleaned and pelletized and then made into building materials, office products, or playground equipment. Up to 100 million pounds a year are being reincarnated into useful second-life items.

Municipal solid waste incinerators have also been advocated as a solution. By burning the waste, its volume is reduced, thereby decreasing the amount of landfill space required to contain it. The heat generated is used to produce steam that turns turbine generators, producing electricity for municipal use or sale to regional electrical networks. If all this sounds too good to be true, it is. Adverse effects include lofting huge amounts of contaminants—including mercury, cadmium, carbon monoxide, nitrous oxides, sulfurated compounds, and even dioxins—into the atmosphere via incinerator smokestacks. Scrubbers and leachers in the combustion line allegedly remove many of these pollutants, but significant levels (as much as several tons a year) may still be emitted. And the ash residues are so concentrated in hazardous materials that only specially lined landfills can only be used to hold them to prevent ground water contamination.

Landfill mining is among the more encouraging solutions. Glass, ferrous metals, plastics, aluminum, rubber, and wood are excavated from old landfill piles and sorted for recycling into second-life products. As pointed out by one southwestern Florida resource manager, the old concept of a landfill as a place where garbage is entombed is no longer valid or acceptable.

Exotic organisms may be another solution. Some common soil bacteria produce polyesters with qualities similar to plastics, and even some rubbers, except that they are biodegradable. The research is new, uncertain and costly. But the bottom line may be the difference in paying for a continuing cleanup with our tax dollars or electing to purchase biodegradable plastics with our income.[5]

EXISTING TREATIES AND LAWS: A GOOD BEGINNING

The MARPOL (MARine POLlution) Treaty is the primary international agreement aimed at protecting the Gulf. Because it is an international treaty, it is restricted to international waters. The treaty consists of a series of annexes, each of which addresses a major pollution problem (shipboard garbage, oil spills, etc.). For example, the Gulf of Mexico has been proposed by the EPA as a "special area" under Annex V of the International Convention for the Prevention of Pollution from Ships. This annex presently prohibits discharging both plastic wastes and nonplastic floating materials. Ships may not discharge nonplastic floating material less than 25 miles from the nearest land, nor within 12 miles any nonplastic or food wastes that have not been ground or pulverized; and if these wastes are ground or pulverized, such discharges may not take place any closer than three miles from the nearest land. The "special area" designation is even more restrictive, forbidding all nonplastic waste disposal in the area except food waste, and even this must be discharged at least 12 miles from the nearest land.

On another front, Congress enacted the Marine Plastic Pollution Research and Control Act of 1988 at the same time it ratified the pertinent annex in the MARPOL Treaty. By adding its own, often more restrictive, stipulations (particularly dealing with marina and seaport garbage), the resulting legislation became much tougher. The laws are in place. But laws are easier to pass than to enforce. And even strict enforcement does not guarantee successful prosecution.

In 1988 the EPA initiated a Gulf of Mexico Program and proclaimed 1992 as the Year of the Gulf. The Gulf of Mexico program is directed toward assessing the most pressing environmental problems, seeking ways to abate pollution, and (most importantly) educating the public. The EPA has already co-sponsored two symposia on the Gulf, one held in Galveston in 1988, and the second convened in New Orleans in 1990. The primary problems facing the Gulf, based on a consensus among participants in the 1988 symposium, were a triad consisting of development (coastal erosion caused by seashore and barrier island development; pass dredging), pollution (toxic substances and pesticides; eutrophication caused by agricultural and industrial point and non-point sources; threats to public health in contaminated water and seafood), and habitat loss (sea grasses, dunes, and wetlands; freshwater diversion from estuaries for flood control and navigation).[6]

Over the first five years, the Gulf of Mexico Program is supposed to produce a comprehensive plan addressing these problems and offering recommendations for alleviation. Future directions will depend, again, on a consensus of the participants. Thus, active participation by the public and interested groups will be of major importance in the coming decade.

Thermal And Radioactive Pollution

A GENIE UNBOTTLED

THE GULF OF MEXICO is a thermally controlled body of water. Temperatures range from 30° C near or at the sea surface to -2° C in the deepest waters. The Gulf of Mexico is also a radioactive body of water, although the amount of radiation emitted (primarily from rocks beneath the seafloor) is so faint as to be considered negligible. These natural (ambient) background levels of radiation have existed for millions of years. Consequently, the animal and plant life in the marine and estuarine waters have adapted to their presence.

THERMAL POLLUTION: GETTING INTO HOT WATER

Then man entered. Suddenly, large-scale electrical generators were being built in coastal regions. Burning coal, oil, or using nuclear energy, the generators produced large amounts of heat—that for efficiency and safety's sake had to be removed. The immediate and obvious solution was to use circulating seawater (up to half a billion gallons a day per facility) to carry it away. Water accepts heat, cools the equipment, and carries the heat elsewhere. It is that "elsewhere" that causes all the problems (see Figure 44).

Heated wastewater discharged into the marine environment is a mixed blessing. In the winter or during cold spells, the receiving area is maintained at a warmer temperature than other areas immediately adjacent but beyond the influence of warm-water flow. Often, the relatively warmer water can be traced as a plume that emerges from the discharge pipe, or outfall, and gradually mixes with the surrounding water body.

Many organisms (for example, manatees, fish, and some species of invertebrates) actively seek warm-water outflows. Because the outflow temperature remains consistently warm throughout the entire year, during both cold and warm weather, the organisms have a thermostable environment. Temperature stress is reduced.

But not all organisms find thermal effluents a blessing. Often, the pulsed flows artificially raise water temperatures beyond the evolutionary capability of the organisms to adapt. Once tolerances are exceeded the organisms die, even though the temperature may drop to acceptable levels thereafter. Such an event, particularly if it disrupts an ecosystem, is categorized as *thermal pollution*.

Thermal pollution causes a multitude of effects in addition to the most

312

Figure 44. Atoms in the marshlands.
Like some bizarre and turreted fortress out of the Arabian Nights, the twin concrete
condensing towers of a nuclear powered electrical generating plant rise from the middle
of the marshes and prairies of the Crystal River area on Florida's central western coast.
Here, mankind matches nuclear productivity with Nature's biological efforts—and hopes
to keep the nuclear genie contained. [Florida Department of Commerce, Division of
Tourism, Tallahassee, Florida]

obvious. Organisms within or around the thermal plume may find conditions
reproductively appealing or attractive for settlement, and undergo rapid population growth. Others that cannot easily adapt to temperature changes (*the-
rmoregulate*) within, or outside the thermal plume, may be reproductively
disrupted. Still others may suffer oxygen deprivation (*anoxia*) when oxygen

levels in the heated water drop owing to diffusion of the gas outward, or its excess usage by other organisms. Resistance to environmental contaminants may decrease in direct proportion to the abnormally high temperature of the water. In short, thermal pollution produces a complex series of impacts that depend on the organisms present, their physiological tolerances, the ecosystems they comprise, and the environment in which they exist.

And it doesn't stop there. Sudden shutdowns of warm-water effluents, particularly during the winter, may also produce thermal (cold) shock to manatees, fish, and invertebrates in the same way that sudden inputs of warm water do. Drastic temperature changes outside the ambient range produce, at the very least, some type of physiological stress; in many instances at the coldest or the hottest end of the continuum, these changes will cause death. Thus any species opting for the tenuous paradise of continually warm water must remain ever adaptable to temperature changes. And though the mobile fauna may be able to escape catastrophic declines or increases, the sessile, or attached, fauna cannot. For the latter it is a Faustian bargain of sorts.

As with any alteration of the environment, not all the effects can be considered detrimental. In Florida, for example, warm-water outfalls at power plants provide refuge for manatees and other aquatic organisms during intense cold snaps and episodic freezes. On the commercial side, aquaculture operations utilize the heated effluents of power plants and factory outfalls to produce constant, year-round temperatures for larval and postlarval culture of marine organisms. Shrimp, lobster, and several species of fishes have all been investigated or are actively undergoing commercial exploitation at this time. Several species of marine algae have also been cultured in artificial warm-water systems, as a food source for other aquacultured animals, a commercial hydroponic crop in and of itself, or as fermentable vegetation to produce methane gas for fuel.

NUCLEAR RADIATION: A RECALCITRANT GENIE

Radioactive substances occur in the environment in a multitude of conditions. Some are natural—for example, radon gas and minute amounts of radium that are found in phosphatic and granitic rocks. Areas along the Gulf of Mexico with potentially high levels of radon gas occur on the west coast of Florida, western Louisiana, and along portions of the Texas coastline.

But a much larger portion of radioactive substances result from human activity. Many radioactive compounds, termed *radionuclides*, are formed as a consequence of nuclear technology. Nuclear-powered electricity-generating plants, nuclear weapons production sites, academic and industrial research laboratories, hospitals, and even just plain radioactive waste ("radwaste") can produce substances that may leak or be accidentally or deliberately discharged into the environment. For example, from 1946 to 1970 the Atomic Energy Commission authorized the disposal of more than 86,000 containers of radwaste, many of which ended up in the Gulf of Mexico. Approximately 44% of all radiation exposure in humans each year comes not from nature but from the consequences of human technology.

Nuclear-powered plants, for example, produce approximately 200 different types of radioactive by-products or isotopes as a consequence of their technology. Around the Gulf of Mexico there is one nuclear generating plant in Florida, one in coastal Louisiana, one operating and one more under construction in Texas, and one in Mexico. Cuba presently has two under construction. While these may seem small numbers, they are nonetheless significant. Consider this: 49 of the 82 presently operating nuclear-powered plants in the United States are intentionally located in coastal areas to allow for coolant water intake and outflow.

The danger from radioactive wastes is fourfold. First, their toxicity is often directly related to the substance itself. The emission of radioactivity can cause serious or fatal consequences to numerous organisms including humans. Radioactive substances may become entrained in food chains or undergo bioconcentration just as hazardous chemicals do. The effects on components of an ecosystem may thereby be magnified throughout the entire food web.

Second, and often of more importance, is the decay rate of a radioactive substance—that is, its half-life. The half-life of a radioactive substance (the duration required to reduce the total existing radioactive emissions in a substance to half of their previous value) may extend from days to decades to millions of years. As an example, 1 pound of radioactive phosphorus 32 (P^{32}) would decay in 14 days to one-half pound of P^{32} and one-half pound of non-radioactive sulfur 32 (S^{32}). Two weeks later only one-fourth pound of P^{32} would remain, with three-fourths pound of S^{32}. Two weeks beyond that one-eighth pound P^{32} would be left, and so on until the majority of the original pound of phosphorus has decayed into inert sulfur.[1]

It is easily seen from this that many radioactive compounds and elements can continue to emit toxic radiation beyond human life spans. For example, radioactive iodine 129 has a half life of 160 million years. This isotope can exert its effects over evolutionary time.

Third, radioactive emissions from one source can induce radioactivity in other compounds or elements, causing them to become toxically radioactive. The environment then remains continuously poisoned as these substances decay through their normal radioactive sequence until they eventually become inert.

Fourth, and perhaps the most vexing of all, is that radioactive waste brings seemingly insurmountable problems of storage and disposal. The high toxicity coupled with the exceedingly long half-lives of some substances means, in effect, that these wastes are forever. Storage or disposal areas are immediately and permanently contaminated. And if such wastes leak into the ecosystem, there is no doubt that many of these radioisotopes will become incorporated in food webs. Because radioactivity acts deleteriously on both the body (somatic effects) and the reproductive system (genetic effects), the target organisms suffer double jeopardy. And if properly encoded in the chromosomes, the parents may pass these mutations on to their offspring.[2]

To illustrate the magnitude of the problem, the EPA has determined that spent fuel rods from nuclear electricity-generating plants need to be stored at least 10,000 years before the radioactive hazard is sufficiently reduced to pose no harm to humans. If such rods had existed and were stored in the pyramids at the beginning of the ancient Egyptian dynasties, the pyramids would still remain hazardous for 3,000 years beyond today!

There remains one other problem associated with nuclear wastes and their production and disposal, perhaps the most important problem of all. Nobody wants it.

And the genie refuses to climb back into the bottle.

PONDERABLES FOR OUR FUTURE

Fact: Radioactive fuel supplies are not limitless. It requires about 160 tons of natural (*unenriched*) uranium to produce 20 tons of *enriched* uranium suitable as nuclear fuel in a typical light-water reactor (LWR), or a ratio of 8 tons *unenriched* to 1 ton *enriched*.

Fact: An LWR seems complex but is functionally simple. Water heated by nuclear fission from *enriched* uranium produces steam to drive turbines, which create electricity. Other water is also used to cool the reactor.

Fact: Of the more than 520 reactors in operation or under construction worldwide, 390 (or 75%) are LWRs.

Fact: Present technology requires about 20 tons of *enriched* uranium per LWR per year, or about 7,800 tons for all LWRs each year.

Fact: Based on present use of *enriched* uranium some 6-7 million tons of *unenriched* uranium will therefore be needed over the next century.

Fact: What is the estimated world's supply of *unenriched* uranium? Six to seven million tons!

Source: W. Hafele. (1990). Energy from nuclear power. *In:* Energy for Planet Earth. *Scientific American*, vol. 263 (3):137-144.

Epilogue

Buena es la que va,
mejor is la que viene;
siete es passada y en ocho muele,
mas molera si Dios quisiere.
*Mariner's dawn watch song
ca. 15th century*[1]

NEARLY 500 YEARS AGO Spanish explorers and merchants arrived in the Gulf of Mexico looking for gold. Today, in our American Mediterranean, where the Spanish conquistadores once plundered the wealth of nations, the modern conquistadores plunder the wealth of the continents and seafloors. Today, black gold has replaced the precious metals and spices; fisheries have taken the place of many agricultural products; and a new industry—tourism—supplements, where it does not supplant, settlement and development.

It is inevitable that modern man, like his Castillian counterparts of old, will find that not only are the supplies of such wealth exhaustible, but the effects of exploitation are too often felt long after the wealth is gone. Today we have begun to learn the hardest of lessons: that we cannot continue to pollute and degrade the environment while we continue to take without giving, to receive without returning.

Although I have documented the myriad problems besetting the Gulf of Mexico and foresee, in many cases, a future rife with continuing adverse environmental impacts, there yet remains hope. The governments of both Mexico and the United States recognize the threats to this part of our mutually shared American Mediterranean and have enacted laws and established programs to protect and study our sea. This is cause for cautious optimism but should not warrant complacency. Public vigilance is ever the watchword if the waters are to remain clear and the beaches clean.

The one firm hope that we who live around the Gulf of Mexico now have is the foreknowledge (gained, to be sure, in retrospect) of the effects of our previous activities. Not only have we the technology to extract, exploit, and expend, we also have the technology to conserve, preserve, and (at the worst) repair any damages we may inflict on our environment. Armed with this new knowledge, and more importantly, putting this knowledge into action, may yet forestall what many experts are predicting could well become a slow but continuing environmental catastrophe both around the shores and within the waters of the Gulf of Mexico. As the peoples and countries of the European Mediterraneans have learned, long-term exploitive use of the natural resources of land-enclosed seas eventually produces environmental crises ranging from polluted beaches to destruction of ecosystems. We here in our own American

Mediterranean must temper the use of our natural resources with reason and reparation. If we do not we may be setting the stage for the collapse of our New World empires, and the world's historians will once again dryly note the passing of another great civilization. It is truly our decision to make.

Today, two great land nations of the Gulf region, the United States and Mexico, and the island republic of Cuba stand together on the shores of this, their own great Mediterranean. Together they share nearly 500 years of history within the Gulf of Mexico. Are the lessons now seen clearly in this hindsight ? Are they held firmly enough and with sufficient understanding to allow proper foresight and planning for the correct and careful use of these environmental treasures? What will the historians and geographers write of our efforts in the next 500 years?

In too many instances over the last five centuries has mankind broken into the treasury of the Gulf of Mexico and squandered its wealth. We need not, we must not, continue along this path. With the ever-increasing involvement of concerned citizens, we can wisely harbor the remaining treasures that Nature has so amply provided. In reading this book you have taken the first step along the avenue of social and environmental involvement. The future of this grand body of water, its majestic biological resources, and all its remaining environmental wealth are in your hands. The year 1992, declared the Year of the Gulf, can be our new beginning. What are you going to do?

> What does your mind seek?
> Where is your heart?
> If you give your heart to each
> and everything,
> you lead it nowhere: you
> destroy your heart.
>
> Nezahualcoyotl
> King of Texcoco, ca. 1450[2]

Footnotes

Prologue
[1] Although Vespucci is popularly credited with the "discovery" that the Gulf of Mexico was a new body of water, debate on the subject has raged since the mid-nineteenth century. For a summary of opposing views see, for example, Galtsoff (1954), chapter 1; Morison (1974), pp. 288-312; Sale (1990) pp. 197, 215-216, 379-380; and the discussion by Weddle (1985), pp. 16-17.

Chapter 1
[1] Just as the original discoverer of the Gulf of Mexico may never be known with certainty, so also unanswered is the question as to who first physically explored much of the actual Gulf area. As Weddle (*op. cit.*) and others have pointed out, several Spanish expeditions came tantalizingly close to the Yucatánian entrance to the Gulf, and then turned back, probably owing to the unwieldiness of the caravels, the continually blowing trade winds, and the rapid currents that rush through the Straits of Yucatán.

[2] If Vespucci was as much a charlatan as some historians would have us believe, this appointment would suggest that he also fooled the administrators of the Casa de Contratacion, and the Spanish monarchy as well. See Lowery (1959), pp. 4-5.

[3] The question of "who discovered what" also applied to coastal and inland geography. Poor reconnoitering and faulty mapmaking often left later historians uncertain as to which features corresponded to those on modern maps. For example, some historians question whether Alvarez de Pineda's "Rio del Espiritu Santo" was the Mississippi River, Mobile Bay, or Galveston Bay. Evidence suggests that Alvarez de Pineda sailed by the Mississippi River, but may never have ascended it. By the same token, de Soto may have come ashore in Florida at Charlotte Harbor, substantially south of the generally accepted landfall at Tampa Bay, and Narvaez may have been lost off Matagorda Bay rather than on the Mississippi. See Weddle (*op. cit.*).

Of additional importance is the fact that many hydrological and geological features are transient at best. River mouths shift, deltas form and decay, embayments fill with sediments, barrier islands wander, erode, and disappear. The coastlines of the 1500-1600s may only have generally resembled those we see today.

[4] "The Narrative of the Expedition of Hernando de Soto by the Gentleman of Elvas." 1557. *In:* Hodge and Lewis (1990), p. 136.

[5] Innes (1969), p. 173; Fuson (1987), pp. 90 ff.

[6] Although every schoolchild knows that the Dutch made their most prominent moves in Nieuw Amsterdam (New York) and the northeast, they also were slicing their share of the New World pie in the Caribbean. The Dutch West Indies Company, begun in 1621, served as a base of operations in the Caribbean.

[7] Buccaneering as a profitable (albeit illegal) enterprise began in the Gulf shortly after 1540 and lasted into the beginning of the eighteenth century. When the pirates ran out of galleons they turned their attention toward the coastal towns where the booty lay stacked on the docks awaiting the next outbound vessel. Operating with relative impunity from bases in the Laguna de Terminos on Yucatán, and the Anclote Keys above Tampa, Florida, the pirates visited nearly every major coastal village,

and the larger towns of Lermna, Villahermosa, Campeche, Tampico, and Vera Cruz in the western Gulf, and Havana, Apalache, the Suwannee River area, and Pensacola in the eastern Gulf. Anything of value was fair game—from pesos, jewelry, bullion, and religious articles, to flour, salt, livestock, and household items. And when piracy failed to yield a profit, there was always poaching of sea turtles and manatees, theft of dye woods, capture of slaves, and smuggling, on which to fall back. See Lowery (*op. cit.*), chapter 1. Weddle also summarizes this nicely (*op. cit.* chapter 21).

[8] The English already had a passing familiarity with parts of the Gulf, having run slaving, pirating, and even some trading expeditions in the mid-1500s. The English captains were all experienced mariners and could not have helped noticing how thinly the Spanish military and civilian lines were stretched around the Gulf. Like two strange bulldogs in a familiar backyard, religious differences kept the Catholic Spanish and Protestant English at each other's throats all around the Gulf. With tacit or open encouragement from Queen Elizabeth I, men of historical renown such as Sir Francis Drake, Sir John Hawkins, and Sir Walter Ralegh looked to the west and challenged Spanish dominance, particularly in the Caribbean and along the east coast of North America.

[9] "One glass is past
and the second now floweth;
more shall run down
if my God so desireth."

Sung at the turning of the hourglass of the first night watch. Retranslated from Morison (*op. cit.*), p. 180.

Chapter 2

[1] Fuson (*op. cit.*), pp. 136, 142, 145.

[2] Ceram (1971), p. 30; Gates, *in* de Landa (1978), pp. iii ff; Weddle (*op. cit.*), p. 33.

[3] For comparative views see Morison (*op. cit.*), p. 116, 120-121; and Wilson, S. M. (1991). The admiral and the chief. Natural History Magazine, March, 1991, pp. 14, 18-19.

[4] A large shell mound at Terra Ceia Island near Bradenton, Florida once had a temple facing the east. De Soto's soldiers destroyed the mound in 1539 to look for freshwater pearls.

[5] Cuban Indians often made the relatively short journey (approximately 90 miles) across the Straits of Florida to trade with the Calusas on Florida's southwestern coast, and to look for a river named "Jordan" in which they might bathe and allegedly be rejuvenated. So many Cuban Indians came to Florida in search of that fabled stream that Senquene, the father of the great Calusa chief Carlos, sequestered them into their own settlement. See Fontaneda's *Memoir* (1575), p. 29.

[6] Not every Spaniard met death. In one of the most famous accounts of capture and cultural adaptation of the time, Hernando d'Escalante Fontaneda, a 13-year-old youth from Cartagena, Colombia, was shipwrecked along the southwestern Florida coast in 1545. Captured by the Calusas, Fontaneda lived with them for approximately 17 years before being ransomed. Juan Ortiz, a young grandee from Seville, was also captured by the Calusa and condemned to be burned at the stake, but was spared when the cacique's daughter pleaded his cause. He eventually rose to the rank of a subchief before being rescued. Gonzalo Guerrero, captured in 1511 by the Mayans and enslaved after his ship went aground on the Alacran Reef, also "went native";

he tattooed his body, let his hair grow, pierced his ears to wear rings, married a subchief's daughter, fathered three children, and attained his own subchiefdom. Nor did the Indians always treat the Spanish dead savagely. Cabeza de Vaca related that bodies of the crew of another vessel, wrecked in an unnamed coastal harbor above Tampa, were later discovered wrapped carefully and respectfully in painted deerskins in a Timucuan (or Tocobagan?) Indian village.

[7] Among the diseases introduced by the Spanish conquest was smallpox, previously unknown in the western hemisphere, and presumably brought in by a Negro slave in 1520. The native Americans also had no resistance to measles. Other introduced pestilences included bubonic plague (brought in by shipboard rats and their fleas, perhaps as early as 1493 on the first Columbus expedition), yellow fever, influenza, tuberculosis, cholera, chicken pox, and at least a score of others. In return, the Indians gave the Old World syphilis, hookworm, and breakbone fever—the latter disease carred by mosquitoes. See Sale (*op. cit.*) p. 304.

[8] Juan Ponce de León first named the coral islets of the Florida Keys *Los Martires*—the martyrs—because the barely awash coral heads at a distance resembled the heads of men in distress. At Key West (*Cayo Hueso*, or "Islet of Bones" in Spanish), the southernmost of the Florida Keys, large numbers of human bones were found, macabre mementoes of a continuing warfare between the Calusas and the Keys Indians.

[9] Many of the tribal names were "Iberianized," and we shall never know what the correct tribal appelation was. See Ceram (*op. cit.*) p. 42; and Sale (*op. cit.*) pp. 95 ff.

[10] Leon-Portilla (1963) discussed this "barbaric" philosophy at length, and noted the poignant response of the Aztecan wise men to the destruction of their religion by the friars in 1524:

> "It was the doctrine of the elders. . .
> allow us then to die,
> let us perish now,
> since our gods are already dead."

See also de Landa (*op. cit.*) p. 35 ff, 47 ff; Gallenkamp (1976), p. 9; Hays (1963), pp. 460-477, 527-537; Innes (*op. cit.*) pp. 19-20. As H. R. Hays wrote so perceptively in 1963: "On the whole, the gods behave badly."

[11] The Copal tree (*Protium copal*) exudes a resin the Mayans used as incense and was an important trade item as well. For further information on Mayan tradesmanship see Andrews, A. P. (1991). America's ancient mariners. Natural History Magazine,October, 1991, pp. 72-75; Hansen, R. D. (1991). The road to Nakbe. *ibid.*, April, 1991, pp. 8, 10, 12, 13-14.

[12] Horses evolved over a 60-million-year period in the New World and were once widely distributed throughout North and South America. They crossed the Bering Strait landbridge several times and spread throughout Asia and Europe, but went extinct in the New World at the end of the Pleistocene era, approximately 100,000 years ago. In 1519, Hernando Cortés reintroduced horses to North America when he landed in Mexico with some 16 animals. Some of these eventually escaped and formed the ancestral stock for the wild horse herds of the eighteenth century.

[13] Fray Diego de Landa (an otherwise careful historian from whom we have most of our early knowledge of the Mayans), in 1562 burned 27 major hieroglyphic scrolls and destroyed more than 5,000 idols because they espoused, in his estimation, nothing but superstitions and falsehoods from the devil. De Landa thus sanctimoniously eliminated most of the knowledge assembled by and for the Mayans over

the previous 2,000 years.

[14] See Gallenkamp (*op. cit.*).

[15] The Temple of the Sun and Temple of the Moon at Teotihuacan were immense structures occupying nearly 475,000 square feet at the base (nearly 11 acres), and rising some 200 feet (20 stories) above the surrounding plaza and avenue. For comparison, the Great Pyramid of Cheops in Egypt occupies 570,000 square feet at the base (13 acres) and presently towers more than 480 feet high (48 stories).

[16] One incident reveals much about the Aztecs. While still in servitude to the more powerful Toltec Colhuacan, the Aztec leaders brazenly requested a Colhuacan princess for marriage to their chief. The Toltecs agreed. Whereupon the Aztecs, after the marriage ceremony, promptly sacrificed the maiden in the hopes that she would become a war goddess for them! The Colhuacan retaliated by expelling the Aztecs from their kingdom. See Farb (1968), p. 164 ff. Innes (*op. cit.* pp. 95-96) provides a more exquisitely macabre version of the marriage story, perhaps one more in keeping with what is known about the Aztec outlook on life.

[17] Interested readers may consult Bernal Díaz del Castillo (1632), Hays (*op. cit.*), Innes (*op. cit.*), and Leon-Portilla (*op. cit.*) for more detail on the Aztec religion. Thompson (1963) discusses both the ancient and the christianized modern Mayan religious ceremonies. Gallenkamp (*op. cit.*) provides a moving summary of the Mayan theocracy in Chapters 7 and 14.

[18] See Díaz del Castillo (*op. cit.*); also William Gates' introduction and summary in his (1978) translation of Diego de Landa's *Relacion de las Cosas de Yucatán.*

[19] Leon-Portilla (*op. cit.*).

[20] Díaz del Castillo (*op. cit.*), p. 191.

Chapter 3

[1] de Tocqueville, A. (1835). Democracy in America. *In:* Mayer, J. P. and M. Lerner (eds.); 1966 p. 312. Harper and Row, Publishers, NY. xciii + 802 pp. In a footnote acidly summarizing the legal machinations, de Tocqueville concluded: "The more I think about it, the more I feel that the only difference between civilized and uncivilized men with regard to justice is this: the former contests the justice of rights, the latter simply violates them."

[2] Farb (*op. cit.*) p. 244.

Chapter 4

[1] Two examples will illustrate this. When Francisco Hernández de Córdoba and many of his crew were grievously wounded at Champotón, Yucatán, Alaminos determined that the quickest way back to Havana was not eastward (the way that they came), but northward to the Florida coast and thence south and eastward (riding the Loop Current) and then through the Florida Straits. The outbound journey required 21 days; the return to Havana took approximately one week. Even so, with Alaminos as pilot (and badly wounded by an arrow to his throat) the vessel ran aground somewhere in the Florida Keys.

Alaminos recovered and became pilot on the de Grijalva expedition back to Yucatán, and eventually a pilot for Hernando Cortés on the expedition that led to the conquest of Mexico. It was Alaminos who used the Florida Current in the Bahama Channel (MacLeish calls it the "Alaminos Memorial Highway") to shove the galleons carrying Cortés' treasure rapidly out into the Atlantic toward Spain. See Galtsoff (*op. cit.*) chapter 1; Díaz del Castillo (*op. cit.*) pp. 14 *et seq*; and MacLeish (1989), pp. 62- 74, 79.

Chapter 5

[1] In a geological and physiographic sense the boundary might be more correctly drawn along the sill from Isla de Cozumel, Yucatán, to Cabo San Antonio, on Cuba's westernmost tip (see Endsheets).

[2] Although Cuba is geographically not part of the Gulf of Mexico as generally defined, the geological and physiographic features found on its northwestern coast argue for its inclusion.

3 For a good general summary and illustrations of these features see Hedgpeth (1953). For more detailed considerations of eastern Gulf of Mexico features see Jones, et al. (1973), particularly figure IIE-28; for the western Gulf see Britton and Morton (1989), figures 1-3. The Minerals Management Service, Gulf of Mexico Regional OCS Office, provided a series of detailed, if somewhat complex, maps (termed "Visuals") to accompany their Environmental Impact Statement of 1982.

[4] Recently acquired evidence suggests that a large asteroid or cometlike object smashed into an area on the north coast of Yucatán near Progreso and formed a huge and now mostly buried crater, termed an "astrobleme." This catastrophic event caused seismic waves or tsunamis inland as far north as Texas and Alabama, and is thought by some scientists to have created atmospheric conditions that resulted in the eventual extinction of the dinosaurs and other fauna and flora around the entire earth.

[5] "Wipe-out" zones are small areas of gas-charged, hydrate-containing, oil-stained sediments often exhibiting large amounts of hydrogen sulfide gas (H_2S) with its characteristic "rotten egg" odor.

Chapter 6

[1] The mid-oceanic ridges, called "the crack around the world," extend around the entire earth, much like the cracks in a broken egg. The zones of subduction are areas of intense volcanic and earthquake activity. In the Pacific Ocean these zones have been called "the ring of fire." The closest ring of fire to the Gulf of Mexico is the volcanic islands of the Antilles on the eastern margin of the Caribbean Plate, and the volcanic mountains of the Central Cordillera running from Mexico southward to Panama on the eastern Margin of the Cocos Plate in the tropical eastern Pacific Ocean. See Decker and Decker (1981).

[2] A complication is that recent evidence from plate tectonics shows that all of the earth's major ocean basins are geologically young, consisting of basaltic lavas erupted less than 200 million years ago.

Chapter 7

[1] Up to 77% of all the earth's fresh waters are held as ice.

[2] The awesome capability of the Mississippi to deposit large sediment loads is matched only by its water capacity. Sediment deposition into the Gulf ranges from 1 to 2 million tons/day, carried by a water discharge estimated to exceed 2 billion cubic yards a day, or about 785 billion cubic yards annually.

[3] Residents of Florida will be familiar with this kind of event. When underground water is removed from the limestone caverns in the central and northern parts of the state, the hydraulic pressure that supported the caverns decreases or is eliminated altogether. The weight of the overlying surface layers causes the caverns to collapse, often extremely rapidly, and a large sinkhole can quickly form, swallowing up houses, cars, and city streets.

[4] See Martinez (1991) for a very readable account.

Chapter 8

[1] It is interesting that sea level in the Gulf of Mexico is about 8 inches higher than along the Atlantic coastline. This is a consequence of prevailing winds from the Caribbean Sea pushing water up into the Gulf. This higher water level produces a hydrostatic head that accounts for the major energy of the Florida Current, which ultimately becomes "the Gulf Stream."

[2] Popular usage notwithstanding, oceanographers restrict the term "Gulf Stream" to the union of the Florida Current with the Antilles Current north of the Bahama Islands and east of Cape Hatteras, North Carolina. The popularized "Gulf Stream" east of Florida is properly called the Florida Current.

[3] Stommel (1965) discusses the alleged effects of the Gulf Stream system on European climate, and points out that the "position and temperature of the large mass of warm water on the [Gulf Stream's] right-hand flank" may be more important. See also MacLeish (*op. cit.*) pp. 10-11, 95-97, 210 ff.

Chapter 9

[1] See Smith and Tirpak (1989) for more data; and Lashof and Tirpak (1990) for an in-depth consideration.

[2] See Hoffmeister (1974), Chapter 10, and particularly Figure 74.

Chapter 10

[1] Laboratory experiments conducted on shore-dwelling fiddler crabs using hyperbaric (high pressure) chambers show that the crabs can survive and adjust in some degree to pressures equivalent to those in the deep sea if applied slowly enough.

[2] Owing to the magnitude and extent of cold deep waters, the average temperature of all the world's oceans is 3.8°C (about 39°F). The average temperature of the oceans at the equator is only 4.9°C (about 41°F). Thus, the oceans of the earth in a general sense form a decidedly cold-water sphere.

[3] For more detailed considerations see chapters in Dietrich (1963), Idyll (1976), Davis (1991), and Thurman (1991).

[4] Oxygen can be dissolved into seawater in a number of other ways, including submarine volcanic gases, chemical breakdown or dissolution of oxygen-containing minerals, the photodissociation of water vapor and its subsequent incorporation in raindrops, and so forth. The problem is that free oxygen is so highly reactive that it almost invariably combines with other elements and is thus removed again from the environment. Those amounts of free oxygen that are produced and survive are negligible when compared to that liberated through photosynthesis. In fact, the presence of free oxygen in the atmosphere (O_2) was a secondary development of life itself on earth. See J. W. Schopf (1983) for a more detailed and technical explanation.

[5] Oceanographers restrict the term "alkalinity" to a rather complex chemical concept. Alkalinity is defined as that amount of hydrochloric acid (HCl) added to 1 liter of seawater at 20°C in order to reduce the pH of the seawater sample to about 4.5. The HCl specifically "unbinds" certain weak acids that are bound to alkaline components in seawater (and are thus neutralized), freeing their H^+ ions and thereby allowing their quantity to be measured.

Chapter 11

[1] Based on the geological record, continental shelves and other shallow water areas may not have emerged from the Archaean seas until about 2.5 billion years ago. See Schopf (*op. cit.*).

[2] Curiously, some chemical states of arsenic are often incorporated by many marine invertebrates and often produce little or no toxic effects.

[3] Diatomaceous oozes are found primarily in cold-water regions south of the Arctic Ocean, and in a circumpolar band around Antarctica. Radiolarian oozes are primarily restricted to deep water areas in the tropical Pacific Ocean. The predominant ooze in the Gulf of Mexico is from calcareous foraminiferans. See Dietrich (*op. cit.*), Chart 2; Thurman (*op. cit.*) Fig. 5-17.

Chapter 12

[1] The pre-Columbian Toltec or Olmec tribes of Guatemala named the god of tempests "Hunrakan" or "Huracan." Interestingly, some Arctic Ocean storms also form in much the same way and exhibit rotational configurations and motions similar to tropical hurricanes. See Businger, S. (1991). Arctic hurricanes. American Scientist, volume 79 (No. 1):18-33.

[2] The lowest barometric readings in the western hemisphere were both recorded in Gulf hurricanes. The infamous "Labor Day Storm" in 1935 measured 26.35 inches (892 millibars). Hurricane Gilbert in 1988 recorded even lower readings at 26.23 inches (888 millibars).

[3] Hurricane Agnes, formed over the Yucatán Peninsula in 1972, was a minimal storm in wind intensity but torrential rains and devastating floods made it one of the costliest natural disasters in U. S. history, with damages exceeding $2 billion.

Chapter 13

[1] In the so-called soft corals the polyps secrete calcareous spicules in a jellylike matrix. The octocorals, the group of soft corals to which the sea whips and sea fans belong, have a central horny skeleton that forms the substructure for the "whip" or "fan," in which the polyps are embedded. The black, flexible "sea twigs" that commonly wash ashore are simply this remnant skeleton denuded of the surrounding polyps and jellylike matrix.

[2] Although the Florida Keys share the waters of both the Atlantic Ocean on their eastern side, and Florida Bay and the Gulf of Mexico on their west, the true Florida Reef Tract is found only along the eastern margin in the Atlantic Ocean.

[3] Alacran Reef is sometimes referred to as an atoll because its somewhat circular outline formed by reef corals resembles that seen in Pacific Ocean atolls. But because it is nonvolcanic in origin and occurs on the continental shelf it is not a true atoll.

[4] See Britton and Morton (1989) for a synopsis of reefs and reeflike areas in the western Gulf of Mexico.

[5] For a summary on oyster bars and how they are formed see Hedgpeth (1953), and L. M. Bahr and W. P. Lanier (1981). The ecology of intertidal oyster reefs of the south Atlantic coast: A community profile. U. S. Fish and Wildlife Service, Office of Biological Services, Washington, DC. FWS/OBS-81/15. 105 pp.

[6] The largest petroleum-exploratory structure in the Gulf was the 62-well slot, 59,000-ton platform of Shell Offshore, Inc., named "Cognac," standing in 1,025 feet of water. In 1988, the "Bullwinkle" platform was erected, which rises 1,615 feet from the seafloor to the top of its derricks, 161 feet taller than the Sears Tower in Chicago. Bullwinkle's huge legs provide a vertical settling and feeding area for benthic and pelagic species from the uppermost levels of the epipelagic zone, just below the sea surface, to the lowermost edges of the photic zone (upper edge of the mesopelagic) where the deep ocean's realm of eternal night begins. Yet even Bullwinkle's glory is transitory. Shell Offshore, Inc. plans to install an auger tension

leg platform (a floating structure moored to the seafloor) in 2,860 feet of water in the Gulf in 1993.

[7] Although the Minerals Management Service requires plugging of all wells and removal of all equipment (including the drilling platform) from the seafloor when a petroleum facility is shut down, provisions in the National Fishing Enhancement Act may allow some abandoned platforms to remain in place or be reset elsewhere under special circumstances. A case in point is a 2,200-ton structure that was disassembled and towed from its position off Louisiana and sunk in 110 feet of water on the continental shelf off Apalachicola, Florida. It is now an actively functioning artificial reef.

Chapter 15

[1] The term "euryhaline" is commonly, but erroneously, used to denote the same concept. The Greek prefix "eurys" means "broad, wide, or far reaching," which is quite a different relationship than that of "polys" which means "many" in the sense of numbers.

[2] The old adage that oysters should not be eaten during the months that have no "r" in their spelling is based partially on the fact that breeding oysters have less desirable culinary characteristics, and breeding usually takes place when the water warms up from May through August.

[3] The term "hermaphrodite" comes from the Grecian fables. Hermaphroditus was the son of the gods Hermes (Mercury) and Aphrodite (Venus), and exhibited both male and female characteristics.

Chapter 16

[1] Some anthropologists have suggested that the Aztecs (and later Mexicans) used large amounts of fiery chili and jalapeno peppers in their foods because the hot, acidic principle helped purge intestinal hookworms that produced a debilitating chronic diarrhea.

[2] Soft-shell crabs are simply blue crabs that have just molted and their chitinous shells have not yet hardened; thus, the entire animal is edible, shell and all.

[3] The lowly shipworm (called teredo) was undoubtedly influential in altering history. Numerous Spanish vessels that ran ashore broke apart as much from worm-weakened timbers as from the effects of sand, reef, and surf. Others simply sank at the docks as worm-riddled hulls gave way. The Caribbean teredos were held by the Spaniards to be more destructive than those of the Mediterranean. Remedies included double-hulling, sandwiching German felt between the planks, and plating the ship-bottoms with copper or brass.

[4] Although most sea cucumbers are toxic, some species serve as human food. In the Pacific Ocean several species are sun-dried and then used in Polynesian and Oriental cookery. These are called "bêche de mer" (that is, "spade of the sea"), or "trepang."

Chapter 17

[1] Some species of frogs in the western Pacific can breed and raise young in salinities approaching 26°/oo.

[2] Blair, et al. (1957), p. 214.

[3] Sea snakes are also open-sea reptiles, occurring both inshore and far out to sea. They presently occur only in the Pacific and Indian Oceans. The Panama Canal could conceivably provide a passageway for one or more eastern Pacific species through the Caribbean and into the Gulf.

[4] See Britton and Morton (1989) pp. 138 ff. for a nice general summary.

[5] All 32 species of marine mammals occurring in the Gulf of Mexico are federally protected under the 1972 Marine Mammal Protection Act.

[6] Manatees are also called "sea cows" for their supposed resemblance to that land mammal, and because they were often observed grazing on underwater vegetation. The scientific family name given to manatees, the Sirenidae, alludes to the fact that early sailors, too long at sea, thought manatees to be mermaids or sirens, particularly when the female manatee was seen cradling her offspring and allowing it to nurse like a human baby. Such romanticisms did not overcome hunger, and manatees were regularly slaughtered and eaten by Indians and Europeans alike, the flesh being said to resemble veal or fine pork.

[7] See Mullin et al. (1991) for a complete summary of these and other cetaceans in the Gulf.

[8] Sir Alistair Hardy points out that benthic species such as crabs, octopus, and skates are also taken by these whales. Additional evidence of benthic feeding proclivities is deduced from numerous sperm whales that became entangled in submarine cables on the seafloor and subsequently drowned. See Hardy (1970), p. 284.

[9] The total number of kills of all species of whales in North America is difficult to estimate because early records simply noted numbers of barrels of whale oil deliverd to dockside, rather than numbers of whales taken. See Reeves, R. R. and E. Mitchell (1988). History of whaling in and near North Carolina. NOAA Technical Report NMFS 65. 28 pp.

[10] The right whale (*Eubalaena glacialis*) was so-named by whalers because it was the "rightest" of the eight species sought, being easily chased, killed, and flensed, as well as providing highly profitable meat and oil. Moreover, the carcass remained afloat after death. Tequesta Indians killed some of these whales by jumping on the whale's back and driving stakes into its blowhole! See Reeves and Mitchelll (*op. cit.*) p. 22.

[11] The Spaniards called the seals "sea wolves" because of their fancied resemblance to that land animal when viewed from a distance. They were first noted by Juan Ponce de León off the Dry Tortugas.

[12] For example, Robins et al. (1966) state that about 1,780 species of birds live and breed on the continent of North America, with 645 species in the United States and northward, and more than 1,100 occurring in Mexico and Central America. A tally of distributional maps in their book shows 404 species occurring somewhere along the Gulf coastal margin from Florida to Yucatán. Data from Kale et al. (1990) show that in Florida alone 179 species of birds breed, and another 300 are winter migrants.

Chapter 18

[1] A category established by the Florida Game and Freshwater Fish Commission, and the Florida Committee on Rare and Endangered Plants and Animals.

[2] Contrarily, although the native orchid flora of Mexico and Central America is well known, and shares many species with Florida, protection in these countries is often judgmental or entirely lacking.

[3] See Austin, D. B. et al. (1990). Endangered plants of the Fakahatchee Strand State Preserve. Rhodora, volume 92 (No. 869):27-35.

[4] In Wilson and Peter (1988).

[5] At the time of this writing, 168 manatees have died in Florida waters in 1991; 66 were killed either directly by humans or through human-related causes. Over 200 were killed in 1990. Human-related causes of death range from boat collisions to being crushed in the doors of a waterway lock leading into Lake Okeechobee.

[6] The potential degradation of the Florida Keys reef system caused by pesticides (Chapter 37) could conceivably result in the loss not only of some 50 species of corals but several hundred species of reef-dwelling fishes and invertebrates as well. The economic loss for the state of Florida would be substantial, affecting fisheries, tourism, and several associated industries.

[7] The red wolf became "officially extinct" in 1975. Recent genetic evidence using DNA analysis suggests that the several putative red wolves presently living in Alligator River National Wildlife Refuge in North Carolina may be hybrids between gray wolves (now extirpated from most of the lower United States) and coyotes (found irregularly distributed throughout the U. S.). Other evidence from the fossil record implies that red wolves may still exist, and if they did crossbreed with other species, it occurred so long ago that their genetic distinctness has been swamped. Some researchers think that red wolves may, in fact, be the progenitors of all other wolf species, thereby becoming a sort of "Adam and Eve Wolf."

Chapter 19

[1] One example of a biotope defined by animals, rather than plants, is a tropical coral reef, where the size, distribution, and areal extent of the sessile coral invertebrates determines much of the structure and composition (species and individuals) of the associated plant and mobile animal communities.

[2] While unequivocal dollar values are difficult to derive owing to the multitude of factors that need to be assessed, the asset value of an acre of wetland has been estimated at $1400-$2800. As one study in Florida showed, the state purchase price of $1200 per acre was a bargain for Florida's taxpayers.

[3] Tabulations by the state's agencies show that in Florida alone at least 32% of the state's upland forests have been converted to agricultural land, and nearly 60% of the wetlands have been destroyed through development. In Louisiana, another water-bound state, the problems are a bit different. There, an estimated 89% of coastal lands lost were a consequence of dredging petroleum navigational canals. See Anonymous (1991). Preliminary assessment of the Louisiana coastal management program. Coastal Management Division, Louisiana Department of Natural Resources, Baton Rouge, LA. 66 pp.

Chapter 20

[1] Seagrasses are not really "grasses" in the sense of land grasses (Family Poaceae) but belong to three spearate water-loving families; the Cymodoceaceae (*Halodule, Syringodium*), Hydrocharitaceae (*Halophila, Thalassia*), and Ruppiaceae (*Ruppia*). Their grasslike look is deceiving.

Chapter 21

[1] For a more complete discussion of Texas and Mexican mangrove systems and their flora and fauna see Britton and Morton (1989), pp. 222-240.

[2] The hypersaline lagoons of the Yucatán peninsula are home to the rare and beautiful pink flamingos that form stately and colorful aggregations as they strut across the shallow mudflats filter-feeding on the many small snails, brine shrimp, and insect larvae.

[3] Britton and Morton (*op. cit.*). For further details on mangroves as functional

ecosystems see Snedaker, S. C. (1989). Overview of ecology of mangroves and information needs for Florida Bay. Bulletin of Marine Science, volume 44 (No. 1):341-347.

Chapter 22

[1] The horseshoe crab is not a true "crab," but rather is more closely related to spiders and their kin, and to extinct giant, scorpionlike arthropods termed *eurypterids* that lived in the Mesozoic era over 400 million years ago. According to Darryl L. Felder of the Center for Crustacean Research at the University of Southwestern Louisiana, Lafayette, genetic evidence suggests that there may be two or possibly three species in the Gulf instead of just one as previously thought.

[2] The commercially valuable "true" blue crab, *Callinectes sapidus*, has an astonishing range, occurring from Nova Scotia southward to Rio de la Plata, Argentina, and throughout the Caribbean Sea. The species has been introduced by man and is apparently flourishing in coastal waters of Denmark, the Netherlands, and France, as well as in the Adriatic, Aegean, western Black Sea, and eastern Mediterranean Sea. There are also records from Lake Hamana-ko in central Japan! Moreover, at least three other species of "blue crabs" occur in the marshes and seagrass beds of the Gulf of Mexico, each more or less blue in color, shaped similarly, often found in the same habitats, and equally tasty. Thus, crab fishermen undoubtedly have sold, albeit inadvertently, other blue-colored swimming crabs in the genus *Callinectes* as "blue crabs." In fact, *Callinectes similis*, called the lesser blue crab, or Gulf crab, occurs around the entire Gulf of Mexico to Yucatán, and is undoubtedly sought and sold under the "blue crab" alias. The author can personally attest to their comestibility, regardless of their correct common name.

Chapter 23

[1] The critical importance of these usually overlooked species is nowhere better emphasized than in the Florida Everglades, where the calcareous blue-green cyanophytes, green algae, and diatoms (called periphyton) that bloom during the rainy season form the driving force, and precipitate the marl substrate in the entire system. See Ferguson-Wood, E. J. and N. G. Maynard (1974). Ecology of the micro-algae of the Florida Everglades; and Gleason, P. J. and W. Spackman, Jr. (1974). Calcareous periphyton and water chemistry in the Everglades; both in: Gleason, P. J. (ed.), (1974); plus the excellent compendium entitled *Cypress Swamps*, edited by K. E. Ewel and H. T. Odum (1984). For another view, see Settles, V. J. (1991). Wetlands mitigation: Changes in the wind? Florida Bar Journal (July/August, 1991):53-55; and Bacchus, S. T. (1992). Looking beyond hydrology. The Palmetto (Winter, 1991):9-12.

Chapter 24

[1] Readers wishing more detailed consideration of these areas, as well as an overview of the entire western coastline of the Gulf of Mexico, are referred to Hedgpeth (1953), Britton and Morton (1989), and Yanez-Arancibia, A. and J. W. Day, Jr. (eds.) (1988). Ecology of coastal ecosystems in the southern Gulf of Mexico: The Terminos Lagoon. Universidad Nacional Autonama de Mexico (in Spanish, with English abstracts).

Chapter 25

[1] The nannoplankton (more correctly "nanoplankton") are rather poorly defined as those nonbacterial, photosynthetic planktonic organisms that range in size from

1 to 50 microns (a micron is a millionth of a meter). Another way to visualize a micron is that 1,000 nanoplankters 1 micron in size would fit on a single serrated tooth on the edge of a postage stamp. The current misspelling was coined by the German planktologist J. Lohmannn in 1911, and has been perpetuated through the literature ever since.

[2] *Trichodesmium*, a blue-green alga which, paradoxically, is red in color, is responsible for blooms that color, and have resulted in the name of, the Red Sea.

[3] Within the Gulf well-known living cyanophyte formations occur at Cape Sable, at the southernmost tip of the Florida peninsula, and in the Laguna de Terminos on the northern Yucatán coastline. Some of the oldest stromatolitic formations are known from Australia, occurring in rocks 3.5 billion years old. Whether cyanophytes were responsible for *all* the ancient formations remains unclear at present. See Walter, M. R., *op. cit.*; and A. H. Knoll (1991). End of the proterozoic eon. Scientific American, volume 265 (No. 4):64-67, 70-73.

[4] The mechanism of calcium carbonate ($CaCO_3$) deposition in cyanophytes is complex and is based on the chemical balances that occur among carbon dioxide (CO_2), carbonic acid (H_2CO_3), and bicarbonates (HCO_3) dissolved in natural waters. Briefly, as algae or other water-dwelling plants use up dissolved CO_2 during photosynthesis, $CaCO_3$ is precipitated. Cyanophytes go the algae one better by extracting CO_2 directly from dissolved HCO_3, which again upsets the balance and causes precipitation of $CaCO_3$, otherwise known as limestone.

[5] The Columbus crab is *Planes minutus*, which in Greek means "small wanderer." The common name alleges that it was the crab seen by Christopher Columbus on Monday, September 17, 1492, while on his way to the New World. From the sighting he concluded that land could not be far off. Had Columbus realized that this small, perpetually pelagic little crab is rarely found anywhere else but on floating seaweed, flotsam, and jetsam far out to sea, the course of world history might have been dramatically altered. The story is probably apocryphal anyway, at least for the species.

Alternatively, there is no valid reason why *Portunus sayi*, the Gulfweed swimming crab, was not the species recorded by Columbus in his logbook. This crab also spends most of its life in the pelagic regions, but does occur inshore on open beaches and lagoons. This, alone, would have made *P. sayi* (in retrospect, at least) a more likely candidate for assuming that land was nearby.

[6] Salps, sea squirts, and other tunicates (subphylum or phylum Urochordata) share chordate features with all vertebrates primarily in their larval stage. The so-called "tadpole larva" of tunicates (vaguely resembling a frog tadpole in shape and movement) possesses a notochord, gill slits, and a hollow, dorsal nerve chord. These are lost or modified in the adult. Similarly, during human development, the fetus changes the notochord to the backbone, dispenses with the gill arches by the end of the first trimester, and incorporates the dorsal nerve chord as the spinal chord. So the next time you see a sea squirt, think: "There, but for the grace of God . . ."

[7] The catchbasket term "radiolaria" is now a term of convenience that has been applied to three groups of planktonic protozoans placed under the scientific name Actinopoda (aktinos = "ray," poda = "feet"). Approximately 7,000 species are known. In addition to silica, some groups have spicules made of strontium sulfate.

[8] Sea birds such as shearwaters, auklets, petrels, and skimmers feed primarily on fish, invertebrates, and their larvae at the sea's surface. These airborne plankton-, pleuston-, and nekton-eaters pointedly emphasize another interaction between the

sea and the sky.

[9] There is often an abrupt change in current velocity along one side of a weedline, that results in the weeds collecting in the "line" along the current gradient. Temperatures inside and outside of the weedline may also be different. See Stommel (*op. cit.*), Frontispiece.

Chapter 26

[1] It is commonly but erroneously believed that the sun is the basis of all life on earth. But without plants sunlight becomes merely unutilized light energy. Many plants (e.g. subterranean fungi, deep sea diatoms, and hydrothermal vent bacteria) have dispensed with sunlight altogether as an energy source.

[2] A simplified food chain might be diatom→krill→blue whale with the arrows indicating direction of energy transfer.

[3] When this blue light is scattered in shallower waters where large amounts of organic material are dissolved, the sea color changes from blue to green.

[4] A prime example of how pollution, productivity, and algal blooms come together in concert was the explosive growth of *Sargassum* weedlines that blew ashore from Texas to Florida in the summer of 1991. The Gulfweed so severely clogged the intake pipes of the cooling system at two electrical power plants north of Tampa that they had to be shut down. At the same time, other large Gulfweed mats washed ashore at St. Petersburg during a red tide episode that killed thousands of fish. Mother Nature may be striking back with a vengeance.

Chapter 27

[1] The United States was one of four nations that voted against the treaty, even though its passage would give the U.S. the greatest benefit owing to its extensive coastlines.

Chapter 28

[1] Minerals Management Service, Outer Continental Shelf Lease Offerings Statistics, September 3, 1991. Prepared by Eileen B. Seiler, Deputy Chief, Office of Program Services, Gulf of Mexico OCS Region; and, MMS: Planning for America's Energy Future & a Quality Environment. Outer Continental Shelf Natural Gas & Oil Resource Management. Brochure.

[2] See Baker (1985) for an excellent introduction to offshore operations and all its attendant complexities.

[3] In 1991 two French petroleum companies, La Total Petroleum and Compagnie Européenne des Pétroles, announced an agreement with President Fidel Castro, and plans to drill for oil off Cuba's northern coast. Successful drilling would gain Cuba some measure of petroleum independence, once predominantly subsidized by the now defunct Soviet Union. However, the potential damage to Florida Keys or peninsular beaches in Florida from oil spills or blow-outs entrained in the Florida Current could be catastrophic.

[4] In world-wide production of crude petroleum, the United States ranks second, behind the ex-Soviet Union, and Mexico ranks fifth. Mexico also ranks fifth in the estimated amount of petroleum reserves, behind Saudi Arabia, Kuwait, the ex-U.S.S.R., and Venezuela.

[5] Petroleum leases are offered at auction in blocks of varying size, with many ranging from approximately 5,000 to 5,700 acres in area. In addition to the "bonus" price paid for the lease by the successful bidder, the federal government imposes a $50,000 performance bond to ensure compliance with operational and environmen-

tal stipulations. Leases are normally for five years, during which time a yearly rental of $3 per acre is charged, and is payable in advance, until the leased tract begins to produce. Then, a yearly charge, called a royalty, is levied against the value of any resources that are produced. The royalty is a percentage determined by the depth of the water over the block; the charge is 16.67% of the product value in water less than 400 meters deep, and 12.5% of the product value in water greater than 400 meters deep. If nothing is produced, the government still assesses a minimum royalty fee of $3 per acre ($15,000 to $17,000 a block). Drilling for oil is therefore expensive even before the first producing well comes in.

[6] In a rather ironic contrast to onshore real estate values, bid prices per acre on the OCS range from a low of $12.92 for a tract off Florida, to a high of $4,967.76 for tracts off Louisiana. As the realtors would say: Location! Location! Location!

[7] The Minerals Management Service recently estimated petroleum reserves in three Gulf of Mexico planning areas being considered for OCS lease sales at 360 million barrels of oil and 3.63 trillion cubic feet of natural gas.

Chapter 29

[1] According to Dr. R. G. Gilmore (*in litt.*) orange roughy is a public relations euphemism for fishes belonging to the deep sea family Trachichthyidae. Trachichthyids, whose common scientific name is "slime heads," occur on rock formations in the Gulf of Mexico at depths below 1,000 feet and are not fished in U. S. waters. As Shakespeare once asked: "What's in a name?"

[2] Dr. R. G. Gilmore also pointed out to the author that the shark fishery bycatch (and all its concomitant wastage of fish) actually surpasses in some cases the commercial shark fishery catch. The latter, in turn, is presently overfishing the western Atlantic stock of several species of sharks.

[3] The notorious "Spiny lobster wars" between Cuban, Bahamian, and American lobstermen off the southeastern coast of Florida in the 1960s provide a good example. Several lobstermen, seeing their livelihood threatened by "foreigners" and "skindivers" actually fired on suspected poachers who approached their offshore traplines—and were eventually sent to prison for their efforts.

Chapter 30

[1] According to the Louisiana State Department of Natural Resources, in the nine immediately coastal parishes of Louisiana more than 30 federal, state, and private parks, refuges, wildlife management areas and commemorative areas exist.

[2] In just the northern Gulf of Mexico alone nearly 1,800 vessels sunk between 1500 and 1945 are recorded.

Chapter 31

[1] A continuing source of contention is that harvesting sugarcane, citrus, and vegetables is extremely labor-intensive. To keep harvesting and processing costs down, some of the larger U.S. growers "import" field labor through labor-pool companies who recruit the workers from Mexico and the Caribbean. The legal or immigrational status of many of these workers is often questionable. More importantly, the legal status is often overshadowed by poor living and working conditions. Many of these migrant workers are considered to be little more than indentured servants. Their word for themselves is "*los esclavos*"—the slaves.

[2] Statistical data from Cuba listed in world compilations is often contradictory and much of it is conditioned as "estimates."

Chapter 32

[1] Salt enriches the U. S. Treasury as well. Salt leases on more than 5,000 acres on the OCS off Louisiana and Texas from 1960 to 1967 brought in $106,000 in revenues. A combined salt-sulfur lease on nearly 143,000 acres off Louisiana in 1988 was worth almost $51 million in bonus revenues. Another $762,000 in rentals accrued from all salt and sulfur offerings. See Minerals Management Service, Outer Continental Shelf Lease Offerings Statistics, September 3, 1991. *ibid.*

[2] Interestingly, much of the salt mined from offshore deposits is used in the extraction process in mining sulfur, rather than being sold on the world food and preservatives market.

[3] Salt has long been a commodity in the Gulf region. The Mayan Indians were collecting thousands of tons of sea salt from salt flats in the estuaries along the northern Yucatán peninsula, and shipping it up and down the coast and into the Mexican interior lowlands for more than a thousand years before the arrival of the conquistadores. The largest salt beds in Central America were located in northern Yucatán, west of Cabo Catoche.

[4] Elemental sulfur results from a complex series of biological and chemical reactions. Put simply, anhydrite caprock over a salt dome is acted on by sulfur-forming bacteria in the presence of methane gas to produce hydrogen sulfide gas and limestone. The limestone traps the gas which is then oxidized to elemental sulfur and water via a series of chemical reactions. Thus, some of Nature's smallest and most primitive life forms (sulfur- and petroleum-producing bacteria) are responsible for much of our lifestyle today.

[5] World leadership in sulfur production changes periodically. The United States, once the largest producer with up to 25% of the world's output, fell behind the ex-Soviet Union. Canada is one of the world's largest exporters at present. See Anonymous (1987). Sulfur & Salt Leasing: Summary of Issues. Gulf of Mexico Outer Continental Shelf. MMS OCS Report MMS 87-0036. 27 pp.

Chapter 33

[1] Britton and Morton (1989), p. 323.

Chapter 34

[1] Sewage is normally treated at three levels: primary, secondary, and tertiary. Primary treatment removes large floating solids and settles other solids out as sludge. Secondary treatment uses aerobic bacteria to digest and thus break down the organic wastes. Tertiary treatment adds chemicals and physical manipulation of the wastewater to reduce pollutants still further or render them harmless.

[2] Coliform bacteria are those microbes normally found as part of the necessary "gut flora" in the digestive tract of humans and other animals. The primary species is *Escherichia coli*, often abbreviated *E. coli*. Presence of inordinately high amounts of this bacteria in a water body, or the human food organisms growing in it (clams, oysters) implies fecal contamination and potential hazards to human health if ingested. However, studies now suggest that this species is an inadequate indicator of poor water quality. Documented outbreaks of serious bacterial pathogens such as *Salmonella* (typhoid fever), *Shigella* (dysentery), and *Klebsiella* (respiratory, intestinal, and genito-urinary infections) have been recorded from waters where coliform bacterial counts met federal levels of acceptance. Instead, *Pseudomonas aeruginosa*, a known coliform pathogen producing eye, ear, and urinary infections in contaminated waters, has been recommended as a replacement indicator for *E. coli*. This

bacterium confirms direct fecal contamination in the water, and has been implicated in more than 50% of all mucosal infections contracted in polluted waters. See Duka, B. J. (1973).

[3] Before ocean dumping of raw sewage was completely regulated in Florida, the area at the offshore end of the Miami Beach outfall was cynically known as "the rose bowl" because of the discoloration of seawater, the effluent and sludge on the seafloor, and the noisome stench in the area.

[4] Although many coliform bacteria, including serious human pathogens that cause cholera, dysentery, and typhoid fever, have a poor survival rate in seawater, a continuing source of inoculation can maintain the number of organisms at a level sufficient to cause disease in susceptible people. The indigenous populace of rural areas, or places where personal hygiene is poor or lacking, may reinfect themselves on a daily basis without exhibiting major symptoms because of an acquired immunity. Not so for visitors. The common gasteroenteritis of tropical regions ("La Turista," "Montezuma's Revenge," "Aztec Two-Step," "The Trots") that produces nausea, vomiting, and diarrhea, may be caused by one or more of these pathogens, plus several others that occur as low-level infections contracted even in seawater.

Chapter 35

[1] The Minerals Management Service classifies an *average large spill* as being 1,000 barrels (42,000 gallons) or greater; an *average medium spill* as 50 to 999 barrels (2,100 to 41,958 gallons); and an *average small spill* as 1 to 49 barrels (42 to 2,058 gallons). Thus, the noted examples are all very large spills. Similarly, the MMS has two categories of accidents. *Minor accidents* are those in which fire or explosion results in equipment or structural damages totaling less than $1 million, and hydrocarbon spillage totals less than 200 barrels (8,400 gallons) during a 30-day period. In *major accidents*, equipment or structural damage exceeds $1 million, hydrocarbon spillage totals 200 barrels or more during a 30-day period, and death or serious personal injuries to humans are involved.

[2] Although the general perception of pollution by petroleum exploration is that of floating patches of oil and tar, other pollutions unavoidably occur. Among these are impacts on ambient water quality produced by drilling muds, drilling fluids, drill cuttings, spills of engine coolants, lubricants, and cleaners, and the effects on existing air quality of the emissions of nitrogen oxides, carbon monoxide, sulfur oxides, volatile organic compounds, and suspended particulate matter from drilling operations.

[3] Final Environmental Impact Statement, Proposed Oil and Gas Lease Sales, 113/115/116 Gulf of Mexico OCS Region. U. S. Department of the Interior, Minerals Management Service Report OCS EIS MMS 87-0077. Chapters and appendices paginated individually.

[4] A study by Professor Fazil Najafi and Murat Baran reads like a doomsday report. A major oil spill in southwestern Florida could prove more catastrophic than the *Exxon Valdez* accident, causing major environmental damages and the loss of billions of dollars in tourism revenues, with the effects lasting for a century or more. See "Oil Spill Impact Assessment and Response Capabilities in South Florida," Report to the Institute of Government, Tallahassee, Florida, June, 1991. Engineering and Industrial Experiment Station, Department of Civil Engineering, University of Florida, Gainesville, FL.

[5] For further details, see the MMS Final Environmental Impact Statement, OCS

EIS 87-0077, *ibid.*; and Managing Oil and Gas Operations on the Outer Continental Shelf, Offshore Minerals Management, MS 646, Washington, DC.

[6] The Congressional bills give ship owners until the year 2015 to make all petroleum-carrying vessels double-hulled. Thus, single-hulled tankers newly built in 1989 could conceivably remain in operation for 25 years before falling under this regulation.

Chapter 36

[1] The EPA Superfund (the Comprehensive Environmental Response, Compensation, and Liability Act, or CERCLA) is a trust fund of $10.1 billion set aside by Congress in 1980 and 1986 to identify and pay for the complete cleanup and restoration of major or long-existing hazardous waste sites, in which the owners are either unlocatable, unable, or unwilling to clean up and restore by themselves. After the site is restored, EPA may then sue for repayment of any costs associated with the cleanup not actually reimbursed by the site owners or agents. The fund is supported from excise taxes on petroleum, chemicals, corporate taxes, general tax revenues, and monies recovered from site owners. The programs are authorized to continue until September 30, 1994. At the beginning of 1990 there were 1,207 currently proposed, or finally accepted, hazardous waste sites in the United States.

[2] The NOAA National Status and Trends Program for Marine Environmental Quality; Technical Memorandum NOS OMA 38, 1987.

[3] Dioxin remains in the news. Recent evidence suggests that the compound may not be as toxic as once thought. The data are based on experimental results in which the male laboratory rats used in the experiment contracted cancer whereas female rats did not, thus introducing a possible experimental bias in the conclusions. The jury is still out in any case.

[4] Smith, G. J. (1987).

[5] See Hall, L. W. and A. E. Pinkney (1985).

[6] *In:* K. Hannum and C. Juniper, 1990. Shades of Green, Buzzworm, The Environmental Journal, pp. 36-41.

Chapter 37

[1] Meristics for pesticide applications are often confusing. For example, 1,000 acres may be treated once per year, or 1 acre may be treated 1,000 times each year. Both treatments constitute a 1,000 acre treatment. But of greater importance are the relative amounts of pesticide applied. If one ounce of pesticide is spread during each treatment, then in the first example 1,000 acres would receive a total of one ounce in a year, whereas the second example would receive nearly 63 pounds in the same period.

[2] See Smith, G. J (*op. cit.*).

[3] *ibid.*

[4] Odenkirchen, E. W. and R. Eisler (1988). Chlorpyrifos hazards to fish, wildlife, and invertebrates: A synoptic review. U. S. Fish and Wildlife Service, Contaminant Hazard Reviews, Biological Report 85 (1.13).

[5] See Eisler, R. (1985). Mirex hazards to fish, wildlife, and invertebrates: A synoptic review. *Op. cit.*, Report 85 (1.1).

[6] TCDD (dioxin), like many poisons, has different toxicities to different species of animals. The degree of toxicity may depend on presence or absence of certain hormones, genetic make-up of the target organism, or prevailing environmental factors. Indeed, dioxin itself acts like a hormone, and some researchers consider it

more of a cancer promoter than a cancer inducer.

[7] Eisler, R. (1986). Dioxin hazards to fish, wildlife and invertebrates: A synoptic review. *Op. cit.*, Report 85 (1.8).

[8] Agent Orange, the infamous defoliant used in Vietnam, was a mixture of two prominent herbicides, 2, 4, 5-T and 2, 4-D. The former was banned by the EPA in 1985. But 2, 4-D has become the third most widely used pesticide in the United States, with over 50 million pounds spread about in 1987.

[9] Not all contamination is deliberate. In early May, 1991, the privately owned Agricultura Nacional de Vera Cruz factory in Cordoba, Mexico, suffered a series of massive explosions that sent clouds of the highly toxic pesticide Parathion into the air. This caused varying degrees of illness in 500 people, required evacuation of another 1,600, and contaminated the local water supply via runoff from fire-fighting equipment. The plant is located 60 miles from the Gulf port city of Vera Cruz.

[10] See Glynn, P., et al. (1989). Condition of coral reef cnidarians from the northern Florida reef tract: Pesticides, heavy metals, and histopathological examination. Marine Pollution Bulletin, volume 20 (No. 11):568-576.

Chapter 38

[1] Some conifers apparently can produce minute amounts of sytrene, a form of "plastic," in their sap.

[2] The Marine Plastic Pollution Research and Control Act of 1987 (P. L. 100-220) makes ocean dumping of plastics illegal. Enforcement and prosecution, however, remain another matter, as our beaches continually illustrate.

[3] Many abandoned or derelict plastic nets, fish traps, and crab and lobster pots continue to capture marine organisms, which then remain trapped but unharvested. This activity is called "ghost fishing." Most of the ghost-fished prey die from starvation. Marine mammals, such as air-breathing bottle-nosed dolphins and sea turtles, drown.

[4] Portions of the Gulf coast barrier islands are natural traps for collecting floating debris owing to the confluence of longshore currents that concentrate the items along certain beaches. Padre Island, Texas, receives debris from much of the western Gulf. Sanibel Island, Florida, a world-renowned shelling beach because of similar current situations, also collects large amounts of debris from the eastern Gulf.

[5] The adaptability of marine organisms toward pollution and debris is amazing. Flotsam, jetsam, and purgamentsam all act as places of attachment for barnacles, bryozoans, sponges, sea squirts, and other members of the fouling community. A favorite hiding place for shallow water octopus and some gobies and blennies is inside discarded glass jars, jugs, and aluminum cans. The author has personally collected hermit crabs living in soda and beer bottles, counted over a hundred spiny lobsters living in an abandoned oil drum, and has seen plastic, metal, and glass articles brought up from over three miles deep that are heavily overgrown with encrusting organisms. Some marine bacteria can actually utilize floating tarballs as an energy source. Others are now being used to digest spilled oil.

[6] At the time of this writing, Florida congressman Andy Ireland (R-Lakeland) introduced a bill (H.R. 3777) specifically directed toward creating a $30 million plan to be implemented by EPA that would direct and coordinate pollution control efforts, oil exploration activities, commercial fishing, recreational usage, and ecological monitoring and research in the Gulf of Mexico. A similar bill (S.R. 1715) had been previously introduced in the Senate by Senator Phil Gramm (R-Texas).

Chapter 39

[1] The speed of radioactive transformation in any element (its rate of decay) cannot be altered. The process is both spontaneous and immutable. The calculated half-life of 4.5 billion years for uranium, for example, means that only about half of the uranium that existed when the earth was first formed (approximately 4.5 billion years ago) still remains. Thus, to paraphrase Will Rogers: "Buy uranium—they ain't making it anymore!"

[2] It is not the dosage rate nor its duration that causes mutations, but rather the total accumulated dosage of radiation that occurred from the time of conception of one or both parents until the time of conception of any offspring. Scientists now believe that every dose of radiation, regardless of how small it might be, can cause some increase in the frequency of mutations. Whether the result affects the biological entity positively, negatively, or appears to be neutral, depends on a multiplicity of factors, including the accumulated dosage and the number of chromosomes that were affected.

Epilogue

[1] Good is that which passeth,
   better is that which cometh;
   seven is past and eight now floweth,
   more shall flow if God desireth.

Sung at the turning over of the final hour glass at the beginning of the daybreak watch. Retranslated from Morison (1974), p. 166.

[2] Leon-Portilla (*op. cit.*) p. 5.

Glossary

Abyssal: That zone of the sea deeper than 3000 meters or about 9900 feet; some authors place its beginning at 2000 fathoms, or 12,000 feet.

Abyssal plain: An expansive area of low relief 2000 meters and deeper extending from the bases of the continental slopes.

Acid: Any chemical compound that reacts with a base to form a salt. See base.

Acid rain: Rainfall containing sulfuric and other acids owing to dissolution therein of gases (primarily sulfur dioxide, SO_2) as it passes through the atmosphere.

Ahermatypic Coral: Coral species not growing sufficiently large or robust enough to form massive reef-like structures.

Alga (pl. algae): A broadly categorical grouping of lower, usually water-dwelling, plants containing chlorophyll but lacking specialized water-conducting tissues, leaves, flowers and seeds.

Alluvial deposit: Sediments eroded, transported and deposited by streams or rivers, forming an important component of the continental shelf.

Alpheids: Any of a group of small shrimplike decapod crustaceans (family Alpheidae) having one much-enlarged claw the finger of which is held "cocked" and then allowed to snap forward producing an audible popping sound. Hence their common name "pistol shrimp" or "snapping shrimp."

American Mediterranean Sea: Oceanographer's term for the bodies of water composing the Gulf of Mexico and the Caribbean Sea.

Amino Acids: An organic acid found in proteins and essential for metabolism. An amine group (NH_2-) is substituted for a hydrogen atom.

Ammonia: A sharp-smelling, colorless, toxic gas (NH_3) often produced as a consequence of putrefaction or decay.

Amphipod: A small, laterally-compressed crustacean of shore to open sea having fixed eyes and one or more claws. Beach-fleas and sand-hoppers are two common examples.

Anadromous: Any of a group of animals (primarily fish) in which the adults ascend freshwater streams and rivers to spawn.

Anaerobic: An environmental condition where oxygen is lacking.

Anglerfish: General term for any fish in which the first two dorsal spines are modified into a movable appendage used as a "lure" to attract their prey.

Anoxia: The total lack of oxygen in a system; hypoxia refers to a reduced amount of oxygen compared to "normal" values.

Antipatharia: Black corals. A group of deeper-living reef-dwelling organisms often whip-like in shape, related to soft corals (Octocorallia).

Aphotic Zone: That depth of the sea offshore beyond which no light penetrates and where photosynthetic activity cannot take place. It occurs at about 100 fathoms or 200 meters of depth.

Aquaculture: The commercial culturing of aquatic organisms in ponds, tanks or other water bodies; sometimes erroneously called "sea farming" (mariculture).

Archipelago: A portion of sea containing numerous geologically related islands, or the island groupings themselves.

Arrow worm: A phylum (Chaetognatha) of small, predatory organisms, having an elongate, transparent, worm-like body with paired lateral fins and a head bearing numerous curved grasping spines. Nearly all species are totally planktonic.

Arroyo: Spanish term for a periodically dry stream or brook.

Atlantic Surface Water: A cold surface water mass originating at the Artic Circle and having a specific salinity and temperature.

Atoll: A circular, platform reef surrounding an interior lagoon and formed when an oceanic volcanic island subsides slowly enough to allow coral reef growth to occur.

Autotrophy: Self-feeding. The mechanism whereby an organism (particularly plants) manufactures nutrients via photosynthesis or chemical synthesis. (See also Heterotrophy.)

Back barrier flats: The sloping landward side of a barrier island usually supporting some form of wetland vegetation.

Backshore: That portion of a seaward beach beyond the landward berm, above all but the highest tides, and therefore usually dry.

Baleen: The finely-divided, horny material forming numerous fringed plates in the upper jaw of plankton-feeding whales. "Whalebone."

Barnacle: A small, marine, filter-feeding crustacean of the fouling community, usually possessing some form of a calcium carbonate shell, and often occurring in large numbers permanently attached to a hard substrate.

Barrier island: A dynamic land form essentially parallel and close to the shore, created by sediment deposition through the action of waves, sea floor relief and long-shore currents, and then maintained by wind or current processes.

Barrier reef: A large, long, complex coral reef built on a seaward platform that usually parallels a shore, and which has a wide and relatively deep lagoon between it and the coastline behind.

Base: Any (often caustic) chemical compounds usually containing a hydroxy radical (-OH) formed of oxygen and hydrogen atoms that form a salt upon reaction with an acid.

Basin: A large depression in the earth's surface of variable depth and form.

Bathyal: The zone of the sea from about 200-3,700 meters (100-2000 fathoms), commonly associated with the continental slopes.

Bayhead: A clearly delimited subtropical wetland vegetational assemblage characterized by the presence of bay trees (genus *Persea*).

Bayou: A small, slow-flowing fresh water or estuarine tributary draining an upland area through coastal swamps or river deltas in eastern Texas, Louisiana, Mississippi and western Florida.

Bay scallop: A commercially exploited estuarine or nearshore marine bivalve of the genus *Argopecten*.

Beaked whale: Any member of the rare group of true whales (family Ziphiidae) whose jaws are formed into a beak containing one or two teeth.

Benzene ring: A chemical symbol consisting of a hexagon which represents the distribution of carbon atoms in the benzene molecule.

Berm: The longitudinal clifflike formation of sand or other beach material produced by wave action, and usually marking the landward limit of high tide, or highest wave reach in a storm.

Bio-accumulation: The acquisition and storage by an organism, via ingestion, respiration or assimilation, of large amounts of (usually toxic) substances from the environment. See Biological concentration.

Bioclastics: The broken sherds of the hard parts of marine organisms.

Bioherm: Any reef or reeflike construction formed by living organisms; e.g. coral reefs, sabellariid worm reefs, oyster bars.

Biological concentration: The ability of an organism to concentrate and store large amounts of potentially hazardous compounds in specific organs in its system.

Biological magnification: The increase in the concentration and storage of potentially hazardous compounds in one organism as a result of its feeding on another having such compounds.

Biological oxygen demand: Oxygen used by bacteria in decomposing organic wastes in a body of water; abbreviated BOD.

Bioluminescence: Light produced through a chemical reaction and physiological mechanism in some organisms, sometimes called living light, cold light, or (erroneously) phosphorescence.

Biomass: The metric dried weight of living tissue of a given organism or group of organisms, usually expressed as milligrams (mg) or grams (g) per volume or unit area.

Biota: All the species of organisms living in a specified area.

Biotope: A geographically delimited assemblage of recurring species of plants and animals in which one or several of the contained species dominates numerically, by size, or distribution, and thus characterizes the assemblage as a whole. For example, a coral reef, a cypress swamp.

Bivalve: Clams, oysters, mussels and their two-shelled relatives.

Blowout: A wide opening in a dune line on a beach begun by some physical alteration (paths, roadways, excavations, construction) and then further enlarged by the wind until the dune is destroyed; also, the runaway flow or eruption of an oil well, usually accompanied by catastrophic fire and massive oil spillage; also, the conical chimneylike cavity produced in a wall or ceiling of a salt mine that results from the fracture or collapse of salt layers, or from the explosion of associated pockets of methane gas during blasting operations.

Blue-green algae: Obsolete name for cyanophytes, a primitive group of simple plantlike organisms appearing dark green or bluish-green owing to their contained pigments.

Bony fish: Any of the order Osteichthyes, fishes having a bony rather than a cartilaginous skeleton, one gill slit, and usually a skin covering of scales or horny plates.

Brackish: Water ranging from 0.5 to 17 parts per thousand salinity.

Brittle star: Five or six-armed starfish (phylum Echinodermata), in which the arms are sharply demarcated from the central disc, are greatly elongated, move laterally in a snakelike motion, and can be cast off as an escape mechanism.

Brotulid: A primarily deep sea heavy-bodied, bottom-dwelling fish with elongate tails (family Brotulidae). Some ichthyologists place brotulids with cusk eels, family Ophidiidae.

Bryozoa: A phylum of microscopic, sessile, colonial invertebrates usually forming encrusting mats or moss-like colonies. Also called moss-animals and Ectoprocta.

Buffer: Any compound which tends to prevent a change in pH in a solution.

Bulkhead: In construction, a concrete or steel sea wall built as a bulwark against waves, currents, or tidal incursions.

Calcareous: Composed of calcium carbonate ($CaCO_3$) or limestone.

Calcareous algae: Red or green algae that deposit calcium carbonate on their stems and fronds.

Caprock: The rocky layer that overlies another substrate and is often exposed at the earth's surface owing to erosion, fire, or weathering processes; also, the calcite-gypsum-anhydrite limestone that caps a rising pillar of salt under a salt dome.

Carapace: The horny outer covering of crustaceans.

Caravels: A type of 15th and 16th century Spanish cargo ship in which the mizzen or other masts were lateen-rigged rather than square-rigged.

Carbamate pesticides: Pesticides of neurotoxic action originally developed from chemicals found in the African calabar bean.

Carbonate sediment: Sediments containing high amounts of calcium or magnesium carbonate; limestone sediments.

Caridean shrimp: A widespread group of marine and freshwater crustaceans having claws on the first *two* pairs of legs (see Penaeidean shrimp).

Celsius: The correct term for the centigrade temperature scale (q.v.).

Cenote: Spanish term for a large, circular well-like depression in karst limestone that was often used by early Indians for religious purposes.

Cenozoic: The present geological era, beginning about 65 million years ago, following the Mesozoic (q.v.).

Centigrade: Commonly used term for the Celsius scale of a thermometer, in which $0°$ and $100°$ indicate the respective freezing and boiling points of water.

Cerith: A small, knobby, conical herbivorous snail common in seagrass beds or mangrove forests.

Chemical degradation: The breakdown of a substance via chemical action.

Chemoautotrophy: The ability of some bacteria to utilize chemical compounds (H_2S) in the absence of light to produce carbon from carbon dioxide.

Chitin: The horny substance that composes the carapace (q.v.) of crustaceans and the integument of insects and some other invertebrates.

Chlorine: A greenish, toxic elemental gas. Chemical symbol: Cl.

Cichlids: A primarily freshwater family (Cichlidae) of fishes found in Africa and South America, and noted for their sport and food value. Some species have been introduced into U.S. waters.

Ciguatera: Poisoning in humans caused by eating certain reef fishes, snails and sea urchins that have ingested a blue-green alga. The name is derived from Cuban fishermen's term for the Caribbean Top Shell, "La Cigua" (*Cittarium (Livona) pica*) which was often implicated in producing the intoxication.

Clam shrimp: Small to microscopic, freshwater crustaceans of the class Ostracoda, having a bivalved shell superficially resembling clams.

Clastics: Rock or shell sherds broken into variably-sized pieces via abrasion and grinding through hydrological activity.

Cloudburst: Local name for sudden, large, rainstorm caused when the supporting air column suddenly gives way releasing the rain.

Cloud forest: The lush, hydric (wet) forests found on mountain sides and higher valleys in the tropics, so-called because clouds form or gather at their level.

Cloudwall: The innermost wall of rain clouds surrounding and defining the eye of a hurricane. Also called wall clouds.

Coastal embayment: Any cusplike physiographic feature found on a mainland coast and forming an enclosed or open bay.

Coastal zone ecological interlock: The ecological and hydrological connection between upland ecosystems and the receiving estuaries.

Coelenterate: Obsolete name for invertebrate organisms carrying stinging cells and belonging to the phylum Cnidaria (once called Coelenterata), including the jellyfish, corals, sea whips, hydroids and their relatives.

Cold saline seeps: Emissions of highly saline waters that seep through fissures and crevices along the Florida Escarpment. (See also Escarpment.)

Coliform bacteria: Bacteria that commonly (but not exclusively) inhabit the intestine of animals, usually belonging to the species *Escherichia coli.* Their presence in a body of water is often used as an indicator of fecal contamination.

Colloidal suspension: Extremely fine particles of a substance (smaller than clay) held in a solvent, not settling out, but not actually dissolved in it either.

Colonial tunicate: A shallow-water encrusting invertebrate organism (phylum Urochordata) composed of numerous individuals united into a gelatinous or leather-like, often brightly colored colony.

Community: The species and individuals of organisms composing clearly defined populations, existing and interacting in specific habitats within a shared environment.

Competition: An ecological concept in which one species attempts to utilize all aspects of its environment more completely than its competitors by sequestering food, living space, or mates.

Conshelf: Jargon for continental shelf.

Continental drift: Popular name for the theory of plate tectonics originally proposed by Dr. Alfred Weggener, which holds that the earth's continents have undergone (and are undergoing) latitudinal and longitudinal movement, coalescence, and separation over geological time.

Continental shelf: The area of the sea floor from the subtidal zone to about 200 meters depth, or where the sea floor begins to slope more decidedly downward.

Continental slope: The area of the sea floor which extends from about the 200 meter line downward to the continental rise just above the beginning of the abyssal plain, at about 1000 meters.

Convective circulation cell: An atmospheric phenomenon in which air is heated through contact with a warm surface (e.g. the sea), becomes lighter and subsequently rises, conveying its contained heat to higher levels.

Coquinoid limestone: A geological formation of permeable fossil sands and shells of the coquina clam (*Donax*) forming a coastal limestone along the eastern and southwestern coast of Florida.

Coral: In general any of a group of colonial or solitary invertebrates possessing stinging cells (phylum Cnidaria), and which secrete a cup of calcium carbonate around the central animal (polyp).

Coriolis force: A force, described in 1835 by the French mathematician G. G. Coriolis, produced by the earth's rotation that causes water and air currents to turn continually toward the right in the Northern Hemisphere.

Cretaceous: A geological period in the Mesozoic era beginning about 135 million years ago and ending about 65 million years ago.

Crustacea: A large polymorphic phylum of marine, freshwater and terrestrial arthropodous invertebrates having a chitinous exoskeleton, jointed legs, two pairs of antennae or "feelers," and gills or gill-like respiratory organs.

Cyanophyta: Primitive plantlike organisms, having attributes of bacteria and algae, and among the oldest living things on earth. Previously called blue-green algae (q.v.).

Cyclone: Any system of winds revolving counterclockwise (in the Northern Hemisphere) around a center of low atmospheric pressure.

Damselfish: Any of several small, brightly colored, pugnacious, rock or reef-dwelling marine fishes of the family Pomacentridae.

Decapoda: As used herein, the order of crustaceans to which crabs, shrimps and lobsters belong, characterized by having ten (deca-) walking legs (-poda) among other attributes.

Deep: Obsolete oceanographic term for any large depression of exceptional depth in the seafloor that occurs below 3000 fathoms.

Delta (delta fan): A fan- or finger-shaped physiographic feature protruding from the general outline of a coast caused by deposits of river-borne sediments.

Depositional fan: A fan-shaped alluvial deposit caused by current or wave activity; also a delta.

Detrital feeder: Any organism that feeds on detritus (q.v.); a detritovore.

Detritus: The finely divided particulate matter left after organic breakdown and decay of vegetation.

Diapirism: The vertical rising and intrusion through overlying geological sediments of columns of salt liquefied as a consequence of long-term downward pressure by surrounding, heavy sedimentary loads.

Diatom: Common name for single-celled, mostly planktonic, algal organisms (family Bacillariophyceae) that construct frustules of nearly pure silica.

Dinoflagellate: Microscopic single-celled, flagella-bearing, often highly ornamented, planktonic algae. Many are capable of bioluminescence; some are a causative agent of red tides.

Dioxin: General name for a class of virulently toxic chemical by-products produced during manufacture of pentachlorophenols (PCP).

Diurnal: In reference to tidal cycles, when a high or low tide occurs only once every 24 hours and 50 minutes, i.e. once each day; also, behaviorally when an organism is active during daylight hours. See semi-diurnal.

DNA: Deoxyribonucleic acid, the major component of genetic material in nearly all organisms on earth.

Down-faulting: The creation of a geological feature through surface rupture and subsequent lowering of the land.

Drift algae: Any large clumps of ex-benthic or floating algae that drift with tides or currents; some form weedlines at sea.

Dune: A hillock or ridge of sand formed primarily by the action of wind on a beach.

Ebb tide: Commonly (but incorrectly) the receding tide; correctly called ebb current, i.e. the tidal current that generally sets to seaward, or in a direction opposite to that of the incoming tide.

Echinoderm: Any member of the phylum Echinodermata; sea urchins, sea cucumbers, sea stars, brittle stars and sea lilies (q.v.).

Ecology: The science that deals with the relationships of living organisms to each other and to their surrounding environment.

Ecosystem: The mutually interacting species of animals and plants existing in a specific environmental situation in a delimited geographical area.

Ecotone: A transitional vegetational assemblage between one biotope and another, and often containing species of both, plus others not found in either.

EIS: Acronym for Environmental Impact Statement; a document supposed to consider or investigate the potential impacts, adverse, benign or favorable, that development or alteration may cause in a specified area.

Emergent plant: A plant species rooted under water but with stalks and leaves growing above the water's surface.

Endemic: A species found only in a given area and nowhere else.

Endosymbiont: Any organism that lives symbiotically within the body or the construction (e.g. tubes, burrows) of another organism.

Enzymes: A proteinlike substance in plant or animal cells that acts as an organic catalyst in chemical reactions, speeding them along but not actually becoming part of the final products.

Eocene: The second earliest epoch in the Cenozoic era, from 54-35 million years ago.

Epibenthic: Living above the sea floor.

Epifauna: The animal species existing on or above a substratum.

Epiphyte: Any organism growing on a plant.

Epizoa: Any organism growing on an animal.

Equatorial current: A major open sea current that normally runs on the surface from east to west across an ocean. Equatorial countercurrents are subsurface currents that flow in the opposite direction beneath them.

Errant: Able to move about; opposite of sedentary.

Escarpment: A geological formation consisting of an elongated, cliff or slope area raised above an adjacent plain.

Estivate: The process similar to hibernation in which some animals reduce their physiological activities, seek a den or excavate a burrow, and enter a kind of torpor during the summer or in long periods of dryness.

Estuary: A semi-enclosed coastal body of water, open to the sea in one or more places, in which sea water is measurably diluted by fresh water entering from the land.

Euryhaline: Said of a water body capable of exhibiting variations in salinity over wide areas. Erroneously equated to polysalinity (q.v.), particularly in regard to marine organisms.

Eutrophication: The over-enrichment of nutrients in a body of water causing unbridled growth of certain organisms.

Exoskeleton: The outer calcareous or chitinous body covering in some invertebrates (for example, insects, crustaceans, echinoderms, corals) to which the interior musculature or other tissue is attached.

Extinction: In biology, the dying out of all populations of a species everywhere in the world, through natural or anthropogenic causes. See extirpation.

Extirpation: The localized extinction of a population of a species through natural or anthropogenic causes. The species may continue to exist elsewhere. See extinction.

Extra tropical cyclone: A low pressure area formed along a primary front outside of the tropics, in which the winds blow counterclockwise in the Northern Hemisphere.

Facies: A geological term for the types of related rock layers that occur in a particular stratigraphic (i.e. layered) sequence.

Fahrenheit: A measure of temperature developed by the German physicist G. D.

Fahrenheit in which the freezing and boiling points of water are 32° and 212°, respectively. (See also Centigrade, Celsius.)

Fathom: A measure of the depth of the sea equivalent to 6 feet or 1.83 meters.

Fauna: All of the animal species occurring in an area.

Fiddler crab: Intertidal and supralittoral crabs (genus *Uca*), the males of which possess a greatly enlarged claw that they wave (like a person playing a fiddle) for signaling purposes.

Filter feeder: Any animal that obtains its food by filtering the flow of water containing such food by passing it through a special anatomical mechanism; examples range from sponges, to clams to baleen whales.

Finback whale: Any large baleen whale of the genus *Balaenoptera,* so called because they possess a small dorsal fin approximately 2/3 the way down their backs (e.g. Sei whale, Blue whale).

Fire ant: A large, reddish brown, mound-building, agressive tropical ant having a toxic bite, introduced into the United States from tropical America.

Flagellum: The whiplike thread of some protozoans used to propel them through the water.

Flatfish: Any benthic marine fish with both eyes on one side of its head. Commercially exploited species include sole, flounder, dab, turbot and their relatives.

Flora: All of the plant species that *may* occur in an area; as opposed to "vegetation" which is all of the plant species that *do* occur in an area.

Florida current: Correct oceanographic name for the rapidly flowing current that passes through the Straits of Florida and along the Florida east coast toward Cape Hatteras. (See also Gulf Stream.)

Florida escarpment: The large, submarine, clifflike formation found at the edge of the Floridan continental shelf from the DeSoto Canyon southward to the Tortugas Terrace.

Flying fish: Small, primarily offshore fishes (families Exocoetidae and Cypseluridae) in which the pectoral fins are greatly elongated and used to allow the fish to glide for considerable distances over the water's surface.

Food chain: Any ecological linkage of different species from micro-organisms to herbivores to top-level carnivores that are connected one to another by their nutritional needs or activities.

Food web: The total number of food chains in an ecosystem.

Foraminifera: Single-celled, amoebalike, planktonic or benthic protozoans often possessing a minute, distinctively coiled or scuptured calcium carbonate shell. Also called **Foraminiferida**.

Foreshore: The beach from the low water mark to high tide level that is inundated more or less daily by the tide (see littoral zone).

Fouling community: The assemblage of sessile marine plants and invertebrates (particularly barnacles, sea squirts, hydroids, algae and clams) that normally forms extensive colonies on hard substrates such as ship hulls, pilings, wharfs and jetties, thereby "fouling" them.

Freshwater: Water containing less than 1 °/oo salts, such as that found in lakes, ponds, and some rivers and springs.

Freshwater marsh: A wetland consisting primarily of reeds, grasses, rushes and their relatives, continually or periodically inundated by fresh water and supporting typical communities of freshwater animals.

Frustule: The upper or lower nested siliceous shell of a diatom.

Fungus: A general term for plant-like organisms that lack chlorophyll, usually reproduce by spores, and obtain nutrients from other living or dead organisms. The mushrooms, molds, smuts, yeasts, mildews and their relatives.

Gale: A wind storm in which continuous winds have attained speeds at least 39 mph but less than 72 mph.

Galleons: Large, three-masted, square-rigged, barrel-hulled 15th-17th century Spanish wooden cargo vessels with raised rear (poop) decks, called stern castles (see caravel).

Geomorphological: Pertaining to the form of parts of the earth.

Geosyncline: A depression or trough formed through geological processes such as sediment loading or down-faulting (q.v.).

Ghost crab: A small, rapidly moving, light colored crab (family Ocypodidae) with long eyestalks commonly seen after dusk on sandy beaches from the Carolinas around the Gulf into the Caribbean.

Glass shrimp: Small, transparent caridean shrimp (families Palaemonidae and Hippolytidae) commonly found in seagrass beds and drift algae. Also called grass shrimp.

Globigerina ooze: A deep sea sediment consisting of the dead shells of amoeboid foraminiferans, usually belonging to the genus *Globigerina*.

Grazer: Ecological term for any (usually planktonic) herbivorous species that subsists primarily on certain plant materials; contrasted with browsers that are non-selective herbivores; the analogy is made with ungulate mammals. Cattle graze, deer browse.

Green turtle: A sea turtle (family Cheloniidae) once hunted extensively for food, particularly to be made into soup.

Groin: An elongate, low, wall-like structure or series of posts extending perpendicularly from shore for the purpose of trapping or slowing sediments eroding from beaches.

Gross primary production: The total amount of carbon produced by plantlike organisms in the plankton.

Ground water: Geological and hydrological term referring to subsurficial water, particularly that contained in aquifers.

Guiana current: A large, fast-moving current derived from the westward-flowing South Equatorial current, that runs north along the Guyana-Venezuela coast of South America and eventually becomes the Caribbean Current.

Gulf Stream: A swift, warm, well-defined current forming at the confluence of the northward flowing Florida Current and Antilles Current off Cape Hatteras and extending to the Grand Banks area. Also, the name popularly but erroneously given to the Florida Current along the east coast of Florida.

Guyot: A flat-topped sea mount ("tablemount") commonly found in deeper waters. All guyots are seamounts; not all seamounts are guyots.

Gyre: A circulating mass of water spun laterally off from a large current system.

Habitat: The sum of environmental, topographical, geological and biological features that form the specific living conditions and area for one or more given species in a biotope. The total number of habitats comprise a biotope. For example, the algae-covered, or sponge-encrusted undersides of a rock ledge may form one or more habitats in a coral reef biotope. See also Niche.

Halides: Chemical compounds containing chlorine, fluorine, bromine or iodine.

Halite: Geological term for salt.

Halophyte: A salt-tolerating plant; any plant capable of living in salty or brackish water conditions.

Hammock: A relatively higher piece of ground in a subtropical swamp that supports less water-tolerant hardwood trees and shrubs.

Hawksbill turtle: A large marine turtle (family Cheloniidae) so named because of its mouthparts which fancifully resemble a hawk's bill, and hunted for its meat and shell products.

Hermatypic coral: Coral species capable of forming reefs, so named after Hermes, the Greek god of reefs.

Heterotrophy: The ability to feed on or gain nutrients from other organisms, and usually, by definition, the inability to manufacture food via photosynthesis.

Hibernation: The physiological process by which some mammals overwinter by reducing their body temperature and slowing their internal activities, thereby inducing torpor. See estivate.

High energy beach: A shoreline subject to considerable wave and current action, thereby preventing accumulation and settlement of sediments smaller than sand size.

Hillocks: Small hill-like mounds on the sea floor.

Humpbacked whale: A large, pelagic, plankton-feeding baleen whale (genus *Megaptera*) with a reduced, humplike dorsal fin.

Hydrocarbons: Generic term for compounds containing carbon (C) and hydrogen (H) in specific chemical configurations, particularly in chains or rings; also that part of an organic molecule containing H and C. Gasoline, benzene (q.v.), fatty acids, wax, and sugar are all hydrocarbons.

Hydrogen: A colorless, odorless gas, highly explosive in the presence of oxygen, and the first and most abundant element in the universe. Chemical symbol: H.

Hydrogen ion concentration: The amount of hydrogen ions released or interacting chemically in a particular solution (measured as pH).

Hydrogen sulfide: A toxic, foul-smelling gas (H_2S), having the odor of rotten eggs, and often liberated as a consequence of decay processes under conditions of low or no oxygen.

Hydrography: The science that deals with the measurement and description of physical features of bodies of marine and fresh water (oceans, seas, lakes, rivers and adjacent coastal areas).

Hydroids: Small, often microscopic, usually stalked, sessile, colonial invertebrate animals (phylum Cnidaria) related to jellyfish, the attached polyps of which often form a major component of a fouling community (q.v.).

Hydrology: The science that deals with the processes of evaporation, precipitation, and movements of the surface and subterranean waters of the earth.

Hydroponic: Using a liquid medium to grow normally terrestrial plants, particularly agricultural crops.

Hydrostatic head: The difference in height of one water mass relative to another, caused by water, current or atmospheric pressures, and which induces current flows via gravity.

Hydrothermal vent: Fissure in the deep sea floor associated with volcanic magmas (molten rock) through which superheated water and steam escapes under great pressure.

Hydrothermal vent communities: A complex assemblage of chemoautotrophic bacteria (q.v.) and deep sea invertebrates (polychaete and pogonophoran worms, clams, crabs) apparently evolutionarily, ecologically, and uniquely associated with hydrothermal vents.

Hydrozoan: The polyps and medusae ("jellyfish") stages of the class Hydrozoa, phylum Cnidaria. (see Hydroids).

Hypersaline: Referring to water bodies having salinities exceeding $40^0/oo$ (ppm), for example, the Laguna Madre or the Great Salt Lake.

Hypoxia: See anoxia.

Ichthyofauna: The total number of fish species in a given area.

Inlet: A more or less permanent opening between two land masses, usually barrier islands, through which seawater can pass into a lagoon or basin behind.

Inorganic: Refers to chemical compounds formed through physical or climatic processes (erosion, dissolution, runoff, etc.) rather than biological events.

Insolation: The effect of the sun's light and heat on an organism.

Intertidal: The zone on a shore between the highest and lowest tides and exposed at least once on each tidal cycle; the littoral zone (q.v.).

Isobath: Contoured lines of equal (iso-) or similar increments of depth (-bath) on an oceanographic chart.

Isomer: Any of several similar and related chemical compounds containing essentially the same number of atoms but held in a different arrangement and thus exhibiting different properties.

Isopod: Small, usually dorso-ventrally flattened marine, freshwater and terrestrial crustaceans with enlarged eyes, a number of more or less uniformly sized (iso-) legs (-pods), and a distinct and often highly ornamented "tail segment." Pill bugs, slaters, sea roaches, and gribbles are common examples.

Isostasy: The geological term for the adjustment that occurs between continents and the seafloor, in which the downward movement of one results in the upward movement of the other.

Isotope: A "variety" of a chemical element which differs from another "variety" of the same element by having alternate numbers of neutrons (an atomic particle) in its atomic nucleus, e.g., Uranium 235 differs from Uranium 238 by having 3 fewer neutrons in its nucleus.

Jetstream: A narrow belt of high-speed winds (150-400 mph) blowing predominantly west to east around the earth at the upper level of the troposphere (10,000-40,000 ft).

Jetty: An artificial construction of boulders or other permanent debris placed to influence currents or protect a harbor or river. See also Groin.

Karst: A geological term for limestones containing solution holes and other hydrological excavations produced by the dissolving action of carbonic acid, usually in rainwater.

Kemp's Ridley: A smaller species of sea turtle (genus *Lepidochelys*) that comes ashore in large egg-laying and breeding "congresses" along the northern Mexican coast. It is extensively hunted for its meat and now is severely threatened with extinction. Also called Atlantic Ridley to distinguish it from the eastern Pacific species.

Key: A small, coralline islet, particularly in south Florida. The word is a corruption of the Spanish "cayo," reef-like island.

Key deer: A miniature race of white-tailed deer found only on Big Pine Key, Florida; a federally protected species.

Killifish: Any of several small (1-2 inches), primarily freshwater, surface-feeding fishes in the family Cyprinodontidae.

Knoll: Geological term for a small, rounded rise on the sea floor (see hillock).

Knot: A unit of speed in which an object travels the equivalent of one nautical mile (6,076 ft) per hour. Thus a vessel traveling at 10 knots (10 kts) will cover 10 nautical miles (60,760 feet) in 1 hour.

Krill: Norwegian name for a small, shrimplike, zooplanktonic crustacean (Euphausiacea) that occurs in enormous numbers in Antarctic waters and forms a major food item for baleen whales.

Lagoon: The semi-enclosed estuarine or marine water body found behind barrier islands or encircled by coral reefs in an atoll.

Land crab: General term for semi-terrestrial marine or freshwater crabs in several families that spend the majority of their lives on land, but which usually must return to water to hatch their eggs.

Larva: The (usually) planktonic stage of an invertebrate and some fishes that precedes the juvenile (and often benthic) stage.

Leptocephalus: Name given to the thin, glasslike planktonic larvae of eels, tarpon, bonefish and their relatives.

Levee: An encircling dike or embankment bordering one or both sides of a sea channel and often constructed to keep river waters from flooding low-lying adjacent lands.

Lichen: A primitive symbiotic plant consisting of an alga and a fungus growing together mutualistically.

Limestone: Geological term for rocks or sediments that contain at least 80% calcium and/or magnesium carbonates.

Lithification: The geological process in which dead organisms or their organic materials are turned to stone (lithified).

Littoral zone: The sea floor between high and low tide marks; the intertidal area.

Loop current: Oceanographer's term for the great current system in the Gulf of Mexico, so named because its path traces a gigantic loop in the Mexico basin.

Lucinid clam: Small, chalky, mud-dwelling estuarine and nearshore bivalves (family Lucinidae), the shells of which often have a distinctive furrow across the upper valve.

Macadam: A type of road surface consisting of crushed gravel embedded in an asphalt binder; named after the engineer who developed it.

Macrofauna: Term for the larger species in a particular animal assemblage. Its opposite is microfauna.

Magnetometer: An instrument that measures the direction and/or intensity of the earth's magnetic field, and often used to search for, locate and examine old wrecks on the sea floor.

Manganese: An important trace element in sea water that also forms large, concretionary nodules (along with cobalt, iron and nickel) around a central core of rocks, shark teeth and whale ear bones. Such deposits sometimes cover vast areas of the sea floor and constitute a potential mineral resource. Chemical symbol: Mn.

Mantis shrimp: Burrowing shrimplike crustaceans (order Stomatopoda) with a long abdomen and rounded, flattened, often highly ornamented tail, having paired, spiny claws that fancifully resemble the arms of a praying mantis insect. Often called "thumb-splitters" because of their pugnacious nature.

Marlin: A large, offshore rounded-bill, gamefish (family Istiophoridae) much sought for sport and culinary potential.

Marsh: Any wetland primarily containing reedy or grassy vegetation. See saltmarsh, freshwater marsh.

Mayfly: Small, short-lived, lacy-winged insects (order Ephemeroptera) that form mating swarms of prodigious numbers over freshwaters in late spring and early summer.

Medusa: The planktonic stage of some members in the phylum Cnidaria (=Coelenterata); a "jellyfish."

Menhaden: A commercially valuable, silvery, herring-like fish (family Clupeidae) occurring in large nearshore schools and forming the basis for the largest commercial fishery in the Gulf; colloquially called "pogy," or "sardine."

Mesozoic: The geological era from about 225 million years to about 65 million years before the present, and consisting of the Triassic, Jurassic and Cretaceous periods; the "age of dinosaurs" and "continental drift."

Metabolic degradation: The breakdown of a substance by an organism as a consequence of its metabolism.

Metamorphosis: The physiological and morphological change occurring in an organism from a non-reproductive kind of body or life-style to the reproductive stage, either as a larvae to an adult (zoea to crab), or from one ecological form to another (free-swimming hydroid medusa to sessile polyp).

Methane: A colorless, odorless gas (CH_4) usually produced through anaerobic breakdown or decay of organic matter; "swamp gas," or "marsh gas."

Mexico Basin: The oceanic basin forming the Gulf of Mexico.

Microbial degradation: Breakdown of substances by bacteria or fungi.

Microfauna: The small (usually microscopic) animal species occurring in a given area. See macrofauna.

Microflora: The small or microscopic plant species occurring in a given area. Most microflora are algae.

Miocene: The geological period in the Cenozoic era occurring from 23 to 6 million years before the present.

Mixed diurnal tide: A tidal cycle in which a high-high, a high-low, a low-high and a low-low tide occur over a cycle; the tides are thus "mixed" and not simple repetitive high and low.

Mojarra: Any of several species of small, plankton-feeding saltwater fishes with protrusible mouths (family Gerreidae).

Molluscs: The phylum of usually shell-bearing marine, freshwater and terrestrial invertebrates composing the snails, clams, chitons, tusk shells, squids and octopus, and their relatives.

Molt: A general term for the sloughing or casting off of an organism's outer covering, and associated with growth (e.g. insects, crustaceans), sexual maturity (birds) or epidermal rehabilitation (snakes).

Montane: Mountainous.

Mosquito fish: A small freshwater and estuarine fish (family Poeciliidae) noted for its predation on mosquito larvae, and so used in mosquito control.

Mud crab: Any of several species of small, carnivorous or scavenging crabs (family Xanthidae) commonly found in shallow-water muddy estuarine areas.

Mudflat: Common term for a muddy area in an estuary exposed at low tide.

Natural gas: Gas (usually methane, 50-90%, plus propane, butane and hydrogen sulfide) produced as a consequence of anaerobic bacterial breakdown of organic materials and usually associated with crude oil deposits.

Nauplius: The first larval stage in many lower marine crustaceans, including white, brown, pink and royal red shrimp, barnacles, capepods, etc.

Nautical mile: A measurement used in marine navigation equal to approximately 6,076 feet, or the equivalent of one minute of arc of a great circle on the earth's sphere.

Neap tide: The lower tides occurring during the first and last quarters of the moon, approximately every two weeks in a tidal cycle.

Needlefish: Elongate, surface-swimming marine and estuarine fish (family Belonidae) with jaws prolonged into a distinct beak.

Nekton: The swimming members of the pelagic and neritic community.

Neritic: That portion of the water column and marine environment occurring over the continental shelf.

Niche: An ecological concept defining the particular "space," behavior and biological relationships occupied or conducted by an organism over time; how an organism "fits" into an environment.

Nitrates: Chemical compounds formed by a union of nitrogen and three oxygen atoms with a metal ($X-NO_3$); nitrites consist of two oxygen atoms ($X-NO_2$).

Nitrifying bacteria: Bacteria living in soil, and in root nodules on some plants, that convert atmospheric nitrogen into nitrates, thus making them available to plants.

Non-targeted organisms: Euphemistic term (NTO) referring to organisms other than those desired to be controlled or killed by pesticide applications.

No-see-um: Colloquial term for extremely small biting midges or gnats; also called sand flies in some areas.

Nuclear generating plant: Jargon for an electricity-generating plant fueled by a nuclear reactor.

Nursery ground: Ecological term for an area (usually in an estuary) in which invertebrate and vertebrate organisms mature before returning to the sea as adults to propogate.

Nutria: A medium to large rodentlike animal with an extremely long tail (70% of body length), webbed hind feet, and large deep orange incisors, introduced from South America and now forming large, commercially exploited, populations in Louisiana, Texas and several midwestern states.

Nutrient flux (or flow): The passage of nutrients through an ecosystem from bacteria through plants to animals and back to bacteria.

Occluded front: Meteorological term for the situation at the juncture of two frontal systems when colder air meets warmer air and raises it aloft, usually creating poor weather conditions.

OCS: Acronym for Outer Continental Shelf, used most often in reference to petroleum explorational activity.

Oil seep: The natural flow or seepage of petroleum from the earth.

Oil slick: The sheen produced on the surface of water by spilled or seeping petroleum products.

Old-growth: Term in ecological forestry applied to forested areas which have a preponderance of very old stands of certain hardwood trees, and which therefore support more stable communities than recently reforested areas.

Oolite: Geological term ("oo" + "lite") for a limestone mineral formed by the successive precipitation and concretion of calcium carbonate around an original nucleus, so called because both in total view and cross-section the mineral looks like a tiny egg.

Organic: General term describing those chemical compounds and products produced by living organisms; opposite of inorganic.

Organochlorine: Chemical term referring to organic compounds in which chlorine, attached to a benzene ring, is a major component; as in a generic class of pesticides such as DDT.

Organophosphorus pesticides: Pesticides composed of organic compounds in which phosphorus, attached to one or more benzene rings, is a major component.

Osmoregulation: The physiological process whereby an organism regulates the intake and excretion of salts from its environment, thus maintaining its internal body fluids in a saline equilibrium.

Overburden: Geological term referring to the layers of sediment and other deposits lying on top of another discrete layer, and which affect the basal layer by their weight or density

Oxygen minimum layer: A discrete layer in the deep sea where dissolved oxygen drops to a minimum value differing from that in waters above and below it.

Oyster bar: A reef-like formation, usually found in estuaries, caused by the settling and growth of numerous Eastern oysters (genus *Crassostrea*) sufficient to raise the colony above the water's surface.

Ozone: A form of oxygen gas (O_3) that occurs in a layer encircling high above the earth which filters ultraviolet radiation produced by the sun.

Patch reef: A small assemblage of hermatypic or non-hermatypic corals usually occurring in isolated "patches" away from a major reef tract.

Peat: A spongy, dense and fibrous, decompositional product of plant matter that often forms widespread layers and deep deposits in marshes and mangrove forests.

Pelagic: Having to do with the open sea beyond the continental shelf.

Penaeidean shrimp: A commercially valuable, marine and estuarine shrimp-like decapod crustacean with small claws on the first *three* pairs of legs (see also Caridean shrimp).

Perennial: Having a growth season extending over several years; recurring more than one year.

Petrochemical sludge: Common term for hazardous or toxic wastes produced during the manufacturing of petroleum-based or derived chemical compounds.

Petroleum: A generic term for biologically-formed hydrocarbons that usually occur as oil, tar, asphalt, and natural gas.

Phosphates: Chemical compounds formed by the union of phosphorus with oxygen atoms, and occurring or required in many biological systems for growth, cell formation, and genetic structures ($X-PO_3$, $X-PO_4$ etc.).

Phosphorescence: Erroneous term for bioluminescence, but more correctly referring to the emission of light from elemental phosphorus caused by its slow and continuing combustion with oxygen in air.

Phosphorus: A waxy, white, light-emitting solid and one of the three most important elements in the biochemical and geochemical cycles in the sea. Chemical symbol: P.

Photolytic degradation: Breakdown of a compound or substance through exposure to light (usually sunlight).

Photosynthesis: A biochemical process evolved in, and unique to, plants and plantlike organisms whereby carbon dioxide and water are combined in the presence of sunlight to produce carbohydrates and oxygen.

Phylum: The highest (and most general) classification for a particular group of living organisms that show biological, morphological and evolutionary relationships to each other.

Plate tectonics: The theory that holds that the occurrence and position of continents and oceanic basins is caused by movement of the earth's crustal plates. Also called continental drift.

Platform reef: A coral reef built upon a previously existing (usually limestone) platform, often itself a previously existing reef.

Pleistocene: The first epoch in the Quartenary period, beginning (according to most geologists) approximately 1 million years ago and lasting until approximately 100,000 years ago.

Pliocene: The last epoch in the Tertiary period, beginning about 12 million years ago and ending about 1 million years ago.

Pluteus: The larval stage of echinoderms; those of sea urchins (Echinoidea) are called echinopluteus, those of brittle stars (Ophiuroidea) are called ophiopluteus.

Pocket harbor: A small, nearly enclosed coastal bay usually occurring inland to a larger and more open embayment, and often sought for safe harbor. Equivalent to "tertiary bay" of some authors.

Pogonophora: A phylum of predominantly threadlike, sediment-dwelling, tube-constructing, mostly deep sea marine worms distinguished by the absence of mouth or digestive tract, and therefore presumably feeding via assimilation of nutrients through the body wall.

Polysaline: Water bodies or organisms having, undergoing, or able to withstand multiple salinity changes. See euryhaline.

Pond apple: A small, water-loving tree (genus *Annona*) found in subtropical and tropical freshwater swamps and producing a soft, apple-shaped edible fruit.

Population: In ecology, a term designating all the interacting individuals of a given species within a community.

Porcelain crab: Small, flattened, rapidly moving, shallow water marine and estuarine anomuran crabs (family Porcellanidae), so-called because of their penchant to shed claws or legs (autotomize) when attacked or molested.

Porcupine fish: Small mostly shallow-water, seagrass dwelling marine fishes (family Diodontidae) whose skin is covered with large spines, and are capable of inflating their body by swallowing large amounts of air or water.

Postlarva: The developmental stage immediately following the larval stage in an invertebrate and some vertebrates, and usually characterized by a distinct change in locomotory, anatomical, behavioral, or physiological characteristics.

Powderpost beetles: Small, bark-burrowing beetles that infest injured or dying hardwood trees and products made from hardwoods. The name comes from the fine powdery excrement produced during the excavations of their galleries.

Prairie (coastal): The large grassy savannah-like areas, usually underlain by marly sediments, occurring in undeveloped parts of Florida.

Pre-Cambrian: The geological era preceding the Cambrian, over 600 million years ago.

Primary production: The rate at which carbon is produced by chemosynthetic or photosynthetic activity.

Primary productivity: The amount of carbon produced by chemosynthesis or photosynthesis by a given organism per unit area and unit of time. More popularly, the production of carbon or carbohydrates by bacteria, algae, or phytoplankton.

Progradation: Geological term for the creation of additional beach or islands via transference of sediments through the action of wind, waves, tides or currents from an existing beach to an area farther offshore.

Propagule: A developing seed, one already sprouted.

Prop root: A type of root commonly found on the trunks of red and white mangrove trees that serve to anchor the trunk more firmly in the sediments.

Proteins: A carbon-based compound containing nitrogen manufactured by living organisms and essential for life.

Protista: Name for one of five major kingdoms of living organisms on earth; specifically the single-celled organisms having a cell wall and a nucleus within; algae (plants) and protozoans (animals).

Pteropod: Small pelagic omnivorous molluscs with curiously shaped shells that swim by flapping a fleshy lobe around the mouth. Commonly called "sea butter-flies." Their empty shells, called "pteropod ooze" carpet miles of the deep sea floor

Puffer fish: Small to medium-sized, usually reef-dwelling marine fishes (family Tetraodontidae) with skin covered by small prickles, and which are capable of swallowing air or water and thus enlarging their bodies when molested. See porcupine fish.

Purgamentsam: Filth, refuse or garbage thrown overboard as waste.

Pygmy sperm whale: A small, toothed whale (genus *Kogia*) superficially resembling a sperm whale, but possessing a distinct dorsal fin which sperm whales lack. Erroneously called pilot whale in some areas.

Quahog: Common name for the edible clam, genus *Mercenaria*. Cherrystones and steamers are smaller and larger individuals, respectively, of the same species.

Quartz: A crystalline, usually translucent, often tinted form of silicon dioxide; a common component of beach sands.

Radioactive: Having the ability to emit alpha, beta or gamma radiation.

Radiolaria: Catchbasket name for the Actinopoda, the microscopic, amoebic pelagic plankton bearing highly ornamented siliceous shells. The empty shells, called "radiolarian ooze" cover parts of the deep sea floor in layers hundreds to thousands of feet thick.

Radionuclide: Any of several compounds formed through the activity of radioactive elements.

Rain forest: A tropical, usually lowland, forest that develops in areas of high rainfall. See also cloud forest.

Raptor: General term for any predatory bird that uses its beak and talons to subdue its prey, e.g., hawks, eagles.

Red crab (deep sea): A large, commercially valuable species of marine crab (family Geryonidae) found in deeper water along the edge of the continental shelf.

Red tide: Common name for large-scale, often irritating or toxic discolorations of sea water caused by the explosive outbreak of populations of microscopic plankton called dinoflagellates.

Reef: Any natural or manmade consolidated and raised area of the sea floor usually composed of rocky substrata or other hard materials, and often forming a hazard to navigation. See bioherm, oyster bar, sabellariid worm reef, serpulid reef.

Refugium: A sanctuary or other place of ecological respite.

Rhizome: A root-like creeping underground stem.

Rifting: Geological term for the sundering or splitting of a land mass or seafloor.

RNA: Ribonucleic acid, a component of living cells involved in the transmission of hereditary information.

Rock shrimp: Any of several species of commercially valuable, marine offshore shrimp (family Sicyoniidae) distinguished by having a heavily sculptured body and extremely short, serrated rostrum or "frontal horn."

Rodent: A mammal belonging to the order Rodentia, an extremely diverse and widespread group of omnivores that includes chipmunks, squirrels, ground squirrels, prairie dogs, rats, mice, voles and their relatives.

Rotifera: The rotifers or wheel animalcules, a group of microscopic freshwater and marine invertebrates distinguished by having a ciliated organ at the front or "head" of the animal that through the rapid circular movement of the cilia appears to be revolving much like a wheel.

Roughneck: Oil industry term for a worker on an oil rig or platform, particularly those associated with drilling operations.

Royal red shrimp: A commercially valuable, bright red, deep water marine shrimp (family Solenoceridae) related to pink, white and brown shrimps.

Sabellariid worm reef: A reef-like structure and a true bioherm (q.v.) found in the surfzone and shallow subtidal zone formed by the coalescence of thousands of tubes of sand constructed by polychaete worms in the family Sabellariidae.

Sailfin molly: A small brightly colored omnivorous, live-bearing fish (family Poeciliidae) of marine, brackish and fresh waters, the males of which are distinguished by having an elongate, sail-like dorsal fin.

Salina: A brackish water area along an estuarine shoreline occasionally inundated by tidal waters and which, owing to the extremely high salt content of the soil, supports only limited vegetation. Also called salt pond or saltern.

Salinity: The amount of salts by weight in parts per thousand (grams) dissolved in a kilogram of seawater; (^{0}/oo).

Salp: Small, spindle- or barrel-shaped, translucent, jelly-like pelagic zooplankton (Tunicata) related to the sessile sea squirts (q.v.). Salps are commonly found in offshore waters where they filter-feed on phytoplankton.

Salt dome: A geological feature caused by uplifting of surrounding rocks and sediments by large deposits of salt which have become liquefied by the weight of overlying sediments (see diapirism).

Saltgrass: A saltmarsh grass (genus *Distichlis*).

Salt marsh: A low-lying coastal area flooded continually by tides in which the primary vegetation consists of salt-tolerant grasses, rushes and sedges.

Salt wedge: The wedge-shaped saline water mass that intrudes on an incoming tide into an estuarine river below the outflowing fresh water.

Sandflea: Local name for a small, filter-feeding crab (family Emeritidae) that superficially resembles a rotund flea (an insect), and found in large numbers in the surfzone of tropical and subtropical sandy beaches.

Sandfly: An extremely small blood-sucking midge frequenting sandy beaches; locally called no-see-ums.

Sapodilla: A tropical fruit-bearing tree (family Sapotaceae) found in south Florida hammocks; locally named the "wild dilly."

Sargassum frogfish: A small, brownish-yellow, predatory anglerfish (genus *Histrio*) found in floating Gulfweed and camouflaged to resemble its habitat.

Savannah: A grassy wetland or marsh often occupying the area shoreward of a barrier island.

Sawgrass: A type of emergent wetland rush (genus *Cladium*) with sharp serrated spinules along the leaf-blade margins, common in the Everglades of southern Florida.

Saxitoxin: A virulent poison produced by some species of dinoflagellates and which is incorporated in the tissues of molluscan shellfish after they have eaten the dinoflagellates.

Scallop: A marine bivalve (family Pectinidae and its relatives); also the adductor (shell-closing) muscle commercially exploited by the seafood industry.

Seafloor: Typically, that part of the earth always covered by seawater, although the intertidal zone becomes exposed at low tides.

Seafloor spreading: The mechanism in plate tectonics by which hot magma, rising to the earth's surface, forces the crustal plates of the seafloor apart. See continental drift.

Sea grass: Any marine or estuarine grass which grows, flowers and produces seeds underwater.

Sea level: Correctly, the height of the surface of the sea at any given time. More popularly, the average height that the sea reaches on a given shore.

Sea level change: Term for the increase in height and subsequent implied encroachment of the sea on low lying coastal areas.

Seamount: A mountain in the sea (often of volcanic origin) rising at least 500 fathoms (3000 feet) or more from the seafloor and having an irregular or sharp summit. See guyot.

Sea scallop: A commercially-exploited deepwater marine bivalve of the genus *Placopecten*; specifically its adductor muscle as seafood. See bay scallop.

Sea snake: Truly marine coastal and pelagic carnivorous snakes (family Hydrophiidae) widely distributed throughout the tropical Indo-West Pacific Ocean, and whose venom is potently neurotoxic. At least one species occurs along the tropical Pacific coast of central and south America.

Sea spider: Small to gigantic (three feet across the legspread or larger) arthropods (phylum Chelicerata, or phylum Pycnogonida of some authorities) having a fanciful resemblance to land spiders in possessing eight to twelve greatly elongated legs attached to a small more or less tubular body. Their relationships to true terrestrial spiders are obscure at best.

Sea squirt: Common name for certain sessile (attached), grape-like or bag-like members of the fouling community (phylum Urochordata), which, when squeezed, eject seawater through one of two siphons.

Sea star: A benthic, star-shaped echinoderm (class Asteroidea) in which the arms are not distinctly demarcated from the central disc, can move only vertically and not laterally, and cannot be easily shed (autotomized); also called starfish.

Sea trout: Common name for some species of shallow-water, seagrass associated, coastal marine and estuarine fishes (family Sciaenidae) that superficially resemble freshwater trout. Sea trout are not related to freshwater trout (which are salmonids) but to drums and croakers.

Sea urchin: Any of numerous species of rounded or flattened, spiny, omnivorous marine echinoderm animals (class Echinoidea) living on or burrowing into shallow or deep sea floors; also called echinoids or sea hedgehogs.

Sediment: Organic or inorganic particles chemically precipitated, secreted by organisms or resulting from their breakdown, or eroded or transported by wind, ice, water or other means, and deposited in a loose and unconsolidated form.

Sedimentary rock: Rocks formed by the accumulation in water, or from weathering, of various-sized particles of geological or biological origin; sandstones, shales, limestones, coal, and salt seams are examples.

Sediment loading: The accumulation of sediments in an area to such a degree that it causes stress on the underlying geological substrata.

Seep: A crack or fissure often found at the base of an escarpment or sea cliff, through which water or other liquids may ooze.

Semi-diurnal: In reference to tidal cycles, those in which a high or low tide occurs once every 12 ½ hours or twice in an approximately 24 hour period, i.e. half (semi-) a day (diurnal) in length of time.

Semiterrestrial: An organism that lives on land but must return to the sea for purposes of breeding or releasing of young.

Senescence: The process of botanical succession in a community caused by deterioration through aging of the individual plants.

Serpulid wormreef: A shallow-water bioherm formed by calcareous tube-building polychaete worms in the family Serpulidae.

Sessile: Said of an organism fixed to the substratum; immobile.

Sheepshead minnow: A common, widely distributed, shallow water fish (family Cyprinodontidae), frequenting fresh and saltwater wetlands, estuaries and nearshore marine environments. Because of its superb osmoregulatory abilities the species is considered to be the most salt-tolerant fish in the world.

Shelf-edge pinnacle: A reef or reeflike formation occurring on the deepwater edge of the continental shelf, and often appearing on fathograms as pinnacles, cones or other sharp-crested formations.

Shellfish: Those marine invertebrate species possessing shelly or horny coverings and used as seafood; e.g. clams, oysters, mussels, scallops, shrimp, crabs and lobsters.

Shell hash: Oceanographic term for sediments composed of broken shells and hard coverings of marine organisms. See bioclastics.

Shoal: Any submerged ridge, bank, bar or area of unconsolidated sediments shallow enough to be a hazard to navigation.

Side-scan sonar: A type of sound echo-ranging that produces an apparent three-dimensional picture of objects on the earth's surface or sea floor.

Silicates: One of the largest and most common groups of minerals consisting of silicon and oxygen united chemically with sodium, calcium, postassium or aluminum often in union with water and forming crystals and other structures in nearly every type of rock. Quartz, feldspar, kaolin, mica, olivine and numerous semi-precious gem minerals are just a few examples.

Sinkhole: A deep, usually circular depression in karst limestone regions caused by dissolution or collapse of the underlying rock through lowering of the water table. See also cenote.

Siphon: A body tube used for water intake and outflow to allow one or more activities including breathing, feeding, chemosensory detection, or propulsion, in molluscs and some other marine invertebrates.

Siphonophora: The group of pelagic, carnivorous, colonial "jellyfish" consisting of man o' war, by-the-wind-sailor, and their relatives.

Sirenian: Manatees and dugongs; "sea cows."

Skate: A small group of bottom-dwelling, subtidal to continental slope, ray-like fishes (family Rajidae) having shortened tails without a venomous spine, broadly rounded pectoral fins, and the body disc usually armed with numerous small spines and prickles. Their distinctive chitinous egg cases that wash ashore are called "mermaid's purses."

Skimmer: Common name for a long-winged tern-like water bird (family Laridae) that flies just above the water's surface and uses its more elongated lower bill to snap up shrimp and small fishes; also called shearwater.

Slough: A low water-retaining area which supports fresh or brackish water wetland trees and shrubs, especially in subtropical areas.

Snook: Any of five species of carnivorous, freshwater and marine fish (family Centropomidae), highly sought for sport and food, and distinguished by a noticeably sloping forehead, underslung jaw, and a distinctive, dark lateral line. Locally called robalo or linesider.

Sodium: Silvery, highly chemically reactive metal, a component of table and sea salt, and one of the most abundant in seawater. Chemical symbol: Na.

Sole: A short-bodied, scavenging and carnivorous, bottom-dwelling, marine and estuarine flatfish (family Soleidae) with both eyes located on the right side of the body. By contrast, the flounders (family Bothidae) have both eyes on the left side of the body.

Solution hole: A small, shallow, usually rounded hole in limestone karst regions caused by dissolution of the sediments by rain or running water. See sinkhole, cenote.

Species diversity: The number of species, and individuals in each, that occurs in a ecologically delimited area.

Species richness: The number of species in an ecologically delimited area. Often erroneously interchanged with species diversity (q.v.).

Spider crab: Any small, omnivorous, marine or estuarine crabs (family Majidae) which superficially resemble spiders because of their long legs and foreshortened bodies.

Spindrift: The sea foam that forms along a beach just above the wave line.

Sponge: Primarily marine, filter-feeding, sessile, colonial invertebrate animals (phylum Porifera) having a body perforated by pores through which water enters and leaves, and characterized by the presence of stiffening spicules of silica or calcium carbonate held in a fibrous matrix called spongin.

Sponge bank: A large, raised area of the seafloor on which the predominant sessile or anchored fauna is sponges.

Spring tide: Higher tides that occur approximately every two weeks during full or new moon. The term "spring" refers to the water rising far up onto the shore rather than to any seasonality. See also neap tide.

Standing crop: The total amount of plankton (or other) organisms, by weight and unit of water volume in a given area.

Stargazer: Any of several bottom-dwelling, subtidal to continental shelf, burrowing, carnivorous fish species (family Uranoscopidae) with large, raised eyes and an electricity-generating organ on the top of the head.

Steering current: The coupling of wind, sea and atmospheric conditions that determines the direction a hurricane or tropical storm will take.

Stone crab: Large, bottom-dwelling, carnivorous and scavenging shallow water marine and estuarine crabs (family Xanthidae) whose robust claws are highly esteemed as seafood.

Stratosphere: That part of the earth's atmosphere above the troposphere, beginning about 5 miles (polar regions) or 11 miles (equatorial regions) above the earth's surface and extending to approximately 60 miles up.

Subantarctic intermediate water: A cold, deep, watermass in the ocean originating in the Antarctic off the continental shelf and flowing northward toward the equator.

Submarine canyon: A canyon or large cleft in the continental shelf, often the site of an old river valley.

Subsidence: The settling or downwarping of an area caused by sediment overloading (q.v.), substratum collapse, isostasy (q.v.) or other geophysical activities.

Subsurficial water: Ground water (q.v.).

Subtidal: That area of seafloor seaward of the intertidal or littoral zone (q.v.).

Subtropical: That area in the Gulf of Mexico geographically defined as between about 27° and 25° N latitude, or where sea surface temperatures in the coldest months rarely fall below 60° F; also the area immediately north of the Tropic of Cancer.

Subtropical underwater: A subsurface water mass in the Atlantic Ocean found predominantly to the north and south of the equator.

Sulfates: Chemical compounds formed by the union of sulfur and oxygen with another element; $(X-SO_4)$.

Sulfur: An amorphous yellowish nonmetallic solid commonly found associated with volcanic or sedimentary deposits. Large deposits occur in Louisiana and Texas. Sulfur is an essential element for life processes. Chemical symbol: S.

Sulfur bottom whale: Whaler's name for a baleen-whale whose underside is sulfurously yellow owing to a growth of yellow diatoms thereon.

Sulfuric acid: A powerful acid (H_2SO_4) used in manufacturing, and which, as a component of acid rain, can be created naturally through a chemical combination of rainwaters and sulfur dioxides (SO_2) produced through automobile emissions. See acid rain.

Sulfur-producing bacteria: Any of a large group of bacteria that derive their energy from the oxidation of sulfur compounds, and which may deposit elemental sulfur within or outside the bacterial cells.

Supersaturation: Chemical term which indicates that a solution under certain physical conditions contains more than the amount of a substance by which it would be considered saturated under normal conditions.

Surf zone: The area on and immediately seaward of a beach between the outermost breaking wave and its farthest uprush on shore.

Swamp: Any low, water-retentive region more or less continually inundated either seasonally or tidally, and containing a large number of trees, often characterized by the predominance of certain species. For example, mangrove swamp, cypress swamp.

Swamp gas: Methane gas, produced through bacterial decomposition of vegetation, and usually occurring in swamps. When it ignites spontaneously it is called will o' the wisp.

Symbiont: Any organism that lives on or in another. The relationship may be necessary for one or both organisms (obligatory), or only temporarily beneficial for either one or the other (facultative).

Talus: Geological term for the rocky debris that accumulates at the base of a slope as a result of gravity; for example, the rubble pile at the seaward base of a coral reef.

Taxonomy: The science of providing organisms with scientific names.

Tectonic alteration: Geological changes in the earth's crust or seafloor caused by plate tectonics (q.v.).

Termites: Wood-dwelling and -eating insects resembling ants that often cause extensive damage to wooden structures. Termites are a necessary part of forest ecosystems, breaking down fallen trees and recycling the nutrients.

Terrigenous: Of the earth; said of deposits formed through terrestrial activities.

Test: The horny outer covering or exoskeleton of some species of marine invertebrates, for example, sea urchins (q.v.).

Thermal degradation: The breakdown of a substance by the application of heat.

Thermal effluent: The heated wastewater discharged from an electricity-generating plant.

Thermocline: The large, vertical or oblique, decreasing temperature discontinuity or gradient that occurs between two layers of water of relatively stable higher and lower temperatures in the sea.

Thermoregulation: The ability of an organism to maintain or adjust its internal temperature in response to external influences.

Tidal channel: A twisting, often ephemeral, shallow channel among mangroves or saltmarsh vegetation created by tidal water runoff during low tide.

Tidal pass: Another name for an inlet, usually between two barrier islands or other points of land.

Tilefish: Deepwater, burrowing, predatory fishes (family Branchiostegidae) with elongate dorsal and ventral fins found on the continental shelf, comprising a commercially valuable fishery.

Toad: An amphibian related to frogs but which possesses parotid glands (venom-secreting glands on the back of the head) whereas frogs do not.

Toadfish: A shallow water, bottom-dwelling or burrowing estuarine and marine fish (family Batrachoididae) with large head, powerful jaws and (in some cases) venom glands associated with pectoral, dorsal or gill spines. Their resemblance to toads is fanciful at best.

Tracheophyte: Any vascular plant, i.e. one having xylem and phloem tissues for transport and/or storage of water and nutrients. For example, trees, shrubs.

Tropical: Reference point to events, localities or biota occurring generally between the old Tropic of Cancer and Tropic of Capricorn adjacent to either side of the equator, or about 24° North and South latitudes of that same line.

Tropical storm: A tropical cyclone in which the wind speed rotates about a defined center between 39 and 73 mph.

Trunkfish: Small, carnivorous, shallow water reef and seagrass dwelling fishes (family Ostraciidae) whose bodies consist of such rigid and bony plates (the "trunk") that swimming is possible only with the dorsal, anal and pectoral fins.

Tubicolous: Animals (particularly polychaete worms) that secrete, or construct and live within some type of tube.

Turbidity: The reduced clarity of a water body caused by suspended matter.

Turbidity current: An extremely dense flow of deep seawater and contained clays, silts, sands and muds that slumps suddenly downward along a continental shelf or slope.

Uplands: Common term for any maritime landforms neither coastal nor wetland in configuration.

Upwelling: The process wherein deeper seawater rises to the sea surface as a result of sinking of other seawaters, or by the effects of offshore currents and winds.

Veliger: The (usually) planktonic larval stage of marine molluscs; some veligers spend their "pelagic" phase within the egg and hatch in an advanced stage of development more resembling the adult snail or clam.

Venus clam: Any member of the family Veneridae, medium to large thick-shelled, commercially valuable clams commonly found in shallow intertidal and subtidal estuarine and marine waters. For example, quahogs, cherrystones.

Vermetid mollusc reef: A true bioherm formed by the coalescence of thousands of calcareous shells of some species of marine snails (family Vermetidae). Locally called "worm rock."

Vermilion snapper: A marine fish (family Lutjanidae) commonly trawled on offshore snapper banks; also, an advertising name for species of freshwater fish (family Cichlidae) raised on fishfarms.

Volcanism: Volcanic activity and its effects.

Wahoo: A large, carnivorous, usually solitary, offshore food and gamefish (family Scombridae) esteemed both for its gastronomic qualities and its fighting ability. The name allegedly comes from the angler's exclamation when he or she first hooks into one.

Warm-temperate: A biogeographical designation for those areas of the earth north or south of the tropics, approximately between 28-35° latitude, and characterized by moderate winter and summer temperatures.

Water lily: Floating and semi-emergent freshwater plants (family Nymphaceae) of ponds, swamps and lakes, so-called because of their large, attractive flowers.

Water mite: Small to nearly microscopic, brightly colored, carnivorous or parasitic freshwater arthropods (order Hydracarina) related to spiders and ticks, found in streams, ponds and lakes.

Watershed: A delineated geographical area supplied and drained by specifically designated surficial and subsurficial water flows or sources, and which delivers water, sediment and dissolved substances to a major river or estuary.

Waterspout: An offshore tornado.

Water strider: Small freshwater, predatory insects (family Gerridae) whose elongate, heavily haired hind legs enable them to walk across the water surface of ponds and lakes.

Wave height: The vertical height of a sea wave measured from the lowest preceding point (trough) to the next highest point (crest); also, the height of breakers or storm waves when they come ashore.

Weedline: Local fishermen's term for the drifting lines of seaweed found offshore and which often support large assemblages of pelagic fish and other organisms.

Wetland: Common term for any area periodically or permanently inundated by shallow fresh or salt waters, with characteristic soil compositions, and which usually supports a characteristic type of vegetation.

Whirligig beetle: A small black, omnivorous, freshwater-dwelling beetle (family Gyrinidae) of ponds and lakes. The name comes from their habit of rapidly swimming in irregular circles at the water's surface.

Willowhead: Local name for a slough or swamp in which willow trees predominate.

Wind forcing: The alteration of water heights and apparent periodicities in a lunar tidal cycle caused by the overriding effects of wind; often seen in shallow estuarine lagoons.

Wisconsin glacial epoch: The period about 20,000-100,000 years ago when the formation of great glaciers lowered world sea levels as much as 300 feet below present stands.

Wormrock: Layman's term for any hard sediments that appear to be, or are actually created by, "worms." The term includes reefs constructed both by gastropod molluscs and polychaete worms.

Xeric: Dry or drought-tolerant, said of plants as well as of their habitats.

Zinc: A bluish-white metal commonly found in association with other metals in the earth and which is often used to form protective coatings in galvanized metals and other compounds. In trace amounts zinc is necessary for life but may be toxic in higher concentrations. Chemical symbol: Zn.

Zonation: The separating of an area into ecological divisions characterized by the occurrence or absence of biota within the zone, by specific biotic sequences observed throughout the zone, or as a consequence of the range of physical factors occuring therein.

Zoogeography: The study of the distribution of animals and the biological, ecological, geological and physical factors affecting that distribution.

Suggestions For Further Reading

A NY SYNOPSIS MUST, by definition, draw heavily on the research and published results of others. This work is no exception. There is a wealth of easily available material dealing with the Gulf of Mexico, but it is scattered throughout both the popular and the scientific literature. I have relied on both sources in an attempt to present as balanced and readable an account as possible.

The following bibliography, which is by no means exhaustive, primarily emphasizes those publications usually available in local public libraries. The reader desiring more technical information should consult the bibliographies in the listed works, the numerous research journals in each scientific discipline, and the abstracting services Bio-abstracts, Marine Biological Abstracts, and Oceanography Abstracts for more detailed articles in the broad scientific literature.

[G] = General works. Suitable for the average reader.

[T] = Technical works. Directed toward the specialist, but usually having some sections of interest to the average reader.

BIBLIOGRAPHIES

Blake, J. B. 1991. Gulf of Mexico programmatic documents and contract deliverables. U.S. Department of the Interior, Minerals Management Service, Gulf of Mexico OCS region, New Orleans, LA. 75 pp. [G]

Gordon, M. R., and L. L. Bane. 1983. Florida marine education resources bibliography. Florida Sea Grant College, Report Number 51, Gainesville, FL. iv + 116 pp. [G]

Renaud, M. L. 1985. Annotated bibliography on hypoxia and its effects on marine life, with emphasis on the Gulf of Mexico. National Oceanographic and Atmospheric Administration (NOAA) Technical Report NMFS 21. iii + 9 pp. [T]

Van Tine, M., and S. C. Snedaker. 1974a. A bibliography of the mangrove literature prepared for the international symposium on biology and management of mangroves. Institute of Food and Agricultural Sciences (IFAS), University of Florida, Gainesville, FL. 153 unnumbered pp. [T]

_____, 1974b. Bibliography and compendium of literature cited sections of papers on mangroves. *IN*: Guidelines for management of mangroves in south Florida. Final Report, U. S. Department of the Interior; Center for Wetlands, University of Florida, Gainesville, FL. iv + 186 pp. [T]

Whittier, H. O. (undated). Florida botanic/ecological bibliography. Privately published, The Florida Native Plant Society and The Florida Conservation Foundation, Winter Park, FL. 278 pp. [G]

CLIMATE AND WEATHER

Anonymous. 1977. Some devastating North Atlantic hurricanes of the 20th century. National Oceanic and Atmospheric Administration Document. NOAA/PA 77019. 12 unnumbered pages.[G]

Bomer, G. W. 1983. *Texas weather.* University of Texas Press, Austin, TX. 265 pp.[G]

Dunn, G., and B. I. Miller. 1964. *Atlantic hurricanes.* Louisiana State University Press, Baton Rouge, LA. 326 pp. [T]

Forrester, F. H. 1981. *1001 questions answered about the weather.* Dover Publications, Inc., New York, NY. 419 pp. [G]

Lashof, D. A., and D. A. Tirpak (eds.). 1990. Policy options for stabilizing global climate. Report to Congress, U. S. Environmental Protection Agency, Washington, DC. Report 21P- 2003.1 [Chapters individually paginated]. [G]

Smith, J. B., and D. A. Tirpak (eds.). 1989. The potential effects of global climate change on the United States. Appendix B—Sea level rise. U. S. Environmental Protection Agency, Washington, DC. Report EPA-230-05-89-052. [Chapters individually paginated] [T]

Tannehill, I. R. 1956. *Hurricanes.* Princeton University Press, Princeton, NJ. 308 pp. [T]

Tufty, B. 1987. *1001 questions answered about hurricanes, tornadoes,and other natural air disasters.* Dover Publications, Inc., New York, NY. xvi + 381 pp.[G]

FAUNA AND FLORA

Abele, L. G., and W. Kim. 1986. An illustrated guide to the marine decapod crustaceans of Florida. State of Florida, Department of Environmental Regulation. Technical Series, Volume 8, Number 1, parts 1 and 2. xvii + 760 pp. [T]

Amos,W. H., and S. H. Amos. 1985. *Atlantic and Gulf coasts.* The Audubon Society Nature Guides. Alfred A. Knopf, New York, NY. 670 pp. [G]

Andrews, J. 1977. *Shells and shores of Texas.* University of Texas Press, Austin, TX. 365 pp. [G]

Bahr, L. M., and W. P. Lanier. 1981. The ecology of intertidal oyster reefs of the south Atlantic coast: A community profile. U. S. Fish and Wildlife Service, Office of Biological Services, Washington, DC. FWS/OBS-81/15. 105 pp. [G]

Bayer, F. M. 1961. *The shallow-water Octocorallia of the West Indian region. A manual for marine biologists.* Martinus Nijhoff, The Hague, Netherlands. 373 pp + 101 text figs. and pls I-XXVII. [T]

Bright, T. G., and L. G. Pequegnat (eds.). 1974. *Biota of the west Flower Garden Bank.* Gulf Publishing Company, Houston, TX. 435 pp. [T]

Britton, J. C., and B. Morton. 1989. *Shore ecology of the Gulf of Mexico.* University of Texas Press, Austin, TX. viii + 400 pp. [G]

Carlton, J. M. 1975. A guide to common Florida salt marsh and mangrove vegetation. Florida Department of Natural Resources, Marine Research Publications. Number 6. 30 pp. [G]

Craig, R. M. 1984. Plants for coastal dunes of the Gulf and South Atlantic coasts and Puerto Rico. U.S. Department of Agriculture, Soil Conservation Service.

Agriculture Bulletin Number 460. 41 pp.[G]

Dawes, C. J. 1974. *Marine algae of the west coast of Florida.* University of Miami Press, Coral Gables, FL. xi + 201 pp. [T]

Duncan, W. H., and M. B. Duncan. 1987. *Seaside plants of the Gulf and Atlantic coasts.* Smithsonian Institution Press, Washington, DC. 409 pp. [T]

Felder, D. L. 1973. An annotated key to crabs and lobsters (Decapoda, Reptantia) from coastal waters of the northwestern Gulf of Mexico. Center for Wetland Resources, Louisiana State University. Sea Grant Publication LSU-SG-73-02. vii + 103 pp. [T]

Gosner, K. L. 1979. *A field guide to the Atlantic seashore.* Peterson Field Guide Series. Houghton Mifflin Company, Boston, MA. 329 pp. [G]

Gunn, C. R., and J. V. Dennis, 1976. *World guide to tropical drift seeds and fruits.* New York Times Book Company, New York, NY. xi + 240 pp. [G]

Harrar, E. S., and J. G. Harrar. 1962. *Guide to southern trees.* Dover Publications, Inc., New York, NY. viii + 709 pp. [G]

Heard, R. W. 1982. Guide to common tidal marsh invertebrates of the northeastern Gulf of Mexico. Mississippi-Alabama Sea Grant Consortium. Report MASGP-79-004. 82 pp. [G]

Hedgpeth, J. W. 1953. An introduction to the zoogeography of the northwestern Gulf of Mexico with reference to the invertebrate fauna. Publications of the Institute of Marine Science, University of Texas. Volume 3, number 1: 109-224.[T]

Hoese, H. D., and R. H. Moore. 1977. *Fishes of the Gulf of Mexico Texas, Louisiana, and adjacent waters.* Texas A&M University Press, College Station, TX. 327 pp. [T]

Hotchkiss, N. 1972. *Common marsh, underwater, and floating-leaved plants of the United States and Canada.* Dover Publications, Inc. New York, NY. 224 pp.[G]

Humann, P. 1991. *Reef fish identification.* Florida Caribbean Bahamas. New World Publications, Inc., Jacksonville, FL. 272 pp. [G]

_____. 1991. *Reef creature identification.* Florida Caribbean Bahamas. New World Publications, Incorporated, Jacksonville, FL. 328 pp. [G]

Idyll, C. P. 1976. *Abyss. The deep sea and the creatures that live in it.* Thomas Y. Crowell Company, New York, NY. xviii + 428 pp. [G]

Kale, H. W., II, and D. S. Maehr. 1990. *Florida's birds. A handbook and reference.* Pineapple Press, Sarasota, FL. 288 pp. [G]

Kaplan, E. H. 1982. *A field guide to coral reefs of the Caribbean and Florida including Bermuda and the Bahamas.* Peterson Field Guide Series. Houghton Mifflin Company, Boston, MA. 289 pp. [G]

Lacefield, E. M. 1975. Survival in the marsh. Louisiana Wildlife and Fisheries Commission, New Orleans, LA. Wildlife Education Bulletin Number 111. 100 pp. [G]

Littler, D. S., M. M. Littler, K. E. Bucher, and J. N. Norris. 1989. *Marine plants of the Caribbean. A field guide from Florida to Brazil.* Smithsonian Institution Press, Washington, DC. 263 pp. [G]

Meinkoth, N. A. 1981. *The Audubon Society field guide to North American seashore creatures*. Alfred A. Knopf, New York, NY. 799 pp. [G]

Morris, P. A. 1975. *A field guide to shells of the Atlantic and Gulf coasts and the West Indies*. Peterson Field Guide Series. Houghton Mifflin Company, Boston, MA. 330 pp. [G]

Mullin, K., W. Hoggard, C. Roden, R. Lohoefener, C. Rogers, and B. Taggart. 1991. Cetaceans on the upper continental slope in the north-central Gulf of Mexico. U.S. Department of the Interior, Minerals Management Service, Gulf of Mexico OCS region, New Orleans, LA. OCS Study/MMS 91-0027. 108 pp. [G]

Odum, W. E, C. C. McIvor, and T. J. Smith. 1982. The ecology of the mangroves of south Florida. A community profile. U. S. Fish and Wildlife Service, Office of Biological Services, Washington, DC. FWS/OBS-81/24. x + 144 pp. [T]

Overstreet, R. M. 1978. Marine maladies: worms, germs and other symbionts from the northern Gulf of Mexico. Mississippi-Alabama Sea Grant Consortium, Gulf Coast Research Labs, Ocean Springs, MS. MASGP-78-021. 140 pp. [T]

Perlmutter, A. 1961. *Guide to marine fishes*. Bramhall House, New York, NY. 431 pp. [G]

Perry, L. M., and J. S. Schwengel. 1955. *Marine shells of the western coast of Florida*. Paleontological Research Institution, Ithaca, NY. 318 pp. [G]

Peterson, R. T. 1947. *A field guide to the birds*. Houghton Mifflin Company, Boston, MA. 290 pp. [G]

Poggie, J. J. 1963. Coastal pioneer plants and habitat in the Tampico region, Mexico. Louisiana State University Press, Baton Rouge, LA. 62 pp. [G]

Rappole, J. H., and G. W. Blacklock. 1985. *Birds of the Texas coastal bend: abundance and distribution*. Texas A&M Press, College Station, TX. 126 pp. [G]

Robbins, C. S., B. Bruun, and H. S. Zim. 1966. *Birds of North America. A guide to field identification*. Golden Press, New York, NY.340 pp. [G]

Sauer, J. D. 1967. Geographic reconnaisance of seashore vegetation along the Mexican Gulf coast. Louisiana State University, Baton Rouge, LA. Coastal Studies Series, Report Number 21. 59 pp. [G]

Schmidley, D. 1981. Marine mammals of the southeastern United States coast and the Gulf of Mexico. U.S. Fish and Wildlife Service, Biological Services Program, Washington, DC. FWS/OBS-80/41. 165 pp. [T]

Smith, F. G. W. 1948. *Atlantic reef corals. A handbook of the common reef and shallow-water corals of Bermuda, Florida, the West Indies, and Brazil*. University of Miami Press, Miami, FL. 112 pp + 41 pls. [T]

Tarver, D. P., J. A. Rodgers, M. J. Mahler, and R. L. Lazor, 1979. *Aquatic and wetland plants of Florida*. Florida Department of Natural Resources, Bureau of Aquatic Plant Research and Control, Tallahassee, FL. 127 pp. [G]

Uebelacker, J. M, and P. C. Johnson (eds.), 1984. Taxonomic guide to the polychaetes of the northern Gulf of Mexico. U. S. Department of the Interior. Minerals Management Service, Gulf of Mexico OCS region, Metairie, LA. Study MMS 84-0049, Volumes 1-7 [individually paginated]. [T]

Voss, G. L. 1976. *Seashore life of Florida and the Caribbean*. Banyan Books, Miami, FL. 199 pp. [G]

Warmke, G. L., and R. T. Abbott. 1962. *Caribbean seashells.* Livingston Publishing Company, Narberth, PA. 348 pp. [G]

Zieman, J. A., and R. T. Zieman. 1989. The ecology of the seagrass meadows of the west coast of Florida. A community profile. U. S. Fish and Wildlife Service, Washington, DC. Biological Report 85 (7.25). ix + 155 pp. [T]

FISHERIES

O'Hara, K., N. Atkins, S. Iudicello, S. G. Criswell, and R. Bierce. 1986. *Marine wildlife entanglement in North America.* Privately published, Center for Environmental Education, Washington, DC. xiv + 218 pp. [G]

Rebel, T. P. 1974. *Sea turtles and the turtle industry of the West Indies, Florida, and the Gulf of Mexico.* University of Miami Press, Coral Gables, FL. 250 pp. [G]

GENERAL BACKGROUND

Anonymous. 1988. The Economist. In: *The world in figures.* G. K. Hall and Company, Boston, MA. 296 pp. [G]

Baker, R. 1985. A primer of offshore operations. Petroleum Extension Service, University of Texas, Austin, TX. vii + 114 pp. [G]

Beccasio, A. D, N. Fotheringham, A. E. Redfield, et al. 1982. Gulf coast ecological inventory: user's guide and information base. U.S. Fish and Wildlife Service, Office of Biological Services, Washington, DC. FWS/OBS-82/55. viii + 191 pp. [G]

Briggs, J. C. 1974. *Marine zoogeography.* McGraw-Hill, New York, NY. x + 475 pp. [G]

Emiliani, C. 1988. *The Scientific Companion. Exploring the physical world with facts, figures, and formulas.* John Wiley and Sons, Incorporated, New York, NY. xii + 287 pp.[G]

Galtsoff, P. S. (ed.). 1954. Gulf of Mexico—its origin, waters, and marine life. Fishery Bulletin, U. S. Fish and Wildlife Service, Volume 55, Number 89: 604 pp. [G]

Gleason, P. J. (ed.). 1974. Environments of South Florida: present and past. Miami Geological Society, Miami, FL. Memoir 2. 452 pp. [G]

Jones, J. I., R. E. Ring, M. O. Rinkel, and R. E. Smith. 1973. A summary of knowledge of the eastern Gulf of Mexico 1973. State University System of Florida. Institute of Oceanography, Tallahassee, FL. xii + 608 pp. [T]

Lynch, M. P., B. L. Laird, N. B. Theberge, and J. C. Jones (eds.). 1976. An assessment of estuarine and nearshore marine environments. Special Report in Applied Marine Science and Ocean Engineering, Number 93 (revised). Virginia Institute of Marine Science, Gloucester Point, VA. xvi + 132 pp. [G]

McConnaughey, B. H., and R. Zottoli. 1983. *Introduction to marine biology.* C. V. Mosby Company, St. Louis, MO. xi + 638 pp. [G]

Minerals Management Service, U.S. Department of the Interior, 1987. Final environmental impact statement proposed oil and gas lease sales 113/115/116 Gulf of Mexico OCS region. OCS EIS MMS 87-0077. xxxvi + 547 pp, appendices A-E.[G]

Morgan, K. O'L., S. Morgan, and N. Quitno. 1990. *1990 State Rankings. A statistical view of the 50 United States.* Morgan Quitno Corporation, Lawrence, KS. 276 pp. [G]

Myers, R. L.,and J. J. Ewel (eds.). *Ecosystems of Florida.* University of Central Florida Press, Orlando, FL. 765 pp. [G]

Odum, H. T., B. J. Copeland, and E. A. McMahan. 1974. *Coastal ecological systems of the United States. Vol. 1.* The Conservation Foundation, Washington, DC. 533 pp. [G]

Palik,T. F., and R. R. Lewis, III. 1983. Southwestern Florida ecological characterization: an ecological atlas. Map narratives. U. S. Fish Wildlife Service, Division of Biological Services, Washington, DC. FWS/OBS-82/47. xvi + 329 pp. [G]

Rezak, R., T. J. Bright, and D. W. McGrail. 1985. *Reefs and banks of the northwestern Gulf of Mexico. Their geological, biological and physical_dynamics.* John Wiley and Sons, New York, NY. 259 pp.[T]

Romans, B. 1775. *A concise natural history of east and west Florida.* [Reprint, 1961. Pelican Publishing Company, New Orleans, LA. 291 pp.] [G]

Russell-Hunter, W. D. 1979. *A life of invertebrates.* Macmillan Publishing Company, New York, NY. xviii + 650 pp. [T]

Schopf, J. W. (ed.). 1983. *Earth's earliest biosphere. Its origin and evolution.* Princeton University Press, Princeton, NJ. xxv + 543 pp. [T]

Wilson, E. O., and F. M. Peter (eds.). 1988. *Bio Diversity.* National Academy Press, Washington, D.C. xiii + 521 pp. [G]

GEOLOGY

Bird, E. C. F. 1970. *Coasts. An introduction to systematic geomorphology.* Volume 4. The Massachusetts Institute of Technology Press, Cambridge, MA. xv + 246 pp. [G]

Decker, R., and B. Decker. 1981. *Volcanoes.* W. H. Freeman and Company, San Francisco, CA. ix + 244 pp. [G]

Hoffmeister, J. E.1974. *Land from the sea. The geologic story of south Florida.* University of Miami Press, Coral Gables, FL. 143 pp. [G]

Martinez, J. D. 1991. Salt Domes. American Scientist, volume 79, number 5: 420-431 (September-October, 1991). [G]

Murray, G. E., 1961. *Geology of the Atlantic and Gulf coastal province of North America.* Harper and Brothers, New York, NY. xvii + 692 pp. [T]

Schwartz, M. L. (ed.). 1973. *Barrier islands.* Benchmark papers in geology. Dowden, Hutchinson and Ross, Inc., Stroudsburg, PA. xiii + 451 pp. [T]

Shepard, F. P., F. B. Phleger, and T. H. van Andel (eds.). 1960. Recent sediments. Northwest Gulf of Mexico. Special Publications, American Association of Petroleum Geologists, Tulsa, OK. 394 pp. [T]

Shepard, F. P., and H. R. Wanless. 1971. *Our changing coastlines.* McGraw-Hill, New York, NY. 579 pp. [G]

HISTORY

Bickel, K. A. 1942. *The mangrove coast. The story of the west coast of Florida.* Paschal-Sawyer Publishers, Sarasota, FL. 277 pp. [G]

Ceram, C. W. 1971. *The first American. A story of North American archaeology.* Harcourt Brace Jovanovich, Inc., New York, NY. xxi + 357 pp. [G]

Davis, D. D. (ed.). 1984. *Perspective on Gulf coast prehistory.* Ripley P. Bullen

Monographs in Anthropology and History, No. 5. University of Florida Press/Florida State Museum, Gainesville, FL. xi + 379 pp. [T]

Díaz del Castillo, B. [1632]. In: Garcia, G. (ed.) 1956. *The discovery and conquest of Mexico.* Farrar, Straus and Cudahy, Publishers, New York, NY. xxxi + 478 pp. [Translation of Bernal Díaz' *The true history of the conquest of New Spain*]. [G]

Dibble, E. F., and E. W. Newton. 1971. *Spain and her rivals on the Gulf coast.* Historic Pensacola Preservation Board, Pensacola, FL. 143 pp. [G]

Douglas, M. S. 1967. *Florida: The long frontier.* Harper and Row, Publishers, New York, NY. x + 307 pp. [G]

Farb, P. 1968. *Man's rise to civilization as shown by the Indians of North America from primeval times to the coming of the industrial state.* E. P. Dutton and Company, New York, NY. xx + 332 pp. [G]

Fontaneda, H. d'Escalante. [ca. 1575]. In: True, D. O. (ed.). 1973. *Memoir of D⁰ d'Escalante Fontaneda respecting Florida.* University of Miami/Historical Association of Southern Florida, Miami, FL. 77 pp. [Translated from the Spanish with notes by Buckingham Smith, Washington DC,1854]. [G]

Fuson, R. H. [Translator]. 1987. *The log of Christopher Columbus.* International Marine Publishing Company, Camden, ME. xviii + 252 pp. [G]

Gallenkamp, C. 1976. *Maya. The riddle and rediscovery of a lost civilization.* David MacKay Company, New York, NY. xii + 220 pp. [G]

Hann, J. J. 1991. *Missions to the Calusa.* University of Florida Press, Gainesville, FL. xv + 460 pp. [G]

Hays, H. R. 1963. *In the beginnings. Early man and his gods.* G. P. Putnam's Sons, New York, NY. 575 pp. [G]

Hodge,F. W., and T. H. Lewis (eds.). 1990. *Spanish explorers in the southern United States, 1528-1543.* Texas State Historical Association, Austin, TX. 411 pp. [Facsimile reprint of Hodge, F. W. and T. H. Lewis (eds.). 1907. *ibid.* Charles Scribner's Sons, New York, NY.] [G]

Innes, H. 1969. *The conquistadors.* Alfred A. Knopf, New York, NY. 336 pp. [G]

Landa, Diego de. [1566] 1978. *Yucatán before and after the conquest.* Dover Publications, Inc., New York, NY. xv + 162 pp. [Translation from the Spanish, with notes, by William Gates of Fray Diego de Landa's *Relación de las cosas de Yucatán,* 1566.] [G]

Leon-Portilla, L. 1963. *Aztec thought and culture. A study of the ancient Nahuatl mind.* University of Oklahoma Press, Norman, OK. xxviii + 241 pp. [Translated from the Spanish by Jack Emory Davis.] [G]

Lowery, W. 1959. *The Spanish settlements within the present limits of the United States, Florida 1562-1574.* Russell and Russell, Incorporated, New York, NY. xix + 500 pp. [G]

Milanich, J., and S. Proctor (eds.) 1978. *Tacachale. Essays on the Indians of Florida and southeastern Georgia during the historic period.* University Presses of Florida, Gainesville, FL. xi + 217 pp. [G]

Morison, S. E. 1974. *The European discovery of America. The southern voyages A.D. 1492-1616.* Oxford University Press, New York, NY. xvii + 758 pp. [G]

Prescott, W. H. 1843. *History of the conquest of Mexico*. Reprint by Random House, The Modern Library, New York, NY. [G] [Undated]

Sale, K. 1990. *The conquest of paradise. Christopher Columbus and the Columbian legacy*. Alfred A. Knopf, New York, NY. 453 pp. [G]

Sprague, J. T. 1848. *The origin, progress, and conclusion of the Florida war*. D. Appleton and Company, New York, NY. 557 pp. + advertising and index. [Facsimile reprint (1964), University of Florida Press, Gainesville, FL.] [G]

Thompson, J. E. S. 1963. *Maya archaeologist*. University of Oklahoma Press, Norman, OK. xvii + 284 pp. [G]

Weddle, R. S. 1973. *Wilderness manhunt. The Spanish search for La Salle*. University of Texas Press, Austin, TX. xiv + 291 pp. [G]

Weddle, R. S. 1985. *Spanish Sea. The Gulf of Mexico in North American discovery 1500-1685*. Texas A&M University Press, College Station, TX. viii + 457 pp. [G]

Willey, G. R. 1949. *Archaeology of the Florida Gulf coast*. Smithsonian Miscellaneous Collections, Smithsonian Institution, Washington, DC. Volume 113. xxiii + 599 pp. 60 pls. [T]

OCEANOGRAPHY

Baker, B. B., Jr., W. R. Deeble, and R. D. Geisenderfer (eds.).1966. *Glossary of oceanographic terms*. U.S. Naval Oceanographic Office, Washington, DC. Special Publication SP-35. vi + 204 pp. [T]

Bascom, W. 1964. *Waves and beaches*. Anchor Books, Garden City, NY. 267 pp. [G].

Davis, R. A., Jr. 1991. *Oceanography. An introduction to the marine environment*. William C. Brown, Publishers, Dubuque, IA. xiv + 434 pp. [G]

Dietrich, G., 1963. *General oceanography, an introduction*. Wiley Interscience, New York, NY. xv + 587 pp. [T]

MacLeish, W. H. 1989. *The Gulf Stream. Encounters with the blue god*. Houghton Mifflin Company, Boston, MA. viii + 243 pp. [G]

Smith, F. G. W., 1973. *The seas in motion*. Thomas Y. Crowell Company, New York, NY. vi + 248 pp. [G]

Stommel, H. 1965. *The Gulf Stream. A physical and dynamical description*. University of California Press, Berkeley, CA. xiii + 248 pp. [T]

Sverdrup, H. U., M. W. Johnson, and R. H. Fleming, 1942. *The oceans, their physics, chemistry, and general biology*. Prentice- Hall, Inc., Englewood Cliffs, NJ. x + 1060 pp. [T]

Thurman, H. V. 1991. *Introductory oceanography*. MacMillan Publishing Company, New York, NY. xi + 526 pp. [G]

Williams, J. 1962. *Oceanography, an introduction to the marine sciences*. Little, Brown and Company, Boston, MA. xiii + 242 pp. [T]

PLANKTON AND PELAGIC SYSTEMS

Fraser, J. 1962. *Nature adrift*. The story of marine plankton. University Press, Aberdeen, Scotland. v + 178 pp. [G]

Hardy, A. 1959a. *The open sea: Its natural history. Part I: The world of plankton*.

Houghton Mifflin Company, Boston, MA. xv + 335 pp. [G]

_____, 1959b. *The open sea: Its natural history. Part II: Fish and fisheries.* Collins Clear-type Press, London, England. xiv + 322 pp. [G]

Hardy, J. T. 1991. Where the sea meets the sky. Natural History Magazine (May 1991): 58-65. [G]

Lallie, C. M., and R. M. Gilmer. 1989. *Pelagic snails.* Stanford University Press, Standford, CA. xiv + 259 pp.[G]

Raymont, J. E. G. 1963. *Plankton and productivity in the oceans.* Macmillan Company, New York, NY. viii + 660 pp. [T]

Schmitt, W. S. 1947. The sun and the harvest of the sea. Smithsonian Institution, Washington, DC. Report for 1946: 295- 314. [G]

POLLUTION

Anonymous. 1984. The sensitivity of coastal environments and wildlife to spilled oil in the southwest Florida region. Research Planning Institute, Inc., Columbia, SC. Special Report RPI/R/84/8/2-20 [To Department of Community Affairs, State of Florida]. iii + 44 pp, appendices A-C. [G]

Anonymous. 1987. A summary of selected data on chemical contaminants in tissues collected during 1984, 1985, and 1986. National Status and Trends Program for Marine Environmental Quality, National Oceanic and Atmospheric Administration, Rockville, MD. NOAA Technical Memorandum NOS OMA 38. 23 pp + appendices A-E. [T]

Blume, A.D., and S. Iudicello. 1987. The Gulf of Mexico as a special area under MARPOL Annex V. Report prepared for the Texas General Land Office by the Center for Environmental Education, Washington, DC. 79 pp.[G]

Delfino, J. J., D. L. Frazier, and J. L. Nepshinsky. 1984. Contaminants in Florida's coastal zone: a review of present knowledge and proposed research strategies. Florida Sea Grant College, Report No. 62. iv + 176 pp. [G]

Dutka, B. J. 1973. Coliforms are an inadequate index of water quality. Journal of Environmental Health, Volume 36 Number 1:39-46. [T]

Eisler, R., 1985 ff 1989. [Named] hazards to fish, wildlife, and invertebrates: A synoptic review. U.S. Fish and Wildlife Service, Washington, DC. Contaminant Hazards Reviews, Biological Reports 85 (1.1 to 1.17). [Note: A continuing series of reports individually paginated on heavy metals, pesticides, polycyclic aromatic hydrocarbons (PAH), polychlorinated biphenyls (PCB) and pentachlorophenol (PCP)]. [T]

Hall, L. W., and A. E. Pinkney. 1985. Acute and sublethal effects of organotin compounds on aquatic biota: an interpretative literature evaluation. CRC Critical Reviews of Toxicology, Volume 14, Number 2:159-209. [T]

O'Hara, K. J., and S. Iudicello, 1987. *Plastics in the ocean: more than a litter problem.* Privately published, Center for Environmental Education, Washington, DC. xvii + 128 pp, Appendices 1, 2. [G]

Smith, G. J. 1987. Pesticide use and toxicology in relation to wildlife: organophosphorus and carbamate compounds. U.S. Fish and Wildlife Service, Washington, DC. Resource Publication No. 170. iii + 171 pp. [T]

Index

Medusae, 142, *219*, 222
Mega Borg, 283, 286, 289
Menéndez de Aviléz, Pedro, 32
Menhaden, 250, 252, 255, 288
Mercury, 22, 89, 269, 293, 295
  poisoning, 295
Mermaids, 327
Meroplankton, 217, *219*, 222, 223
Mesopelagic zone, 231, *232*
Mesozoic era, 60, 63
Mestizos, 40
Metamorphosis, 142, 192, 223
Metazoan animals, 89
Methane, 67, 188, 247, 269, 281, 333
Methylmercury chloride, 95
Mexico, agricultural products of, 265
Mexico Basin, 52-53, 55
Miami, 102
Microbes, *90*, 91, 232, 279
  pathological, 134
Microfauna, 188
Microflora, 191
Microlayer, pollution in, 224
Mid-Atlantic Ridge, 56, 59
Middle Grounds, Florida 68
Migration, 165, 166, 169, 185, 327
Migratory feeders, 214
Millipedes, 146
Minerals Management Service, 243, 244, 261, 269, 286, 323, 326, 331, 332, 334
Mining,
  landfill, 310
  mineral, 267-69
  phosphate, 267
  room-and-pillar, 66
  salt, 66, 67, 333
  solution, 67
  value of, 269
Missions, 24, 28-29, 33
Mississippi Delta, 52, 53, 66, 68, 128, *130*, 133, 197, 233
Mississippi River, 23, 24, 25, 45, 55, 62, *63*, 64, 65, 70, 71, 81, 93, *108*, 127, 128, 133, 159, 177, 197, 199, 268, 281, 292, 305, 319, 323
Mississippi Sound, 254
Missouri River, *63*
Mites, 146
Mobile, 277, 286, 291, 297
Mobile Bay, 23, 26, 128, 131, 121, 127, 254, 319
  river valley of, 62
Moctezuma, 39
Mollusca, 65, 136, 139, 144, 147-48, 150, *155*, 188
  and toxins, 296
  vermetid, 114, 117
Molybdenum, 96
Monitoring programs, 210

Monkfish, 256
Monofilament line, 272
Montanes, 212, 216
Moonpool, *242*
Mosquito control, *299*, 304, 305
Mosquitoes, 192, 208, 215, 299, 300, 321
Moss animals, see Bryozoans
Moss, Spanish, 205
Motor vehicles, 245, 247
Mound builders, 41
Mountain-rimmed plains, 216
Mountains, submerged, 53
Mud, 187
Mud flats, 128, 130, 166, 177
Mud puppies, 156
Mudlumps, *54*, 55, 114
Muds, sulfur, 94
Mullet, 250
Mussels, 57 , 147, 234
Mutagenic products, 293, 337
Mysidaceans, 146
Nannoplankton, 218, 329-30
Naples, 121
Narváez, Pánfilo de, 23, 319
National Audubon Society, 194
National Park Service, 194
Natural gas, 236, 241-47, 268
Nauplius, *219*
Navigational charts, 45
Nearshore fish, 255
Negro slaves, 43
Nekton, 226, 227, *232*
Nematode worms, 144-45, 207
Neurotoxins, 298
Neuston, 224-26
New Orleans, 127, 244, 286, 291
Newts, 156
Nicaragua, 56
Nickel, 252, 269, 295
Nitrates, 89, 91, 92, 132, 281, 282
Nitrification, 93
Nitrites, 89, 91, 92, 132, 281, 282
Nitrogen, 89, *90*, 91, 92-93, 188, 279, 281
Nitrogen oxides, 247
"Noah" factor, 170
Northers, 99, 101-2
Notochord, 222
Nuclear power plants, 96, *313*, 314-16
Nursery grounds, 179, 256
Nutrients,
  ambient, 279
  excess, 277, 279-82
  flux, 198
  production, 198
  sea grass, 181
Octopus, 147, 336
Offshore continental shelf, 241, 243-46, 333
Offshore economic zone, 240
Offshore sandy plain communi-

ties, 176
Offshore species, 255
Ohio River, *63*
Oil, 236, 241, 244-47, 268
  as pollutant, 283-90
  cargo, size of, 287
  consumption of, 246
  on continental shelf, 241
  pollution, 285
  refineries, 245
  reserves, 246, 267
  revenues of, 244-45
  seeps, 55, 286
  types of, 241-43, *242*
  values of, 245
Oil and gas
  exploration, 51
  leases, 186, 243-45, 288, 331-32
Oil drilling platforms, 236, 241, *242*, 245, 260
  locations of, 243, 331
Oil industry, 47
Oil pipelines, 284
Oil platforms, 118, 119, *120*, 121, 176, *242*, 285, 325
Oil spills, 283-90, 331, 334
  clean-up costs of, 287, 288
  effects on ecosystems, 287
  number of, 284
  probability of, 286
  recovery from, 287
Oilfield supply bases, 245
Okaloosa darter, 170
Old-growth ecosystems, 287
Oligochaetes, 145
Olmecs, 37
Omnivores, 185, 217, 223, 226
Oolites, 64
Opalinates, 141
Ophiuroidea, 148, 150
Orange roughy, 256, 332
Orca Basin, 82
Orchids, 169, 327
Orizaba and Cofre de Perote, 53, 378
Ortiz, Juan, 320
Osmoregulation, 133-34, 205
Ostracods, 146
Outfall, 312
Overburden, 65
Overfishing, 121, 253
Oxygen, 86, 89, 131, 134, 196, 225, 229, 232, 234, 279, 280, 291, 296, 302, 324
  dependency, 199
  deprivation, 313-14
  minimum layer, 86
Oyster
  bars, 176, 287, 288, 325
  beds, 114-17, *116*, 128, 147, 254
  fishing, 253, 255
  leases, 254
Oysters, 134-41, 191, 201, 234, 326

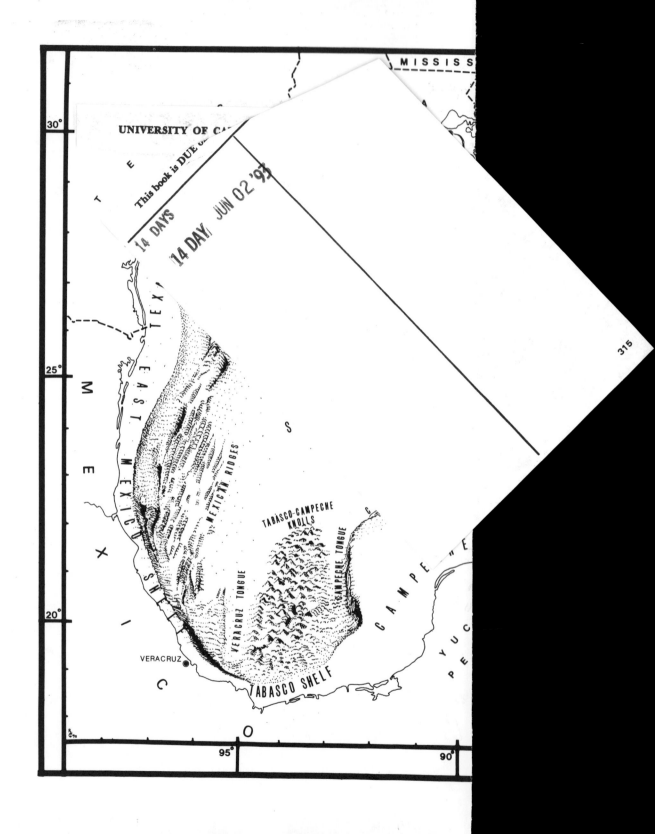